DATE DUE

			PRINTED IN U.S.A.

SOMETHING ABOUT THE AUTHOR

ISSN 0276-816X

something
ABOUT THE
AUThOR

**Facts and Pictures about Authors
and Illustrators of Books for Young People**

EDITED BY
ANNE COMMIRE

VOLUME 50

GALE RESEARCH COMPANY
BOOK TOWER
DETROIT, MICHIGAN
48226

Editor: Anne Commire

Associate Editors: Agnes Garrett, Helga P. McCue

Senior Assistant Editor: Dianne H. Anderson

Assistant Editors: Elisa Ann Ferraro, Eunice L. Petrini, Linda Shedd

Sketchwriters: Marguerite Feitlowitz, Rachel Koenig

Researcher: Catherine Ruello

Editorial Assistants: Catherine Coray, Joanne J. Ferraro, Nigel French

Permissions Assistant: Susan Pfanner

In cooperation with the Young People's Literature staff

Editor: Joyce Nakamura

Senior Assistant Editor: Heidi Ellerman

Assistant Editor: Marla Fern Gold

Research Assistants: Michael P. Beaubien, Carolyn Kline

Production Manager: Mary Beth Trimper

External Production Assistants: Linda Davis, Anthony J. Scolaro

Internal Production Associate: Louise Gagné

Internal Senior Production Assistant: Sandy Rock

Internal Production Assistant: Candace Cloutier

Layout Artist: Elizabeth Lewis Patryjak

Art Director: Arthur Chartow

Special acknowledgment is due to the members of the *Contemporary Authors* staff
who assisted in the preparation of this volume.

Chairman: Frederick G. Ruffner

President: Thomas A. Paul

Publisher: Dedria Bryfonski

Associate Editorial Director: Ellen T. Crowley

Director, Biography Division: Christine Nasso

Senior Editor, Something about the Author: Adele Sarkissian

Library of Congress Catalog Card Number 72-27107

ISBN 0-8103-2260-9
ISSN 0276-816X
Computerized photocomposition by
Typographics, Incorporated
Kansas City, Missouri
Printed in the United States

Contents

5

F

G

H

J

K

L

M

Introduction

As the only ongoing reference series that deals with the lives and works of authors and illustrators of children's books, *Something about the Author (SATA)* is a unique source of information. The *SATA* series includes not only well-known authors and illustrators whose books are most widely read, but also those less prominent people whose works are just coming to be recognized. *SATA* is often the only readily available information source for less well-known writers or artists. You'll find *SATA* informative and entertaining whether you are:

—a student in junior high school (or perhaps one to two grades higher or lower) who needs information for a book report or some other assignment for an English class;

—a children's librarian who is searching for the answer to yet another question from a young reader or collecting background material to use for a story hour;

—an English teacher who is drawing up an assignment for your students or gathering information for a book talk;

—a student in a college of education or library science who is studying children's literature and reference sources in the field;

—a parent who is looking for a new way to interest your child in reading something more than the school curriculum prescribes;

—an adult who enjoys children's literature for its own sake, knowing that a good children's book has no age limits.

Scope

In *SATA* you will find detailed information about authors and illustrators who span the full time range of children's literature, from early figures like John Newbery and L. Frank Baum to contemporary figures like Judy Blume and Richard Peck. Authors in the series represent primarily English-speaking countries, particularly the United States, Canada, and the United Kingdom. Also included, however, are authors from around the world whose works are available in English translation, for example: from France, Jean and Laurent De Brunhoff; from Italy, Emanuele Luzzati; from the Netherlands, Jaap ter Haar; from Germany, James Krüss; from Norway, Babbis Friis-Baastad; from Japan, Toshiko Kanzawa; from the Soviet Union, Kornei Chukovsky; from Switzerland, Alois Carigiet, to name only a few. Also appearing in *SATA* are Newbery medalists from Hendrik Van Loon (1922) to Sid Fleischman (1987). The writings represented in *SATA* include those created intentionally for children and young adults as well as those written for a general audience and known to interest younger readers. These writings cover the spectrum from picture books, humor, folk and fairy tales, animal stories, mystery and adventure, science fiction and fantasy, historical fiction, poetry and nonsense verse, to drama, biography, and nonfiction.

Information Features

In *SATA* you will find full-length entries that are being presented in the series for the first time. This volume, for example, marks the first full-length appearance of Raymond Abrashkin, Hermann Hesse, Ann Jonas, Margaret Landon, Robin McKinley, Eleanor Roosevelt, Cynthia Rylant, Audrey Wood, and Don Wood.

Brief Entries, first introduced in Volume 27, are another regular feature of *SATA*. Brief Entries present essentially the same types of information found in a full entry but do so in a capsule form and without illustration. These entries are intended to give you useful and timely information while the more time-consuming process of compiling a full-length biography is in progress. In this volume you'll find Brief

Entries for Grace Chetwin, Lisa Eisenberg, Delia Ephron, Jean Ferris, Beau Gardner, Winfried Opgenoorth, Donna Paltrowitz, Stuart Paltrowitz, Ann Rinaldi, and S. D. Schindler, among others.

Obituaries have been included in *SATA* since Volume 20. An Obituary is intended not only as a death notice but also as a concise view of a person's life and work. Obituaries may appear for persons who have entries in earlier *SATA* volumes, as well as for people who have not yet appeared in the series. In this volume Obituaries mark the recent deaths of V. C. Andrews, Danny Kaye, Alistair MacLean, Rebecca Hourwich Reyher, Yuri Suhl, and others.

Revised Entries

Since Volume 25, each *SATA* volume also includes newly revised and updated entries for a selection of *SATA* listees (usually four to six) who remain of interest to today's readers and who have been active enough to require extensive revision of their earlier biographies. For example, when Beverly Cleary first appeared in *SATA* Volume 2, she was the author of twenty-one books for children and young adults and the recipient of numerous awards. By the time her updated sketch appeared in Volume 43 (a span of fifteen years), this creator of the indefatigable Ramona Quimby and other memorable characters had produced a dozen new titles and garnered nearly fifty additional awards, including the 1984 Newbery Medal.

The entry for a given biographee may be revised as often as there is substantial new information to provide. In this volume, look for revised entries on Emily Arnold, Paul deKruif, Fritz Eichenberg, Milton Meltzer, Gary Paulsen, and Uri Shulevitz.

Illustrations

While the textual information in *SATA* is its primary reason for existing, photographs and illustrations not only enliven the text but are an integral part of the information that *SATA* provides. Illustrations and text are wedded in such a special way in children's literature that artists and their works naturally occupy a prominent place among *SATA*'s listees. The illustrators that you'll find in the series include such past masters of children's book illustration as Randolph Caldecott, Walter Crane, Arthur Rackham, and Ernest H. Shepard, as well as such noted contemporary artists as Maurice Sendak, Edward Gorey, Tomie de Paola, and Margot Zemach. There are Caldecott medalists from Dorothy Lathrop (the first recipient in 1938) to Richard Egielski (the latest winner in 1987); cartoonists like Charles Schulz, ("Peanuts"), Walt Kelly ("Pogo"), Hank Ketcham ("Dennis the Menace"), and Georges Rémi ("Tintin"); photographers like Jill Krementz, Tana Hoban, Bruce McMillan, and Bruce Curtis; and filmmakers like Walt Disney, Alfred Hitchcock, and Steven Spielberg.

In more than a dozen years of recording the metamorphosis of children's literature from the printed page to other media, *SATA* has become something of a repository of photographs that are unique in themselves and exist nowhere else as a group, particularly many of the classics of motion picture and stage history and photographs that have been specially loaned to us from private collections.

Indexes

Each *SATA* volume provides a cumulative index in two parts: first, the Illustrations Index, arranged by the name of the illustrator, gives the number of the volume and page where the illustrator's work appears in the current volume as well as all preceding volumes in the series; second, the Author Index gives the number of the volume in which a person's biographical sketch, Brief Entry, or Obituary appears in the current volume as well as all preceding volumes in the series. These indexes also include references to authors and illustrators who appear in *Yesterday's Authors of Books for Children* (described in detail below). Beginning with Volume 36, the *SATA* Author Index provides cross-references to authors who are included in *Children's Literature Review*.

Starting with Volume 42, you will also find cross-references to authors who are included in the *Something about the Author Autobiography Series* (described in detail below).

Character Index—New Feature

If you're like many readers, the names of fictional characters may pop more easily into your mind than the names of the authors or illustrators who created them: Snow White, Charlotte the Spider, the Cat in the

Hat, Peter Pan, Mary Poppins, Winnie-the-Pooh, Brer Rabbit, Little Toot, Charlie Bucket, Lassie, Rip Van Winkle, Bartholomew Cubbins—the list could go on and on. But who invented them? Now these characters, and several thousand others, can lead you to the *SATA* and *YABC* entries on the lives and works of their creators.

Making its first appearance in Volume 50, the Character Index provides a broad selection of characters from books and other media—movies, plays, comic strips, cartoons, etc.—created by listees who appear in all the published volumes of *SATA* and *YABC*. This index gives the character name, followed by a "*See*" reference indicating the name of the creator and the number of the *SATA* or *YABC* volume in which the creator's bio-bibliographical entry can be found. As future *SATA* volumes are published, additional characters will appear in a cumulative Character Index that will be published annually in *SATA*. (The cumulative Illustrations and Author Indexes will continue to appear in each *SATA* volume.)

It would be impossible for the Character Index to include every important character created by *SATA* and *YABC* listees. (Several hundred important characters might be taken from Dickens alone, for example.) Therefore, the *SATA* editors have selected those characters that are best known and thus most likely to interest *SATA* users. Realizing that some of your favorite characters may not appear in this index, the editors invite you to suggest additional names. With your help, the editors hope to make the Character Index a uniquely useful reference tool for you.

What a *SATA* Entry Provides

Whether you're already familiar with the *SATA* series or just getting acquainted, you will want to be aware of the kind of information that an entry provides. In every *SATA* entry the editors attempt to give as complete a picture of the person's life and work as possible. In some cases that full range of information may simply be unavailable, or a biographee may choose not to reveal complete personal details. The information that the editors attempt to provide in every entry is arranged in the following categories:

1. The "head" of the entry gives

    —the most complete form of the name,
    —any part of the name not commonly used, included in parentheses,
    —birth and death dates, if known; a (?) indicates a discrepancy in published sources,
    —pseudonyms or name variants under which the person has had books published or is publicly known, in parentheses in the second line.

2. "Personal" section gives

    —date and place of birth and death,
    —parents' names and occupations,
    —name of spouse, date of marriage, and names of children,
    —educational institutions attended, degrees received, and dates,
    —religious and political affiliations,
    —agent's name and address,
    —home and/or office address.

3. "Career" section gives

    —name of employer, position, and dates for each career post,
    —military service,
    —memberships,
    —awards and honors.

4. "Writings" section gives

    —title, first publisher and date of publication, and illustration information for each book written; revised editions and other significant editions for books with particularly long publishing histories; genre, when known.

5. "Adaptations" section gives

> —title, major performers, producer, and date of all known reworkings of an author's material in another medium, like movies, filmstrips, television, recordings, plays, etc.

6. "Sidelights" section gives

> —commentary on the life or work of the biographee either directly from the person (and often written specifically for the *SATA* entry), or gathered from biographies, diaries, letters, interviews, or other published sources.

7. "For More Information See" section gives

> —books, feature articles, films, plays, and reviews in which the biographee's life or work has been treated.

How a *SATA* Entry Is Compiled

A *SATA* entry progresses through a series of steps. If the biographee is living, the *SATA* editors try to secure information directly from him or her through a questionnaire. From the information that the biographee supplies, the editors prepare an entry, filling in any essential missing details with research. The author or illustrator is then sent a copy of the entry to check for accuracy and completeness.

If the biographee is deceased or cannot be reached by questionnaire, the *SATA* editors examine a wide variety of published sources to gather information for an entry. Biographical sources are searched with the aid of Gale's *Biography and Genealogy Master Index*. Bibliographic sources like the *National Union Catalog*, the *Cumulative Book Index*, *American Book Publishing Record*, and the *British Museum Catalogue* are consulted, as are book reviews, feature articles, published interviews, and material sometimes obtained from the biographee's family, publishers, agent, or other associates.

For each entry presented in *SATA*, the editors also attempt to locate a photograph of the biographee as well as representative illustrations from his or her books. After surveying the available books which the biographee has written and/or illustrated, and then making a selection of appropriate photographs and illustrations, the editors request permission of the current copyright holders to reprint the material. In the case of older books for which the copyright may have passed through several hands, even locating the current copyright holder is often a long and involved process.

We invite you to examine the entire *SATA* series, starting with this volume. Described below are some of the people in Volume 50 that you may find particularly interesting.

Highlights of This Volume

EMILY ARNOLD......defines illustration as "the need to be linked to someone else, to connect with a *subject outside of oneself*....[It is] at the heart of the impulse to illustrate, and is still the inspiration for all my drawing." As a child, Arnold focused her artistic ability on creating totally complete books—always with male protagonists and always including "copyright date, flap copy, and author's bio." In adulthood, however, her first ventures into publication were concerned with illustrating children's books by other authors. After nineteen years and one hundred books, Arnold began writing as well as illustrating stories for children. "I write for several hours in the morning, and devote the afternoon, and sometimes the evening to illustration work."

FRITZ EICHENBERG......is a German-born artist and illustrator whose favorite mediums are lithographs, wood engravings, and woodcuts. A product of the German *Gymnasium*, an educational system that was "brutal in demanding obedience," Eichenberg took "refuge in literature" to escape his environment. Later, as a student at the State Academy of Graphic Arts, he discovered wood engravings while illustrating his book, *Till Eulenspiegel's Merry Pranks*. Teaching himself the technique, Eichenberg "fell in love with wood, a medium that suited me." During Hitler's rise to political power, Eichenberg, who foresaw disaster for Germany, left his homeland and settled in New York City. There he established a successful career in illustration, which eventually led to equally successful careers in writing and teaching. Among his many diverse accomplishments in the field of art is the distinction of being the founder of the

Graphic Arts Center in New York. Eichenberg, who perceives art as a vocation, advises his students: "Be willing to offer your life, if necessary, to it."

ROBIN McKINLEY......, as an only child, found "the world of books much more satisfactory than the real world." Her introverted teenage years were spent riding horses (a lifelong interest), reading, and inventing stories. "Writing has always been the other side of reading for me," she says. "It never occurred to me not to make up stories." Today, McKinley is a popular author, reteller, and 1985 Newbery Medal-winner for her book, *The Hero and the Crown,* her second novel about the fantasy land of Damar, where "hope, honor, and duty" prevail. "As an important adjunct to hope and honor, I am obsessed with the idea of freedom," says McKinley. She describes herself as a medium for her stories rather than a creator of them, and claims to write by "ear." "As the story grows, I hear people talking to each other and I hear the names they call each other, the unfamiliar words they use."

MILTON MELTZER......"early became a slave to the printed word, devouring library shelves from one end to the other." A biographer and historian, Meltzer has toiled with volumes of words, producing over sixty books that reflect his interest in man's struggle for freedom and justice. "What links them all is the fact that each one has fought for unpopular causes," he says. A champion of the underdog, Meltzer believes that writers of history books for young people must strive to show human behavior honestly and must offer readers room to explore their own ideas and to interpret events with their own judgment.

CYNTHIA RYLANT......is a versatile writer of picture books, poetry, short stories, and novels. Growing up with her grandparents and later living alone with her mother, Rylant credits those years with the development of her positive attitude toward life and her ability to translate that attitude into stories. Her grandparents taught her "how hard life can be sometimes, but always,...for everything we lose, we will get something back." Her mother gave Rylant a wealth of material for her books. "*Waiting to Waltz: A Childhood* is full of [my mother's] spirit: the constant fascination with small-town people, the involvement with animals, and the feeling, always, that you really are not like everyone else," says Rylant.

URI SHULEVITZ......, award-winning illustrator and author of children's books, uses a visual approach when he creates his books. Beginning with his first book in 1963, Shulevitz found that by "writing with pictures" he could communicate the action of a story and evoke additional images for it. "First I visualized the action, and then I thought of how to say it in words," explains Shulevitz. By using this visual technique, Shulevitz is able to channel his natural inclination of thinking through images into his writing. "One 'listens' with one's eyes, and 'sees' through one's ears and fingers. For me, it is the small chaos preceding creation."

AUDREY and DON WOOD......, husband-and-wife team, create children's books from their home in Santa Barbara, California. Although each artist approaches his material differently, they both agree on what basic ingredients a children's book requires. "Rhythm is crucial in a picture book, a children's book should be delightful for the adults, who often read to their children," says Audrey Wood. Don Wood agrees, but adds "point of view" as another necessary component in a good book. "When I'm planning my illustrations, I often pretend I have a camera and am moving it around.... It's fun to play with point of view." Because the Woods see their picture books as dramatic representations of stories, they "tell" their stories using characters based on their family and friends, often staging their books as though they were theater performances.

These are only a few of the authors and illustrators that you'll find in this volume. We hope you find all the entries in *SATA* both interesting and useful.

Yesterday's Authors of Books for Children

In a two-volume companion set to *SATA, Yesterday's Authors of Books for Children (YABC)* focuses on early authors and illustrators, from the beginnings of children's literature through 1960, whose books are still being read by children today. Here you will find "old favorites" like Hans Christian Andersen, J. M. Barrie, Kenneth Grahame, Betty MacDonald, A. A. Milne, Beatrix Potter, Samuel Clemens, Kate Greenaway, Rudyard Kipling, Robert Louis Stevenson, and many more.

Similar in format to *SATA, YABC* features bio-bibliographical entries that are divided into information categories such as Personal, Career, Writings, and Sidelights. The entries are further enhanced by book illustrations, author photos, movie stills, and many rare old photographs.

In Volume 2 you will find cumulative indexes to the authors and to the illustrations that appear in *YABC*. References to these authors and illustrators can also be located in the *SATA* cumulative indexes.

By exploring both volumes of *YABC*, you will discover a special group of more than seventy authors and illustrators who represent some of the best in children's literature—individuals whose timeless works continue to delight children and adults of all ages. Other authors and illustrators from early children's literature are listed in *SATA*, starting with Volume 15.

Something about the Author Autobiography Series

You can complement the information in *SATA* with the *Something about the Author Autobiography Series (SAAS)*, which provides autobiographical essays written by important current authors and illustrators of books for children and young adults. In every volume of *SAAS* you will find about twenty specially commissioned autobiographies, each accompanied by a selection of personal photographs supplied by the authors. The wide range of contemporary writers and artists who describe their lives and interests in the *Autobiography Series* includes Joan Aiken, Betsy Byars, Leonard Everett Fisher, Milton Meltzer, Maia Wojciechowska, and Jane Yolen, among others. Though the information presented in the autobiographies is as varied and unique as the authors, you can learn about the people and events that influenced these writers' early lives, how they began their careers, what problems they faced in becoming established in their professions, what prompted them to write or illustrate particular books, what they now find most challenging or rewarding in their lives, and what advice they may have for young people interested in following in their footsteps, among many other subjects.

Autobiographies included in the *SATA Autobiography Series* can be located through both the *SATA* cumulative index and the *SAAS* cumulative index, which lists not only the authors' names but also the subjects mentioned in their essays, such as titles of works and geographical and personal names.

The *SATA Autobiography Series* gives you the opportunity to view "close up" some of the fascinating people who are included in the *SATA* parent series. The combined *SATA* series makes available to you an unequaled range of comprehensive and in-depth information about the authors and illustrators of young people's literature.

Please write and tell us if we can make *SATA* even more helpful to you.

Acknowledgments

Grateful acknowledgment is made to the following publishers, authors, and artists
for their kind permission to reproduce copyrighted material.

AMERICAN LIBRARY ASSOCIATION. Sidelight excerpts from an article "Beyond Fact" by Milton Meltzer in *Beyond Fact: Nonfiction for Children and Young People,* compiled by Jo Carr. Copyright © 1982 by American Library Association. Reprinted by permission of the American Library Association.

ANNICK PRESS LTD. Illustrations by Michael Martchenko from *Mortimer* by Robert Munsch. Text copyright © 1985 by Robert N. Munsch. Illustrations copyright © 1985 by Michael Martchenko./ Illustration by Michael Martchenko from *Angela's Airplane* by Robert N. Munsch. Text copyright © 1983 by Michael Martchenko./ Illustration by Michael Martchenko from *The Boy in the Drawer* by Robert N. Munsch. Copyright © 1982 by Robert N. Munsch./ Illustration by Michael Martchenko from *Thomas' Snowsuit* by Robert Munsch. Text copyright © 1985 by Robert Munsch. Illustrations copyright © 1985 by Michael Martchenko. All reprinted by permission of Annick Press Ltd.

ASSOCIATED BOOK PUBLISHERS. Illustration by Martin Ursell from *The Song of Pentecost* by W. J. Corbett. Text copyright © 1982 by W. J. Corbett. Illustrations copyright © 1982 by Methuen Children's Books Ltd. Reprinted by permission of Associated Book Publishers.

ATHENEUM PUBLISHERS. Illustration by Susan Seddon Boulet from "The Butterfly with No Keys" in *The Candlemaker and Other Tales* by Victoria Forrester. Text copyright © 1984 by Victoria Forrester. Illustrations copyright © 1984 by Susan Seddon Boulet./ Illustration by Yasuko Koide from *May We Sleep Here Tonight?* by Tan Koide. Text copyright © 1981 by Tan Koide. Illustrations copyright © 1981 by Yasuko Koide. Both reprinted by permission of Atheneum Publishers.

BANTAM BOOKS, INC. Illustration by Ron Wing from *The Magic of the Unicorn* by Deborah Lerme Goodman. Text copyright © 1985 by R. A. Montgomery. Illustrations copyright © 1985 by Bantam Books, Inc./ Jacket illustration from *Demian* by Hermann Hesse. Copyright © 1965 by Harper & Row, Publishers./ Detail of cover illustration from *Dancing Girls* by Margaret Atwood. Copyright © 1977, 1982 by O. W. Toad Ltd. Cover copyright © 1985 by Griesbach and Martucci. All reprinted by permission of Bantam Books, Inc.

BELITHA PRESS LTD. Illustration by Barry Wilkinson from *Jonah and the Great Fish,* retold by Ella K. Lindvall. Copyright © 1983 by Belitha Press Ltd. Illustrations copyright © 1983 by Chris Molan. Reprinted by permission of Belitha Press Ltd.

BOREALIS PRESS LTD. Illustration by Steven Collier from *Martin's Starwars* by Joan Lyngseth. Copyright © 1978 by Joan Lyngseth and Borealis Press Ltd. Reprinted by permission of Borealis Press Ltd.

BRADBURY PRESS. Jacket illustration by Ann Grifalconi from *Underground Man* by Milton Meltzer. Copyright © 1972 by Milton Meltzer./ Jacket illustration by Neil Waldman from *Dogsong* by Gary Paulsen. Text copyright © 1985 by Gary Paulsen. Jacket illustration copyright © 1985 by Bradbury Press./ Jacket illustration by Jon Weiman from *Sentries* by Gary Paulsen. Text copyright © 1986 by Gary Paulsen. Jacket illustration copyright © 1986 by Bradbury Press./ Jacket illustration by Jon Weiman from *Tracker* by Gary Paulsen. Copyright © 1984 by Gary Paulsen./ Jacket illustration by Jon Weiman from *Dancing Carl* by Gary Paulsen. Text copyright © 1983 by Gary Paulsen. Jacket illustration copyright © 1983 by Bradbury Press./ Illustration by Stephen Gammell from "The Brain Surgeon" in *Waiting to Waltz: A Childhood,* poems by Cynthia Rylant. Text copyright © 1984 by Cynthia Rylant. Illustrations copyright © 1984 by Stephen Gammell./ Illustration by Stephen Gammell from *The Relatives Came* by Cynthia Rylant. Text copyright © 1985 by Cynthia Rylant. Illustrations copyright © 1985 by Stephen Gammell. All reprinted by permission of Bradbury Press.

CHILD'S PLAY (INTERNATIONAL) LTD. Illustration by Don Wood from *The Big Hungry Bear* by Don and Audrey Wood. Copyright © 1984 by M. Twinn./ Illustration by Don Wood from *Quick as a Cricket* by Audrey Wood. Copyright © 1982 by M. Twinn./ Illustration by Audrey Wood from *Balloonia* by Audrey Wood. Text and illustrations copyright © 1981 by Audrey Wood./ Illustration from *Tugford Wanted to Be Bad* by Audrey Wood. Copyright © 1983 by Audrey Wood./ Illustration from *The Princess and the Dragon* by Audrey Wood. Text and illustrations copyright © 1981 by Audrey Wood. All reprinted by permission of Child's Play (International) Ltd.

COWARD, McCANN & GEOGHEGAN, INC. Illustration by Pamela Allen from *Bertie and the Bear* by Pamela Allen. Copyright © 1983 by Pamela Allen./ Illustration by Pamela Allen from *Who Sank the Boat?* by Pamela Allen. Copyright © 1982 by Pamela Allen. Both reprinted by permission of Coward, McCann & Geoghegan, Inc.

THOMAS Y. CROWELL, INC. Illustration by Emily Arnold McCully from *Last Look* by Clyde Robert Bulla. Text copyright © 1979 by Clyde Robert Bulla. Illustrations copyright © 1979 by Emily Arnold McCully./ Illustration by Deborah Kogan Ray from *The White Marble* by Charlotte Zolotow. Text copyright © 1963 by Charlotte Zolotow. Illustrations copyright © 1982 by Deborah Kogan Ray. Both reprinted by permission of Thomas Y. Crowell, Inc.

DELACORTE PRESS. Sidelight excerpts from *Violins and Shovels: The WPA Arts Project* by Milton Meltzer. Reprinted by permission of Delacorte Press.

DIAL BOOKS FOR YOUNG READERS. Illustration by Rosekrans Hoffman from *Three Sisters* by Audrey Wood. Text copyright © 1986 by Audrey Wood. Illustrations copyright © 1986 by Rosekrans Hoffman. Reprinted by permission of Dial Books for Young Readers.

DLM, INC. Illustration by Carmen Mowry from *Andersen Stories for Pleasure Reading* by Edward W. Dolch, Marguerite P. Dolch and Beulah F. Jackson. Copyright © 1956 by DLM Teaching Resources. Reprinted by permission of DLM, Inc.

DODD, MEAD & CO. Illustrations by Ashley Wolff from *The Bells of London* by Ashley Wolff. Copyright © 1985 by Ashley Wolff. Reprinted by permission of Dodd, Mead & Co.

DOUBLEDAY & CO., INC. Illustration by Harvey Dinnerstein from *Remember the Days: A Short History of the Jewish American* by Milton Meltzer. Copyright © 1974 by Milton Meltzer. Reprinted by permission of Doubleday & Co., Inc.

E. P. DUTTON, INC. Illustration by Emily Arnold McCully from *The Thing in Kat's Attic* by Charlotte Towner Graeber. Text copyright © 1984 by Charlotte Towner Graeber. Illustrations copyright © 1984 by Emily Arnold McCully./ Illustration by Martin Ursell from *The Song of Pentecost* by W. J. Corbett. Text copyright © 1982 by W. J. Corbett. Illustrations copyright © 1982 by Methuen Children's Books Ltd./ Illustration by Diane Goode from *When I Was Young in the Mountains* by Cynthia Rylant. Text copyright © 1982 by Cynthia Rylant. Illustrations copyright © 1982 by Diane Goode. All reprinted by permission of E. P. Dutton, Inc.

FARRAR, STRAUS & GIROUX, INC. Sidelight excerpts from *Autobiographical Writings* by Hermann Hesse, edited by Theodore Ziolkowski./ Photograph by Jason Laure from *Joi Bangla! The Children of Bangladesh* by Jason Laure and Ettagale Laure. Copyright © 1974 by Jason Laure./ Sidelight excerpts from *World of Our Fathers: The Jews of Eastern Europe* by Milton Meltzer./ Illustration by Uri Shulevitz from *The Fool of the World and the Flying Ship,* retold by Arthur Ransome. Illustrations copyright © 1968 by Uri Shulevitz./ Illustration by Uri Shulevitz from *The Golem* by Isaac Bashevis Singer. Text copyright © 1982 by Isaac Bashevis Singer. Illustrations copyright © 1982 by Uri Shulevitz./ Illustration by Uri Shulevitz from *The Treasure* by Uri Shulevitz. Copyright © 1986 by Uri Shulevitz./ Illustration by Uri Shulevitz from *The Strange and Exciting Adventures of Jeremiah Hush* by Uri Shulevitz. Copyright © 1986 by Uri Shulevitz./ Illustration by Uri Shulevitz from *The Fools of Chelm and Their History* by Isaac Bashevis Singer. Text copyright © 1973 by Isaac Bashevis Singer. Illustrations copyright © 1973 by Uri Shulevitz. All reprinted by permission of Farrar, Straus & Giroux, Inc.

GARRARD PUBLISHING CO. Illustration by Marguerite Dolch from *True Cat Stories* by Marguerite P. Dolch. Copyright © 1975 by Marguerite P. Dolch. Reprinted by permission of Garrard Publishing Co.

GREENWILLOW BOOKS. Illustration by Ann Jonas from *The Quilt* by Ann Jonas. Copyright © 1984 by Ann Jonas./ Illustration by Ann Jonas from *Holes and Peeks* by Ann Jonas. Copyright © 1984 by Ann Jonas./ Jacket illustration by Ted Bernstein from *The Door in the Hedge* by Robin McKinley. Copyright © 1981 by Robin McKinley./ Illustration by Uri Shulevitz from *Hanukah Money* by Sholem Aleichem. Copyright © 1978 by Uri Shulevitz./ Jacket illustration by David McCall Johnston from *The Hero and the Crown* by Robin McKinley. All reprinted by permission of Greenwillow Books.

HARCOURT BRACE JOVANOVICH, INC. Jacket illustration by Sidney Butchkes from *The Sweeping Wind* by Paul deKruif. Copyright © 1962 by Paul deKruif./ Illustration by Zadig from *Hunger Fighters* by Paul deKruif. Copyright 1926, 1927, 1928 by The Curtis Publishing Co. Copyright 1928 by Harcourt Brace Jovanovich, Inc. Copyright 1955 by Paul deKruif./ Sidelight excerpts from *Life among the Doctors* by Paul deKruif. Copyright 1949 by Paul deKruif. Copyright renewed © 1977 by Eleanor Lappage deKruif./ Sidelight excerpts from *The Sweeping Wind, a Memoir* by Paul deKruif. Copyright © 1962 by Paul deKruif./ Illustration by Fritz Eichenberg from *Ape in a Cape: An Alphabet of Odd Animals* by Fritz Eichenberg. Copyright 1952 by Fritz Eichenberg./ Illustration by Fritz Eichenberg from *Dancing in the Moon: Counting Rhymes* by Fritz Eichenberg. Copyright 1955 by Fritz Eichenberg./ Illustration by Don Wood from *King Bidgood's in the Bathtub* by Audrey Wood. Text copyright © 1985 by Audrey Wood. Illustrations copyright © 1985 by Don Wood./ Illustration by Don Wood from *Moonflute* by Audrey Wood. Text copyright © 1980, 1986 by Audrey Wood. Illustrations copyright © 1980 by Don Wood. All reprinted by permission of Harcourt Brace Jovanovich, Inc.

HARPER & ROW, PUBLISHERS, INC. Illustration by Emily Arnold McCully from *Journey from Peppermint Street* by Meindert De Jong. Text copyright © 1968 by Meindert De Jong. Illustrations copyright © 1968 by Emily Arnold McCully./ Illustration by Emily Arnold McCully from *First Snow* by Emily Arnold McCully. Copyright © 1985 by Emily Arnold McCully./ Illustration by Emily Arnold McCully from *Stand in the Wind* by Jean Little. Text copyright © 1975 by Jean Little. Illustrations copyright © 1975 by Emily Arnold McCully./ Illustration by Emily Arnold McCully from *Her Majesty, Grace Jones* by Jane Langton. Text copyright © 1961 by Jane Gillson Langton. Illustrations copyright © 1972 by Emily Arnold McCully./ Sidelight excerpts from an article "Growing Up in Nazi Germany" by Charles Hannam in *A Boy in That Situation: An Autobiography.*/ Photograph by Martin Hesse from *The Hesse/Mann Letters,* edited by Anni Carlsson and Volker Michels. Copyright © 1975 by Harper & Row, Publishers, Inc./ Illustration by Deborah Kogan Ray from *Sunday Morning We Went to the Zoo* by Deborah Kogan Ray. Copyright © 1981 by Deborah Kogan Ray./ Illustration by Margaret Ayer from *Anna and the King of Siam* by Margaret Landon. Copyright 1943, 1944 by Margaret Mortenson Landon./ Illustration by Leonard Everett Fisher from *All Times, All Peoples: A World History of Slavery* by Milton Meltzer. Text copyright © 1980 by Milton Meltzer. Illustrations copyright © 1980 by Leonard Everett Fisher./ Sidelight excerpts and photographs from *This I Remember* by Eleanor Roosevelt. Copyright 1949 by Anna Eleanor Roosevelt./ Sidelight excerpts from *This Is My Story* by Eleanor Roosevelt. Copyright 1937 by Anna Eleanor Roosevelt./ Illustration by Uri Shulevitz from *The Second Witch* by Jack Sendak. Text copyright © 1965 by Jack Sendak. Illustrations copyright © 1965 by Uri Shulevitz./ Illustration by Sarah Wilson from *Beware the Dragons!* by Sarah Wilson. Copyright © 1985 by Sarah Wilson. All reprinted by permission of Harper & Row, Publishers, Inc.

HASTINGS HOUSE, PUBLISHERS. Illustrations by Hans Helweg from *Olga Carries On* by Michael Bond. Text copyright © 1976 by Michael Bond. Illustrations copyright © 1976 by Hans Helweg. Both reprinted by permission of Hastings House, Publishers.

HERDER & HERDER, INC. Photographs from *Portrait of Hesse: An Illustrated Biography* by Bernhard Zeller. Copyright © 1963 by Rowohlt Taschenbuch Verlag Gmbtt, Reinbek bei Hamburg. English translation © 1971 by Herder & Herder, Inc. All reprinted by permission of Herder & Herder, Inc.

HERITAGE PRESS. Illustration by Fritz Eichenberg from *The Idiot* by Feodor Dostoevski./ Illustration by Fritz Eichenberg from *Crime and Punishment* by Feodor Dostoevski. Both reprinted by permission of Heritage Press.

HOLIDAY HOUSE, INC. Illustration by Fritz Eichenberg from *Padre Porko: The Gentlemanly Pig* by Robert Davis. Copyright 1939, 1948 by Robert Davis./ Jacket illustration by Allen Davis from *The Diary of Trilby Frost* by Dianne Glaser. Copyright © 1976 by Dianne Glaser. Both reprinted by permission of Holiday House, Inc.

HOLT, RINEHART AND WINSTON GENERAL BOOK. Illustration by Jim Spence from *Pop and Peter Potts* by Clifford B. Hicks. Text copyright © 1984 by Clifford B. Hicks. Illustrations copyright © 1984 by Holt, Rinehart and Winston. Reprinted by permission of Holt, Rinehart and Winston General Book.

THE HORN BOOK, INC. Sidelight excerpts from *Illustrators of Children's Books: 1946-1956,* compiled by Bertha M. Miller and others. Copyright © 1958 by The Horn Book, Inc./ Sidelight excerpts from an article "Interview with Ann Jonas" by Sylvia and Kenneth Marantz, May/June, 1987 in *Horn Book.*/ Sidelight excerpts from an article "The Illustrator's Notebook," edited by Lee Kingman in *Horn Book.* Copyright © 1978 by The Horn Book, Inc./ Sidelight excerpts from an article "Writing with Pictures" by Uri Shulevitz, February, 1982 in *Horn Book.* All reprinted by permission of The Horn Book, Inc.

HOUGHTON MIFFLIN CO. Jacket illustration by Heather Cooper from *Bluebeard's Egg and Other Stories* by Margaret Atwood. Copyright © 1983, 1986 by O. W. Toad Ltd./ Jacket illustration by Diane de Groat from *Daphne's Book* by Mary Downing Hahn. Text copyright © 1983 by Mary Downing Hahn. Jacket illustration copyright © 1983 by Diane de Groat. Both reprinted by permission of Houghton Mifflin Co.

HOUNSLOW PRESS. Illustration by Peter Whalley from *Colombo's 101 Canadian Places* by John Robert Colombo. Text copyright © 1983 by J. R. Colombo. Illustrations copyright © 1983 by Peter Whalley. Reprinted by permission of Hounslow Press.

JEWISH PUBLICATION SOCIETY. Photographs by Stephen Epstein from *The Jews in America: A Picture Album* by Milton Meltzer. Text copyright © 1974, 1985 by Milton Meltzer. Both reprinted by permission of Jewish Publication Society.

ALFRED A. KNOPF, INC. Illustration from *Bread—and Roses: The Struggle of American Labor, 1865-1915* by Milton Meltzer. Copyright © 1967 by Milton Meltzer. Reprinted by permission of Alfred A. Knopf, Inc.

LITTLE, BROWN & CO., INC. Illustration by Eric von Schmidt from *Chancy and the Grand Rascal* by Sid Fleischman. Copyright © 1966 by Albert S. Fleischman./ Illustration by Eric von Schmidt from *Humbug Mountain* by Sid Fleischman. Copyright © 1978 by Albert S. Fleischman. Both reprinted by permission of Little, Brown & Co., Inc.

LODESTAR BOOKS. Jacket illustration by Andrew Rhodes from *Popcorn Days and Buttermilk Nights* by Gary Paulsen. Copyright © 1983 by Gary Paulsen./ Photographs from *Eleanor Roosevelt, with Love: A Centenary Remembrance* by Elliott Roosevelt. Copyright © 1984 by Elliott Roosevelt. All reprinted by permission of Lodestar Books.

JAMES LORIMER & CO. Illustration by Ann Blades from *Anna's Pet* by Margaret Atwood and Joyce Barkhouse. Text copyright © 1980 by Margaret Atwood. Illustrations copyright © 1980 by Ann Blades. Reprinted by permission of James Lorimer & Co.

LOTHROP, LEE & SHEPARD BOOKS. Illustration by Pamela Allen from *Mr. Archimedes' Bath* by Pamela Allen. Copyright © 1980 by Pamela Allen. Reprinted by permission of Lothrop, Lee & Shepard Books.

MACMILLAN PUBLISHING CO. Illustration by Uri Shulevitz from *The Magician,* adapted by Uri Shulevitz. Copyright © 1973 by Uri Shulevitz./ Illustration by David Small from *Eulalie and the Hopping Head* by David Small. Copyright © 1982 by David Small. Both reprinted by permission of Macmillan Publishing Co.

McGRAW-HILL BOOK CO. Illustration by Brinton Turkle from *Danny Dunn and the Fossil Cave* by Jay Williams and Raymond Abrashkin. Copyright © 1961 by Jay Williams and the Estate of Raymond Abrashkin. Reprinted by permission of McGraw-Hill Book Co.

WILLIAM MORROW & CO., INC. Illustration by Ann Jonas from *Where Can It Be?* by Ann Jonas. Copyright © 1986 by Ann Jonas. Reprinted by permission of William Morrow & Co., Inc.

THOMAS NELSON, INC. Jacket illustration by Richard Cuffari from *The Foxman* by Gary Paulsen. Copyright © 1977 by Gary Paulsen. Reprinted by permission of Thomas Nelson, Inc.

NEW DIRECTIONS PUBLISHING CORP. Cover photograph by A. K. Coomaraswamy from *Siddhartha* by Hermann Hesse. Copyright 1951 by New Directions Publishing Corp./ Illustration by Fritz Eichenberg from *A Child's Christmas in Wales* by Dylan Thomas. Both reprinted by permission of New Directions Publishing Corp.

NEW CANADA PUBLICATIONS. Illustration by Barry Zaid from *The Chocolate Moose* by Gwendolyn MacEwen. Text copyright © 1982 by Gwendolyn MacEwen. Illustrations copyright © 1982 by Barry Zaid. Reprinted by permission of New Canada Publications.

OXFORD UNIVERSITY PRESS. Illustration by Alison Lester from *Thing* by Robin Klein. Text copyright © 1982 by Robin Klein. Illustrations copyright © 1982 by Alison Lester./ Illustration by William Papas from *Armenian Folk Tales and Fables,* translated by Charles Downing. Copyright © 1972 by Charles Downing./ Illustration by William Papas from *Captain Pamphile's Adventures* by Alexandre Dumas. Translated by Douglas Munro. English translation copyright © 1971 by Douglas Munro. All reprinted by permission of Oxford University Press.

CLARKSON N. POTTER, INC. Sidelight excerpts from *The Wood and the Graver* by Fritz Eichenberg. Copyright © 1977 by Fritz Eichenberg. Reprinted by permission of Clarkson N. Potter, Inc.

PRICE/STERN/SLOAN PUBLISHERS, INC. Illustration by Robin James from *Ming Ling* by Stephen Cosgrove. Copyright © 1983 by Price/Stern/Sloan Publishers, Inc. Reprinted by permission of Price/Stern/Sloan Publishers, Inc.

RANDOM HOUSE, INC. Illustration by Aurelius Battaglia from *Mother Goose.* Copyright © 1973 by Random House, Inc./ Wood engraving by Fritz Eichenberg from "William Wilson" in *Tales of Edgar Allan Poe.* Copyright 1944 by Random House, Inc./ Photographs from *Hermann Hesse, Pilgrim of Crisis: A Biography* by Ralph Freedman. Copyright © 1978 by Ralph Freedman./ Illustrations by Susan Jeffers from *Black Beauty* by Anna Sewell, adapted by Robin McKinley. Text copyright © 1986 by Random House, Inc. Illustrations copyright © 1986 by Susan Jeffers./ Illustration by Fritz Eichenberg from *Jane Eyre* by Charlotte Bronte./ Illustration by Fritz Eichenberg from *Wuthering Heights* by Emily Bronte. All reprinted by permission of Random House, Inc.

REGENSTEINER PUBLISHING ENTERPRISES, INC. Illustration by Joann Daley from *The Haunted Motorcycle Shop* by Harriette Abels. Copyright © 1978 by Regensteiner Publishing Enterprises, Inc. Reprinted by permission of Regensteiner Publishing Enterprises, Inc.

CHARLES SCRIBNER'S SONS. Illustration by Uri Shulevitz from *The Silkspinners* by Jean Russel Larson. Text copyright © 1967 by Jean Russell Larson. Illustrations copyright © 1967 by Uri Shulevitz./ Illustration by Uri Shulevitz from *One Monday Morning* by Uri Shulevitz. Copyright © 1967 by Uri Shulevitz. Both reprinted by permission of Charles Scribner's Sons.

SIMON & SCHUSTER, INC. Jacket illustration by Paul Bacon from *Lady Oracle* by Margaret Atwood. Copyright © 1976 by Margaret Atwood. Reprinted by permission of Simon & Schuster, Inc.

STEMMER HOUSE PUBLISHERS, INC. Illustration by Fritz Eichenberg from *Poor Troll: The Story of Ruebezahl and the Princess,* retold by Fritz Eichenberg. Copyright © 1983 by Fritz Eichenberg. Reprinted by permission of Stemmer House Publishers, Inc.

THE VIKING PRESS. Illustration by Emily A. McCully from *Friday Night Is Papa Night* by Ruth A. Sonneborn. Text copyright © 1970 by Ruth A. Sonneborn. Illustrations copyright © 1970 by Emily A. McCully. Reprinted by permission of The Viking Press.

VIKING KESTREL. Illustration by Stephen Marchesi from *Winnie Mandela: The Soul of South Africa* by Milton Meltzer. Text copyright © 1986 by Milton Meltzer. Illustrations copyright © 1986 by Stephen Marchesi./ Illustration by Donna Diamond and photograph by Dorothea Lange from *Dorothea Lange: Life through the Camera* by Milton Meltzer. Text copyright © 1985 by Milton Meltzer. Illustrations copyright © 1985 by Donna Diamond./ Illustration by Donna Ruff from *Eleanor Roosevelt: First Lady of the World* by Doris Faber. Text copyright © 1985 by Doris Faber. Illustrations copyright © 1985 by Donna Ruff. All reprinted by permission of Viking Kestrel.

FREDERICK WARNE LTD. Cover illustration by Jonathan Rosenbaum from *Getting to Know Me* by Elizabeth T. Billington. Copyright © 1982 by Elizabeth T. Billington. Reprinted by permission of Frederick Warne Ltd.

WATSON-GUPTILL PUBLICATIONS. Illustration and Sidelight excerpts by Uri Shulevitz from *Writing with Pictures: How to Write and Illustrate Children's Books* by Uri Shulevitz. Copyright © 1985 by Uri Shulevitz. Both reprinted by permission of Watson-Guptill Publications.

WESTERN PUBLISHING CO., INC. Illustration by Joan Elizabeth Goodman from *Good Night, Pippin* by Joan Elizabeth Goodman. Copyright © 1986 by Joan Elizabeth Goodman. Reprinted by permission of Western Publishing Co., Inc.

THE WESTMINSTER PRESS. Illustration by Dick Teicher from *A Boat to Nowhere* by Maureen Crane Wartski. Copyright © 1980 by Maureen Crane Wartski. Reprinted by permission of The Westminster Press.

Sidelight excerpts from *The Imagineers* by Pamela Allen, number 5, 1983. Reprinted by permission of Pamela Allen./ Sidelight excerpts from an article "Milton Meltzer" by Lee Bennett Hopkins in *More Books by More People.* Copyright © 1974 by Lee Bennett Hopkins. Reprinted by permission of Curtis Brown Ltd./ Sidelight excerpts from an article "An Interview with Margaret Atwood" by Catherine Sheldrick Ross and Cory Bieman Davies in *Canadian Children's Literature,* number 42, 1986. Reprinted by permission of *Canadian Children's Literature.*/ Sidelight excerpts from an article "Whatever You Make of It" by Robert Munsch in *Canadian Children's Literature,* number 43, 1986. Reprinted by permission of *Canadian Children's Literature.*/ Sidelight excerpts from an article "American Bicentennial

Reading" by Milton Meltzer. Copyright © 1975 by Children's Book Council, Inc. Reprinted by permission of Children's Book Council, Inc./ Sidelight excerpts from an article "Margaret Atwood: 'Poems and Poet' " by Joyce Carol Oates in *New York Times Book Review,* May 21, 1978. Copyright © 1978 by The New York Times Co. Reprinted by permission of The New York Times, Inc./ Jacket illustration by David Palladini from *Beauty: A Retelling of the Story of Beauty and the Beast* by Robin McKinley. Copyright © 1978 by Robin McKinley. Reprinted by permission of David Palladini./ Sidelight excerpts from an article "Anna and I" by Margaret Landon in *Town & Country,* December, 1952. Reprinted by permission of *Town & Country.*/ Sidelight excerpts from an article "Writing for Young Adults" by Maureen Crane Wartski in *Writer,* December, 1986. Reprinted by permission of Maureen Wartski.

Appreciation also to the Performing Arts Research Center of the New York Public Library at Lincoln Center for permission to reprint the theater stills from "The King and I."

PHOTOGRAPH CREDITS

Pamela Allen: Ron Allen; Margaret Atwood: Graeme Gibson; Joseph Robert Colombo: Bill Brooks; Fritz Eichenberg: Antonie Eichenberg; Joan Elizabeth Goodman: Robert Zuckerman; Mary Downing Hahn: Norman Jacob; Ann Jonas: Donald Crews; Robin McKinley: Helen Marcus; Milton Meltzer: Catherine Koren; Gary Paulsen: *News Tribune and Herald* (Duluth, Minn.); Uri Shulevitz: Donald Wallace; Sarah Wilson: Edward Williams.

something
about the
author

ABELS, Harriette S(heffer) 1926-
(H. R. Sheffer)

PERSONAL: Born December 1, 1926, in Port Chester, New York; daughter of Mitchell (a department store executive) and Matilda (Smith) Sheffer; married Robert H. Abels (in design and marketing), September 5, 1949; children: Barbara (Mrs. Ben-David), David M., Carol (Mrs. Horowitz). *Education:* Attended Furman University, 1944-45. *Religion:* Jewish. *Home and office:* 14674 Valley Vista Blvd., Sherman Oaks, Calif. 91403. *Agent:* Cantrell-Colas Inc., 229 East 79th St., New York, N.Y. 10021.

CAREER: Employed as a medical secretary, 1946-49; writer, 1963—. *MEMBER:* P.E.N. (secretary of Los Angeles branch, 1977-79), Romance Writers of America, Southern California Council on Literature for Children and Young People.

WRITINGS—For children; fiction, except as noted: *The Circus Detectives* (illustrated by Susan Jeffers), Ginn, 1971; *Mystery on the Delta,* Lantern Press, 1971; *Call Me Clown* (illustrated by Jim Lamb), Childrens Press, 1977; *The Haunted Cottage* (illustrated by Joann Daley), Childrens Press, 1978; *The Haunted Motorcycle Shop* (illustrated by J. Daley), Childrens Press, 1978; *The Creature of Saxony Woods* (illustrated by J. Daley), Childrens Press, 1979; *Dollhouse Miniatures* (nonfiction), Childrens Press, 1980; *Emmy, Beware!* (illustrated by Richard Wahl), Childrens Press, 1981; *September Storm* (illustrated by Scott Gustafson), Childrens Press, 1981.

For young adults; romance novels: *Follow Me, Love,* Avalon, 1978; *A Special Love,* Tempo, 1982; *A New Love for Lisa,* Tempo, 1983; *Cupid Confusion,* Tempo, 1984; *First Impression,* Tempo, 1984; *A Good Sport,* Tempo, 1985; (with Joyce Schenk) *Seaside Heights,* Signet Vista, 1985; *Lucky in Love,* Tempo, 1985.

"Galaxy I" series; for children; science fiction; illustrated by Rodney Furan and Barbara Furan; edited by Howard Schroeder; published by Crestwood House, 1979: *A Forgotten World; The Green Invasion; Medical Emergency; Meteor from the Moon; Mystery on Mars; Planet of Ice; The Silent Invaders; Strangers on NMA-6; Unwanted Visitors.*

"Our Future World" series; for children; nonfiction; illustrated by Vista III Design; edited by H. Schroeder; published

HARRIETTE S. ABELS

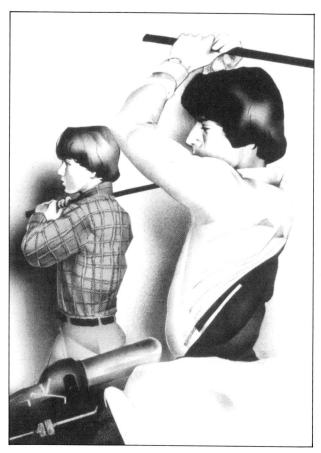

Chuck swung the heavy crowbar at the wall. ■ (From *The Haunted Motorcycle Shop* by Harriette Abels. Illustrated by Joann Daley.)

by Crestwood House, 1980: *Future Business; . . . Communication; . . . Family; . . . Food; . . . Government; . . . Medicine; . . . Science; . . . Space; . . . Travel.*

Under pseudonym H. R. Sheffer; "Teammates" series; for children; fiction; illustrated by Vista III Design; edited by H. Schroeder; published by Crestwood House, 1981: *The Last Meet; Moto-Cross Monkey; Partners on Wheels; Sarah Sells Soccer; Second-String Nobody; Street-Hockey Lady; Swim for Pride; Two at the Net; Winner on the Court; Weekend in the Dunes.*

Under pseudonym H. R. Sheffer; "Movin' On!" series; for children; nonfiction; edited by H. Schroeder; published by Crestwood House: *Airplanes,* 1982; *Paddlewheelers,* 1982; *Race Cars,* 1982; *Trains,* 1982; *Vans,* 1982; *Cycles,* 1983; *Great Cars,* 1983; *R.V.'s,* 1983; *Tractors,* 1983; *Trucks,* 1983.*

Contributor of articles and stories to periodicals, including *Highlights for Children* and *Jack and Jill.*

WORK IN PROGRESS: Young adult problem novel co-authored with Joyce Schenk.

SIDELIGHTS: "I first started writing as a child. Although I've limited my career to writing for children and young adults, I'm now attempting adult category novels."

HOBBIES AND OTHER INTERESTS: Travel, archeology, art (especially Impressionism).

ABRASHKIN, Raymond 1911-1960 (Ray Ashley)

PERSONAL: Born in 1911, in Brooklyn, N.Y.; died August 25, 1960, in Weston, Conn.; married wife, Evelyn; children: William H., John W. *Education:* City College (now of the City University of New York), B.S. 1931. *Residence:* Weston, Conn.

CAREER: Film producer, teacher, and author of books for children. Teacher in New York City public schools, 1931-40; free-lance writer, 1946-60. Former editor for Reynal and Hitchcock. *Wartime service:* U. S. Maritime Service, World War II. *Awards, honors:* Silver Lion Award for best American film from Venice International Film Festival, and Academy Award nomination from Academy of Motion Picture Arts and Sciences, both 1954, both for "The Little Fugitive"; Young Reader's Choice Award from Pacific Northwest Library Association, 1961, for *Danny Dunn and the Homework Machine,* and 1963, for *Danny Dunn on the Ocean Floor.*

WRITINGS—All for children; "Danny Dunn" series; all written with Jay Williams; all science fiction: *Danny Dunn and the Anti-Gravity Paint* (illustrated by Ezra Jack Keats), Whittlesey House, 1956; . . . *on a Desert Island* (illustrated by E. J. Keats), Whittlesey House, 1957; . . . *and the Homework Machine* (illustrated by E. J. Keats), McGraw, 1958; . . . *and the Weather Machine* (illustrated by E. J. Keats), McGraw, 1959; . . . *on the Ocean Floor* (illustrated by Brinton Turkle), Whittlesey House, 1960; . . . *and the Fossil Cave* (illustrated by B. Turkle), Whittlesey House, 1961.

The following "Danny Dunn" books were written by J. Williams who continued the series following Abrashkin's death: *Danny Dunn and the Heat Ray* (illustrated by Owen Kampen), McGraw, 1962; . . ., *Time Traveler* (illustrated by O. Kampen), Whittlesey House, 1963; . . . *and the Automatic House* (illustrated by O. Kampen), Whittlesey House, 1965; . . . *and the Voice from Space* (illustrated by Leo Summers), McGraw, 1967; . . . *and the Smallifying Machine* (illustrated by Paul Sagsoorian), McGraw, 1969; . . . *and the Swamp Monster* (illustrated by P. Sagsoorian), McGraw, 1971; . . . *Invisible Boy* (illustrated by P. Sagsoorian), McGraw, 1974; . . ., *Scientific Detective* (illustrated by P. Sagsoorian; Junior Literary Guild selection), McGraw, 1975; . . . *and the Universal Glue* (illustrated by P. Sagsoorian), McGraw, 1977.

Recordings; all for children: "Busy Policeman Joe [and] Tall Fireman Paul," music by Tom Glazer, read by Leon Janney, RCA Victor, 1960; (with T. Glazer) "On the Ranch: A Story-Song Record for Your Child to Grow On," performed by Cisco Houston and others, RCA Victor, 1961; "Music for Ones and Twos," performed by T. Glazer, CMS Records, 1972. Also "The Emperor's Clothes."

Under pseudonym Ray Ashley, author and producer of film "Little Fugitive," Little Fugitive Productions, 1953. Also composer of several operas for children; education editor, *PM* newspaper; contributor to periodicals, including *Ladies' Home Journal.*

ADAPTATIONS—Plays: "Danny Dunn and the Homework Machine," adapted by Julie Mandel, Metromedia-on-Stage, 1969.

Recordings: "Danny Dunn and the Homework Machine," Golden Records, 1969; "Danny Dunn and the Swamp Monster," read by Jay Williams, one read-along cassette with book and teacher's guide, Listening Library, 1984.

"It is!" he exclaimed. "It's clicking like anything!" ■(From *Danny Dunn and the Fossil Cave* by
Jay Williams and Raymond Abrashkin. Illustrated by Brinton Turkle.)

SIDELIGHTS: Born in Brooklyn, New York, Abrashkin received his B.S. degree from City College in New York in 1931 and taught in the New York City public school system from 1931 to 1940.

Following his World War II tour of duty in the U. S. Maritime Service, he became editor at Reynal and Hitchcock. From 1946 until his death he devoted himself to free-lance work. He was an education editor of the now defunct newspaper *PM*, a composer of numerous children's records and children's operas, an author and a motion-picture producer.

In 1953 Abrashkin wrote and co-produced the film "Little Fugitive" under his pseudonym Ray Ashley. The movie's main character, seven-year-old Richie Andrusco, is confronted with the gruesome belief that he has murdered his twelve-year-old brother, the result of a cruel hoax engineered by his brother and friends. Young Andrusco wrestles with his dilemma by running away from his tenement home and finds himself in Coney Island, where he indulges himself in the enjoyment of the place and in his newly found freedom. The *Christian Science Monitor* called the film "an engaging and unhackneyed film. . . . The story has a great deal of humor, some pathos, and a sympathetic identification with its small hero's experiences which invites the spectator into a kaleidoscopic child-world of wonders, joys, bewilderments, and passing terrors."

Abrashkin explained how they discovered the unknown child actor Richie Andrusco climbing onto a horse on a Coney Island merry-go-round. "We asked him if he wanted some help climbing up, and it was the way he turned around and said 'No!' that drew us to him. His first tests were not perfect, but it was amazing how quickly he improved. At the beginning of the filming we were wasting takes at the ratio of about fifteen to one. At the end, about one out of every two was good." [*New York Herald Tribune*, October 18, 1953.[1]]

The film won the Silver Lion Award for best American film from the Venice International Film Festival and an Academy Award nomination from the Academy of Motion Picture Arts and Sciences. It was produced for a final cost of under $100,000.

In 1956, the first of the "Danny Dunn" books written with Jay Williams was published. At the time Abrashkin was almost completely paralyzed by illness and unable to speak. He would point to letters on a drawing of a typewriter keyboard which would represent an entire word—a shorthand system the two men had developed.

The "Danny Dunn" series was extremely popular among young people, who wrote fan letters averaging one thousand a year. Although Abrashkin died after the fifth book was published, the series was continued by Jay Williams until his own death in 1978.

(From the movie "Little Fugitive," starring Richie Andrusco. Copyright 1953 by Little Fugitive Production Co.)

Abrashkin died at his home in Weston, Connecticut at the age of forty-nine on August 25, 1960. In 1969 *Danny Dunn and the Homework Machine* was adapted into a play for young people and into a children's record.

FOR MORE INFORMATION SEE: Time, November 2, 1953. Obituaries: *New York Times,* August 26, 1960; *Publishers Weekly,* September 12, 1960; Felice Levy, compiler, *Obituaries on File,* Volume 1, Facts on File, 1979.

ALLEN, Pamela 1934-

PERSONAL: Born April 3, 1934, in Devonport, Auckland, New Zealand; daughter of William Ewart (a surveyor) and Esma (a homemaker; maiden name, Griffith) Griffiths; married William Robert Allen (head of Visual Art School, Sydney College of Art), December 12, 1964; children: Ben, Ruth. *Education:* Elam School of Art (now Auckland University College), Diploma of Fine Art, 1954; attended Auckland Teachers Training College, 1955-56. *Agent:* Curtis Brown, 27 Union St., Paddington, Sydney, N.S.W. 2021, Australia.

CAREER: Author and illustrator, 1979—. Art teacher in secondary schools in New Zealand, 1956-58, 1960-64. *Member:*

Australian Society of Authors, Children's Book Council of Australia. *Awards, honors:* Picture Book of the Year commendation from the Children's Book Council of Australia, and New South Wales Premier's Literary Award, children's book category, both 1981, and Australian Book Publishers Association Book Design Award commendation, 1980-81, all for *Mr. Archimedes' Bath;* Children's Book of the Year Award from the Children's Book Council of Australia, and New South Wales Premier's Literary Award, children's book category, both 1983, and International Board on Books for Young People honour diploma for illustration (Australian entry), 1984, all for *Who Sank the Boat?;* Children's Book of the Year Award from the Children's Book Council of Australia, 1984, for *Bertie and the Bear.*

WRITINGS—All self-illustrated: *Mr. Archimedes' Bath,* Lothrop, 1980; *Who Sank the Boat?,* T. Nelson (Australia), 1982, large print edition, 1985, Coward, 1983; *Bertie and the Bear* (Junior Literary Guild selection), T. Nelson, 1983, Coward, 1984; *A Lion in the Night,* T. Nelson, 1985, Putnam, 1986; *Simon Said,* T. Nelson, 1985; *Watch Me,* T. Nelson, 1985; *Herbert and Harry,* T. Nelson, 1986; *Mr. McGee,* T. Nelson, 1987. Contributor to *School* (New South Wales).

Illustrator; all published by Heinemann (New Zealand), except as noted: Jan Farr, *Mummy, Do Monsters Clean Their Teeth?,*

1975; J. Farr, *Mummy, How Cold Is a Witch's Nose?*, 1976; T. E. Wilson, *Three Cheers for McGinty,* 1976; T. E. Wilson, *McGinty Goes to School,* 1976; T. E. Wilson, *McGinty the Ghost,* 1976; T. E. Wilson, *McGinty in Space,* 1976; J. Farr, *Big Sloppy Dinosaur Socks,* 1977; J. Farr, *Mummy, Are Monsters Too Big for Their Boots?,* 1977; N. L. Ray, *The Pow Toe,* Collins (Australia), 1979; Sally Fitzpatrick, *A Tall Story,* Angus & Robertson (Australia), 1981.

WORK IN PROGRESS: "Fancy That!," Simon Did, and *Watch Me Now,* all for T. Nelson (Australia).

SIDELIGHTS: "I was born in Devonport, Auckland, New Zealand in 1934 during the depression. My father and mother were both born in New Zealand while my grandparents came from England.

"I lived all my childhood in Devonport going to the local primary school in Vauxhall Road and then on to St. Cuthbert's College in Auckland. All I knew about myself was that I wanted to draw. I persuaded my parents to let me go from there to art school—the Elam School of Art as it was then. I completed my Diploma of Fine Art after four years and went on to training college to become an art teacher in a secondary school.

"It was only after I had a child of my own that I became really aware of children's picture books. It was during my own children's pre-school years when I was involved with the Birkenhead Play Centre that I came to know young children so well.

"In 1978, our family moved to Sydney, and it was then that I attempted to write and illustrate my first book, *Mr. Archimedes' Bath.*

"... I had just arrived with my husband and two children to live permanently in Sydney. I had been illustrating Jan Farr's writing in New Zealand. These books were inexpensive editions of paperback books using two colours and retailing then

**Was it the sheep
who knew where to sit
to level the boat
so that she could knit?**

■ (From *Who Sank the Boat?* by Pamela Allen. Illustrated by the author.)

and danced.

PAMELA ALLEN

for about $1.00. My first published illustrations were for Jan Farr's, *Mummy, Do Monsters Clean Their Teeth?* . . . in 1975.

"I wanted to illustrate a picture book in full colour. I had visions of making a livelihood and a meaningful role for myself in this field. I ended up on Collins doorstep where Anne Ingram and Margaret Jones (editors of the children's books) gave me an hour of their time. They were not encouraging about illustrating work but said that if I could both write and illustrate a book, then they could be interested. I walked out of their office an author.

"How do you write a good picture book for children? I was examining myself—my skills and my priorities. 1. I had an art school background, historically out of touch, but I could draw. 2. I knew children well—young children—I had had two of my own and had been deeply involved in a pre-school cooperative. . . .

"I put as my *first* priority—*the child*. But I did not know how to write. I had read somewhere that 'words cage thought.' I had thoughts. Wasn't the intention of a book, any book, to communicate a thought? I would step behind the words and concentrate on communicating the thought or the idea. So I put as my *second* priority—*the idea*. I used as a springboard for myself the book, *Rosie's Walk* by Pat Hutchins. In *Rosie's Walk,* you can observe for yourself that words are not the sole means of communication.

"My idea was the *displacement of water*. I knew that the young child did not know consciously why the water rose, but that baths with Mum or Dad were a universal experience. I also knew that for me a picture book with a young child was not the same experience as an adult with a book. There was *me* and the *child*. The book was the catalyst for the loving time we shared. When I read *Where the Wild Things Are* to my children, we always had a wild rumpus—screeching and jumping and bouncing on the bed if it were bedtime. I feel Maurice Sendak could have filled the page with noises to prompt those parents who did not do the same.

(From *Bertie and the Bear* by Pamela Allen. Illustrated by the author.)

"In our house a book and cuddle were one and the same thing. A book and a piece of sticking-plaster could make it 'all better.' The idea of the displacement of water was rich with possibilities for the parent to participate, extend and have fun. I did not see the need to duplicate in words that which could be understood from the illustrations. I already knew from experience that if you restricted yourself (in almost anything), because you were restricted, you were better able to develop control and skill; and you were not plagued by excesses, extravagances and irrelevancies. Things did not fall apart. So I set about using as few words as possible, *accurately*.

"My *third* priority became *the text*. My *fourth* priority became *the art work and visual layout*. Finding the ultimate form of *Mr. Archimedes' Bath* was labourious and largely arrived at consciously (to fit 32 pages, of course). The key hinged on everyone getting in and out of the bath on every page . . . boring to say but there to observe. *Mr. Archimedes' Bath* is the first book that I both wrote and illustrated. I believe that I will improve and that I am improving. The longer I 'hang in there,' the better I will become.

"I became conscious of some of the strengths of this book from the children—strengths which I had not been conscious of when I did it, such as the importance of the 'particular' as opposed to the 'general.' I discovered the delight which . . . children found in the wrinkled bottom of Mr. Archimedes and in the guilty look of the animals when they think they are blamed.

"Although I am writing for the non-reader, this is the very child who is in the process of accumulating reading skills. So for me, the print must be large and simple. And in the case of *Who Sank the Boat?* the repetitive line can soon be recognised. The publisher here suggested that the repetitive line be in italics. I said we must consult a language expert to see how it affected those learning to read. The answer came back, 'No italics.' You can only have large, simple print, of course, if you have very few words.

"*Who Sank the Boat?* is the second book I wrote and illustrated. . . . The title I gave it was, 'The Last Straw,' but I was persuaded by Bob Sessions, the publisher, that *Who Sank the Boat?* was a better title.

"The idea for *Who Sank the Boat?* existed alongside the idea for *Mr. Archimedes' Bath*. It was a complete piece of theatre which I could see and hold in my hand as you can hold an onion. Shirley Hughes' [at a] seminar in Sydney likened a picture book to an onion. I knew exactly what she meant. A picture book has a form, and that form is complete in itself. When it is finished, it is not going anywhere. When I came to use words, I found I had far too many. I was unravelling the happening in a thin line—like letting out a fishing line. I shook myself and said, 'What is it you're on about?' Who sank the boat, of course. Once I had asked the question, it all fell into place quite quickly.'' [*The Imagineers*, number 5, 1983. Amended by Pamela Allen.[1]]

"The medium and technique I employed in the illustrations for *Mr. Archimedes' Bath* was sepia ink and water colors. In *Who Sank the Boat?* I used black ink and water colors, that's in the major illustrations and in the minor illustrations on the left hand side, pen and sepia ink. In *Bertie and the Bear*, again black ink and water colors.

"About my illustrative style, my concern and the emphasis that I've put on my books is not in the illustrations. I think that you can't have a good picture book if you've got a poor text and to me it's important that you have a good text, and the illustrations, for me, come almost naturally. I draw easily and I make them come alive. I don't think my illustrations have changed very much from *Mr. Archimedes' Bath* to *Bertie and the Bear*.

"The art school I attended influenced my illustration. I've always been able to draw. The school's aim was that the students be able to paint like Rembrandt and Augustus John. No art school today has those aims. When I went to art school I drew still lifes. I drew from life and I drew plaster casts, six hours at a time with the aim of having the skill of Rembrandt.

Can anyone tell me where all this water came from? ■ (From *Mr. Archimedes' Bath* by Pamela Allen. Illustrated by the author.)

"I get tremendous support from librarians. I hear from librarians and teachers and children. I've been invited into schools more times than I'm able to accept.

"I'm interested in children and books which work with children. I don't actually see my work separated from that context.

"I see myself as an author/illustrator. I feel that you can't really separate a book into parts if it's a picture book, it's a picture *book*, it's a *book* and a *book* includes text and illustration. To separate it, is to break it into pieces and it can never stand up that way. I think if you've got a good story or a strong text and you've got poor illustrations, you can still have a good book. But if you've got poor text and beautiful illustrations, the most beautiful illustrations in the world, you've almost always got a poor book. My aim is toward the text. I think my strength is that I'm writing with a small child in mind. I see my books as being read aloud, they only come into existence when they're read aloud. And it's the fun that I can make happen with that triangle which is probably my strength."

"I am having so much fun playing games with picture books that I can't think of anything else I'd rather be doing."[1]

HOBBIES AND OTHER INTERESTS: Sailing.

FOR MORE INFORMATION SEE: The Imagineers (Australia), number 5, 1983; *Review* (Australia), December, 1984.

ALMOND, Linda Stevens   1881(?)-1987

OBITUARY NOTICE: Born about 1881 in Seaford, Del.; died January 10, 1987, in Plymouth Meeting (one source cites Philadelphia), Pa. Author of children's books. Almond is best known for carrying on the "Peter Rabbit" series after Beatrix Potter, the original author, stopped writing them in 1921. *Peter Rabbit's Easter, . . . And the Little Girl, . . . And The Old Witch Woman, . . . Goes A-Fishing,* and *. . . And the Two Terrible Foxes* are among the numerous titles she authored. She also wrote the "Buddy Bear" series, "Penny Hill" stories, and short stories and articles for children's magazines, including *Youth's Companion* and *Child Life.*

FOR MORE INFORMATION SEE: American Authors and Books: 1640 to the Present Day, 3rd revised edition, Crown, 1972. Obituaries: *Philadelphia Inquirer,* January 13, 1987; *Detroit Free Press,* January 14, 1987; *USA Today* (Arlington), January 14, 1987; *Chicago Tribune,* January 15, 1987; *Washington Post,* January 17, 1987.

ANDREWS, V(irginia) C(leo)   (?)-1986

OBITUARY NOTICE: Born June 6, in Portsmouth, Va.; died of cancer, December 19, 1986, in Virginia Beach, Va.; buried in Olive Branch Cemetery, Portsmouth, Va. Artist and author of novels and short stories. Andrews was the author of seven gothic novels whose phenomenal commercial success reportedly made her the fastest-selling author in America. All originally published as paperbacks by Pocket Books, her tales of terror and suspense, very popular with adolescents, have sold more than thirty million copies. *Flowers in the Attic,* the 1979 book that catapulted Andrews from obscurity to international fame, is the story of four children locked in an attic by their scheming mother and tortured by their sadistic grandmother. It is also her first novel to be made into a motion picture, scheduled for release in 1987. The six books that followed are *Petals on the Wind, If There Be Thorns, Seeds of Yesterday, My Sweet Audrina, Heaven,* and *Dark Angel.* Andrews, an invalid most of her life, supported herself for years as a commercial artist and fashion illustrator before seriously pursuing her writing career. Her first literary sales were stories for confession magazines.

FOR MORE INFORMATION SEE: New York Times Biographical Service, Arno Press, 1980; *Contemporary Authors,* Volume 97, Gale, 1981. Obituaries: *Detroit Free Press,* December 20, 1986; *Milwaukee Journal,* December 20, 1986; *Los Angeles Times,* December 21, 1986; *New York Times,* December 21, 1986; *Washington Post,* December 21, 1986; *White Plains Reporter-Dispatch,* December 21, 1986; *Chicago Tribune,* December 22, 1986; *Variety,* December 24, 1986; *Time,* January 5, 1987; *School Library Journal,* March, 1987.

ARNOLD, Emily   1939-
(Emily Arnold McCully)

PERSONAL: Born July 1, 1939, in Galesburg, Ill.; daughter of Wade E. (a writer) and Kathryn (a teacher; maiden name, Maher) Arnold; married George E. McCully (a historian), June 3, 1961 (divorced, 1975); children: Nathaniel, Thaddeus. *Ed-*

ucation: Brown University, B.A., 1961; Columbia University, M.A., 1964. *Residence:* Greenwich Village, N.Y. and Chatham, N.Y. *Agent:* Harriet Wasserman Literary Agency, Inc., 137 East 36th St., New York, N.Y. 10016.

CAREER: Worked in advertising and as a free-lance magazine artist, 1961-67; illustrator of children's books, 1966—; writer, 1975—. Teacher at workshops at Brown University, Boston University, St. Clements, Cummington Community of the Arts, and Rockland Center for the Arts. *Member:* Authors Guild, Writers Community, PEN American Center, Cummington Community for the Arts, Phi Beta Kappa. *Awards, honors:* Gold Medal from Philadelphia Art Directors, 1968, for an advertisement; illustrator of National Book Award winner, *Journey from Peppermint Street,* 1969; *Hurray for Captain Jane!* was a Children's Book Council Showcase Title, 1972; Brooklyn Art Books for Children citation from the Brooklyn Museum and the New York Public Library, 1975, for *MA nDA LA;* Juvenile Award from Council of Wisconsin Writers, 1979, for *Edward Troy and the Witch Cat;* National Endowment for the Arts grant in creative writing, 1980; New York State Council on Arts fiction grant, 1982; finalist, National Book Award, 1982, for *A Craving; Picnic* was chosen one of *School Library Journal*'s Best Books of the Year, 1984, received the Christopher Award, 1985, and was included in the International Biennale at Bratislava, 1985.

WRITINGS: A Craving (novel), Avon, 1982; (under name Emily A. McCully) *Picnic* (ALA Notable Book; Junior Literary Guild selection), Harper, 1984; (under name Emily Arnold McCully) *First Snow* (Junior Literary Guild selection), Harper, 1985; *Life Drawing* (adult novel), Delacorte, 1986; *The Show Must Go On,* Western, 1987; *School* (Junior Literary Guild selection), Harper, 1987; *New Baby,* Harper, 1988;

EMILY ARNOLD

Christmas Gift, Harper, 1988; *You Lucky Duck,* Western, 1988; *The Grandma Mixup,* Harper, 1988.

Illustrator; under name Emily Arnold McCully: George Panetta, *Sea Beach Express,* Harper, 1966; Emily Cheney Neville, *The Seventeenth Street Gang,* Harper, 1966; Marjorie W. Sharmat, *Rex,* Harper, 1967; Natalie S. Carlson, *Luigi of the Streets,* Harper, 1967; Liesel M. Skorpen, *That Mean Man,* Harper, 1968; Felice Holman, *Year to Grow,* Norton, 1968; Barbara Borack, *Gooney,* Harper, 1968; Meindert De Jong,

Journey from Peppermint Street, Harper, 1968; Seymour Simon, *Animals in Field and Laboratory: Science Project in Animal Behavior,* McGraw, 1968; Barbara K. Wheeler and Naki Tezel, *The Mouse and the Elephant,* Parents' Magazine Press, 1969; Jan Wahl, *The Fisherman,* Norton, 1969; Pierre Gripari, *Tales of the Rue Broca,* translated by Doriane Grutman, Bobbs, 1969; Virginia O. Baron, editor, *Here I Am! An Anthology of Poems Written by Young People in Some of America's Minority Groups,* Dutton, 1969; Janet Luise Swoboda Lunn, *Twin Spell,* Harper, 1969.

Pedro sat on the kitchen floor, pushing two little cars around and around the legs of his bed. ■ (From *Friday Night Is Papa Night* by Ruth A. Sonneborn. Illustrated by Emily Arnold McCully.)

Imagine—that whole endless sea held back by my sand and gravel bags! ■ (From *Journey from Peppermint Street* by Meindert De Jong. Illustrated by Emily Arnold McCully.)

Jane H. Yolen, *Hobo Toad and the Motorcycle Gang,* World Publishing, 1970; Jeanne B. Hardendorff, *Slip! Slop! Gobble!,* Lippincott, 1970; Ruth A. Sonneborn, *Friday Night Is Papa Night* (Junior Literary Guild selection), Viking, 1970; Mildred Kantrowitz, *Maxie,* Parents' Magazine Press, 1970; Phyllis M. Hoffman, *Steffie and Me,* Harper, 1970; J. B. Hardendorff, *The Cat and the Parrot,* Lippincott, 1970; Miska Miles (pseudonym of Patricia Miles Martin), *Gertrude's Pocket,* Little, Brown, 1970; Betsy Byars, *Go and Hush the Baby,* Viking, 1971; Alix Shulman, *Finders Keepers,* Bradbury, 1971; Arnold Adoff, *Ma nDA LA,* Harper, 1971; Sam Reavin, *Hurray for Captain Jane!,* Parents' Magazine Press, 1971; Helen E. Buckley, *Michael Is Brave,* Lothrop, 1971; Evelyn C. Nevin, *Extraordinary Adventures of Che Che McNerney,* Scholastic Book Services, 1971; Seymour Simon, *Finding Out With Your Senses,* McGraw, 1971; Louise McNamara, *Henry's Pennies,* F. Watts, 1972; Arthur Miller, *Jane's Blanket,* Viking, 1972; Lynn Schoettle, *Grandpa's Long Red Underwear,* Lothrop, 1972; Lee Bennett Hopkins, editor, *Girls Can Too!,* F. Watts, 1972; Jane Langton, *The Boyhood of Grace Jones,* Harper, 1972; A. Adoff, *Black Is Brown Is Tan,* Harper, 1973; Constance C. Greene, *Isabelle the Itch,* Viking, 1973; M. Kantrowitz, *When Violet Died,* Parents' Magazine Press, 1973; Mary H. Lystad, *That New Boy,* Crown, 1973; Thomas Rockwell, *How to Eat Fried Worms,* F. Watts, 1973; Anne Norris Baldwin, *Jenny's Revenge,* Four Winds Press, 1974; J. Langton, *Her Majesty, Grace Jones,* new edition, Harper, 1974; M.

Miles, *Tree House Town,* Little, Brown, 1974; M. W. Sharmat, *I Want Mama,* Harper, 1974.

Jean Little, *Stand in the Wind,* Harper, 1975; Susan Terris, *Amanda, the Panda and the Redhead,* Doubleday, 1975; Sylvia Plath, *The Bed Book,* Harper, 1976; Ianthe Thomas, *My Street's a Morning Cool Street,* Harper, 1976; Rita Golden Gelman and Joan Richter, *Professor Coconut and the Thief,* Holt, 1977; Miranda Hapgood, *Martha's Mad Day,* Crown, 1977; Elizabeth Winthrop, *That's Mine,* Holiday House, 1977; A. Adoff, *Where Wild Willie,* Harper, 1978; Betty Baker, *No Help at All,* Greenwillow, 1978; B. Baker, *Partners,* Greenwillow, 1978; Russell Hoban, *The Twenty-Elephant Restaurant,* Atheneum, 1978; Glory St. John, *What I Did Last Summer,* Atheneum, 1978; Nancy Willard, *The Highest Hit,* Harcourt, 1978; C. C. Greene, *I and Sproggy,* Viking, 1978; Sarah Sargent, *Edward Troy and the Witch Cat,* Follett, 1978; Kathryn Lasky, *My Island Grandma,* F. Warne, 1979; Barbara Williams, *Whatever Happened to Beverly Bigler's Birthday?,* Harcourt, 1979; Clyde Robert Bulla, *Last Look,* Crowell, 1979; Mirra Ginsburg, *Ookie-Spooky,* Crown, 1979.

Edith Thacher Hurd, *The Black Dog Who Went into the Woods,* Harper, 1980; Pat Rhoads Mauser, *How I Found Myself at the Fair,* Atheneum, 1980; Tobi Tobias, *How We Got Our First Cat,* F. Watts, 1980; Jane Breskin Zalben, *Oliver and Allison's Week,* Farrar, 1980; Brooke M. Varnum, *Play and Sing . . . It's Christmas! A Piano Book of Easy-to-Play Carols,* Macmillan, 1980; Vicki Kimmel Artis, *Pajama Walking,* Houghton, 1981; Kathleen Benson, *Joseph on the Subway Trains,* Addison-Wesley, 1981; Beatrice Gormley, *Mail-Order Wings,* Dutton, 1981; Jeannette Eyerly, *The Seeing Summer,* Lippincott, 1981; Alice Schertle, *The April Fool,* Lothrop, 1981; Charlotte Zolotow, *The New Friend,* Harper, 1981; B. Gormley, *Fifth Grade Magic,* Dutton, 1982; Marion M. Markham, *The Halloween Candy Mystery,* Houghton, 1982; E. T. Hurd, *I Dance in My Red Pajamas,* Harper, 1982; B. Williams, *Mitzi and the Terrible Tyrannosaurus Rex,* Dutton, 1982; B. Williams, *Mitzi's Honeymoon with Nana Potts,* Dutton, 1983; Laurie Adams and Allison Coudert, *Alice and the Boa Constrictor,* Houghton, 1983; Corrine Gerson, *Good Dog, Bad Dog,* Macmillan, 1983; B. Gormley, *Best Friend Insurance,* Dutton, 1983; Christopher Smart, *For I Will Consider My Cat Jeoffry,* Atheneum, 1984; M. M. Markham, *The Christmas Present Mystery,* Houghton, 1984; *The Playground,* Golden Books, 1984; B. Williams, *Mitzi and Frederick the Great,* Dutton, 1984.

Charlotte T. Graeber, *The Thing in Kat's Attic,* Dutton, 1985; B. Gormley, *The Ghastly Glasses,* Dutton, 1985; B. Williams, *Mitzi and the Elephants,* Dutton, 1985; Mary Stolz, *The Explorer of Barkham Street,* Harper, 1985; Barbara M. Joosse, *Fourth of July,* Knopf, 1985; Jane O'Connor, *Lulu and the Witch Baby,* Harper, 1986; Jane R. Thomas, *Wheels,* Clarion Books, 1986; B. Joosse, *Jam Day,* Harper, 1987; J. O'Connor, *Lulu Goes to Witch School,* Harper, 1987; Ruth Shaw Redauer, *Molly,* Simon & Schuster, 1987; R. S. Redauer, *Molly Goes Hiking,* Simon & Schuster, 1987; Doreen Rappaport, *The Boston Coffee Party,* Harper, 1987; B. Gormley, *Richard and the Vratch,* Avon, 1988; R. S. Redauer, *Molly Goes to the Library,* Prentice-Hall, 1988; *Breakfast by Molly,* Prentice-Hall, 1988.

(Contributor) William Abrahams, editor, *The O'Henry Collection: Best Short Stories,* Doubleday, 1977. Also contributor of short stories to *Massachusetts Review, Dark Horse,* and *Cricket.*

WORK IN PROGRESS: An adult novel, *To the Careless;* several picture books for children, including *Zaza's Big Break.*

You may pick the peppers out. ■ (From *The Thing in Kat's Attic* by Charlotte Towner Graeber. Illustrated by Emily Arnold McCully.)

ADAPTATIONS: "That Mean Man" (filmstrip), Creative Reading Program, 1969; "Picnic" (cassette; filmstrip with cassette), Weston Woods, 1986.

SIDELIGHTS: Born **July 1, 1939,** in Galesburg, Illinois. "I started drawing when I was about three. My mother decided to 'harness' my talent by having me draw ear after ear, hand after hand, and so on, until I got it right. By the time I was five, I was doing fairly ambitious drawings of men with trouser cuffs, buttons and pleats. I was quickly routed past finger painting and other more personally expressive types of art. From the outset, I was very concerned with subject matter. This has sometimes been inhibiting. To this day, I cannot imagine what my work would *look like* if I were a painter or sculptor instead of an illustrator. In fact, I wrote a novel *Life Drawing* in which I explored this question through my protagonist who is a painter, not an illustrator. The need to be linked to something else, to connect with a *subject outside of oneself* is, I think, at the heart of the impulse to illustrate, and is still the inspiration for all of my drawing.

"As a child I also wrote and illustrated stories, binding them into book form, complete with copyright date, flap copy, author's bio. My main characters were always boys. It seemed to me that their lives were *infinitely* better than girls' simply because they weren't as restricted. I envied them their freedom and action-packed lives, and my stories and art reflected this with lots of excitement and drama, and no pretty little girls sitting around not getting their dresses dirty. It didn't take me too long to realize that my early efforts at self-publishing were not purely artistic initiatives. I was imitating the adult world, and indeed wanted to be done with childhood as soon as possible.

"My role models were always men. I even preferred male writers and artists. Howard Pyle's *Robin Hood* was a favorite, as were *Treasure Island* and *Robinson Crusoe.* I also devoured John R. Tunis' sports series, and another about boys shipping out and traveling all over the world. Of course, I read *Little Women,* but was much more taken with *Little Men.* Adventure comic strips were also important to me, not only for their subject matter, but because I admired the economy of the dramatic techniques employed. Biographies were another source of stimulation and inspiration. I remember a particular series in which each book had a silhouette of the subject on the cover. The silhouette—the power and mystery of black on white, the strong *presence* it lent to the subject—was a big part of the attraction for me. The silhouette, in itself, somehow promised wonders.

"When I was about twelve I became absolutely fascinated with fairy tales and read them over and over. I'm sure this had to do with my awakening sexuality. The tales about princesses and maidens were essentially useless to me. I preferred the darker tales, like *Rumpelstiltskin.*

"My parents had an extensive library, and from an early age, I did a lot of copying, mostly from a book of American artists. I was particularly drawn to scenes of the twenties and thirties because they gave me a glimpse into my parents' lives, about which I was very curious. And I copied the works of the Ashcan School over and over, and even set up a stand at the end of our driveway when I was nine where I sold my renderings of their works. [The Ashcan School, also referred to as the Eight, comprised Arthur B. Davies, Maurice Pendergast, Ernest Lawson, William Glackens, Everett Shinn, Robert Henri, John Sloan and George Luks, who came together in 1908 to exhibit their paintings of everyday American life. They organized the crucial 1913 New York Armory Show, which introduced modern European art to the U.S.]. I took an oil

painting class when I was twelve or thirteen, and while the adult students were doing still lifes and decorative scenes, I would paint a tramp on a park bench.

"I could sense that all of this made my mother very uneasy. She was apprehensive that people wouldn't like my work and that it would be hard for me to make a living. It was always assumed that I would support myself by drawing, and though this may have injected some tension, I never let it influence what or how I drew. I insisted on gritty, significant subject matter.

"In high school I was blessed with a wonderful art teacher—a classic, tweedy, pipe-smoking illustrator whose work appeared in publications like *Field and Stream.* He helped me to see that my initial sketches were generally better than my reworked finishes. He helped me to value my naturally quick, spontaneous style of execution.

"I was a maverick in every sense. The Long Island town in which I was raised was very conventional, particularly during the fifties, and quite wealthy—full of Republicans. The community was founded by A. T. Stewart, a department store magnate, who built himself a hunt club that eventually became a hotel, and a dozen beautiful Victorian houses, known as The Twelve Apostles, for his friends. Around this nucleus, the

As Fran started up the walk, Monica called after her, "Watch out for the bears!" ■ (From *Last Look* by Clyde Robert Bulla. Illustrated by Emily Arnold McCully.)

town sprang up. The community had an interesting sense of history, but was like a place under glass: there were no blacks, no Jews, no minorities of any stripe. I was the only remotely left-wing person all through school, and made a lot of noise and mischief about it. I was a leader in school, and my drawing ability gave me an undeniable mystique, but still I felt horribly out of sync and isolated though in the midst of things. In fact I presented myself as a midwesterner. My mother and I were born in Illinois and went back every year to visit. I spent many hours poring over books about the Midwest. I was motivated to assume this identity not so much out of a yearning for the prairies, but out of alienation from my present surroundings.

"New York City was a much more immediate and lasting influence. My father, a documentary scriptwriter and producer for NBC, worked in Manhattan, and I loved to visit him there. I remember how impressed I was when he told me that one could walk all over Midtown underground—how I loved that maze beneath Rockefeller Center! From the time I was twelve or so, I could go alone into New York by train. I went to museums, particularly the Museum of Modern Art, and spent a lot of time sketching people in Union Square Park, still one of my favorite spots. New York City fueled my ambitions for an active life in the arts, theatre and publishing. I had visions of having a glamorous career as an illustrator for the *Saturday Evening Post*.

"I went to Brown University because it was one of the few colleges in the country offering courses (at Rhode Island School

"They call that beginner's luck," she said. ■ (From *Stand in the Wind* by Jean Little. Illustrated by Emily Arnold McCully.)

of Design) in illustration. During my freshman year I took life drawing, painting and a course in illustration for which we had to do a children's book. Although this was the area in which people said I showed the most talent, I had virtually no interest at that point in children's books. As a matter of fact, I all but stopped drawing in college, except for portraits, which I did to earn spending money. I was tired of the freakishness that seemed to be part of being an artist. For years, people stood around me as I drew, marvelling that I could reproduce someone or something. I threw myself into other activities— theatre, for example—which I hadn't done before. I also felt an urgency to study, to read literature, and to stretch my intellect. I became passionate about art history, and chose this discipline as my major. These were happy years. I grew a lot, and made important, intimate friendships. I think, too, that on some subliminal level, I was trying to escape what for me had always constituted my vision of the 'real world': that one day I would grow up and draw for money."

1961. "After graduation I married and moved to New York, the locus for all of my old artistic ambitions. I wanted to do *everything,* and had experience in very little. My husband did graduate study in history. After an agonizing job search, I finally landed a position with an art studio where, as a female, I was relegated to errand-running. Only the men were permitted to do paste-up, but I practiced on the sly and eventually left for a slightly better job as mat-cutter with an advertising agency. This, too, proved maddeningly limiting, and so I enrolled in a graduate art history program at Columbia concentrating on seventeenth-century iconography, which seemed to me a broader approach to studying human history. Still, I grew weary of making so many verbal descriptions of art works, and felt constrained by the curatorial cast of mind of the people around me. I went back to drawing and painting on my own."

1963-64. "With my husband's Belgium-American scholarship, we moved into a garret in Brussels. I researched my thesis and worked on my art. Unfortunately, everything I did then was destroyed in a fire. I would go out to sketch people and scenes and then put them together in a sort of collage. This was very new for me, and I cultivated a freewheeling work style. For years I was faithful to the surface, and now I was having trouble getting beneath it.

"My husband accepted a position at a college in Pennsylvania and with it we settled outside Philadelphia. I got my first illustration job—mostly spots for book reviews—on the *New York Herald Tribune*. We used a messenger service that shuttled between Philadelphia and New York because most of my assignments were overnight jobs. This was very exciting. During this time I was also making the rounds with my portfolio. I did illustrations for men's magazines, pharmaceutical companies, lots of book covers. I came to children's books in a roundabout way.

"I did several posters for WPAT [New Jersey radio station], one of which was used as an advertisement in the New York subways. An editor at Harper & Row saw it and called to ask if I would like to try my hand at picture books. At first, it wasn't easy for me to recapture a child's sensibility. But as I went along, that came more naturally, and having children of my own certainly helped."

In a typical thirty-two page picture book, Arnold is given the manuscript and the number of colors permitted—generally three: black and two others "that will, in combination produce a third color that's fairly interesting." [Lael Locke, "Silent Stories, Moving Pictures," *The Paper: The Monthly Guide to the Berkshires and the Hudson Valley,* April, 1984.[1]]

How the text should be broken up, lay out of pages, setting, and visual characters are left to Arnold's discretion. "The whole point of a picture book is that it's a collaboration that should be completely open-ended, and the only way most editors feel they can effect that is by letting the illustrator take the manuscript and expand it any way he or she can, rather than follow the dictates of the author, which would limit the final product to the author's sensibility. The illustrations should ideally be an expansion of the author's idea. . . . The manuscripts that are least successful describe too much, so that the illustrator is somewhat hampered by them and has to do exactly what the author says."[1]

"When my children were young I would occasionally ask them to pose for me, but generally I work without models. I do, however, consult the picture collection at The New York Public Library. Most of my picture book illustrations came from my imagination. I do a lot of revising, but it's not because a drawing, or part of one, isn't accurate; it's because I'm working through layers of perspective. Even when I find I must work on a drawing over and over, I want the finish to have a spontaneous, sketch-like quality. Characterization is, for me, the most important aspect of book illustration. It is through the characters that the reader enters the story."

After nineteen years spent illustrating some 100 books by other authors, Arnold went solo with *Picnic,* a story told entirely in water-color paintings. "I wanted to capture the tenderness and sweetness you find in families that are very close and happy," said Arnold of her story about a family of mice who go off for a picnic in the country and discover that the youngest mouse has somehow fallen out of their pickup truck. The story unfolds in two directions—that of the family searching for its youngest member and that of the mouse and the experiences it has on its own. "The story is . . . about the job of coming back after two separate adventures. The little mouse who's lost is not utterly miserable—the mouse finds a way of coping with the situation, and I think that's a very important part of the story."[1]

Arnold first created the mouse family to illustrate a piano lesson book of Christmas carols. As she worked she became more and more taken with them, and started making up stories for them. The first image series was of the truck and the little one falling out. The rest of the tale came together around that. "From the beginning, this was a story that came to me in pictures, not words."

A sequel to *Picnic,* entitled *First Snow* was published in 1985. "It's about the family going back to the same place in winter and the youngest mouse's fear of going down a very steep slope on a sled. It's another very simple story, but it's funny and has to do with really essential feelings that little kids have—being afraid of sensations, and then experiencing them and loving it. One of the first powerful senses in the world has to do with being lost, being afraid, being separated from the parents briefly. That's what's so wonderful about children's books . . . because they can't be terribly complicated, they get at things that are . . . basic and universal."[1]

Arnold lived for some years until 1966 in a small town in New Hampshire in an eighteenth-century house. While maintaining a career in illustration, she also raised organic flower and vegetables, baked bread, canned fruits and vegetables and made preserves. During this time, she also began writing adult fiction. Her first story appeared in *The Massachusetts Review* and was selected for inclusion in *The O. Henry Collection: Best Short Stories, 1977.* In the late 1970s, Arnold divorced and relocated to Brooklyn, New York, where she began work

on her first novel, *A Craving,* 1982, which was nominated for the prestigious National Book Award.

When asked about her typical day, she replied, "If I am working on a novel or a long story, I write for several hours in the morning and devote the afternoon, and sometimes the evening, to illustration work. I can do art work for many hours at a time. There is something mesmerizing about the physicality of visual work, and of course, knowing that a finished product is just hours away makes it hard for me to stop."

She divides her time between a loft in Manhattan's Greenwich Village and a house in Chatham, New York. "I work the year round, although during the summer in the country, I play tennis every day, keep up my gardens and generally have a more relaxed life. Chatham is near the Jacob's Pillow Dance Festival, and I have become very interested in modern dance. Although I haven't sketched dancers or dances that I have seen, I am sure that certain fleeting images of bodies in motion have stayed with me and found expression in later drawings."

To aspiring writers and artists, Arnold advises: "Don't worry about what other people are doing. Don't try to emulate. Work from what is inside you, crying out—however softly, however timidly—for expression."

—Based on an interview by Marguerite Feitlowitz

Even in washing windows Alexander the Great was a one-man circus. ■ (From *Her Majesty, Grace Jones* by Jane Langton. Illustrated by Emily Arnold McCully.)

(From *First Snow* by Emily Arnold McCully. Illustrated by the author.)

Arnold's works are included in the Kerlan Collection at the University of Minnesota.

HOBBIES AND OTHER INTERESTS: Theater (acting), gardening, cooking, travel, tennis.

FOR MORE INFORMATION SEE: Lee Kingman and others, compilers, *Illustrators of Children's Books: 1957-1966,* Horn Book, 1968; Martha E. Ward and Dorothy A. Marquardt, *Illustrators of Books for Young People,* Scarecrow, 1975; Zena Sutherland and Mae Hill Arbuthnot, *Children and Books,* 5th edition, Scott, Foresman, 1977; Doris de Montreville and Elizabeth D. Crawford, editors, *Fourth Book of Junior Authors and Illustrators,* H. W. Wilson, 1978; L. Kingman and others, compilers, *Illustrators of Children's Books: 1967-1976,* Horn Book, 1978; Ruth M. Noyce, "Profile: The Staccato Touch: Emily Arnold McCully," *Language Arts,* October, 1979; *Newsday,* May 16, 1982; *Los Angeles Times Book Review,* June 6, 1982; *Washington Post,* June 20, 1982; *Los Angeles Herald Examiner,* July 4, 1982.

ATWOOD, Margaret (Eleanor) 1939-

PERSONAL: Born November 18, 1939, in Ottawa, Ontario, Canada; daughter of Carl Edmund (an entomologist) and Margaret (Killam) Atwood; divorced; children: Jess. *Education:* University of Toronto, B.A., 1961; Radcliffe College, M.A., 1962; Harvard University, graduate study, 1962-63 and 1965-

MARGARET ATWOOD

67. *Politics:* "William Morrisite." *Religion:* "Pessimistic Pantheist." *Home:* Toronto, Ontario, Canada. *Agent:* Phoebe Larmore, 228 Main St., Venice, Calif. 90291. *Office:* c/o Oxford University Press, 10 Wynford Dr., Don Mills, Ontario, Canada.

CAREER: Worked during her early career as cashier, waitress, market research firm writer, and film script writer; University of British Columbia, Vancouver, lecturer in English literature, 1964-65; Sir George Williams University, Montreal, Quebec, lecturer in English literature, 1967-68; University of Alberta, Edmonton, lecturer, 1969-70; York University, Toronto, Ontario, assistant professor of English literature, 1971-72; University of Toronto, Ontario, writer-in-residence, 1972-73; writer; University of Alabama, Tuscaloosa, lecturer, 1985; New York University, lecturer, 1986. House of Anansi Press, Toronto, editor and member of board of directors, 1971-73. *Member:* Canadian Civil Liberties Association (member of board of directors, 1973-75), Amnesty International, Writers' Union of Canada (vice-chairman, 1980-81), International P.E.N. (Canadian chapter; president 1984-85). *Awards, honors:* E. J. Pratt Medal, 1961; President's Medal from the University of Western Ontario, 1965; Governor General's Award, 1966, for *The Circle Game,* and 1986, for *The Handmaid's Tale;* first prize in Canadian Centennial Commission Poetry Competition, for *The Animals in That Country;* Union League Civic and Arts Foundation Prize from *Poetry,* 1969; D.Litt., Trent University, 1973, Concordia College, 1980; LL.D., Queen's University, 1974; Bess Hoskins Prize from *Poetry,* 1974; City of Toronto Book Award, Canadian Bookseller's Association award, and Periodical Distributors of Canada Short Fiction Award, all 1977, all for *Lady Oracle;* St. Lawrence Award for fiction, 1978, for *Dancing Girls;* Radcliffe Graduate Medal, 1980; Molson Award, 1981; Guggenheim fellowship, 1981; Companion of the Order of Canada, 1981; Welsh Arts Council International Writer's Prize, 1982; Periodical Distributors of Canada and the Foundation for the Advancement of Canadian Letters Book of the Year Award, 1983; Toronto Arts Award for writing and editing, 1986.

WRITINGS—Juvenile: *Up in the Tree* (self-illustrated), McClelland & Stewart, 1978; (with Joyce C. Barkhouse) *Anna's Pet* (illustrated by Ann Blades), James Lorimer, 1980.

Novels: *The Edible Woman,* McClelland & Stewart, 1969, Atlantic-Little, Brown, 1970; *Surfacing,* McClelland & Stewart, 1972, Simon & Schuster, 1973; *Lady Oracle,* Simon & Schuster, 1976; *Life before Man,* McClelland & Stewart, 1979, Simon & Schuster, 1980; *Bodily Harm,* Simon & Schuster, 1981; *Encounters with the Element Man,* Ewert, 1982; *Murder in the Dark,* Coach House Press, 1983; *Unearthing Suite,* Grand Union Press, 1983; *The Handmaid's Tale,* McClelland & Stewart, 1985, Houghton, 1986.

Poetry: *Double Persephone,* Hawkshead Press, 1961; *The Circle Game,* Contact Press, 1966; *The Animals in That Country,* Atlantic-Little, Brown, 1968; *The Journals of Susanna Moodie,* Oxford University Press, 1970; *Procedures for Underground,* Atlantic-Little, Brown, 1970; *Power Politics,* Anansi, 1971, Harper, 1973; *You Are Happy,* Oxford University Press, 1974, Harper, 1975; *Selected Poems,* Oxford University Press, 1976, Simon & Schuster, 1978; *Two-Headed Poems,* Oxford University Press, 1978, Simon & Schuster, 1981; *True Stories,* Oxford University Press, 1981; *Snake Poems,* Salamander Press, 1983; *Interlunar,* Oxford University Press, 1984; *Selected Poems II,* Oxford University Press, 1986.

Other: *Survival: A Thematic Guide to Canadian Literature,* Anansi, 1972; (with others) *Canadian Imagination: Dimen-*

Sally thinks: the egg is alive, and one day it will hatch. But what will come out of it? ■ (Jacket illustration by Heather Cooper from *Bluebeard's Egg and Other Stories* by Margaret Atwood.)

sions of a Literary Culture, Harvard University Press, 1977; *Dancing Girls* (short stories), McClelland & Stewart, 1977, published as *Dancing Girls and Other Stories,* Seal Books, 1978; *Days of the Rebels: 1815-1840,* Natural Science, 1977; (with Catherine M. Young) *To See Our World* (essay) GLC Publishers, 1979; *Second Words: Selected Critical Prose* (nonfiction), Anansi, 1982; *Bluebeard's Egg* (short stories), McClelland & Stewart, 1983, Houghton, 1986; *The New Oxford Book of Canadian Verse in English,* Oxford University Press, 1982; (editor with Robert Weaver) *The Oxford Book of Canadian Short Stories in English,* Oxford University Press, 1986.

Work is represented in more than 100 anthologies, including *How Do I Love Thee: Sixty Poets of Canada (and Quebec) Select and Introduce Their Favourite Poems from Their Own Work,* edited by John Robert Colombo, M. G. Gurtig (Edmonton, Alberta), 1970; *Five Modern Canadian Poets,* edited by Eli Mandel, Holt (Toronto), 1970; *72: New Canadian Stories,* edited by David Helwig and Joan Harcourt, Oberon Press, 1972. Contributor of poetry to *Tamarack Review, Canadian Forum, New Yorker, Atlantic, Poetry, Kayak, Quarry, Prism,* and other magazines; contributor of short stories, reviews, and critical articles to *Harper's, Canadian Literature, Maclean's, Saturday Night, Alphabet, Elipse,* and other periodicals.

ADAPTATIONS: "The Poetry and Voice of Margaret Atwood" (record), Caedmon, 1978.

WORK IN PROGRESS: A novel.

SIDELIGHTS: "I was born in the Ottawa General Hospital . . . in 1939. Six months later I was backpacked into the Quebec bush. I grew up in and out of the bush, in and out of Ottawa, Sault Ste. Marie and Toronto. I did not attend a full year of school until I was in grade eight. This was a definite advantage. My parents are both from Nova Scotia, and my 'extended family' lives there.

"I began writing at the age of five, but there was a dark period between the ages of eight and sixteen when I didn't write. I started again at sixteen and have no idea why, but it was suddenly the only thing I wanted to do. My parents were great readers. They didn't encourage me to become a writer, exactly, but they gave me a more important kind of support; that is, they expected me to make use of my intelligence and abilities and they did not pressure me into getting married. . . . Remember that all this was taking place in the 1950s, when marriage was seen as the only desirable goal. My mother is a very lively person who would rather skate than scrub floors; she was a tomboy in youth and still is one. My father is a scientist who reads a great deal of history and has a mind like Leopold Bloom's. But as far as I know, the only poems he ever composes are long doggeral verses, filled with puns, which he writes when he has the flu." [Joyce Carol Oates, "Margaret Atwood: 'Poems and Poet,'" *New York Times Book Review,* May 21, 1978.[1]]

Besides an early interest in writing, Atwood remembered having an equally strong interest in reading. " . . . Beatrix Potter, very early on. A. A. Milne. These are books that were read to me. *Winnie the Pooh, Alice in Wonderland, Alice Through the Looking Glass*—children's classics, in other words, of those times. When I started to read myself, I remember being heavily into E. Nesbit and Edgar Allan Poe that some fool had put in the children's library. I terrified myself in grade six with Poe. *Grimm's Fairy Tales* I had very early—the unexpurgated complete version which my parents bought by mistake, not realizing that it was full of people being put into barrels full of nails and rolled down the hill into the sea.

" . . . I have only the vaguest of memories of Dick, Jane, Spot, and Puff. I know we had them at school, but they didn't leave much of an impression. There were a lot of collections of fairy tales—*The Yellow Fairy Book,* all the Andrew Lang books. I read all the ones I could get my hands on, that they had in the school library. I probably read books that were somewhat too old for me at the time. I remember reading *Moby Dick* early on, not really understanding it that well but finding it quite fascinating. Things like *Robinson Crusoe* and *Gulliver's Travels,* which were originally written for adults but people put them in children's libraries because they don't have any sex in them. Fenimore Cooper, of course—I read some of those. Mark Twain I liked a lot—*Tom Sawyer* and *Huckleberry Finn.* Again, *Huckleberry Finn* is an adult's book; it's very scary in parts. And I read comic books. I read a lot of comic books. It was the comic book generation. My brother collected them so we had a huge number, somewhat disapproved of, but our parents knew we read other things too, so it wasn't a problem. People traded them a lot. Saturday afternoons we sat around and traded comic books and read them.

" . . . I read *Batman, Superman, Captain America, Wonder Woman, Donald Duck, Mickey Mouse, Little Lulu.* All of that I read, and Archie and Veronica and Betty, *Casper the Friendly Ghost.* He was actually a bit later than our generation. Then there were some crime comics that were kind of bloody and there were horror comics. But I think my favorite was Plastic Man who could transform himself into anything, but you could always tell because it was red and blue.

" . . . I was never big on *The Little Engine That Could* and that kind of morally encouraging tale about machinery. Protestant ethic, goal-oriented books I wasn't so keen on. I was much more keen on dragons and magic and those things. And some of the comic books stuff fed right into that, because that's exactly what it is.

"The Bible I was familiar with because of Sunday school, translated into cute little fables—people in bedsheets. Remember the coloured pictures that they used to give you? That was quite useful in later life, although I didn't think so at the time. I read the *Boys Own Annual,* with all those stories; old, old copies of it are in my grandfather's attic. About the turn of the century they had all those stories of adventures in caves and recovering lost treasures—the Rider Haggard, Alan Quartermain, *King Solomon's Mines* kinds of boys' adventure stories, really. Nobody ever told me they were supposed to be for boys only. So I read them. I read some Ernest Thompson Seton and animal stories—Sir Charles G. C. Roberts, *Wild Animals I Have Known, Kings in Exile.* They were quite sad. The animals always died. They were quite depressing. I used to cry over them—it was terrible. I read *Little Women* at one stage. And Arthur Conan Doyle; at about age ten or eleven I devoured all of Sherlock Holmes and some of his other knights-in-armour fraudulent historical romances. I also read a lot of 'classical Victorian fiction.' I read *Pride and Prejudice* at an early age. I read *Wuthering Heights,* of course. And I read Dickens. I read some things that were too old for me that I didn't really understand and that depressed and upset me. Victor Hugo was too depressing. . . . " [Catherine Sheldrick Ross and Cory Bieman Davies, "An Interview with Margaret Atwood," *Canadian Children's Literature,* number 42, 1986.[2]]

Atwood was well known for writing award-winning poetry, fiction, and criticism before writing her first children's book. "I don't think of poetry as a 'rational' activity but as an aural one. My poems usually begin with words or phrases which appeal more because of their sound than their meaning, and the movement and phrasing of a poem are very important to

"Goodbye toad," she said. "I hope you find a home that is cool and dark and under something."
■ (From *Anna's Pet* by Margaret Atwood and Joyce Barkhouse. Illustrated by Ann Blades.)

me. But like many modern poets I tend to conceal rhymes by placing them in the middle of lines, and to avoid immediate alliteration and assonance in favor of echoes placed later in the poems. For me, every poem has a texture of sound which is at least as important to me as the 'argument.' This is not to minimize 'statement.' But it does annoy me when students, prompted by the approach of their teacher, ask, 'What is the poet *trying to say?*' It implies that the poet is some kind of verbal cripple who can't quite 'say' what he 'means' and has to resort to a lot of round-the-mulberrybush, thereby putting the student to a great deal of trouble extracting his 'meaning.'

" . . . I find it necessary, in order to write about a place, to have actually been there. I can invent characters, but I am absolutely dependent on the details of the material world to make a space for my characters to move around in. . . . Cultural attitudes in novels are not usually invented by the novelist; they are reflections of something the novelist sees in the society around her."[1]

Up in the Tree was her first book for children. It was illustrated and hand-lettered by the author and dedicated to her daughter, Jess. It was followed by *Anna's Pet* in collaboration with her aunt, Joyce Barkhouse. " . . . *Up in the Tree* was one of about six rather nonsensical books that I wrote in fairly quick succession during a period when I was feeling quite dippy. . . . I do write rhymed Christmas cards for people, rhymed birthday cards, rhymed satirical verse, and that kind of thing. So writing children's books was not completely out of the question.

(Detail of cover illustration from *Dancing Girls* by Margaret Atwood.)

"The other book, *Anna's Pet,* which was prose, I was approached to write and I wrote it along with my aunt, who had been one of the first people to encourage my writing. So I thought it would be fun to do a book with her. She had the knowledge of how to write with a limited vocabulary for kids because she writes children's books.

"They gave us a grade level, and she was used to writing for grade levels, so we worked it out together. She said, 'You can use this word; you can't use that one; we can use this tense of these words but not those tenses' and all that, which I knew nothing about.

"The story itself has an interesting history. It's based on a little story that she had written many years ago in phonetics because someone had asked her to do that. And she has based the story on my brother, who did take worms to bed and who hid snakes under his pillow and things like that. She had been visiting us at the time when my brother had taken a snake to bed and it had gone away, unknown to my mother. It had crawled into the wood stove to be where it was warm; so that when my mother opened the stove to light the fire in the morning, there was the snake. She said, 'I think the snake would be happier outside.'

" . . . Obviously I thought it would be more interesting to have a little girl who dug up worms. Lots of kids dig up worms. It is stereotypical to have little boys who dig up worms, but little girls do it too and I saw no reason why not."[2]

"You can only have that optimistic, happy-ending perspective on the world in children's literature. It doesn't ring true in serious adult literature because we know the world isn't entirely like that. We know that we would like the world to be

(Jacket illustration by Paul Bacon from *Lady Oracle* by Margaret Atwood.)

like that, but we know that there is a gap; whereas in children's literature you can wholeheartedly endorse that optimistic perspective because you are dealing with wish-fulfillment. You can give full play to your wish-fulfillment and have everything turn out absolutely right and nobody's ever going to die, there's never going to be any tragedy, the princess will be rescued, and the prince will be restored to his right mind. Have you ever noticed how often the princes go out of their minds in *Grimms' Fairy Tales?* But it will all be set right and that's very reassuring. I think that it's reassuring for kids to be read that kind of book, because, Lord knows, they'll have the other stuff soon enough. So better they should have a foundation of happy endings in childhood so that they can have some kind of feeling of cessation of anxiety and of expectations fulfilled which will carry them on through later life when things don't always work out that neatly.

"You can be definitely sillier. There's more room for play. I play around quite a lot anyway. But you can do it in a more overt and simple-minded way, I think. At least I can.... There's a certain delight in complicated triple-syllable rhymed endings. There's a delight in doing those kinds of things with words. Kids have that delight and they will do it themselves.''[2]

When asked why she writes, the Canadian author responded, "I guess I've never felt the necessity of thinking up a really convincing answer to that one, although I get asked it a lot. I suppose I think it's a redundant question, like 'Why does the sun shine?' . . . It's a human activity. I think the real question is, 'Why doesn't everyone?' . . . ''[1]

Atwood is well known for her adult novels as well as for numerous short stories, television plays, children's books, critical works, and volumes of poetry. Her latest works have made political statements. *The Handmaid's Tale,* for example, tells the story of a coup by the fundamentalist religious right in the United States and the political dangers that ensue. "I think there are political elements in just about everything I've ever written—if by political you mean who's got the power and how did they get it, and how do they maintain it, and what is it power to do?"

"When you begin to write, you're in love with the language, with the act of creation, with yourself partly; but as you go on, the writing—if you follow it—will take you places you never intended to go and show you things you would never otherwise have seen. I began as a profoundly apolitical writer, but then I began to do what all novelists and some poets do; I began to describe the world around me." [Lindsy Van Gelder, "Margaret Atwood," *Ms.,* January, 1981.[3]]

FOR MORE INFORMATION SEE: Poetry, July, 1972; *West Coast Review,* January, 1973; *New York Times Book Review,* March 4, 1973, April 6, 1975, September 26, 1976, May 21, 1978, February 3, 1980; *Saturday Review,* April, 1973; *New Leader,* September 3, 1973; *American Poetry Review,* November/December, 1973, March/April, 1977; *Contemporary Literary Criticism,* Gale, Volume II, 1974, Volume III, 1975, Volume IV, 1975, Volume VIII, 1978, Volume XIII, 1980, Volume XV, 1980; *Canadian Literature,* spring, 1974; *Ontario Review,* spring-summer, 1975; *Saturday Night,* September, 1976; *Washington Post Book World,* September 20, 1976, January 27, 1980; *Publisher's Weekly,* August 23, 1976; *Modern Fiction Studies,* autumn, 1976; *New York Times,* December 23, 1976, January 10, 1980, February 8, 1980; *New Orleans Review,* Volume V, number 3, 1977; *Christian Science Monitor,* June 12, 1977; *Book Forum,* Volume IV, number 1, 1978; *Canadian Children's Literature,* number 12, 1978; *Chicago Tribune,* January 27, 1980, February 3, 1980; *People,*

May 19, 1980; Sherill Grace, *Violent Duality: A Study of Margaret Atwood,* Vehicule Press, 1980; Arnold Davidson and Cathy Davidson, editors, *The Art of Margaret Atwood: Essays in Criticism,* Academic Press, 1980; Catherine Sheldrick Ross and Cory Bieman Davies, "An Interview with Margaret Atwood," *Canadian Children's Literature,* number 42, 1986; Lindsy Van Gelder, "Margaret Atwood," *Ms.,* January, 1987.

BACON, Margaret Frances 1895-1987 (Peggy Bacon)

OBITUARY NOTICE—See sketch in *SATA* Volume 2: Born May 2, 1895, in Ridgefield, Conn.; died January 4, 1987, in Kennebunk, Me. Educator, artist, illustrator, and author. Noted for her good-natured satires and humorous caricatures, Bacon wrote and illustrated many books for children, including *The Lion-hearted Kitten, Mercy and the Mouse, The Ballad of Tangle Street, Off with Their Heads, The Ghost of Opalina; or, Nine Lives, The Good American Witch,* and *The Magic Touch.* She also illustrated more than three dozen books, including *The Adventures of Tom Sawyer, Treasury of Cat Stories,* and *The Cat Who Rode Cows.* In addition, Bacon contributed stories, poems and drawings to *Vogue, Vanity Fair,* and *New Yorker,* among other magazines, taught art for more than thirty years, and exhibited her paintings, drawings, and prints worldwide. Among her awards and honors is the American Academy and Institute of Arts and Letters Gold Medal, which Bacon won in 1980 for her lifelong contribution to graphic art and illustration.

FOR MORE INFORMATION SEE: Contemporary Authors, Permanent Series, Volume 2, Gale, 1970; *Current Biography,* H. W. Wilson, 1940, March, 1987; *Illustrators of Books for Young People,* Scarecrow Press, 1975; *Illustrators of Children's Books,* Horn Book, 1967; *Who's Who in American Art,* 16th edition, Bowker, 1984. Obituaries: *New York Times,* January 7, 1987; *West Palm Beach Evening Times,* January 8, 1987.

BAKER, Eugene H.

BRIEF ENTRY: Baker received his M.A. and Ph.D. in education from Northwestern University in Chicago, Illinois. He has worked as a teacher and principal in Chicago's North Shore suburbs, and as vice president of curriculum and materials development for Zachary's Workshop Ltd., in Lake Forest. His "I Want to Be" series, a collection of more than two dozen career books for children published by Children's Press, highlights career options in simple, fictional narratives. A wide range of titles include: *I Want to Be an Architect* (1969), illustrated by Felix Palm; *I Want to Be a Forester* (1969), illustrated by Darrell Wiskur; and *I Want to Be a Bank Teller* (1972), illustrated by Jim Temple. Baker's "Junior Detective" series for would-be Sherlock Holmes readers includes tips on sleuthing, as in *Secret Writing: Codes and Messages* (Child's World, 1980) and *Shadowing the Suspect* (Child's World, 1980). He has also written juvenile books on safety, history, and values, as well as professional instructional texts for educators on teaching methods.

Children, you are very little,
And your bones are very brittle;
If you would grow great and stately,
You must try to walk sedately.

—Robert Louis Stevenson

Hark, hark,
The dogs do bark,
The beggars are coming to town;
Some in rags,
And some in tags,
And one in a velvet gown.

(From *Mother Goose*. Illustrated by Aurelius Battaglia.)

BATTAGLIA, Aurelius 1910-

PERSONAL—Education: Attended Corcoran School of Art.

CAREER: Muralist; illustrator of books for children. Has worked as an instructor for the Walt Disney Studios and as an illustrator for magazines and newspapers. *Wartime service:* U.S. Navy, World War II, educational film producer. *Awards, honors: Mother Goose* was chosen one of Child Study Association's Children's Books of the Year.

ILLUSTRATOR—All for children: Pat-a-Cake: A Baby's Mother Goose, Simon & Schuster, 1948; John E. Bechdolt, *Little Boy with a Big Horn,* Simon & Schuster, 1950; Kathryn Jackson and Byron Jackson, *The Cat Who Went to Sea, and Other Cat Stories,* Simon & Schuster, 1950; Jane W. Watson, *Pets for Peter,* Simon & Schuster, 1950; Margaret Bradford Boni, editor, *Fireside Book of Folk Songs,* Simon & Schuster, 1952; Leslie Waller, *Our American Language: A Book to Begin On,* Holt, 1960; *Captain Kangaroo's Read-Aloud Book,* Random House, 1962; *Captain Kangaroo's Sleepytime Book,* Random House, 1963; *Captain Kangaroo's Storybook,* Random House, 1963; Kathleen N. Daly, *My Elephant Book,* Golden Press, 1966; Odille Ousley, adapter, *The Little Pig Who Listened,* Ginn, 1966; *Stories to Read to the Very Young,* Random House, 1966; Janet Fulton, *Raggedy Ann,* Golden Press, 1969; Mary J. Fulton, *Detective Arthur on the Scent,* Golden Press, 1971; Bertha M. Parker, *The New Golden Dictionary,* Golden Press, 1972; *Mother Goose,* Random House, 1973; M. J. Fulton, *Detective Arthur, Master Sleuth,* Golden Press, 1974; Annie Ingle, *The Big Farm Book,* Platt, 1976; *Little Brown Bear,* Platt, 1977; Sarah Leslie, *Seasons,* Platt, 1977; *Three Little Pigs,* Random House, 1977; *Animal Homemakers,* Platt, 1978; *Baby's Seasons,* Platt, 1978; *A Farm,* Platt, 1978; *My First Mother Goose Book,* Golden Press, 1980; *Animal Sounds,* Golden Press, 1981; Mabel Watts, *Hiram's Red Shirt,* Golden Press, 1981.

FOR MORE INFORMATION SEE: Martha E. Ward and Dorothy A. Marquardt, *Illustrators of Books for Young People,* 2nd edition, Scarecrow, 1975.

BELL, Neill 1946-

BRIEF ENTRY: Born January 19, 1946, in Washington, D.C. A free-lance writer since 1980, Bell has taught anthropology and sociology at the university level, acted as teacher and administrator of an elementary school, and worked as a newspaper reporter, columnist, and photographer. Interested in nonfiction books for children, he has written *Book of Where; or, How to Be Naturally Geographic* (Little, Brown, 1982) and *Only Human: Why We Are the Way We Are* (Little, Brown, 1983) for middle graders. "I believe that kids can be stimulated to explore themselves and the world around them if they have the opportunity to read books that encourage them," Bell said. Using cartoon illustrations and a personable yet challenging tone, *Book of Where* provides an understanding of geography concepts such as scale, maps, and the globe. According to *Booklist, Book of Where* "gets some key lessons across in a refreshingly unpedantic fashion." In the same style, *Only Human,* dedicated to "Adam, Eve, and all the kids," examines evolution, genetics, and anthropology. *Home:* 7070 Black Bart Trail, Redwood Valley, Calif. 95470.

FOR MORE INFORMATION SEE: Contemporary Authors, Volume 118, Gale, 1986.

BERENDS, Polly B(errien) 1939-

PERSONAL: Born December 1, 1939, in Chicago, Ill.; daughter of Curtis (in advertising) and Mary Hastings (Reid) Berrien; married Jan Berends (a horticulturist), April 22, 1967; children: Jan Berrien, Andrew Lukas. *Education:* Skidmore College, B.A., 1961; Union Theological Seminary and Columbia University, M.A., 1963.

CAREER: Golden Press, New York City, picture book editor, 1963-65; Random House, New York City, children's book editor, 1963-72; writer and pastoral counselor, 1975—. Research associate at New York Institute of Metro-psychiatry, 1975—.

I am right. I am not alone. There is a duck in the elevator with me. A white duck with orange feet. ■ (From *The Case of the Elevator Duck* by Polly Berrien Berends. Photograph from the movie adaptation. Produced by Learning Corporation of America, 1976.)

WRITINGS—Juvenile: *Games to Play with the Very Young* (illustrated by Denman Hampson), Random House, 1967; *Who's That in the Mirror?* (illustrated by Lilian Obligado), Random House, 1968; *I Heard Said the Bird,* Random House, 1969; *Vincent, What Is It?,* Random House, 1969; *The Case of the Elevator Duck* (illustrated by James K. Washburn), Random House, 1973; *Ladybug and Dog and the Night Walk* (illustrated by Cyndy Szekeres), Random House, 1980; *Ladybug and Dog Tales,* Lothrop, 1983; *Ozma and the Wayward Wand* (illustrated by David Rose), Random House, 1985. Also translator of *Toto and the Aardvark,* for Doubleday.

Other: *Whole Child/Whole Parent,* Harper, 1975, revised edition, 1982.

ADAPTATIONS: "The Case of the Elevator Duck" (film), Learning Corporation of America, 1976.

WORK IN PROGRESS: Now See Here: Spirituality and Mental Health; Gently Lead (or How to Teach Your Children about God) While Finding Out for Yourself; two juvenile books, *Baby Bear's Perfect Christmas* and *The Star Child.* ∎

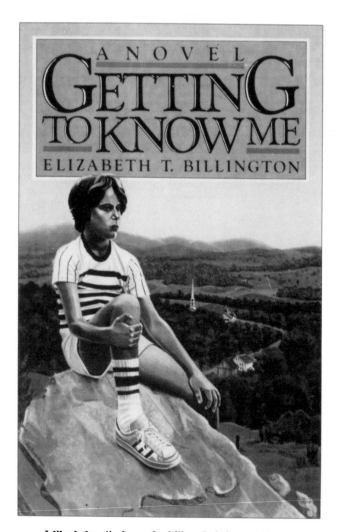

I liked the climb up the hill and sitting on the large rocks at the top, looking at Leeford far below. ∎
(Cover illustration by Jonathan Rosenbaum from *Getting to Know Me* by Elizabeth T. Billington.)

BILLINGTON, Elizabeth T(hain)

PERSONAL: Born in New York, N.Y.; daughter of Henry Alden and Alice (Fisk) Thain; married Richard Billington (a publisher); children: Richard Alden. Address: c/o Frederick Warne & Co., Inc., 101 Fifth Ave., New York, N.Y. 10003.

CAREER: Writer, 1966—.

WRITINGS: Adventure with Flowers, Warne, 1966; *Understanding Ecology* (illustrated by Robert Galster), Warne, 1968, revised edition, 1971, new edition published as *Ecology Today* Kaye & Ward, 1977; (editor) *Randolph Caldecott Treasury,* Warne, 1978; *Part-Time Boy* (juvenile; illustrated by Diane De Groat), Warne, 1980; *Getting to Know Me,* Warne, 1982; *The Move,* Warne, 1984.

WORK IN PROGRESS: Fiction for children.

SIDELIGHTS: Billington's works are included in the de Grummond Collection at the University of Southern Mississippi.

BOULET, Susan Seddon   1941-

PERSONAL: Born July 10, 1941, in Sao Paulo, Brazil; daughter of Eric Joseph (a farm manager) and Josephine (Eleanor) Seddon; married Larry Boulet, September 2, 1967 (died March, 1980); children: Eric Lawrence. *Education:* Attended Aliance Francaise, Sao Paulo, Brazil and Laney College, Oakland, Calif. *Religion:* Catholic. *Home and office:* 5249 Manila, Oakland, Calif. 94618.

CAREER: Has worked as a teacher, 1957-61, a secretary, 1961-62, and in the ticket office for an airline, 1963-70. Free-lance artist and illustrator, 1970—. *Exhibitions:* Rainbow Show, Palace of the Legion of Honor, San Francisco, Calif.; Village Gallery, Sacramento, Calif.; The Illuminarium Gallery, Larkspur Landing, Calif.; Community Congregational Church, Tiberon and Belevedere, Calif.; Whole Life Expo, Moscone Center, San Francisco, Calif. Work is in private collections in Europe, South America, South Africa, Southwest Asia and the United States.

ILLUSTRATOR: Victoria Forrester, *The Candlemaker and Other Tales,* Atheneum, 1984; V. Forrester, *Poor Gabriella: A Christmas Story,* Atheneum, 1986. Also illustrator of book jackets, greeting cards and posters.

When at home alone I sit
And am very tired of it,
I have just to shut my eyes
To go sailing through the skies—
To go sailing far away
To the pleasant Land of Play;
To the fairy land afar
Where the little people are;
Where the clover-tops are trees,
And the rain-pools are the seas,
And the leaves, like little ships,
Sail about on tiny trips;
And above the daisy tree
   Through the grasses,
High o'erhead the Bumble Bee
   Hums and passes.

              —Robert Louis Stevenson

(From "The Butterfly with No Keys" in *The Candlemaker and Other Tales* by Victoria Forrester. Illustrated by Susan Seddon Boulet.)

CAMPBELL, (Elizabeth) Andréa 1963-

PERSONAL: Born November 30, 1963, in Ottawa, Canada; daughter of Alphonses Patrick (a professor of English) and Elizabeth (a homemaker; maiden name, McLean) Campbell. *Education:* Attended Seneca College, Toronto, 1982-83 and University of Ottawa, 1984-86. *Home:* 11 Crownhill St., Ottawa, Ontario K1J 7K1, Canada.

CAREER: Children's Aid Center, Toronto, Ontario, Canada, file clerk, 1983-84. *Member:* Ottawa Rowing Club.

ILLUSTRATOR—All written by father, A. P. Campbell: *A True Story: Albert the Talking Rooster,* Borealis, 1974; *The Pollywog Who Didn't Believe . . . He'd Be a Frog,* Borealis, 1975; *The Little Red Cart,* Borealis, 1979.

SIDELIGHTS: ''My father is the author of the books I have illustrated. He chose me as his illustrator because he loved the innocence of childrens' drawings which showed how children perceive the world. He thought children would enjoy reading books with children as illustrators and would be able to identify better with the story than with an adult's interpretation of the story.

''Although I have not been drawing in the past few years, I have discovered photography which I have a great passion for. I am aiming for a career in journalism which involves some photography and creativity. My choice of career was influenced by my love of travelling and my interest in politics and photography.''

HOBBIES AND OTHER INTERESTS: Darkroom film development, playing the violin, jogging, skiing, playing soccer, dancing to a good band and drinking strong coffee.

CARRIER, Lark 1947-

BRIEF ENTRY: Born in 1947 in Montana. Carrier credits her first eleven years in the Rocky Mountains with shaping her views of the world and nature. A graduate of the Parsons School of Design, she works for a Boston design company and has written and illustrated three picture books for pre-schoolers and middle graders. In her first book, *There Was a Hill . . .* (Picture Book Studio, 1985), an Ezra Jack Keats Award nominee, ''soft, muted colors, highlighted by luminous white, create forms that are strong and pleasing,'' according to *Booklist.* Half pages with beginning phrases flip open to expose the concluding phrases and changing images. ''It is almost like watching clouds [sic] shapes change and evolve,'' observed *School Library Journal.* Carrier again used pastel colors and effusive white in *A Christmas Promise* (Picture Book Studio, 1986), about a young girl, an evergreen tree, and the birds and animals who make the tree their home. Carrier's third book is titled *Wolfman and Cody* (Picture Book Studio, 1987).

CHETWIN, Grace

BRIEF ENTRY: Born in Nottingham, England. A teacher and author of fantasy books, Chetwin earned a degree in philosophy from Southampton University and has taught high school in England and New Zealand. Besides a passion for writing, she has had a lifelong involvement in dance, including running her own dance company in New Zealand for four years. She has also produced operas and plays at the amateur level. Characters Meg and her sister appear in Chetwin's first two books

for middle graders. The two girls become trapped in the fantasy world of Halloween Wood in *On All Hallows' Eve* (Lothrop, 1984), while Welsh lore is combined with modern-day computer technology in *Out of the Dark World* (Lothrop, 1985). For young adults, *Gom on Windy Mountain* (Lothrop, 1986), first in the ''Tales of Gom'' series, is an adventure involving wizardry, telepathy, and Gom's struggle against the evil Skeller. ''Chetwin evocatively describes her mountain scenes, develops real and fascinating characters, and uses fantasy elements imaginatively,'' noted *Booklist.* The second book of the series is in progress. Chetwin has also written *The Atheling* (Bluejay Books, 1987), the first volume of a science fiction tetralogy for adults. Currently at press are two picture books and a young adult novel. *Home:* 37 Hitching Post Lane, Glencove, N.Y. 11542.

COLOMBO, John Robert 1936-

PERSONAL: Born March 24, 1936, in Kitchener, Ontario, Canada; son of J. A. (a film producer) and Irene (a housewife; maiden name, Nicholson) Colombo; married Ruth Brown (a teacher), May 11, 1959; children: Jonathan, Catherine, Theodore. *Education:* Attended Waterloo College, Waterloo, Ontario, 1956-57; University of Toronto, B.A. (with honors), 1959, graduate study, 1959-60. *Home:* 42 Dell Park Ave., Toronto, Ontario, Canada M6B 2T6.

CAREER: Author and poet. University of Toronto Press, Toronto, Ontario, editorial assistant, 1959-60; Ryerson Press, Toronto, assistant editor, 1960-63; McClelland & Stewart, Toronto, advisory editor and editor-at-large, 1964-70. Occasional instructor at Atkinson College, York University. Has given poetry readings throughout Canada and in the United States,

John Robert Colombo with son, Theo.

United Kingdom, and eastern and western Europe. Representative for Canadian poetry, Commonwealth Arts Festival, Cardiff and London, 1965; former advisor, Canada Council and Ontario Arts Council. *Member:* League of Canadian Poets (provisional coordinator), P.E.N. (Canada), Science Fiction Research Associates (United States), North York Arts Council (honorary patron).

AWARDS, HONORS: Centennial Medal, 1967; Certificate of Merit from the Ontario Library Association, 1978, for contribution to research; named Esteemed Knight of Mark Twain, 1978, for contribution to literature; recipient of Order of Cyril and Methodius (first class) from Bulgaria, 1980, for popularizing Bulgarian letters; has also received numerous Canada Council grants and other grants for specific undertakings.

WRITINGS—Poetry: *Miraculous Montages,* Heinrich Heine, 1966; *Abracadabra,* McClelland & Stewart, 1967; *Neo Poems,* Sono Nis, 1970; *The Great Collage,* Oasis, 1974; *The Sad Truths,* PMA Books, 1974; *Variable Cloudiness,* Hounslow, 1977; *Private Parts: New Poems by John Robert Colombo,* Hounslow, 1978; *Selected Poems of John Robert Colombo,* Black Moss Press, 1982.

Editor—Poetry books, except as noted: *The Varsity Chapbook* (anthology), Ryerson, 1959; (with Jacques Godbout) *Poetry 64/Poésis 64* (anthology), Ryerson, 1963; *The Mackenzie Poems,* Swan Publishing, 1966; *The Great Wall of China: An Entertainment,* Delta Canada, 1966; *William Lyon Mackenzie Rides Again!,* The Guild of Hand Printers, 1967; (with Raymond Souster) *Shapes and Sounds: Poems of W.W.E. Ross* (anthology), Longmans, Green (Canada), 1968; *John Toronto: New Poems by Dr. Strachan,* Oberon Press, 1969.

How Do I Love Thee? (anthology), Hurtig, 1970; *The Great San Francisco Earthquake and Fire,* Fiddlehead Poetry Books, 1971; *New Direction in Canadian Poetry* (anthology), Holt, 1971; *Rhymes and Reasons* (anthology), Holt, 1971; *Praise Poems,* Weed Flower Press, 1972; *Leonardo's Lists,* Weed Flower Press, 1972; *Translations from the English: Found Poems,* PMA Books, 1974; *Proverbial Play,* The Missing Link Press, 1975; *Trio: 21 Poems . . . in English Translation* (anthology), International Festival of Poetry, 1975; *Mostly Monsters,* Hounslow, 1977; *The Poets of Canada* (anthology), Hurtig, 1978; *Dark Times: Selected Poems of Waclaw Iwaniuk,* translated by Jagna Boraks and others, Hounslow, 1979; *The Great Cities of Antiquity,* Hounslow, 1979; *Poems of the Inuit* (anthology), Oberon, 1981; *Far from You: Selected Poems of George Skvor/Pavel Javor,* translated by Ron D.K. Banerjee, Hounslow, 1981; *Songs of the Indians* (anthology; two volumes), Oberon, 1983; (with M. Richardson) *We Stand on Guard: Poems and Songs of Canadians in Battle* (anthology), Doubleday (Canada), 1985.

Compiler: *Colombo's Canadian Quotations,* Hurtig, 1974; *Colombo's Little Book of Canadian Proverbs, Graffiti, Limericks and Other Vital Matters* (illustrated by P. Whalley and D. Shaw), Hurtig, 1975; *Colombo's Concise Canadian Quotations,* Hurtig, 1976; *Colombo's Canadian References,* Oxford, 1976; *The Poets of Canada,* Hurtig, 1978; *Colombo's Book of Canada,* Hurtig, 1978; (with others) *CDN SF&F: A Bibliography of Canadian Science Fiction and Fantasy,* Hounslow, 1979; *Colombo's Book of Marvels,* NC Press, 1979; *Colombo's Names and Nicknames,* NC Press, 1979; *Colombo's Hollywood: Wit and Wisdom of the Moviemakers,* Collins, 1979, published as *Popcorn in Paradise,* Holt, 1980 (published in England as *Wit and Wisdom of the Moviemakers,* Hamlyn, 1980); *Other Canadas: An Anthology of Science Fiction and Fantasy,* McGraw-Hill Ryerson, 1979.

The Canada Colouring Book (illustrated by Emma Hesse), Hounslow, 1980; *Blackwood's Books,* Hounslow, 1981; (with Michael Richardson) *Not to Be Taken at Night: Classic Canadian Tales of Mystery and the Supernatural* (anthology), Lester & Orpen Dennys, 1981; *222 Canadian Jokes* (illustrated by Peter Whalley), Highway, 1981; *Friendly Aliens,* Hounslow, 1981; *Windigo,* Western Producer Prairie Books, 1982; *Colombo's Last Words* (illustrated by P. Whalley), Highway, 1982; *Years of Light: A Celebration of Leslie A. Croutch,* Hounslow, 1982; *Colombo's Laws* (illustrated by P. Whalley), Highway, 1982; *Rene Levesque Buys Canada Savings Bonds, and Other Great Canadian Graffiti* (illustrated by David Shaw), Hurtig, 1983; *Colombo's Canadiana Quiz Book,* Western Producer, 1983; *Colombo's 101 Canadian Places* (illustrated by P. Whalley), Hounslow, 1983; *The Toronto Puzzle Book,* McClelland & Stewart, 1984; *Toronto's Fantastic Street Names* (monograph), Bakka Books, 1984; *Canadian Literary Landmarks,* Hounslow, 1984; *Great Moments in Canadian History* (illustrated by P. Whalley), Hounslow, 1984; *1001 Questions about Canada,* Doubleday (Canada), 1986.

Translator—Published by Hounslow, except as noted: Robert Zend, *From Zero to One,* Sono Nis, 1973; (and editor with Nikola Roussanoff) *Under the Eaves of a Forgotten Village: Sixty Poems from Contemporary Bulgaria* (illustrated by Maryon Kantaroff), 1975; (with Irene Currie) Paul Eluard and Benjamin Péret, *152 Proverbs Adapted to the Taste of the Day,* Oasis, 1975; (with Susana Wald) Ludwig Zeller, *When the Animal Rises from the Deep the Head Explodes,* Mosaic Press/ Valley Editions, 1976; (and editor with N. Roussanoff) *The Balkan Range: A Bulgarian Reader,* 1976; (with N. Roussanoff) Lyubomir Levchev, *The Left-Handed One: The Poems of Lyubomir Levchev,* 1977; (with N. Roussanoff) Andrei Germanov, *Remember Me Well,* 1978; (with N. Roussanoff) Dora Gabe, *Depths,* 1978; (and editor) George Faludy, *East and West: Selected Poems of George Faludy,* 1978; (with Susana Wald) Ludwig Zeller, *Mirages,* Oasis, 1977; (and editor with Waclaw Iwaniuk) Ewa Lipska, *Such Times: The Selected Poems of Ewa Lipska,* 1981; (with Petronela Negosanu) Marin Sorescu, *Symmetrics: Selected Poems of Marin Sorescu,* 1982;

Yoho National Park, a wilderness area of 507 square miles . . . is in British Columbia. ■ (From *Colombo's 101 Canadian Places* by John Robert Colombo. Illustrated by Peter Whalley.)

Selected Translations, Black Moss, 1982; R. Zend, *Beyond Labels,* 1982; George Faludy, *Learn This Poem of Mine by Heart,* 1983.

Also author of plays and documentaries for Canadian Broadcasting Corporation. Contributor to periodicals, including *Globe and Mail* and *Toronto Star.* Member of editorial board, *Tamarack Review,* 1960-82.

SIDELIGHTS: "I have been called 'the Master Gatherer' for my many compilations of Canadiana. These include such standard popular reference works as *Colombo's Canadian Quotations* and *Colombo's Canadian References,* but also such unusual collections, as *Other Canadas* (the country's first collection of science fiction and fantasy), *René Lévesque Buys Canada Savings Bonds and Other Great Canadian Graffiti* (the first selection of graffiti from Canadian walls), *Mostly Monsters* (found poems based on fantastic literature), not to mention *Poems of the Inuit* and *Songs of the Indians* (the first comprehensive anthologies of native lyrics). I am an inveterate collector and a chronic list-maker. My mission (in part at least) is to make inventories and make accessible previously snubbed materials from the tributaries and mainstreams, the highways and byways, of the Canadian people. Such literary material reveals the human spirit and sheds some light on life in the northern half of the North American continent."

Colombo has been a guest of the Writers' Unions of the Soviet Union, Romania, and Bulgaria.

HOBBIES AND OTHER INTERESTS: Reading.

FOR MORE INFORMATION SEE: Times Literary Supplement, May 13, 1983.

CORBETT, W(illiam) J(esse) 1938-

PERSONAL: Born February 21, 1938, in Warwickshire, England; son of William Jesse (a saw maker) and Dora (a housewife; maiden name, Ruffles) Corbett. *Education:* Attended school in England. *Politics:* "I hate extremes so I would say liberal." *Religion:* Church of England. *Home and office:* 6 Selborne Grove, Billesley, Birmingham 13, England. *Agent:* Murray Pollinger, 4 Garrick St., London WC2E 9BH, England.

CAREER: Writer. Has been employed as a merchant seaman, factory-hand, soldier, furniture-remover, building-site laborer, dishwasher, and others. *Awards, honors:* Whitbread Literary Award, children's book category, 1982, and selected one of *School Library Journal*'s Best Books, 1983, both for *The Song of Pentecost.*

*WRITINGS—*For children: *The Song of Pentecost* (illustrated by Martin Ursell), Methuen, 1982, Dutton, 1983; *Pentecost and the Chosen One* (illustrated by M. Ursell), Methuen, 1984; *The End of the Tale* (illustrated by Tony Ross), Methuen, 1985; *Pentecost of Lickey Top,* Methuen, 1987.

WORK IN PROGRESS: "I have just finished some short stories for Penguin/Puffin, and one story for a separate short-story book for young children. I am now working on a novel about the Peninsular Wars for children. It is about children involved in those times. It will take about a year to finish."

SIDELIGHTS: "Mine was an ordinary working family, living on an ordinary council estate. My earliest memories are of air-raid sirens, of bombs whistling down as we crouched in the

W. J. CORBETT

Anderson shelter in the back-garden. And then in the morning the 'all-clear' and the scampering for much prized schrapnel pieces. My older brother, John, would take me by the hand and lead me on such expeditions. He was an avid collector of such relics as well as of books and easily the greatest influence in my early life. He was always bringing home armfuls of treasure from the city's second-hand bookshops. Piles of *Astounding* science fiction, *Boy's Own* annuals, books about the castles of England with map-pockets, all beautifully illustrated, stacks of *Romance of the Nation* issues that you were supposed to bind yourself. Once a complete set of *Just William,* all red-bound, dusty volumes of Dickens, half/filled stamp and postcard albums, school prize day books (the winners long, long dead), and all with the peculiar odor of pages years unturned—I wonder where they all went? And then there were the childhood trips to the Lickey Hills, Stratford-upon-Avon, Henley-in-Arden—John striding ahead with an old army haversack stuffed with the obligatory bottle of cold tea and fish-paste sandwiches. He never tired of pointing out the scarred walls of Kenilworth Castle, and I, on cue, never tired of parroting in my short-trousered voice, 'Cromwell done that.'

"But all that was so long ago. My education was scant. I left school at age fifteen having failed every examination placed before me. I was good at English literature, though. I remember once starting an essay with the line, 'He was a plump bespectacled gentleman of some fifty summers . . . ,' which annoyed my teacher no end. From that moment I began to respect him, even though he continued to sneer at my math. After all, hadn't he read at least one Dickens novel? Two years ago a TV company made a film about me. That particular teacher wrote to me, remembering.

"As I said . . . I left school, at first quite pleased to turn wheels on lathes, for it was a living. But I grew to hate it. The thing that rankled was, I could no longer blame Cromwell, only myself. So I went to sea in a sieve. As a sixteen-year-old boy I thoroughly enjoyed peeling potato mountains on deck and counting the flying fishes. I saw a lot of the world but never, alas, the hills of the Chankly Bore. But I did see at age eighteen the parade ground of Aldershot, for all at once His Majesty called me up for National Service. I quite liked it, for not

Uncle was shoved inside by the Great Aunts, who proceeded to secure the tiny door shut. ■ (From *The Song of Pentecost* by W. J. Corbett. Illustrated by Martin Ursell.)

only could I begin to blame Cromwell again, but I became a physical training instructor in our old model army. But after two years it was back to drifting again. And the sieve was for real this time. Nothing much happened from age twenty to forty. Just a long series of dead-end jobs, but with a life-long love of reading to ease the tedium.

"Then suddenly I was thrown out of work with no chance of ever getting another job. So what to do? I did what I should have done many years ago. Instead of picking up a pen merely to sign on the dole, I picked one up and wrote a poem. Then another, and then a short story. And soon I was writing about a harvest mouse called Pentecost. He, too, was in search of a better life. Together we rediscovered the Lickey Hills of my childhood. I never found Mr. Lear's Chankly Bore. Instead I invented my own. That marvellous man would have smiled and approved, I'm sure.

"My books are now in several languages, including Japanese. Needless to say, I am bemused and proud."

CURRY, Peggy Simson 1911-1987

OBITUARY NOTICE—See sketch in *SATA* Volume 8: Born December 30, 1911, in Dunure, Ayrshire, Scotland; died after a long illness, January 20, 1987, in Casper, Wyo. Educator, poet, and author of western fiction. Known as the poet laureate of Wyoming, Curry was also an award-winning short story writer and novelist. She received the Golden Spur Award from Western Writers of America in 1971 for her juvenile novel, *A Shield of Clover*, and for short stories in 1957 and 1976. An instructor in creative writing at Casper College, Curry wrote a guide for writers entitled *Creating Fiction from Experience*. Her poetry volumes include *Red Wind of Wyoming* and *Summer Range*, and among her novels are *Fire in the Water*, *So Far from Spring*, and *The Oil Patch*. She was also a contributor to *Boys' Life*, *Christian Science Monitor*, *Good Housekeeping*, *New York Times*, *Reader's Digest*, *Saturday Evening Post*, and other periodicals. Her poet's column appeared in the Sunday edition of the *Chicago Tribune*.

FOR MORE INFORMATION SEE: Contemporary Authors, New Revision Series, Volume 12, Gale, 1984; *The Writers Directory: 1986-1988,* St. James Press, 1986. Obituaries: *Baltimore Sun,* January 22, 1987; *Detroit Free Press,* January 23, 1987; *Washington Post,* January 24, 1987; *Seattle Times,* January 25, 1987.

DAVIES, Joan 1934-
(Joan Lyngseth)

PERSONAL: Born January 29, 1934, in Saskatchewan, Canada; daughter of Arthur (a farmer and store owner) and Emily (a store owner; maiden name, Hague) Davies; married Delmar Milton Lyngseth (an assistant deputy minister of the Canadian government), July 29, 1957; children: Russell Blake. *Education:* Sheffield College of Commerce, diploma, 1957; Carlton University, B.A. (first class honors), 1962; University of Saskatchewan, B.A. (summa cum laude), 1961, M.A., 1963. *Home and office:* 477 Lisgar St., Ottawa, Ontario, Canada K1R 5H2. *Agent:* Nancy Colbert, Colbert Agency, 303 Davenport Rd., Toronto, Ontario, Canada M5R 1K5.

CAREER: Free-lance writer. *South Yorkshire Times,* Rotherham, England, junior reporter, 1951-55, senior reporter, 1955-56; government of Saskatchewan, Regina, Saskatchewan, information officer, 1957-58, television script writer, 1964; Carlton University, Ottawa, Ontario, teaching assistant, 1965-67; Algonquin College, Ottawa, literature teacher, 1967-70; Written Word, Inc., Ottawa, owner and free-lance writer, 1981—. *Member:* Writers' Union of Canada. *Awards, honors:* Imperial Order of Daughters of the Empire National Short Story Competition, first prize for "Waste Sad Time," 1965.

JOAN DAVIES

WRITINGS: (Under name Joan Lyngseth) *Martin's Starwars* (juvenile fantasy; illustrated by Steven Collier), Borealis, 1978; (contributor; under name Joan Lyngseth) Marilyn Berg, editor, *Common Ground: Stories by Women,* Press Gang, 1980; *Wine and Wheat* (autobiographical account), Western Producer Prairie Books, 1984.

WORK IN PROGRESS: A collection of short stories and a novel.

SIDELIGHTS: "There was a time when I was charmed out of my cotton socks by the ubiquitous tales of young boys (never girls apparently) who had a close brush with death and then were confined to their beds for months or even a year. Sometimes when a poor invalid recovered, he remained lame or delicate and couldn't become an athlete or a champion horseman. Of course, these little boys were always from well-to-do families, so they were cosseted by a nanny and provided with all the books they could read. Eventually they became learned; often they became wonderful writers. I pitied their afflictions and envied their opportunities and achievements.

"But I too had an opportunity not given to everyone, even though I grew up as healthy as a dandelion, and the world was at war.

"I was born on the Saskatchewan prairie during the depression and drought of the early 1930s. My father, an English immigrant, desperately wanted to be a wheat farmer, but Russian thistle was the only plant which could survive on his land after the topsoil had dried out and blown away. The last crop seen in the district for years was eaten by grasshoppers. After that the families of farmers were fed and clothed by charities and government handouts.

"We were fortunate. We had relatives in England who sent tickets to take us 'home' to Sheffield. I was one year old at the time.

"Four years later, World War II began. Instead of being sent to school, I was evacuated to live with a farm family in a safe place in the country. That experience ended when an air base was built nearby and German bombers began searching for it.

"Back with my family in Sheffield, I found that schools were closed because of air raids. There were no classes and no television, and my parents were occupied day and night running a store. With nothing else to do, I learned to read, and read whatever was available on my parents' bookshelves.

"It was an odd assortment. At eight I was stumbling through *The Life of Tolstoy* and extracting what I could from *Lust for Life,* a lurid biography of Vincent Van Gogh; I was misunderstanding *How Green Was My Valley,* weeping over Mary Webb's novels and luxuriating in *Palgrave's Golden Treasury.* The gift of a Beatrix Potter story left me astonished at a mother who said 'I am affronted' when a kitten lost a mitten. My mother would have said, 'Then you had better learn to knit.'

"School closure until the Luftwaffe bombers no longer made raids in the daytime was not entirely as satisfactory from my point of view as falling ill and being confined to bed and books for months, but it produced something akin to the desired result. True, I didn't become learned, but I did develop an ardent desire to become a writer.

"At nine, after I had discovered libraries, I wrote plays on an antique typewriter. The machine was so elementary that it needed ink pouring onto a felt pad so that the type faces could

As I pulled the trigger, a beam of white light shot out, melting a large hole through the snowman's middle. ■ (From *Martin's Starwars* by Joan Lyngseth. Illustrated by Steven Collier.)

pick up the ink and transfer it onto paper. The plays were elementary too. They were conglomerations of plagiarized material from the legends and fairy stories I had read. I typed the scripts with two fingers, and in costumes made from nightgowns and dressing gowns, a friend and I performed to whatever audience we could lure into our garage. The stage was a few planks precariously balanced on bricks. Each actor took several parts, changing costume in full view. But those pale and thin little invalid boys had an advantage other than some months with nothing to do but read. They had rich parents who could later on put them in excellent English public schools and then provide them with a modest but adequate income which preserved them from want when they decided to devote their lives to writing.

"The closest I could get to achieving that end was becoming a journalist.

"The invalids' parents provided them with the grand tour around Europe to round out their education. I emigrated (if one can emigrate to the place where one was born) and lived in Saskatchewan for seven years. After that I made my home in Ottawa.

"When I was neither learning nor teaching, I was writing. Chiefly I wrote the things other people paid me to write. I still do that, working on contract, but now I spend much more time writing the things I want to write in the way I want to write them.

"It has taken years to accumulate skill and confidence, and to learn to juggle time like a circus performer tossing hats. And the truth is, I still envy those little boys who, at an impressionable age, spent a year lying pale and wan and reading.

"To a young person wanting to create with words, my advice is always: if you happen to have rich parents who abominate TV, then fall ill at about the age of ten for one year and insist on a nurse who is highly literate. If you are, like almost every other North American creative writer, born with good health and wage-earning parents, then read. Read one book a day until you find yourself waiting impatiently for the new spring and fall publications.

"The advice is probably as old as the alphabet, but there should be a warning sign posted with it. I have wasted a lot of energy in past years because no one pointed out the 'Caution. Detour Ahead' sign.

"From time to time I have, and still do, become infatuated by an author's style. But now I no longer try to incorporate its more obvious charms into my own style. The only good that came out of such covetous behaviour is that I can now imitate almost any style a paying client asks for (though for the life of me I can't imagine why anyone would want to reproduce some of the styles I am asked to copy).

"I have concluded that a writer's style is as unique and inescapable as his or her fingerprints. It is there to be discovered, refined, and polished, but it cannot be changed in any fundamental way. Making a radical change almost certainly ensures that the new style will not say the things that the combination of the writer's experience, perceptions, and responses to the world dictate.

"In my case I am sure that my style is my personality. I use a spare, stripped-down style. A superfluous adjective offends me, an unnecessary clause pains me. And I react in much the same way to my home and to my social life. I give no houseroom to anything which is merely a temporary diversion and has no practical purpose or moving beauty. My friendships are few but deeply satisfying.

"Perhaps there has never been a time when I have not loved someone else's style more than my own. But though my word-child is neither brilliant nor remarkable for beauty, it is good mannered and I grow fond of it. It responds by becoming increasingly cooperative and accommodating.

"Provided I am writing about something familiar, we have a comfortable relationship. True, *Martin's Starwars* is a science fiction fantasy, but the adventures in it are friendly territory to me. They are largely based on material I read as a child. *Wine and Wheat* is about the life of my parents on the prairies and about Sheffield during World War II. My short stories are often drawn from my experience as a newspaper reporter. Now I am working on a novel about an old woman travelling across Canada by train, and to help it speak with an authentic voice, I am planning a train trip from coast to coast."

DAVIS, Grania   1943-
(Mama G.)

BRIEF ENTRY: Born July 17, 1943, in Milwaukee, Wis. A writer who has lived in Mexico, Japan, Central America, Europe, and India, Davis is fascinated with Asian myths. Two books for elementary-school readers, *The King and the Mangoes* (1975) and *The Proud Peacock and the Mallard,* (1976) both published by Dharma Publishing, are collections of

Buddhist tales. *The Rainbow Annals* (Avon, 1980), a fantasy for "the most mature," according to *Kliatt,* "reads like a Tibetan myth." In it, the Monkey God and his demoness lover Drolma are reincarnated as mortals several times and do battle with Black Shen, an evil magician. Davis provides "a wonderfully detailed picture of the life of nomads, farmers and merchants of Tibet as well as a history of its religion and philosophy," added *Kliatt.* Another book strongly based on a mythological theme, *Moonbird* (Doubleday, 1986) is a fantasy about a young teenager who lives on Bali. "The mythological undercurrents are a nice change of pace from technologically based science fiction," observed *Voice of Youth Advocates.* In addition to several books for adults, Davis has produced the "Mama G." column in the *Marin Scope* since 1973, "Travel and Gourmet" column in *Penthouse Letters,* and has contributed to science fiction and fantasy magazines. She has also worked as a travel agent and teacher. *Agent:* Jane Butler, c/o Virginia Kidd, Literary Agent, 538 East Harford St., Milford, Pa. 18337.

FOR MORE INFORMATION SEE: Contemporary Authors, New Revision Series, Volume 16, Gale, 1986.

deKRUIF, Paul (Henry)   1890-1971

PERSONAL: Surname pronounced "da Krife"; born March 2, 1890, in Zeeland, Mich.; died February 28, 1971; son of Hendrik (a farm implement dealer) and Hendrika J. (Kremer) deKruif; first marriage ended in divorce; married Rhea Elizabeth Barbarin, December 11, 1922 (died 1957); married Eleanor Lappage, September 1, 1959; children: (first marriage) Hendrik, David. *Education:* University of Michigan, B.S., 1912, Ph.D., 1916. *Home:* Wake Robin, Holland, Mich.

CAREER: University of Michigan, Ann Arbor, assistant professor of bacteriology, 1916-17, 1918-20; Rockefeller Institute for Medical Research, New York, N.Y., associate in pathology, 1920-22; free-lance writer and popularizer of medical science, beginning 1922. Former consultant to Chicago Board of Health, Michigan State Health Department, National Foundation for Infantile Paralysis, secretary of general scientific committee, 1940; President's Birthday Ball Commission for Infantile Paralysis Research, co-founder, 1934, and longtime secretary. *Military service:* U.S. Army, Sanitary Corps, 1917-18; served in France; became captain.

WRITINGS: (Contributor) *Civilization in the United States: An Inquiry by Thirty Americans,* edited by Harold Stearns, Harcourt, 1922; *Our Medicine Men* (collection of articles from *Century* magazine), Century, 1922; (collaborator on medical background) Sinclair Lewis, *Arrowsmith,* Harcourt, 1925; *Microbe Hunters,* Harcourt, 1926, published as *Dr. Ehrlich's Magic Bullet and the Discoveries of Eleven Other Microbe Hunters,* Pocket Books, 1940; *Hunger Fighters,* Harcourt, 1928; *Seven Iron Men,* Harcourt, 1929; *Men Against Death,* Harcourt, 1932; (with Sidney Howard) *Yellow Jack* (play produced in New York, 1934), Harcourt, 1933; (with wife, Rhea deKruif) *Why Keep Them Alive?,* Harcourt, 1936; *The Fight for Life,* Harcourt, 1938; *Toward a Healthy America,* Public Affairs Committee, 1939; *Activities of the National Foundation for Infantile Paralysis in the Field of Virus Research,* National Foundation for Infantile Paralysis, 1939.

Health Is Wealth, Harcourt, 1940; *Kaiser Wakes the Doctors,* Harcourt, 1943; *The Male Hormone,* Harcourt, 1945; (with R. deKruif) *Life among the Doctors,* Harcourt, 1949; *A Man against Insanity,* Harcourt, 1957; *The Sweeping Wind, a Memoir,* Harcourt, 1962.

Regular contributor to magazines, including *Country Gentlemen* and *Ladies' Home Journal*, beginning 1925, and *Reader's Digest*.

ADAPTATIONS: "Yellow Jack" (motion picture), Metro-Goldwyn-Mayer, 1938; "Fight for Life" (motion picture), Columbia, 1940; "Dr. Ehrlich's Magic Bullet" (motion picture; based on *The Microbe Hunters*), Warner Bros., 1940; "Yellow Jack" (radio play), The Theatre Guild, 1946.

SIDELIGHTS: **March 8, 1890.** Born in Zeeland, Michigan of Dutch ancestry, deKruif inherited a love for books from his mother. ". . . From my earliest boyhood I remembered her as a tremendous reader. She had read Dicken's *Tale of Two Cities* aloud to me and his *Child's History of England* over and over. She was, in her obscure western Michigan way, an authority on George Eliot and Mark Twain, and I remember her reading deep in *Anna Karenina*—which she considered a bit too rough for me—reading, preoccupied by the star-crossed lives of Anna and Vronsky. Her reading of illicit love would have got her severe censure by the Calvinistic elders of our village of Zeeland, Michigan, had they known. . . .

"In my boyhood in our family my father would be stony silent for days, gloomy, preoccupied, only opening his mouth to read the inevitable chapter of the Bible after every meal. He was a tough, totally self-made man whose formal schooling had ended at the second grade. He was a natural mathematician who

PAUL deKRUIF

would offhand give me the answer to a stated problem in college algebra without so much as having heard of a quadratic equation. He solved the fiscal angles of profit and loss in his hard-driving farm-implement business at a glance. He had contempt for the economic calfishness of his farmer customers and foreclosed them without too much mercy.

"My father made what was big country money in those early nineteenth-century days but then often tossed a part of these profits away in bold investments, such as an as yet unsuccessful paper milk bottle, and in Portland cement companies. These disasters made him furious, not at himself but at my mother, who was then reduced to tears. Outside our home he was considered a jolly man; his round face smiled and his round belly shook with hearty laughter.

"He was true to my mother, who feared him and loved him. 'Your father was a hard man,' my mother summed him up to me just before she died. On his black days, for minor peccadilloes, he bared my back and had at me with a horsewhip with the abandon of a Captain Bligh. Afterward he seemed to feel better and might take us out for an auto ride—for a spin as he called it—and then would like as not treat us to an ice-cream soda.

"He was determined to get me away from our small town, wanting me to become an engineer or a doctor or a 'rattling attorney' though he never made it clear to me why an attorney should rattle. Yet he had no great hopes for me, considering me a coward because I couldn't keep what he called 'a stiff upper lip'—I whimpered when he beat the hell out of me. The streak of cowardice in me must have stemmed partly from fear of my father. I do not blame him because I now know that for many years—beneath his being outwardly robust—he was, subclinically, a sick man; and his irritability was that of an undiagnosed diabetic. In his last years, slowly starving to death under diabetic treatment on scant calories, he became gentler to me." [Paul deKruif, *The Sweeping Wind, a Memoir*, Harcourt, 1962.[1]]

1908. A magazine article about Nobel Prize winner and bacteriologist Dr. Paul Ehrlich prompted deKruif to study premedicine.

1912. Received a B.S. degree from the University of Michigan. Having won a Rockefeller research fellowship, he became a researcher in bacteriology under Professor Novy of the University of Michigan. "Novy was the Nestor of American microbe hunters. He was the world's authority on the spirochetes of relapsing fever; one of these corkscrew microbes bears his name. He was the first person to cultivate artifically the trypanosome of deadly Nagana. . . . He had got his science working under Robert Koch in Berlin and Emile Roux at the Institut Pasteur in Paris."[1]

1912-1916. Worked and studied for a Ph.D. degree in microbiology at the University of Michigan.

1917. Served as a captain with the Army Sanitary Corps in France, doing research on the bacteria of gas gangrene during World War I.

1919. After the war, deKruif returned to research and teaching at the University of Michigan, where he met and fell in love with a young laboratory assistant, Rhea Barbarin. Although already married and the father of two boys, deKruif was determined to get a divorce and remarry. In order to do this, he attempted to earn money as a free-lance writer, and wrote to journalist Henry L. Mencken for advice. ". . . A mad plan formed in my head . . . to make a new life, to make enough money to take care of my family responsibilities and at the same time to kick free to marry the unattainable Rhea. It was crazy and wild. How did I know she would be so foolish and brave as to marry me even if it were possible?

"I . . . wrote a letter to Henry L. Mencken—never having met him, he never having heard of me—telling him my admiration of the clear way he described the phenomenon of catalysis, asking his advice as to whether a young scientific man should dare to try popular writing on the side. In four days the first of many years of sharp, gay, brilliant, often obscene notes came back from Mencken telling me certainly it was worth while to try it.

"Now, somewhat neglecting my blood-dissolving streptococci, I worked into the night on a sketch—satirical in a style deriving from Mencken—examining the scientific pretenses of an eminent professor. How lucky for me that my new mentor didn't think it good enough for his *Smart Set*. Its sarcasm was not too funny and could only have hurt an old man who had indeed been kind to me. But, having been asked to contribute to a highbrow magazine, I thought I was a writer. To tough-faced Tom Le Blanc, my lab assistant, a sailor veteran of the war, I confided that I was going to add writing to microbe hunting. His sneering reply was memorable. 'You—a writer?' he asked. 'Ha—that's just as if you'd announce to me you were going to be a capitalist. What would you use for money, kiddo?'"[1]

1920. Hired as an associate at the Rockefeller Institute for Medical Research in New York City.

1922. Series of articles on the medical profession that were originally printed in *Century* magazine were published in book form as *Our Medicine Men*. Although the book was published anonymously, it contained criticisms of some of his colleagues from the Rockefeller Institute. Consequently, he was asked to resign from the institute, which forced him to turn his energies toward writing. DeKruif wrote scientific and medical articles for popular magazines.

December 11, 1922. Having been granted a divorce from his first wife, he married Rhea Barbarin. ". . . Rhea held my hand as the sun peeped out of the gray for a moment and shone on the bride, and we laughed and believed the old superstition that this meant we were going to be happy. Some of our friends could not believe me to be a fit man for this good girl with the honest, wide-apart gray eyes. Rhea herself knew they had reasons for their doubts; like van Gogh's mysterious young Arlésienne, La Mousmée, her eyes often looked with just a touch of sadness into the inscrutable future. But there was this about Rhea: she was brave.

"She stuck to the rugged task—the taming of a turbulent man—till at last our days became not only halcyon but happy. That was her victory. Ahead of us surely lay a long life's late golden afternoon. We were strong for our ages and I was confident

(From the movie "Yellow Jack," starring Robert Montgomery. Produced by Metro-Goldwyn-Mayer, 1938.)

(From the movie "Fight for Life." Released by Colombia Pictures, 1940.)

of knowing tricks to keep us so. We worked together closer year by year; it was as if we were tossing passes in life's rough game without having to look where the other one was.''[1]

1925. Sinclair (''Red'') Lewis' book *Arrowsmith,* a novel about a physician, was published. Lewis collaborated with deKruif on the medical background of the book. The two-year collaboration took Lewis and deKruif to the Caribbean, England, and France. "On the *S.S. Guiana* Red and I both wore steamer caps and carried walking sticks. We were trying to seem like world travelers. Red was almost one, though he had not been in Africa, Asia, or the lands of the South Pacific. Red gave the impression of an eminent British author lately escaped from Sauk Centre, Minnesota. He look[ed] distinguished—a lurid, brilliant personality. He looked anything but dull and dreary. Except for my stylish steamer cap and trench stick I could have passed for a Michigan Dutchman coming into town on a wagon load of turnips. On the *S.S. Guiana* we did not have to be impressive. There was nobody on the grimy little cargo boat one could awe. Red was rehearsing for greater things to come.

"The first morning out Red unlimbered his Corona in our cabin and we settled down to build the skeleton of a novel— still tentatively called *Barbarian*—but gradually becoming *Arrowsmith.* It was for me as if to be in a new wonderful world to be working with Sinclair Lewis. It was astoundng how rapidly he developed the scientific and spiritual agonies of Martin Arrowsmith, a tough young man hell bent to become a microbe hunter. . . .''[1]

The collaboration resulted in an acknowledgment by Lewis in the book's preface and twenty-five per cent of the royalties going to deKruif. "What about the credit for who wrote *Arrowsmith?* Over the years it has become plain that the majority of people who have talked to me about *Arrowsmith* had no idea I'd had anything to do with it at all. Then there is a small school of friends who erroneously believe it was not really Sinclair Lewis but deKruif who wrote it. Nothing could be farther from the truth. Sinclair Lewis wrote it. Yet there is evidence that, during the early phases of the book's composition, Red thought I'd been of some help to him.

"Permit me here to deliver a judgment in the style of Judge Bridlegoose. This verdict has aged in the wood of my head over many years. In my own Bridlegoosean opinion, *Arrowsmith,* as a work of art, was in part improbable. All the science in it might have happened, though none of it did actually happen. The storied fictional protagonist, Max Gottlieb, was more than improbable. He was a muddy mélange of my revered chief, Professor Novy, and of Jacques Loeb, who was my master in a philosophy of the mechanistic conception of life, of God a mathematician, of God a Univac, of God a superstition, of God a childish concept, of God nonexistent. . . .

"Of one character Novy would have approved fully. That was Leora. In her he would have detected, as many have done, a replica of Rhea. Leora was, as Lewis called her, the undemanding wife every man dreams of. 'Why not end the book with the death of Leora; why not call the book *Leora?*' Alf Harcourt asked Red after reading the manuscript. Red flew into a fury. He threatened to withdraw the book before pub-

(From the movie "Dr. Ehrlich's Magic Bullet," starring Edward G. Robinson. Copyright 1940 by Warner Brothers Pictures Corp.)

lication and said he'd sail back to England never to return. Who was Alf to tamper with this masterpiece? Then Alf took me aside, 'Take Red back to town and cool him off,' he said. This I did in my role of bouncer in charge of the great American novelist's unstable and capricious genius. It was a rugged job.

"Why did I stick by it? Well, because Red had taught me to let my imagination go. Without that, I couldn't have begun to write the book about the microbe men. I couldn't have become a writer without apprenticeship to Red's wild genius. . . . At Fontainebleau in 1923, after reading the completed first draft of *Arrowsmith* I thought it was a fine book and was proud to have had some part in it and said so with exclamation points in the margins of the manuscript. What I think of it now is that it's okay not to be more widely identified with its composition. Red did me an unwitting favor by not giving me joint top billing on the cover. Red was right, ethically. Apprentices are not supposed to have their names on a product."[1]

1926. Wrote *Microbe Hunters,* which became a best-seller that was published in a total of eighteen languages and sold over a million copies. "Before the publication of *Microbe Hunters.* . . , Alf Harcourt gave Rhea a kindly warning. We must not hope too much. The book trade was showing not much interest in my off-beat opus, said Alf. We'd be lucky if it sold out its first printing—2800 copies.

"Immediately upon publication the sales of the book exploded in our faces. 'One of the noblest chapters in the history of mankind,' wrote Henry Mencken. 'A book for those who love high adventure, who love clear, brave writing,' reported William Allen White. 'Accurate as to facts, absolutely,' pronounced the good gray pathologist, Dr. Ludvig Hektoen. . . . It shortly passed one hundred thousand copies in sales, and before its great day was over—though it sells steadily today, not really slackening its pace in thirty years—it became one of the big nonfiction books of the decade.'"[1]

The book's success earned deKruif a reputation as a medical writer. It was followed by *The Hunger Fighters,* which described the work of those men who researched food yield. "From my earliest writing days I'd felt the need of teachers. I'd begun by aping authors who seemed to talk my own innate language. H. G. Wells was the first of these but I'd had to leave him when he became preoccupied by what he thought was the desperate need of our all clubbing together in a world state. This seemed to me to destroy his knack of telling a true story. Then Henry Mencken's boisterous demolition of political, ecclesiastical, and academic dignitaries held me enthralled, and I tried to apply Henry's unique technique to the deflation of the prevailing poopdom among doctors. The results of my attempted imitation of Mencken were not outstanding. I didn't know all the good and bad about that most wonderful profession. It must be admitted that Sinclair Lewis taught me technically while I was aiding him with *Arrowsmith,* yet that great satirist's contempt for certain human weaknesses among plain people was something I could not imitate because it was something I did not feel.

"For a moment I had luck, kicking free of all literary influence to tell in my own way, and in my own style, reeking with rhetoric, stories of the only men I truly knew, certain microbe hunters. But when that vein ran out, where would I go from there? Nowhere, so it seemed, excepting back to the bleak life of a feature writer. But I didn't want to be a feature writer. I wanted to be a writer. And I was hell bent to be a writer no matter how long it might take me to get down what I secretly believed was in me, if only one book that might have a chance to live as a human story. From Ernest Hemingway I learned that I'd have to start from scratch, to begin all over.

"I wrote *Seven Iron Men* in Fleetwood in the winter of 1928-29. As a book it turned out a flop, not even *d'estime*. 'So you've taken up muckraking?' said Carl Sandburg. 'It's the most cruel book I've ever read,' said our Wall Street friend, Tommy Thomas. 'Cruel to whom?' I asked. 'To Mr. Rockefeller, of course.' Mr. Rockefeller had done our country a great service. He'd got the Mesabi iron into orderly, businesslike hands, ready for the U.S. Steel Corporation. His ethics in so doing? Ethics are not in question in the great epic of American business, explained Tommy. 'Before you started the story, you should have realized that, in times of financial stringency, many properties inevitably change hands.' Tommy's economic insight was simple and profound.

"Right now in a futile moment I wish the clock could be turned back, to give me a chance to take a second whack at

(From *Hunger Fighters* by Paul deKruif. Illustrated by Zadig.)

(Jacket illustration by Sidney Butchkes from *The Sweeping Wind* by Paul deKruif.)

this seven-iron-men story as it might have been told—with the writing savvy picked up in the thirty years that have gone by. The trouble with the book was I didn't know how to write it. I overwrote it, attempting to make myself a belle-lettrist, trying to create even a musical movement in it, naming parts of it *andante, allegro, più presto* and *fugato*. This was phony. What came out was pseudo-music all in a high key and all in the same rhythm and hysterical. If I had only been enough of a writer to have written it straight and plain and deadpan, it could then have had humor. The facts behind it were so bizarre that, if they'd been underwritten, readers might have thought what funny, contrasting characters go to make up our wild, woolly land."[1]

1932. "We bought twenty-nine acres of deep wooded dunes we had found on the shore of Lake Michigan. This hideaway was ten miles from Holland, Michigan, and our nearest all-year-round neighbors were nearly two miles distant. I'll never forget our first walk alone through that forest toward the big lake. The hills were dotted white with three-petalled trillium wake robins. 'Let's call it "Wake Robin"' said Rhea. . . .

"Together we cut a clearing in the woods two hundred feet from the edge of the bank above Lake Michigan's shore. Together we cut down the big trees with a crosscut saw. With a wedge and maul and a double-bitted Michigan ax we cut the big logs into firewood. Rhea learned to swing the maul and the ax like a lumberjack. Then that early summer there arose a little house, the first we could call our own. Rhea called it

'The Shack'—it had one room with a lean-to for an in-a-door bed and another lean-to for a kitchen and our facilities were a simple outdoor Chick Sales from which it was pleasant to regard the blue of the lake in the early morning."[1]

1933. "Rhea—her own architect—began to design and expand our shack into a split-level, low, rambling house; its gray-green hand-split shakes made it look as if it were part of the woods. . . .

"About a year after the publication of *Men Against Death* came a letter from the cantankerous and powerful poet, Ezra Pound. His letter assured me *Men Against Death* displayed honesty and sincerity, despite its economic ineptitude. Why did I persist in writing success stories about many medical achievements, with never a mention of a man-made cause of death more murderous than all the billions of microbes put together?

"Pound pointed out it was poverty that was the big killer. Despite our knowledge of the microbic and metabolic causes of human suffering, the trouble was that there was not enough money to make that knowledge operative and to enforce it. He was far from a communist but he had an economic panacea for poverty, namely Social Credit as expounded by the Scottish engineer, Major C. H. Douglas. I'd never heard of Douglas but if Pound said Social Credit was the answer, that was enough for me. I was that suggestible. I bought and studied all the writings of Major Douglas. A parable by the good Major excited me. He asked me to imagine a company of people crossing a desert. Some few had big water bottles but the great majority were equipped only with little ones. This was our economic order. The throats of those with the little water bottles became parched; their lips became cracked and black. Yet there were, potentially, water and big bottles enough for everybody.

"That's humanity today—when power to produce anything for everybody is limitless. At Wake Robin life seemed to me to be as simple as that.

". . . In the beginning of the deep depression I was dominated by the economic philosophy of Boss Kettering, who seemed convinced that what America mainly lacked was enough science. All we needed was more research to stimulate more industry to give more men work for greater production. . . ."[1]

1934. "My writing took a fundamental turn. We began to search out and report upon the misery of a part of humanity that could not be blamed for its suffering. Rhea and I began

(From the movie "Arrowsmith," starring Ronald Colman and Helen Hayes. Produced by United Artists, 1932. Based on the novel by Sinclair Lewis, on which Paul deKruif collaborated.)

to study the needless sickening and dying of children. Here is our Simple Simon economics: little rich girls and boys didn't have to be deprived of a single calorie or a solitary unit of vitamin to give enough death-fighting food and vitamins to all spindly-legged undernourished poor little boys and girls."[1]

Two years later a book about forgotten children entitled *Why Keep Them Alive?* was published.

1937. When the National Foundation for Infantile Paralysis was formed by President Roosevelt, deKruif became secretary to the general scientific advisory committee. "The new foundation was to set out to fight the paralytic terror on every front; to finance the discovery of science for its prevention; to broadcast to doctors knowledge of modern treatment that might prevent the horrible deformities visiting those maltreated when they are stricken; to help communities organize themselves to make self-supporting citizens of those wrecked by the paralytic aftermath of the pestilence. It was to be planned, co-ordinated by the best scientific brains in the nation. And when a polio epidemic loomed, the new foundation would instantly pour in money to pay the experts, the community's physicians and healthmen and its nurses to co-ordinate (this had not yet become for me a dirty word) to make a field test of a preventitive (if any) upon all children whose parents might demand it.

"This work began to take a lot of time away from my proper job of writing. My friend and publisher, Mr. Alfred Harcourt, was worried about me. 'You're going to have to choose between staying a writer and becoming a public health organizer,' he said, with a critical gleam in his dark eyes. As for myself, I was flattered."[1]

1940. Resigned from the National Foundation for Infantile Paralysis. Interested in an extension of public health facilities, deKruif wrote *Health is Wealth*. That same year, he became contributing editor to *Reader's Digest*, a post he held for over twenty years.

September, 1948. After years of successfully regulating her diabetes, deKruif's mother succumbed to the disease. "She pushed aside the oxygen mask, gasping: 'Give me the injection, the needle!' She wanted a shot of papaverine. Those were her last words, a testimony to her experimenter's spirit. This was my mother.

"She had hated her fears. Five weeks before she had conquered a big one, making her first airplane flight non-stop Los Angeles to Chicago. She was almost 82 and that was her great day. My father had died of diabetes, at 60; my mother had diabetes too, but insulin and other medical science had kept her vivid, alert, active and really alive up to her last moments, far beyond life's normal expectancy. None of that science was known when my father died in 1917.

"The day my mother died it dawned on me that the 30 years since my father's death were the greatest decades in history. More life-saving science had been discovered in the past 30 years than in the preceding 30 centuries.

"A very great deal of it had concentrated its power on my mother, to keep her alive so long and strong. How her eyes would have snapped to realize that she had been a participant in this most astounding of all revolutions. 'Rest easy, mother,' I said, looking at her for the last time." [Paul deKruif, *Life Among the Doctors*, Harcourt, 1949.[2]]

1957. Wife Rhea died. ". . . When Rhea's eyes closed in her last sleep at exactly two in the morning of July 9 . . . after a

terrible two weeks' fight to keep breathing, suddenly, nothing was the same for me any more. . . . From a full life that seemed too good to be true, it has become an existence so torn, so mutilated that it does not seem to matter whether it goes on one more day."[1]

1959. Married Eleanor Lappage.

1962. Last book, *The Sweeping Wind, a Memoir* was published.

February 28, 1971. Died of a heart attack in Holland, Michigan. "The power in the hands of the plainest physician is the best gift of God, so far, to mankind."[2]

The Microbe Hunters and *The Hunger Fighters* were best sellers, with the former selling more than a million copies in a total of eighteen languages.

FOR MORE INFORMATION SEE: Stanley Kunitz and Howard Haycraft, editors, *Junior Book of Authors*, H. W. Wilson, 1934; *Newsweek*, August 26, 1940, March 15, 1971; *Current Biography 1942*, H. W. Wilson, 1943; S. J. Kunitz and H. Haycraft, editors, *Twentieth Century Authors*, H. W. Wilson, 1942; *Reader's Digest*, December, 1946, January, 1947; Paul deKruif, *Life Among the Doctors*, Harcourt, 1949; Paul Henry deKruif, *The Sweeping Wind, a Memoir*, Harcourt, 1962; *Current Biography 1963*, H. W. Wilson, 1964; *Current Biography 1971*, H. W. Wilson, 1972.

Obituaries: *Detroit Free Press*, March 2, 1971; *New York Times*, March 2, 1971; *Washington Post*, March 3, 1971; *Variety*, March 10, 1971; *Newsweek*, March 15, 1971; *Time*, March 15, 1971; *Antiquarian Bookman*, March 17, 1971.

DODSON, Susan 1941-

PERSONAL: Born January 19, 1941, in Pittsburgh, Pa.; daughter of Charles W. (an attorney) and Louise (a housewife; maiden name, Williams) Dodson. *Education:* Attended California State College, California, Pa., 1958-60, and Art Institute of Pittsburgh, 1960-62. *Home and office:* New York, N.Y.

CAREER: Free-lance textile artist and author of novels for young adults. *Awards, honors: The Creep* was selected one of New York Public Library's Books for the Teen Age, 1980.

*WRITINGS—*For young adults: *The Creep*, Four Winds, 1979; *Have You Seen This Girl?*, Four Winds, 1982; *Shadows across the Sand*, Lothrop, 1983.

SIDELIGHTS: "I am writing in the young adult field, and since I myself had unusual experiences and a difficult time during those years I find myself going back over that period, reworking it to better conclusions, possibly to help teenagers and hopefully to entertain them."

DOERKSEN, Nan 1934-

BRIEF ENTRY: Born March 3, 1934, in Speedwell, Saskatchewan, Canada. Doerksen has written numerous articles and short stories for various religious publications, as well as three books for children. She was a practicing registered nurse from 1957-1960, and continues to volunteer her time with senior citizens and the mentally handicapped. "Love of God, family, and nature are probably the strongest motivational forces in my life and writing," she said. She received her bachelor's degree in nursing from the University of New Brunswick, Fredericton, in 1978 and her master's in 1981. Doerksen's books for children are titled *Bears for Breakfast* (Kindred, 1983), *The First Family Car* (Kindred, 1986), and *Rats in the Sloop* (Ragweed, 1986). She is currently working on a book of animal stories for children, puppet scripts for Social Services, and a novel based on her nursing experience in northern Canada. Doerksen is active in church groups and has held various church offices. *Home:* 732 Fenety St., Fredericton, New Brunswick, Canada E3B 4H2.

DOLCH, Edward William   1889-1961

PERSONAL: Born August 4, 1889, in St. Louis, Mo.; died in 1961, in Santa Barbara, Calif.; son of Edward William (a businessman) and Ida Catherine (a housewife; maiden name, Scheirer) Dolch; married Marguerite Pierce (an author and lecturer), 1915 (died, 1978); children: Eleanor Dolch LaRoy, Marguerite, Catherine Dolch McAndrew, Edward William, Jr., John Parker. *Education:* Washington University, St. Louis, Mo., B.A., 1915; University of Wisconsin, M.A., 1918; University of Illinois, Ph.D., 1925. *Religion:* Congregationalist. *Residence:* Santa Barbara, Calif.

CAREER: Teacher, and author of numerous books on reading and vocabulary for adults and children. University of Wisconsin, assistant professor, 1917-18; University of Illinois, professor of education, 1924-54. Lecturer. *Member:* American Education Research Association, Illinois Association of Supervisors and Directors of Education, National Society for the Study of Education, National Council on Research in Elementary English. *Awards, honors:* The Psychology and Teaching of Reading was included as one of the best education books of the year, 1931.

WRITINGS—All published by Garrard, except as indicated: *Manual of Business Letter Writing,* Ronald, 1922; *Outlining for Effective Writing,* Harper & Brothers, 1923; *Reading and Word Meanings,* Ginn, 1927; *The Psychology and Teaching of Reading,* Ginn, 1931, 2nd edition, Garrard, 1951, reprinted, Greenwood, 1970; (compiler with B. R. Buckingham) *A Combined Word List,* Ginn, 1936; *A Manual for Remedial Reading,* 1939, 2nd edition, 1945; *Teaching Primary Reading,* 1941, 3rd edition, 1960; *Better Spelling,* 1942; *Helping Handicapped Children in School,* 1948; *Problems in Reading,* 1948; *Helping the Educationally Handicapped,* 1950; *Helping Your Child with Reading,* 1954, 2nd edition, 1956; *Methods in Reading,* 1955; *Helping Your Child with Arithmetic,* 1957; *Helping Your Child with Spelling,* 1960; *The Dolch List of 220 Basic Sight Words and Suggestions for Teaching Them,* [Nashville], 1965.

"Basic Vocabulary" series; all with wife, Marguerite P. Dolch; all for children; all published by Garrard: *Animal Stories in Basic Vocabulary* (illustrated by daughter, Marguerite Dolch), 1952; *"Why" Stories . . .* (illustrated by M. Dolch), 1952; *Folk Stories . . .* (illustrated by M. Dolch), 1952; *Dog Stories . . .* (illustrated by Bernette Johnson and Robert S. Kerr), 1954; *Wigwam Stories . . .* (illustrated by R. S. Kerr), 1956; *Tepee Stories . . .* (illustrated by R. S. Kerr), 1956; *Pueblo Stories . . .* (illustrated by R. S. Kerr), 1956; *Elephant Stories . . .* (illustrated by Dee Wallace), 1956; *Circus Stories . . .* (illustrated by D. Wallace), 1956; *Navaho Stories . . .* (illustrated by Billy M. Jackson), 1957; *Lodge Stories . . .* (illustrated by B. M. Jackson), 1957; *Lion and Tiger Stories . . .* (illustrated by Charles Forsythe), 1957; *Bear Stories . . .* (illustrated by C. Forsythe), 1957; *Horse Stories . . .* (illustrated

by C. Forsythe), 1958; *Irish Stories . . .* (illustrated by Carmen Mowry), 1958; *More Dog Stories . . .* (illustrated by E. Harper Johnson), 1962.

"First Reading Book" series; all with M. P. Dolch; all for children; all published by Garrard: *On the Farm* (illustrated by Don Robertson and Midge Robertson), 1958; *In the Woods* (illustrated by Robert P. Borja), 1958; *Zoo Is Home* (illustrated by R. P. Borja), 1958; *Tommy's Pets* (illustrated by D. Wallace), 1958; *Monkey Friends* (illustrated by C. Forsythe), 1958; *Friendly Birds* (illustrated by Carol Rogers), 1959; *I Like Cats* (illustrated by Pauline Adams), 1959; *Dog Pals* (illustrated by Fran Matera), 1959; *Big, Bigger, Biggest* (illustrated by F. Matera),1959; *Some Are Small* (illustrated by Larry Kettelkamp), 1959; *Once There Was an Elephant* (illustrated by William Moyers), 1961; *Once There Was a Rabbit* (illustrated by Robert Patterson), 1961; *Once There Was a Cat* (illustrated by Carl Hauge and Mary Hauge), 1961; *Once There Was a Dog* (illustrated by Tom O'Sullivan), 1962; *Once There Was a Monkey* (illustrated by Kenyon Shannon), 1962; *Once There Was a Bear* (illustrated by Gerald McCann), 1962.

"Folklore of the World" series; all with M. P. Dolch; all for children; all published by Garrard: *Stories from Japan* (illustrated by Lucy Hawkinson and John Hawkinson), 1960; . . . *Mexico* (illustrated by Ernest De Soto), 1960; . . . *Hawaii* (illustrated by Ted Schroeder), 1960; . . . *India* (illustrated by Gordon Laite), 1961; . . . *Alaska* (illustrated by Carl Heldt), 1961; . . . *Spain* (illustrated by Don Bolognese), 1962; . . . *It-*

EDWARD WILLIAM DOLCH

The people who were watching it all laughed and laughed as the King and Queen and all the King's men ran down the street. ■ (From *Andersen Stories for Pleasure Reading* by Edward W. Dolch, Marguerite P. Dolch, and Beulah F. Jackson. Illustrated by Carmen Mowry.)

aly (illustrated by Colleen Browning), 1962; . . . *France* (illustrated by G. Laite), 1963; . . . *Old Russia* (illustrated by James Lewicki), 1964; . . . *Old Egypt* (illustrated by G. Laite), 1964; . . . *Old China* (illustrated by Seong Moy), 1964; . . . *Canada* (illustrated by Gil Miret), 1964.

"Pleasure Reading" series; all with M. P. Dolch and Beulah F. Jackson; all for children; all published by Garrard: *Bible Stories for Pleasure Reading* (illustrated by John Slocum and Y. Cuypers-Fransen), 1950; *Fairy Stories* . . . (illustrated by M. Dolch and Y. Cuypers-Fransen), 1950; *Famous Stories* . . . (illustrated by J. Slocum, Y. Cuypers-Fransen and R. S. Kerr), 1951; *Aesop's Stories* . . . (illustrated by M. Dolch), 1951; *Gospel Stories* . . . (illustrated by M. Dolch), 1951; *Old World Stories* . . . (illustrated by M. Dolch), 1952; *Far East Stories* . . . (illustrated by M. Dolch), 1953; *Greek Stories* . . . (illustrated by M. Dolch and R. S. Kerr), 1955; *Andersen Stories* . . . (illustrated by C. Mowry), 1956; *Robin Hood Stories* . . . (illustrated by C. Mowry), 1957; (reteller) Daniel Defoe, *Robinson Crusoe* . . . (illustrated by E. De Soto), 1958; (reteller) Jonathan Swift, *Gulliver's Stories* . . . (illustrated by Billy M. Jackson), 1960; (reteller) Sir Walter Scott, *Ivanhoe* . . . (illustrated by George Foster), 1961.

Contributor to periodicals, including *Education, School Review, English Journal, Elementary English, Journal of Higher Education, Elementary School Journal, Educational Outlook, Chicago Schools Journal, Journal of Educational Research, School Review,* and *Reading Teacher.*

WORK IN PROGRESS: New editions to be published by Developmental Learning Materials and Teaching Resources Co.

SIDELIGHTS: Dolch devoted his entire life to education, as a teacher, researcher, and author. After graduating from Washington University with a B.A., he became a teacher of English, leaving that position to become an assistant professor at the University of Wisconsin. There he became interested in the child development point of view in education.

While working on his Ph.D. in elementary education at the University of Illinois, Dolch began writing magazine articles for educational journals. His thesis, *Reading and Word Meanings* was published two years after he received his doctorate in 1925. "Training is most effective when it is directed toward the performance of definite, clearly defined jobs. This is true in reading as well as in other fields. Our training of students in reading will be most effective if we identify *reading jobs* and train directly for their performance." [E. W. Dolch, "Rapid Reading with a Purpose," *The School Review: A Journal of Secondary Education,* University of Chicago Press, October, 1951.[1]]

Teachers at the University of Illinois began bringing Dolch their poor readers. In his efforts to help these remedial readers, he discovered how a few common words opened doors for reading to them. After seven years of research he developed 'The Dolch 220 Basic Sight Service Words.' Besides research in vocabulary, Dolch devised methods for teaching remedial reading. "The schools of our country are dedicated to the education of all the children of all the people. This is an ideal toward which we progress year by year. Teachers, administrators, school board members and citizens have this ideal before them and are trying to realize it. We have worked hard to overcome the barrier of ignorance on the part of many citizens as to the need for education. We have worked hard to overcome the barrier of lack of money in the home and in the school fund. We have worked to overcome the difficulty of the scattering of children in rural neighborhoods. Now we are working to overcome the barrier of handicap, whether physical, mental, or emotional." [E. W. Dolch, "Preface," *Helping Handicapped Children in School,* Garrard, 1948.[2]]

During his later years Dolch was Professor Emeritus of Education at the University of Illinois and was widely recognized for his research in education, his writing, his teaching, and his knowledge of how children learn to read. The books that he wrote and the games that he designed with his wife for the teaching of reading were the results of their actual teaching experiences and research. For many years Dolch worked with educators and parents showing them how children learn and what effective methods and materials can be used to stimulate an interest in reading and arithmetic in students.

"The school's efforts, even when exerted with the utmost earnestness and wisdom, may still be thwarted by the pupil's attitude or his lack of capability. Suppose, as is often the case, that a boy [or girl] is attending school on compulsion, feeling all the while an antagonism to anything the school presents to him. The school can force such a [child] to come into contact with the various fields of endeavor that it presents, but it cannot force upon him any educative relationship to them. It can compel him to 'know of' various facts about nature, mankind, or man's activities; it cannot force him to make the effort that alone brings understanding, reaction, and pleasure. Thus a pupil may quite thwart the school's endeavor to lend a hand in his education; as a matter of fact, a large percentage of pupils do so thwart it to a greater or less[er] degree." [Edward W. Dolch, Jr., "Defining Education for the Layman," *Educational Review,* June, 1923.[3]]

After his retirement, Dolch lived with his wife, who was also his co-author and co-creator of his books and educational games, in California until his death in 1961.

FOR MORE INFORMATION SEE: Educational Review, June, 1923; *School Review,* October, 1951; *Elementary English,* February, 1958.

DOLCH, Marguerite Pierce 1891-1978

PERSONAL: Born December 16, 1891, in St. Louis, Mo.; died March, 1978, in Santa Barbara, Calif; daughter of Parker Hall (a newspaper publisher) and Eleanor (an elementary school teacher; maiden name, Whittaker) Pierce; married Edward William Dolch (an educator, author and lecturer), 1915 (died, 1961); children: Eleanor Dolch LaRoy, Marguerite, Catherine Dolch McAndrew, Edward William, Jr., John Parker. *Education:* University of Illinois, A.B., M.A.; also attended Washington University, St. Louis, Mo. *Residence:* Santa Barbara, Calif.

CAREER: Author of reading for children and lecturer on education.

WRITINGS—"Basic Vocabulary" series; all with husband, Edward W. Dolch, except where indicated; all for children; all published by Garrard: *Animal Stories in Basic Vocabulary* (illustrated by daughter, Marguerite Dolch), 1952; "*Why*" *Stories* . . . (illustrated by M. Dolch), 1952; *Folk Stories* . . . (illustrated by M. Dolch), 1952; *Dog Stories* . . . (illustrated by Bernette Johnson and Robert S. Kerr), 1954; *Wigwam Stories* . . . (illustrated by R. S. Kerr), 1956; *Tepee Stories* . . . (illustrated by R. S. Kerr), 1956; *Pueblo Stories* . . . (illustrated by R. S. Kerr), 1956; *Elephant Stories* . . . (illustrated by Dee Wallace), 1956; *Circus Stories* . . . (illustrated by D.

MARGUERITE PIERCE DOLCH

Wallace), 1956; *Navaho Stories . . .* (illustrated by Billy M. Jackson), 1957; *Lodge Stories . . .* (illustrated by B. M. Jackson), 1957; *Lion and Tiger Stories . . .* (illustrated by Charles Forsythe), 1957; *Bear Stories . . .* (illustrated by C. Forsythe), 1957; *Horse Stories . . .* (illustrated by C. Forsythe), 1958; *Irish Stories . . .* (illustrated by Carmen Mowry), 1958; *More Dog Stories . . .* (illustrated by E. Harper Johnson), 1962; (sole author) *True Cat Stories* (illustrated by M. Dolch), 1975.

"First Reading Book" series; all with E. W. Dolch, except where indicated: all for children; all published by Garrard: *On the Farm* (illustrated by Don Robertson and Midge Robertson), 1958; *In the Woods* (illustrated by Robert P. Borja), 1958; *Zoo Is Home* (illustrated by R. P. Borja), 1958; *Tommy's Pets* (illustrated by D. Wallace), 1958; *Monkey Friends* (illustrated by C. Forsythe), 1958; *Friendly Birds* (illustrated by Carol Rogers), 1959; *I Like Cats* (illustrated by Pauline Adams), 1959; *Dog Pals* (illustrated by Fran Matera), 1959; *Big, Bigger, Biggest* (illustrated by F. Matera), 1959; *Some Are Small* (illustrated by Larry Kettelkamp), 1959; *Once There Was an Elephant* (illustrated by William Moyers), 1961; *Once There Was a Rabbit* (illustrated by Robert Patterson), 1961; *Once There Was a Cat* (illustrated by Carl Hauge and Mary Hauge), 1961; *Once There Was a Dog* (illustrated by Tom O'Sullivan), 1962; *Once There Was a Monkey* (illustrated by Kenyon Shannon), 1962; *Once There Was a Bear* (illustrated by Gerald McCann), 1962; (sole author) *Once There Was a Coyote* (illustrated by C. Hague and M. Hague), 1975.

"Folklore of the World" series; all with E. W. Dolch, except where indicated; all for children; all published by Garrard:

Stories from Japan (illustrated by Lucy Hawkinson and John Hawkinson), 1960; *. . . Mexico* (illustrated by Ernest De Soto), 1960; *. . . Hawaii* (illustrated by Ted Schroeder), 1960; *. . . India* (illustrated by Gordon Laite), 1961; *. . . Alaska* (illustrated by Carl Heldt), 1961; *. . . Spain* (illustrated by Don Bolognese), 1962; *. . . Italy* (illustrated by Colleen Browning), 1962; *. . . France* (illustrated by G. Laite), 1963; *. . . Old Russia* (illustrated by James Lewicki), 1964; *. . . Old Egypt* (illustrated by G. Laite), 1964; *. . . Old China* (illustrated by Seong Moy), 1964; *. . . Canada* (illustrated by Gil Miret), 1964; (sole author) *Animal Stories from Africa* (illustrated by Lee J. Morton), 1975; (sole author) *Stories from Africa* (illustrated by Vincent D. Smith), 1975.

"Pleasure Reading" series; all with E. W. Dolch and Beulah F. Jackson; all for children; all published by Garrard: *Bible Stories for Pleasure Reading* (illustrated by John Slocum and Y. Cuypers-Fransen), 1950; *Fairy Stories . . .* (illustrated by M. Dolch and Y. Cuypers-Fransen), 1950; *Famous Stories . . .* (illustrated by J. Slocum, Y. Cuypers-Fransen and R. S. Kerr), 1951; *Aesop's Stories . . .* (illustrated by M. Dolch), 1951; *Gospel Stories . . .* (illustrated by M. Dolch), 1951; *Old World Stories . . .* (illustrated by M. Dolch), 1952; *Far East Stories . . .* (illustrated by M. Dolch), 1953; *Greek Stories . . .* (illustrated by M. Dolch and R. S. Kerr), 1955; *Andersen Stories . . .* (illustrated by C. Mowry), 1956; *Robin Hood Stories . . .* (illustrated by C. Mowry), 1957; (reteller) Daniel Defoe, *Robinson Crusoe . . .* (illustrated by E. De Soto), 1958; (reteller) Jonathan Swift, *Gulliver's Stories . . .* (illustrated by

But Tiger, the big striped cat, thought Grandmother's chair was his chair. ■ (From *True Cat Stories* by Marguerite P. Dolch. Illustrated by the author.)

Billy M. Jackson), 1960; (reteller) Sir Walter Scott, *Ivan-hoe* . . . (illustrated by George Foster), 1961.

WORK IN PROGRESS: New editions to be published by Developmental Learning Materials and Teaching Resources Co.

SIDELIGHTS: Dolch, author and lecturer, worked closely with her husband, Edward, on their books for children and teachers. Her daughter, Eleanor Dolch LaRoy, commented about her mother's work as a lecturer. "My mother's sense of drama and storytelling could capture an audience of teachers or children. She often shared the platform with my father demonstrating his materials and principles.

"She would sometimes ask teachers to bring to the platform one of their difficult remedial reading cases and right there in front of everyone she would start teaching that child. First she would find a topic, any topic, in which the child was truly interested and briefly talk with him about it. As might be expected, the topic very often was animal pets. Hence, many of the Dolch books are true animal stories.

"One day on the platform in front of a large audience of teachers in a big school auditorium there sat a little boy silently, sullenly facing my mother. The topic of animals did not bring a response; baseball did not bring a response. Then my mother noticed that the child was staring fascinatedly at her front teeth. Her dentures were loose! 'You're teeth are wiggling,' said the little boy. Right then and there my mother and the little boy had a fascinating discussion and demonstration about false teeth. Immediately following they played enthusiastically some word card game, and finally together read a page in a book. As my mother handed the child the book for him to keep, and he proudly walked off the stage, there was a loud applause from the audience of teachers.

"Her formula was simple: get the child's attention; hold his attention; have fun; and have successful reading—no matter what. No matter who the child is, what his level is, or where you may be working.

"Not all of remedial reading cases presented were small children. Some were very large and grown up children. For a long time there was a prized possession displayed in our home. It was a stuffed raccoon, a gift to my parents from a teenage boy who had successfully read his first book, the Dolch 'First Reading Book' *In the Woods*. I remember my parents' surprise at the ceremonial presentation of this gift at one of their lectures."

The Dolch Reading Program combined common sense, practical principles evolved from their research and study. Their daughter explained how her parents wrote their books. [They] . . . wrote in a scientifically determined easy basic vocabulary. However they chose two particular subjects of interest to everyone regardless of age, namely, true animal stories and authentic folk stories. There are eighteen books of true animal stories and thirty books of folk tales. In addition, there are thirteen classics that have been retold, including Bible stories. Dr. and Mrs. Dolch felt everyone should be able to read the classics of literature as part of his heritage. Of the folklore, four of the books are American Indian folk stories from different parts of the United States.

"Dr. and Mrs. Dolch did all this work together as a team. Together, for years, as they lectured about reading, they traveled over the United States and to each country from which the folk stories came, with the exception of China and Russia. They wanted the stories that they used to be as authentic as possible to reflect the different countries and also have the form which had held interest of all ages for so many generations of people.

"Dr. Dolch researched the word lists which they used and painstakingly controlled the vocabulary in each book. Mrs. Dolch was the story-teller writer. She found a basic vocabulary was very appropriate for stories that had been a part of a people's oral traditions, that had been retold again and again for generations to entertain adults and children alike.

"The true animal stories were gathered from newspaper items, magazines, and personal accounts. All were reported as true in the adult press and media. Retelling them in a basic vocabulary takes nothing from their wonder and interest to people of every age.

"The basic vocabularies used were the famous 'Dolch 220 Basic Service Words,' the 'Dolch 95 commonest nouns,' the 'Dolch 684 Story-tellers' Vocabulary,' and the 'Dolch First One-Thousand Words' learned by children. All of the total sixty-one Dolch children's books, (true animal stories, folklore, and classics) are amazingly written within the basic vocabulary. Professor Dolch believed that a life-long reading habit was based on the thrill of reading many interesting books easily and pleasurably."

DREVES, Veronica R. 1927-1986

OBITUARY NOTICE: Born October 29, 1927, in Sioux City, Iowa; died after a long illness, September 30, 1986, in Bellevue, Wash. Consultant and author. Dreves was a child development specialist for the National Conference of Catholic Bishops, U.S. Catholic Conference, White House Conference on Families, and the Catholic Archdiocese of Seattle. She also founded and directed Beginning Families, a non-profit agency which counsels parents of young children, and directed the Center for Young Children. She wrote *Discover Me, The Joy in Me, Celebrate,* and the "Wonder of God" series of books and music for young children. In 1970 Dreves was awarded a distinguished service award from Briar Cliff College.

FOR MORE INFORMATION SEE: American Catholic Who's Who 1980-1981, Volume 23, National Catholic News Service, 1979. Obituaries: *Seattle Times,* October 2, 1986; *Sioux City Journal,* October 6, 1986.

EDELMAN, Elaine

BRIEF ENTRY: Born in Minneapolis, Minn. Edelman graduated from Sarah Lawrence College in New York, and has worked as a television producer, free-lance filmmaker, publishing company editor, and free-lance writer, poet, and instructor. Her first children's book, *Boom-de-Boom* (Pantheon, 1980, illustrated by Karen Gundersheimer, was called "a rare pleasure" by *Publishers Weekly.* It is the story of Gertrude, the fat lady, who leads a line dance through the busy town and back to her house, where: "They're dancing still, in Gertrude's room, all the people who boom-de-boom, 1-2-3, 1-2-3." *I Love My Baby Sister (Most of the Time)* (Lothrop, 1984), illustrated by Wendy Watson, is told through the eyes of a three-year-old who cannot wait for her infant sister to grow up so they can be friends. "A positive, knowing evocation of early childhood," reported *Booklist.*

Edelman has also co-written a book of poetry for adults; a play titled "Mother of Pearl," which was first produced at Company Theatre of Los Angeles in June, 1972; television documentaries for WNBC-TV and WNET-TV, both in New York City; and the series "Profile of Communism" (Anti-Defamation League of B'nai B'rith), sound filmstrips which won awards at the 1963 and 1965 American Film Festivals. She also contributes articles and poems to magazines and newspapers, including *Esquire, McCall's, Vanity Fair,* and *New York Times Book Review,* and is represented in anthologies, including *Young North American Poets* (Spring Rain Press, 1974). Edelman is the recipient of the 1970 Harcourt, Brace, Jovanovich Poetry Fellowship, University of Colorado Writers' Conference, and a grant from the Dramatists Guild in 1973. She is a member of New Dramatists, Writers Guild, and PEN America. *Agent:* Gloria Loomis, Watkins-Loomis, 150 E. 35th St., New York, N.Y. 10016.

FOR MORE INFORMATION SEE: International Who's Who in Poetry, International Biographical Center, 1982; *Contemporary Authors,* Volume 113, Gale, 1985; *Directory of American Poets and Fiction Writers,* Poets and Writers, Inc., 1985; *International Authors and Writers Who's Who,* 10th edition International Biographical Centre, 1986.

EICHENBERG, Fritz 1901-

PERSONAL: Born October 24, 1901, in Cologne, Germany; came to United States in 1933, naturalized in 1940; son of Siegfried (a merchant) and Ida (a merchant; maiden name, Marcus) Eichenberg; married Mary Altmann, 1926 (died, 1937); married Margaret Ladenburg, 1941 (divorced, 1965); married Antonie Ida Schulze-Forster (a graphic designer), January 7, 1975; children: (first marriage) Suzanne Eichenberg Jensen; (second marriage) Timothy. *Education:* Attended School of Applied Arts, Cologne, 1916-20; State Academy of Graphic Arts, Leipzig, M.F.A., 1923. *Religion:* Society of Friends

FRITZ EICHENBERG

(Quakers). *Home and studio:* 142 Oakwood Dr., Peace Dale, R.I. 02883.

CAREER: Graphic artist and illustrator of classics and other books. Started as newspaper artist in Germany, 1923, and worked as artist and traveling correspondent for Ullstein Publications, Berlin, before settling in United States; WPA Art Project, New York, N.Y., 1935-40; New School for Social Research, New York, N.Y., member of art faculty, 1935-45; Pratt Institute, Brooklyn, N.Y., professor of art, 1947-72, chairman of department of graphic arts, 1956-63, founder-director of Graphic Arts Center, 1956-72; University of Rhode Island, Kingston, professor of art, 1966-71, chairman of department, 1966-69; Albertus Magnus College, New Haven, Conn., professor of art, 1972-73.

EXHIBITIONS: One-man shows, including New School for Social Research, 1939, 1949; Associated American Artists Gallery, 1967, 1977, 1987; Pratt Manhattan Center Gallery, 1972; Klingspor Museum (retrospective), Offenbach, Germany, 1974; International Exhibition Foundation, 1979-81. Work has been shown in Xylon international exhibitions in Switzerland, Yugoslavia, and other countries, in U.S. Information Agency traveling exhibits, and in Society of American Graphic Artists shows. Work represented in collections, including Pushkin Museum, Boston Public Library, National Gallery of Art, Hermitage Museum (Leningrad), National Museum (Stockholm), Vatican Museum (Rome), Bibliotheque Nationale (Paris), Metropolitan Museum of Art, Philadelphia Museum of Art. Member of Pennell Committee, Library of Congress, 1959-65, and Yale University Library, 1979. *Member:* National Academy of Design, Royal Society of Arts (London; fellow), Society of American Graphic Artists.

AWARDS, HONORS: Puss in Boots was included in the American Institute of Graphic Arts' Fifty Books of the Year, 1937; illustrator of Newbery honor book, *Have You Seen Tom Thumb?,* 1943; *New York Herald Tribune*'s Spring Book Festival Award, 1942, for *Mischief in Fez;* Joseph Pennell Medal from Pennsylvania Academy of Fine Arts, 1944, for a wood engraving; first prize from National Academy of Design, 1946, for print; Caldecott honor book from the American Library Association, 1953, for *Ape in a Cape: An Alphabet of Odd Animals;* Silver Medal from Limited Editions Club, 1954; Lewis Carroll Shelf Award, 1962, for *Padre Porko: The Gentlemanly Pig* and 1968, for *No Room: An Old Story Retold;* grant from John D. Rockefeller III Fund, 1968; D.F.A. from Southeastern Massachusetts University, 1972, University of Rhode Island, 1974, Pratt Institute, 1976, California College of Arts and Crafts, 1978, Marymount College, 1984, and Stonehill College, 1985; named one of the "Outstanding Educators of America," 1973; S.F.B. Morse Medal from National Academy of Design, 1973, for a wood engraving; National Book Award nomination, 1980, for *Endangered Species, and Other Fables with a Twist;* Rhode Island Governor's Award for the Arts, 1981, for contributions to the world of art; *Rainbows Are Made: Poems by Carl Sandburg* was selected one of *New York Times* Best Illustrated Children's Books, 1982.

WRITINGS: Ape in a Cape: An Alphabet of Odd Animals (juvenile; self-illustrated), Harcourt, 1952; *Art and Faith* (booklet; self-illustrated), Pendle Hill, 1952; *Dancing in the Moon: Counting Rhymes* (juvenile; self-illustrated; ALA Notable Book), Harcourt, 1955, reissued, 1975; (translator with William Hubben) Helmut A. P. Grieshaber, *H.A.P. Grieshaber,* Arts, 1965; (author of text) Naoko Matsubara, *Nantucket Woodcuts,* Barre Publishers, 1967; (contributor) *Education in the Graphic Arts,* Boston Public Library, 1969.

How glad I was to behold a prospect of getting something to eat! I was now nearly sick.... ■
(From *Jane Eyre* by Charlotte Brontë. Illustrated by Fritz Eichenberg.)

(Editor) *Artist's Proof: A Collector's Edition of the First Eight Issues of the Distinguished Journal of Print and Printmaking,* New York Graphic Society, 1971; (translator and illustrator) Desiderius Erasmus, *In Praise of Folly,* Aquarius, 1972; *The Print: Art, Masterpiece, History, Techniques,* Abrams, 1975; *Yours in Peace, Prints with a Message,* Fellowship of Reconciliation, 1977; *The Wood and the Graver: The Work of Fritz Eichenberg,* C.N. Potter, 1977; *Endangered Species, and Other Fables with a Twist* (self-illustrated), Stemmer House, 1979; *The Artist and the Book,* Yale University Library, 1979; *Dance of Death* (self-illustrated), Abbeville Press, 1983; (reteller) *Poor Troll: The Story of Ruebezahl and the Princess* (self-illustrated), Stemmer House, 1983; *Bell, Book and Candle* (self-illustrated), American Library Association, 1984; *Artist on the Witness Stand* (self-illustrated), Pendle Hill, 1984.

Illustrator: *Puss in Boots,* Holiday House, 1936; Joel Chandler Harris, *Uncle Remus Stories,* limited edition, Peter Pauper Press, 1937; Moritz A. Jagendorf, *Till Eulenspiegel's Merry Pranks,* Vanguard, 1938; Therese Lenotre, *Mystery of Dog Flip,* translation from the French by Simone Chamoud, Stokes, 1939; Robert Davis, *Padre: The Gentlemanly Pig,* Holiday House, 1939, enlarged edition, published as *Padre Porko: The Gentlemanly Pig,* 1948; Rosalys Hall, *Animals to Africa,* Holiday House, 1939.

Stewart Schackne, *Rowena, the Skating Cow,* Scribner, 1940; Eula Griffin Duncan, *Big Road Walker,* Stokes, 1940; Babette

Deutsch, *Heroes of the Kalevala: Finland's Saga* (ALA Notable Book), Messner, 1940; Jonathan Swift, *Gulliver's Travels,* Heritage Press, 1940, junior text edition, 1947, new edition, 1961; Richard A. W. Hughes, *Don't Blame Me* (short stories), Harper, 1940; William Shakespeare, *Tragedy of Richard the Third,* Limited Editions, 1940; Henry Beston, *The Tree That Ran Away,* Macmillan, 1941; Marjorie Fischer, *All on a Summer's Day,* Random House, 1941; Irmengarde Eberle, *Phoebe-Bell,* Greystone Press, 1941; Ivan S. Turgenev, *Fathers and Sons,* translation from the Russian by Constance Garnett, Heritage Press, 1941; Mabel Leigh Hunt, *Have You Seen Tom Thumb?* (ALA Notable Book), Stokes, 1942; Charlotte Brontë, *Jane Eyre* [and] Emily Brontë, *Wuthering Heights* (companion volumes), Random House, 1943; Henrik Ibsen, *Story of Peer Gynt,* retold by E. V. Sandys, Crowell, 1943; I. Eberle, *Wide Fields: The Story of Henry Fabre,* Crowell, 1943; Eleanor Hoffmann, *Mischief in Fez,* Holiday House, 1943; Leo N. Tolstoi, *Anna Karenina,* translation from Russian by C. Garnett, two volumes, Doubleday, 1944, two volumes in one, 1946, deluxe edition, Garden City Publishing, 1948; Edgar Allan Poe, *Tales,* Random House, 1944; Mark Yeats, *Sancho and His Stubborn Mule,* W. R. Scott, 1944; Rose Dobbs, *No Room: An Old Story Retold,* Coward, 1944; Feodor M. Dostoevski, *Crime and Punishment,* translation from the Russian by C. Garnett, Heritage Press, 1944.

Stephen Vincent Benét, *The Devil and Daniel Webster,* Kingsport, 1945; F. M. Dostoevski, *The Grand Inquisitor,* Haddam House, 1945; Glanville W. Smith, *Adventures of Sir Ignatius Tippitolio,* Harper, 1945; Anna Sewell, *Black Beauty,* Gros-

(From *Crime and Punishment* by Feodor Dostoevski. Wood engraving, "Before the Murder," by Fritz Eichenberg.)

Eichenberg posing for "Before the Murder."

(From *A Child's Christmas in Wales* by Dylan Thomas. Illustrated by Fritz Eichenberg.)

set, 1945; Terence H. White, *Mistress Masham's Repose,* Putnam, 1946; E. Brontë, *Wuthering Heights,* Random House, 1946; Maurice Dolbier, *The Magic Shop,* Random House, 1946; Felix Salten, compiler, *Favorite Animal Stories,* Messner, 1948; F. M. Dostoevski, *The Brothers Karamazov,* translation from the Russian by C. Garnett, revised with introduction by Avrahm Yarmolinsky, Limited Ediitons, 1949; Ruth Stiles Gannett, *Wonderful House-Boat-Train,* Random House, 1949.

Rudyard Kipling, *The Jungle Book,* Grosset, 1950; Mark van Doren, *The Witch of Ramoth,* Maple Press, 1950; Wilkie Collins, *Short Stories,* Rodale Books, 1950; (with Vassily Verestchagin) L. N. Tolstoi, *War and Peace,* translation from the Russian by Louie Maude and Aylmer Maude, two volumes in one, Heritage Press, 1951; Margaret Cousins, *Ben Franklin of Old Philadelphia,* Random House, 1952; Dorothy Day, *Long Loneliness* (autobiography), Harper, 1952; Nathaniel Hawthorne, *Tale of King Midas and the Golden Touch,* Limited Editions, 1952; Johann Wolfgang von Goethe, *Story of Reynard the Fox,* translation by Thomas J. Arnold from the original German poem, Heritage Press, 1954; F. M. Dostoevski, *The Idiot,* translation from the Russian by C. Garnett, revised with introduction by A. Yarmolinsky, Heritage Press, 1956; Elizabeth J. Coatsworth, *The Peaceable Kingdom and Other Poems,* Pantheon, 1958; Edna Johnson and others, compilers, *Anthology of Children's Literature,* 3rd edition (Eichenberg did not illustrate earlier editions), Houghton, 1959, 4th edition, 1970.

F. M. Dostoevski, *The Possessed,* translation from the Russian by C. Garnett, Heritage Press, 1960; L. N. Tolstoi, *Resurrection,* translation by Leo Wiener, revised and edited by F. D. Reeve, Heritage Press, 1963; Jean Charlot, *Posada's Dance of Death,* Graphic Arts Center, Pratt Institute, 1965; Etienne Decroux, *Mime: The Art of Etienne Decroux,* Pratt Adlib Press, 1965; Dylan Thomas, *A Child's Christmas in Wales,* limited edition, New Directions, 1969.

L. N. Tolstoi, *Childhood, Boyhood, Youth,* translation by L. Wiener, Press of A. Colish, 1972; John M. Langstaff, adapter, *The Two Magicians,* Atheneum, 1973; F. M. Dostoevski, *A. Raw Youth,* translation by C. Garnett, Limited Editions, 1974; Avon Neal, *Pigs and Eagles,* Thistle Hill Press, 1979; E. A. Poe, *Eleanora,* Penmaen Press, 1979.

Johann Jakob Christoffel von Grimmelshausen, *The Adventurous Simplicissimus,* translated by John P. Spielman, Limited Editions, 1981; Allen Hoffman, *Kagan's Superfecta and Other Stories,* Abbeville Press, 1981; Lee Bennett Hopkins, editor, *Rainbows Are Made: Poems by Carl Sandburg* (ALA Notable Book), Harcourt, 1982; F. M. Dostoevski, *The House of the Dead,* translated by C. Garnett, Limited Editions, 1982; D. Thomas, *Rebecca's Daughters,* New Directions, 1982; Georges Bernanos, *Diary of a Country Priest,* Limited Editions, 1986.

Contributor of articles to periodicals, including *American Artist, Artist's Proof, Friends Journal, Publishers Weekly, Horn*

Book, and *Print.* Founder and chief editor, *Artist's Proof: An Annual of Prints and Printmaking,* Pratt Institute, 1960-72.

WORK IN PROGRESS: Beachcomber's Bestiary; Aritst's Logbook, an autobiography.

SIDELIGHTS: "I was born in Cologne, Germany in **1901,** the year Queen Victoria died. The strongest memory of my childhood is the day when my father took me through the streets of Cologne, window-shopping for a pet mouse. I was four years old, and could not have known it was the last time I would see my father walking. From then on he was bedridden with Parkinson's disease until his death ten years later.

"My mother, a wonderul woman, loved classical music intensely; it was her source of strength. She took care of the small business and raised three children.

"For eleven years I suffered through the Gymnasium—the program was brutal in demanding unconditional obedience. There was no poetic intermingling and art was out of the question. Beatings were frequent. Looking back, attempting to analyze the effect those years had, I realize that what I became was in some way based on the brutal treatment I received in school. The only teacher I adored taught German literature, a decent man who never hit anyone and took an interest in my work. He predicted that one day I would become a good writer.

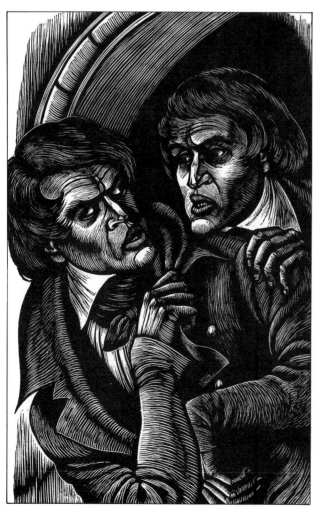

(From "William Wilson" in *Tales of Edgar Allan Poe.* Wood engraving by Fritz Eichenberg.)

I took refuge in literature because I had the urge to know what life—apart from my horrible environment—was all about. In a militaristic atmosphere you either succumb to it or become a rebel. I became a rebel.

"Anti-semitism was nonexistent in those days. My parents did not attend synagogue and I was raised in a nonreligious atmosphere. We really did not think of ourselves as Jews or as German-Jews; we were *Germans.*

"I lived through the First World War with all the trimmings. The bombing of Cologne was on a minor scale, but it was a bombing and we spent nights in the cellar together with the rest of the people of our little neighborhood.

"During this time I wrote a school essay on *The Dance of Death* (which I would later illustrate). Why that particular subject caught my attention, I owe to the times—it was the war years, bombs were falling, trains arrived with prisoners of war. We all thought a lot about death in those days. My grandfather, who owned an internationally-famous matzoh bakery, was given the 'privilege' of picking prisoners of war to work for him for no pay. I remember, in particular, a German-speaking Russian Jewish soldier who befriended me one summer. I was a tiny shrimp of a lad, and we struck up a wonderful relationship. I remember his uniform of a great blouse and a hat with an emblem on it. I saw in him, not a prisoner of war, not a soldier, but a *human being.* This experience and the deep feelings it aroused in me were probably the beginnings of my pacifism.

"The war ended in 1918. Everything was in smithereens. Soldiers came back wearing the red arm bands of the Socialists. And so the new era began. And I would eventually play a political part in it, lampooning Hitler in my newspaper cartoons.

"After my painful experience as a student in the Gymnasium, I drew a breath of fresh air and began attending evening life drawing classes at the ancient School of Applied Arts. In my spare time, I sketched animals in the zoo.

"It was suggested to me that I learn a graphic art medium in order to earn a living. I served a tough apprenticeship in lithography at the DuMont Schauberg printing plant in Cologne, spending most of my time rubbing litho ink. My first assignments were drawing wine labels on stone and designing ads and posters for Tietz, a large department store in Cologne.

"In 1919, I took a job in the art department at Tietz. I was eighteen years old, and in the beginning spent my salary in night clubs drinking with a friend. With that out of my system, I spent my money on books.

"I made the acquaintance of a man who ran a small bookstore in Cologne. He would leave me alone to browse for hours. There, among other wonders, I discovered J. C. Grimmelshausen's *The Adventurous Simplicissimus,* which many years later, I would illustrate. The most important find was Frans Masereel's *Book of Hours.* A Belgian pacifist in exile in France, he was the first artist to create a book from a collection of woodcuts without words. He was obsessed with the challenge of expressing his ideas without the benefit of text. For him, illustration had to stand on its own merit. His *Ein Bilderoman,* comprised of 60 woodcuts, also deeply influenced me. I still see Masereel as one of my guiding lights.

"Eventually I became the staff artist at Tietz. After a year and a half on the job, I decided that what I needed most was to perfect my skills as a graphic artist. I proposed this to the

(From *The Idiot* by Feodor Dostoevski. Wood engraving, "Nastasya, the Bride," by Fritz Eichenberg.)

director of the department store and asked whether he would send me to the State Academy of Graphic Arts in Leipzig. To my astonishment he agreed, and I went off to study for two years. As a master student under Hugo Steiner-Prag I was allowed to pursue whatever project I wanted. It was there that I first became acquainted with boxwood and gravers. I also illustrated my first book, *Till Eulenspiegel's Merry Pranks,* as well as Jonathan Swift's *Gulliver's Travels* and Dostoevsky's *Crime and Punishment,* all of which were published while I was still a student. This was a great boost to my ego, which was always a little shaky.

"I had made my first lithographs as an apprentice, and executed my first wood engravings, teaching myself the technique. I fell in love with wood, a medium that suited me. Though I have sometimes tried to go back to lithography, it has never been more than an interlude and I have always come back to wood engraving."

1926. Married Mary Altmann. "Mary was a wonderful woman whom I met at the Academy in Leipzig. After our daughter was born, Mary went back to Berlin and I followed her. In Berlin I landed in the lap of a big empire: Ullstein Publications, a publications factory which produced everything from kiddy stuff to newspapers, magazines and books of every sort. I was a staff artist and traveling correspondent for many of the publications. I wrote articles and illustrated them, made posters and cartoons for Ullstein and other German publishers. These were exhilerating years when theatre, films, dance and literature were flourishing, until suddenly a man named Hitler, whom I had lampooned in my cartoons, became Reichs Chancellor.

"The ten years spent in Berlin were fun. My name was known, there were invitations to every big occasion, but it was not

(From *Padre Porko: The Gentlemanly Pig* by Robert Davis. Illustrated by Fritz Eichenberg.)

enough. I had great enthusiasm for the revolution in Germany. The Weimar Republic (1919-1933) gave me some hope for my country's future. I met many of the people involved in the new government both socially and on my assignments. They were honorable but so outnumbered they could not reverse the direction in which Germany was headed. It was tremendously disappointing to see the slow but widening disillusionment, to see people hand over the reins to Hitler. That experience put an end to my affection for anything I would call 'German.'

"By 1932, before Hitler was politically a menace, I was finished with Germany. I wanted to get out because I could 'smell' bad times ahead. I felt that Berlin was soon to become a death trap. I wanted to explore the free world, to find a place for myself, my wife and my child. I began my quest by heading to Mexico as a correspondent for the Ullstein Publications. I had dreamed for years of seeing the murals of Diego Rivera, of seeing artists working in a revolutionary setting. I started in Venezuela, then went on to Colombia and Guatemala, from Guatemala to Mexico, and from Mexico to El Paso, Texas. Then I covered the 1933-34 World's Fair in Chicago. Traveling I had made many friends in a very short time. Many of them begged me to stay, telling me it wasn't necessary to return, that I could send for my wife and child. But I wanted to bring them back to the United States myself."

On his way back to Germany, Eichenberg passed through New York. "From the moment I set eyes on New York City, I fell in love with its soaring skyline and teeming millions. I knew we could make a new beginning there. So despite the warnings of my new American friends, I went back to Berlin. Although my wife assured me that she would follow wherever I had decided to go, she made it clear that she felt I was making a mistake to leave Berlin. This was 1933, everyone felt I was overreacting. I still had my passport stamped 'Correspondent.' I felt it was now or never.

"As a correspondent, I had travelled abroad on a luxury steamer, first class, all expenses paid. However, when I returned to America with my family it was on a small line via Ellis Island, like any other immigrant.

"America filled my bill emotionally, and much later on, financially as well. I didn't know a thing about the Depression when we landed in New York. Money didn't interest me—I only needed enough to cover my expenses. But I discovered that as an artist, there wasn't much hope for employment during the Depression years."

Settled in New York City where he found J. Johnson Co., a purveyor of engraver's boxwood on Fulton Street which supplied him for many years. During this period Eichenberg made prints of city scenes both realistic and allegorical. Many were done under the famous Federal Artist's project of the Depression-born Works Progress Administration (WPA). "Here, in America, I finally felt freedom. Here you could die in peace, or as luck would have it, be picked up by a marvelous organization called the WPA."

"The Federal Arts Project [provided] work for the artist at a salary of $22.75 per week—democracy in action! Good art material [was] provided, including boxwood and tools, the deadlines were generous, and [there was] no censorship of any kind. My fellow artists—well-known names among them—were congenial, and a spirit of camaraderie prevailed. The theme chosen by the artists [reflected] the difficult problems of the day; [there was little abstract work] and plenty of social and political commentary. Strong influences from south of the border—from the prophets of the Mexican revolution, Orozco, Rivera and Siqueiros—[were] in evidence." [Fritz Eichenberg, *The Wood and the Graver,* Clarkson N. Potter, 1977.[1]]

(From *Wuthering Heights* by Emily Brontë. Illustrated by Fritz Eichenberg.)

9 bears saying their prayers

(From *Dancing in the Moon: Counting Rhymes* by Fritz Eichenberg. Illustrated by the author.)

Yak with a pack

(From *Ape in a Cape: An Alphabet of Odd Animals* by Fritz Eichenberg. Illustrated by the author.)

"Someone suggested that I see Alvin Johnson at The New School for Social Research in New York City. Johnson had recently created a program he called University in Exile, employing intellectuals and academics who had been thrown out of Italy, Germany and other European countries. Some emigrés could hardly speak English, but it didn't matter; he gave them a means to survive. I taught one or two evenings at the New School, then Johnson suggested I speak to Frida Kirchway, editor of *The Nation,* a gutsy and venerable magazine. She hired me to draw cartoons. So between The New School, *The Nation* and WPA, I earned about $60.00 a week, enough to take care of my family.

"My mother, two sisters and their families were still living in Cologne but I managed to get them out just before *Kristallnacht,* and then the great pogrom which swept Germany and Poland at the end of 1938. I didn't have much money, but my many friends in America provided the affidavits of support required by the Department of Immigration. I don't know what I would have done had my family landed in Auschwitz. I would have gone berserk. I admire people who came out and continued to live after such atrocities.

"At first, my entire extended family lived with us at our small house in Westchester, New York—my mother until she died at the age of eighty-six.

"In 1936, I broke into children's books in the U.S. with *Puss and Boots.* I became fast friends with Helen Gentry who did the book design. Both the woodblock prints and type were hand-set, and the book was chosen as one of the Fifty Books of the Year by the American Institute of Graphic Arts—a small fanfare, but one that would open the door to bigger and better things."

1936. Commissioned by George Macy, editor of Heritage Press and The Limited Editions Club to illustrate Feodor Dostoevsky's masterpiece, *Crime and Punishment.* "I had illustrated *Crime and Punishment* as a student, but I didn't tell Macy that! The earlier illustrations, which I'd executed at the age of twenty, were rather immature.

"The trials of the intervening years [had] given me new insight into Dostoevsky's stricken characters: the feverish Raskolnikov; gentle Sonya; Svidrigailov, the tempter; and the captain's mad wife. Crime, exile, and redemption—what a challenge for an artist at a time when his world seems to be falling apart."[1]

1937. Wife died of cancer. "She died suddenly and the loss demolished me completely. She was only thirty-one years old. She died on the operating table. Neither she nor I were prepared for it. She loved life, she loved me and our daughter. We were just beginning.

Became a Quaker in **1940.** "I lived alone for four years after Mary's death and in 1941 married Margaret Ladenburg with whom I had one son, Timothy."

1947. Became chairman of the Department of Graphic Arts at Pratt Institute, a position he held until 1972.

1948-49. George Macy commissioned Eichenberg to select and illustrate a *magnum opus.* "I chose without hesitation Dostoevsky's *The Brothers Karamazov.*

"For more than a year I [loved, suffered, and sinned] with the doomed Karamazovs, drawn into the whirlpool of their lives, redeemed in the end by the saintliness of Alyosha, the young-

est son. Day after day, month after month, I [traced] and [scratched] and [scraped] the drama of this epic out of the dark surface of a lithostone covered with lithographic touch. One by one, fifty lithographs [emerged], expertly etched and printed in the workshop of George Miller, the wizard of the lithostone who worked with George Bellows, Thomas Benton, Diego Rivera, and other greats of the past."[1]

In conjunction with his work on *The Brothers Karamazov,* Eichenberg illustrated a special wood engraved edition of *The Grand Inquisitor* for Haddam House. "An editor friend of mine persuaded me to make a special edition of *The Grand Inquisitor,* that great drama-within-a-drama in *The Brothers Karamazov,* about the second coming of Christ who silently vanquishes his relentless vicar on the earth with a kiss of mercy. I made three very small engravings: 'Portrait of Dostoevsky,' 'The Crown of Thorns,' and 'The Grand Inquisitor,' the scene in which Christ leaves the Grand Inquisitor and begins to walk upstairs, into freedom and, of course, into more trouble. It was an especially intriguing challenge to execute that same great scene on lithostone as well as on a block of boxwood, and compare their graphic impact. The engravings were made before I began the lithographs for the book and in my final estimation are better than the lithographs.

"I am the most severe critic of my work. I am quite satisfied with my illustrations for *The Brothers Karamazov.* It was hard work—I made fifty-three lithographs in all. But the reason I feel proud of these particular illustrations is that I feel Dostoevsky would have approved of my interpretation.

"I have to respect the text I illustrate. I must accept it—body and soul. And this, of course, can limit my vocabulary as an artist. How many great books are there, after all? On the other hand, I have alway wanted to illustrate Lao Tzu's thirty-one sayings. I have tried again and again, and have found that this book is *too great* a thing for me to do. Perhaps it is too Oriental, or too spiritual. Or perhaps it is that such profound poetry is not meant to be illustrated.

"You never know when you begin a book whether or not the illustration will work. In some cases, it has worked beyond my expectations, for example, 'Heathcliff Under the Tree,' in Bronte's *Wuthering Heights.* Wherever I travel, people approach me asking for my signature on that particular print. This has rarely happened with my illustrations of Dostoevsky or Tolstoy. It seems that many people identify with my interpretation of Heathcliff. And yet, when I made the illustration, I had no idea it would be such a powerful and compelling image."

1956. Founded the Graphic Arts Center in New York. "Though many Germans returned to Germany after the war, I had no emotional urge to go back. In 1956, I returned as the Chairman of the Graphic Arts Department of Pratt Institute to see what had gone on in the art world since Hitler. I visited every art school in Europe from Italy to Scandinavia. It was a test for myself; I wanted to see how I'd react. I saw the old Gymnasium which I had hated. It was completely demolished. And that, I must say, was a deep satisfaction."

1957. *Ape in a Cape: An Alphabet of Odd Animals* cited as Caldecott honor book. "After a year of at times depressingly hard struggle with a major classic [*The Brothers Karamazov*], I [tried] to relax and escape into the brighter world of the children's book. The result: two picture books of my own concoction, *Ape in a Cape,* a simple ABC and *Dancing in the Moon,* with funny counting rhymes. They [caught] on, not only with my own children but also with Margaret McElderry,

Even playful Beni was stretched on his back, and the cat hardly moved her legs. ■(From *Poor Troll: The Story of Ruebezahl and the Princess,* retold by Fritz Eichenberg. Illustrated by the author.)

then with Harcourt, Brace, and to my surprise these books are still in print. Certain children's books appeal to young and old alike. Albert Einstein—of all people—liked my ABC, so I dedicated my second, the counting rhymes, to him! I admit, it took some nerve, but then I knew the child in him.''[1]

1958. Illustrated *The Peaceable Kingdom and other Poems* for Pantheon. ''I derived benefit from spending much of my childhood in the company of animals, and began sketching them as a child. Never to be without sketch pad at the zoo or circus proved more profitable to me than years of study at art school. Graver and boxwood seem ideally suited to produce a great variety of textures, from the softness of fur to the sharpness of fang and claw.

''After doing many children's books, I discovered that I do best with very heavy, tragic material—perhaps because my life has not been an easy one. There are things an artist must get off his chest. By doing well in performing an almost impossible chore, the artist finds some relief from the burden he shoulders. But of the many children's books I have illustrated over the years, I am most fond of T. H. White's *Mistress Masham's Repose.*

''This country is not geared toward illustrated books. Parents want illustrated books for their young children, but nobody in America is interested in seeing writers such as Ernest Hemingway or Theodore Dreiser illustrated. However, I still work for the Limited Editions Club, which publishes 1,000 examples of an illustrated book. Out of 220 million people in the States it is difficult to sell out an edition. It goes without saying that the pay is terrible. For some of my most popular books, such as *Jane Eyre* or *Wuthering Heights* (which I worked on for over a year) I made only two thousand dollars, with no royalties. If money entered into it, I wouldn't make art because it is impossible to earn a living. I have been lucky merely to subsist on my earnings as an artist.''

1966-71. Served as professor of art and later chairman of the Art Department at the University of Rhode Island. ''In the eyes of many of my students, art is a job which doesn't pay well. That has never made any difference to me. I advise them to become printmakers in order to generate a wider audience for their work. Many of the illustrations I did were made into prints which landed in countries all around the world. India . . . the Soviet Union . . . I have seen my prints in the hands of the Pope and in the hands of Premier Khrushchev. My work seems to cut across party lines, and this gives me deep satisfaction.''

When he begins a project, Eichenberg reads the text first, ''even if it is a book, such as *Gulliver's Travels,* with which I am very familiar. While I read, I make thumbnail sketches. I select some to show the publisher. Most are expendable, since they don't claim to be art work, but they help give a sense to the designer of what the final illustrations will be. In the second phase, I do more finished drawings, including more details of character and composition. I don't use models, but create characters from my imagination. When I have a finished drawing, I wrap the drawing around the wood block and attach it with adhesive. With a pointed instrument, I trace the black lines of the drawing onto the darkened surface of the wood.

''My approach to the woodblock is not a purely mechanical or technical one, but is intimate, highly personal, emotional, and sensual. The first cut made into the darkened surface of a woodblock with the point of a steel blade or a burin releases hidden forces that one can hardly gauge beforehand. The steel ignites a spark, a source of light spreading slowly over the face of the block as the image emerges, white against black.

This to me constitutes the neverending [stet] excitement—the suspense, the challenge, the surprise, as the graver and the wood take over, guide your eye and hand, create and develop the drama in a wealth of textures, light and shadow.''[1]

''Before you know it, you are trusting the wood, trusting that your tools will go in the right direction. I never slip. I never make mistakes. It is as if some mysterious power is with me, joins me as I work.

''I take great interest in the theatre and in it find a metaphor for wood engraving. One can equate the stage with a rectangular block of wood. The play begins in darkness. Then suddenly, a light comes from somewhere and hits that dark space—illuminating, perhaps, a human face. The light lands on the forehead, and then moves down the actor's body. The body casts a shadow. There is the source of light, there is movement, and there is a sense of *expectation.* The anticipation, the empathy and associations built up in this initial and dramatic stage impression is electrifying. The audience is in suspense—so many questions are raised by that first dash of light.

''What you try to do as an illustrator is to make the action clear, understandable. After the book is published there is no possibility for a child to approach you, illustration in hand, and ask 'What did you mean by this?' as my young son Timothy sometimes did. When he felt he needed explanations it was a warning to me that I had done something wrong. No explaining would make any impression on him. He would simply respond to my justifications saying, 'I still don't *see* it.' So I would check over the illustration, and indeed find that I hadn't been clear enough, or had misinterpreted the text. Children are very severe and accurate critics. If I read Kipling's *Jungle Book* to my children for, say, the tenth time, I deviated at all from the way Kipling *would have meant* me to express his text in an oral rendition (the time I attempted to make sound effects of seagulls screeching, for example), the children would say, 'Don't exaggerate.' It was not my business in their eyes to imitate seagulls. It was not really part of the story, of Kipling's rhythms, and so the children were merely irritated by my effort. I think if we gave the task of book or art reviewing over to children, we would get much closer to the source.

''My children were accustomed to seeing me work from morning till night. Work always came first, which is not particularly ideal for children. I remember working on a book while my son, then only five-years-old, stood by silently watching. I always maintained contact with them through my work. And through my work, they became fond of me.''

1975. Married Antonie Ida Schulze-Forster, a well-known graphic designer from Germany who has designed all of Eichenberg's own books.

Also the author of many books, Eichenberg feels most comfortable with his illustration. ''I'm not sure I can do justice to the word with my writing. Writing is very important to me, and the feeling of deficiency I experience in relation to my own writing is very pronounced. I have so much admiration for great writers that I feel a little self-conscious about it. People say that I write beautifully, but I sincerely doubt it. The crux of the matter lies in the fact that I write in my second language, English. I wasn't born with it, and so the finesse has escaped me. Not to be born with a language and at the same time yearning to express the finest sensitivities is a curse. I can understand why Immanuel Kant ended up in an insane asylum. You come to a point where you want to be more perfect than God. But we are limited in so many ways.

Bagheera would call, "Come along, Little Brother!" ■ (From *The Jungle Book* by Rudyard Kipling. Illustrated by Fritz Eichenberg.)

Then he took a turn up and down stamping his feet. ■ (From *Black Beauty: The Autobiography of a Horse* by Anna Sewell. Illustrated by Fritz Eichenberg.)

"Dream of Reason," a self-portrait of Eichenberg surrounded by several of the authors he has illustrated. (Wood engraving, circa 1975.)

"There are so many different approaches to art. How do you explain Picasso? Or Klee? Or Warhol? Each had a different motivation. Art is a vocation—you can't recommend it to someone and it can't really be taught. You have to jump into the pool and sink or swim. Don't imitate anyone. You must be able to engage your own resources. The challenge is, how deep can you go? And what can you do to improve yourself, to gain experience? We all have different experiences and we either go down under their weight or we grow by them. I warn my students not to have a commercial interest in what they are doing. Art must be an obsession—you must be willing to offer your life, if necessary, to it. This is not always a comfortable position to be in. It should be quite obvious when one reads the life of a Beethoven or Michelangelo or Goya that you don't make art because you want to make money; you do it because you *have to*. Even if no one else cares—*you* care."

—Based on an interview by Rachel Koenig

Eichenberg's works are included in the Kerlan Collection of the University of Minnesota.

HOBBIES AND OTHER INTERESTS: Book collecting over a seventy-year period.

FOR MORE INFORMATION SEE: Howard Simon, *500 Years of Art in Illustration*, Garden City Publishers, 1942; *American Artist*, December, 1944, May, 1964, October, 1975; Bertha E. Mahony and others, compilers, *Illustrators of Children's Books: 1744-1945*, Horn Book, 1947; Richard Williamson, *Book Illustrators*, Kingsport Press, 1952; *Graphis*, Volume XIII, number 43, 1952, May, 1980; *American Artist*, May, 1956, October, 1975; *Publishers Weekly*, February 4, 1957, May 7, 1979; B. M. Miller and others, compilers, *Illustrators of Children's Books: 1946-1956*, Horn Book, 1958; *Horn Book*, February, 1960, December, 1980; Muriel Fuller, editor, *More Junior Authors*, H. W. Wilson, 1963; *Library of Congress Quarterly*, April, 1965; Lee Kingman and others, compilers, *Illustrators of Children's Books: 1957-1966*, Horn Book, 1968.

Edna Johnson and others, editors, *Anthology of Children's Literature*, 4th edition, Houghton, 1970; *Rhode Islander*, August 12, 1973; *Idea* (Tokyo), January, 1974; *Contemporary American Illustrators of Children's Books*, Rutgers University Art Gallery, 1974; Martha E. Ward and Dorothy A. Marquardt, *Illustrators of Books for Young People*, Scarecrow, 1975; *Biography News*, November, 1975; *Print*, September, 1976; Emily Chewning, "Eichenberg's Confessions," *Print*, May, 1976; L. Kingman and others, compilers, *Illustrators of Children's Books: 1967-1976*, Horn Book, 1978; *Illustrator's Notebook*, Horn Book, 1978; *Six Decades of Prints by Fritz Eichenberg*, Catalogue International Exhibitions Foundation, 1979; *Fritz Eichenberg and the Books*, Yale University Library, 1979; Robert Ellsberg, "Fritz Eichenberg: An Undimmed Sense of Wonder," *Friends Journal*, October, 1982; "Fritz Eichenberg Named 1984 Arbuthnot Lecturer," *School Library Journal*, December, 1982; "The Eichenberg Impact," *Commonweal*, September, 1983; Jim Roginski, compiler, *Newbery and Caldecott Medalists and Honor Book Winners*, Libaries Unlimited, 1983; Nancy Roberts, "Fritz Eichenberg, Gentle Witness for Peace," *Christian Century*, November, 1983.

Thanks to my friends for their care in my breeding,
Who taught me betimes to love working and reading.
                                                —Isaac Watts

EISENBERG, Lisa   1949-

BRIEF ENTRY: Born April 19, 1949, in Flushing, N.Y. Eisenberg graduated from Swarthmore College in 1971, and worked as a writer and editor at various publishing companies in New York and California. She began free-lance writing in 1979. "In my writing I combine an interest in children, education, and, most importantly, humor," she said. This is evident from her riddle-and-joke books, written with Katy Hall. Each riddle book is a bundle of one-liners about a particular subject. In *Fishy Riddles* (Dial, 1983), illustrated by Simms Taback, readers are asked what Cinderella Dolphin wore to the ball ("Glass flippers!"), and what a frightened skin diver is called ("Chicken of the Sea!"). *School Library Journal* wrote: "You get the picture, and every fish (or other marine creature) riddle you've ever groaned at is here.... Needless to say, kids will love it." Other titles in the series are *Chicken Jokes and Puzzles* (Scholastic Book Services, 1976), *A Gallery of Monsters* (Random House, 1980), *Pig Jokes* (Scholastic Book Services, 1983), and *Buggy Riddles* (Dial, 1986).

Her young adult reading series, "Laura Brewster" (Pitman, 1978) and "South City Cops" (Fearon, 1984), are fast-action detective stories with male and female heroes. In the first series, insurance investigator Laura Brewster must solve six mysterious deaths. *Falling Star* is about actor Guy Garrison, whose body has disappeared. "Characters are kept to a minimum, and there's just the right amount of action and tension to keep readers involved," observed *Booklist*. Other books in the series include *Killer Music, Tiger Rose,* and *Golden Idol*, Laura's last adventure, in which she must retrieve a gold statue in Hong Kong. The "South City Cops" series follows the exploits of police team Kate Brightwater and Eddy Hall. Titles include *Hit Man, Kidnap,* and *The Payoff Game*. Eisenberg also writes for *3-2-1 Contact. Home:* 102 Eastwood Ave., Ithaca, N.Y. 14850.

FOR MORE INFORMATION SEE: Contemporary Authors, Volume 110, Gale, 1984.

ELLISON, Lucile Watkins   1907(?)-1979

PERSONAL: Born about 1907, in Pennington, Ala.; died of cancer, December 20, 1979, in Washington, D.C.; married George Ellison, 1935. *Education:* Received degree from Mississippi State College for Women (now Mississippi State University for Women). *Residence:* Washington, D.C.

CAREER: Worked as a reporter and teacher in Meridian, Mass.; served National Education Association as member of field services staff and as assistant secretary of National Committee for the Defense of Democracy through Education, about 1937-61, executive secretary of citizenship committee, 1961-70.

WRITINGS—Juvenile; all illustrated by Judith Gwyn Brown; all published by Scribner: *Butter on Both Sides* (short stories), 1979; *The Tie That Binds,* 1981; *A Window to Look Through* (novel), 1982.

SIDELIGHTS: Ellison began writing stories for children in 1974, after learning that she was terminally ill with cancer. She regarded her writing as therapy, a chance to relive her childhood in Alabama. As she told the *Washington Post*, she chose to write about her own childhood for other children because "I realized that I had a year to live. And I realized that things had happened to me that will never happen again."

Lucile Watkins Ellison with husband, George.

FOR MORE INFORMATION SEE: Washington Post, December 17, 1979. Obituaries: *Washington Post,* December 22, 1979.

EPHRON, Delia 1944-
(Delia Brock)

BRIEF ENTRY: Born July 12, 1944, in Los Angeles, Calif. Ephron turned a humorous article she published in *New York Times Magazine* into the critically-acclaimed *How to Eat Like a Child: And Other Lessons in Not Being a Grown-up* (Viking, 1978) illustrated by *New Yorker* cartoonist Edward Koren. The essays cover the proper behavior concerning birthdays, Christmas, sibling torture, pets, and assorted other rites of childhood. "Ephron's clever observations document children's behavior in a hilarious fashion," observed *Library Journal. Teenage Romance: Or How to Die of Embarrassment* (Viking, 1981), also illustrated by Koren, is written in the same format, with pointed jabs at the trials of being a teenager. "Ephron offers another collection of pure delight, evocations of adolescence with a smitch of pathos contained in the comedy," noted *Publishers Weekly.* Among topics covered are how to make a pass, to hang out, have a slumber party, and hide pimples. Ephron is also the author of *Santa and Alex* (Little, Brown, 1983), illustrated by Elise Primavera, for younger readers. Alex stays up to sneak a peek at Santa Claus, and is surprised to be invited along on the delivery route.

Twelve essays make up the collection for *Funny Sauce: Us, the Ex, the Ex's New Mate, the New Mate's Ex, and the Kids* (Viking, 1986). Geared toward adults, a tongue-in-cheek tone is utilized to present the funnier side of not-so-funny extended family situations. Under the name Delia Brock, Ephron co-authored with Lorraine Bodger *Gladrags* (Simon & Schuster, 1975) which details simple ways for transforming old clothes into new garments, *The Adventurous Crocheter* (Simon & Schuster, 1972), and *Crafts for All Seasons* (Universe, 1980). *Residence:* Los Angeles, Calif.

FOR MORE INFORMATION SEE: New York Times, November 17, 1978; *Readers Digest,* March, 1979, August, 1979; *Saturday Evening Post,* May, 1979; *People,* October 12, 1981; *Nation,* November 21, 1981; *Washington Post Book World,*

August 22, 1982; *New York Times Book Review,* September 5, 1982; *Contemporary Authors, New Revision Series,* Volume 12, Gale, 1984; *New York Times Magazine,* September 14, 1986.

FERRIS, Jean 1939-

BRIEF ENTRY: Born January 24, 1939, in Fort Leavenworth, Kan. Author of children's books. Ferris went to Stanford University, where she received her B.A. in 1961 and M.S. in 1962. She then began a career as a clinical audiologist until 1976. Her first children's book, *Amen, Moses Gardenia* (Farrar, Straus, 1983), is about teenage depression and suicide. "Very well written, possibly useful in working with depressed adolescents. . . . The reader is able to follow [the main character's] confused reasoning about what her problems are and the solutions to them. The end is hopeful and optimistic," wrote *The Voice of Youth Advocates. The Stainless Steel Rule* (Farrar, Straus, 1985) is about friendship and the breach of trust. *Publishers Weekly* called the book "a taut, compelling novel, with moments of high humor and characters that will challenge readers as well as appeal to them." Ferris' latest juvenile novel, *Invincible Summer* (Farrar, Straus, 1987), is about a teenager with leukemia. She is also the author of *Music: The Art of Listening* (William C. Brown, 1985), a manual with accompanying cassette tapes. Ferris is the recipient of a 1984 grant from the Society of Children's Book Writers, and is a member of that society, as well as the Southern California Council on Literature for Children and Young People. *Home:* 2278 San Juan Rd., San Diego, Calif. 92103.

FOR MORE INFORMATION SEE: Contemporary Authors, Volume 116, Gale, 1986.

FitzGERALD, Cathleen 1932-1987

OBITUARY NOTICE: Born July 1, 1932, in Dublin, Ireland; died of cancer, January 11, 1987, in New York, N.Y. Educator, editor, and author. FitzGerald wrote *Let's Talk about Words* and *Let's Talk about Bees,* as well as scripts for children's radio and television programs. A former teacher, FitzGerald was managing editor and, later, executive editor, of Grolier's *New Book of Knowledge* for children. She also served in the firm's international division as editorial advisor for the *Japanese Book of Knowledge.*

FOR MORE INFORMATION SEE: Contemporary Authors, 33-36, revised edition, Gale, 1973. Obituaries: *Publishers Weekly,* January 30, 1987.

GARDNER, Beau

BRIEF ENTRY: Born in Oceanside, N.Y., Gardner graduated from Pratt Institute and is a professional graphic designer. In 1974 he founded Beau Gardner Associates, Inc., in New York City. He has used his talents to create a series of picture books for children that are intended to challenge the observer's imagination. His first, *The Turn About, Think About, Look About Book* (Lothrop, 1980), presents abstract pictures which look different each time the reader turns the book—on its side, upside-down, then on its other side. "Attractive to the eye for its bright colors, intriguing to the mind for its ingenuity, the book stimulates the observer to perceive the manifold possibilities of interpretive seeing," observed *Horn Book. The Look Again . . . And Again, and Again, and Again Book* (Lothrop,

1984), is filled with more of the same. "Gardner offers children a zesty game to play and the chance to use imagination, maybe even to decide that they can discern objects different from his, as they study the intriguing graphics," wrote *Publishers Weekly.* Both of these books have been selected by the American Institute of Graphic Arts Book Show for excellence in design. Gardner is also the creator of *The Upside Down Riddle Book* (Lothrop, 1982), compiled by Louis Phillips; *Have You Ever Seen. . .? An ABC Book* (Dodd, 1986); and *Guess What?* (Lothrop, 1985), where readers try to guess what animal is represented by the small, abstract section presented. "Teachers, librarians, and parents will find this a true imagination stretcher that can be used in a variety of ways with both individual children and groups," noted *Booklist. Residence:* Long Island, N.Y.

GLASER, Dianne E(lizabeth)   1937-

PERSONAL: Born August 29, 1937, in Bronx, N.Y.; daughter of James and Elizabeth Jackson; married Marvin E. Glaser (a creative director), November 9, 1957; children: Tamara, Sean, Carey, Dane, Amber, Quinn, Tristan. *Education:* Attended University of Alabama, Huntsville, 1956-57. *Home and office:* 1135 McNichol Lane, Chattanooga, Tenn. 37421.

CAREER: Writer, 1971—. *Awards, honors: The Diary of Trilby Frost* was named one of American Library Association's Books of the Year, 1977.

WRITINGS—For children: *Amber Wellington, Daredevil* (illustrated by husband, Marvin Glaser), Walker, 1975; *Amber Wellington, Witchwatcher,* Walker, 1976; *The Diary of Trilby Frost* (ALA Notable Book), Holiday House, 1976; *Summer Secrets,* Holiday House, 1977; *The Case of the Missing Six* (illustrated by David K. Stone), Holiday House, 1978.

GOODMAN, Deborah Lerme   1956-

PERSONAL: Maiden name is pronounced *Ler*-mee; born October 31, 1956, in New York, N.Y.; daughter of Joseph A. and Madeline (Brunks) Lerme; married John Goodman (a woodworker), May 2, 1982. *Education:* Carnegie-Mellon University, B.F.A., 1978; George Washington University, M.A.T., 1981. *Politics:* Liberal Democrat. *Home and office:* 8 Fairmont Ave., Cambridge, Mass. 02139.

CAREER: Merrimack Valley Textile Museum, North Andover, Mass., Children's Museum, Boston, Mass., and Museum of Our National Heritage, Lexington, Mass., educator, 1978-80; Smithsonian Institution, Washington, D.C., education coordinator, 1981-84; writer and creator of games, 1984—. *Member:* American Craft Council, Museum Education Roundtable.

WRITINGS—Juvenile: The Magic Shuttle, Smithsonian Institution, 1982; (with Marjorie L. Share) *Bee Quilting* (nonfiction), Smithsonian Institution, 1984; *The Throne of Zeus,* Bantam, 1984; *The Magic of the Unicorn,* Bantam, 1985; *The Trumpet of Terror,* Bantam, 1986; *Vanished!,* Bantam, 1986; *You See the Future,* Bantam, 1988.

Contributor to magazines, including *Fiberarts, Threads, Faces, Cobblestone,* and *Pennywhistle Press.*

Dear Diary,
This is my very first thing to write for posterity. ■ (Jacket illustration by Allen Davis from *The Diary of Trilby Frost* by Dianne Glaser.)

The unicorn cleans the water in [the] well.... ■ (From *The Magic of the Unicorn* by Deborah Lerme Goodman. Illustrated by Ron Wing.)

WORK IN PROGRESS: Magazine articles.

GOODMAN, Joan Elizabeth   1950-

PERSONAL: Born June 18, 1950, in Fairfield, Conn.; daughter of Milton Joel (an architectural engineer) and Fayalene (a psychiatric social worker; maiden name, Decker) Goodman. *Education:* Attended L'Accademia di Belle Arti, Rome, 1969-70; Pratt Institute, B.F.A., 1973. *Home:* 684 Washington St., 1-B, New York, N.Y. 10014. *Agent:* Paige Gillies, Publisher's Graphics, 251 Greenwood Ave., Bethel, Ct. 06801.

CAREER: Village Voice, New York, N.Y., type specker, 1968-69; Hallmark Cards, Kansas City, Mo., greeting card artist, 1974-76; free-lance author and illustrator.

WRITINGS—Self-illustrated: *Teddy Bear, Teddy Bear,* Grosset, 1979; *Bear and His Book,* Simon & Schuster, 1982; *Right's Animal Farm,* Western, 1983; *Amanda's First Day of School,* Western, 1985; *The Secret Life of Walter Kitty,* Western, 1986; *Good Night, Pippin,* Western, 1986; *The Bunnies' Get Well Soup,* Western, 1987; *Edward Hopper's Great Find,* Western, 1987; *Hillary Squeak's Dreadful Dragon,* Western, 1987.

Illustrator; all published by Troll, except where indicated: David Cutts, reteller, *The Gingerbread Boy,* 1979; Olive Blake, *The Grape Jelly Mystery,* 1979; Ruben Tanner, *The Teddy Bear's Picnic: A Counting Book,* Dutton, 1979; Carol Beach York, *Johnny Appleseed,* 1980; Judith Grey, *Yummy, Yummy,* 1981; Rose Greydanus, *Hocus Pocus, Magic Show!,* 1981; Robyn Supraner, *The Case of the Missing Rattles,* 1982; Eileen Cur-

ran, *Easter Parade,* 1985; R. Supraner, *The Cat Who Wanted to Fly,* 1986.

WORK IN PROGRESS: A sequel to *The Secret Life of Walter Kitty,* entitled *Happy Birthday Benjamin!;* a sequel to *Amanda's First Day of School,* entitled *Amanda and Baby Wiggles; Rio Goes to Sleep* deals with bedtime monsters; *Max and Lulu,* a story about two contentious cats.

SIDELIGHTS: "I was born in Fairfield, Connecticut. My father was an architectural engineer. My mother was a very talented painter, but she kept that hidden until her early seventies when she began doing beautiful impressionistic oils. My older brother is a very fine artist. His work appears regularly in *Scientific American.* My grandmother lived with us and she, too, was an artist. Being surrounded by artists it seemed inevitable that I should be drawn to art.

"I feel lucky that I found out very early on what I loved doing and I've just stuck with it.

"My Nana taught me how to use her oil paints as soon as she could trust me not to eat them. They *did* look delicious but I traded off the need to taste them for the greater need to keep on painting. Since then many other things have looked delicious; acting in particular. Even though I've been very preoccupied with the theatre at different times, I've always kept painting as my main goal.

"I went to Pratt Institute because being an art major was not enough. I wanted to be surrounded by ART and to live in a community of ARTISTS. My first year at Pratt I worked part-time for the *Village Voice* as a type specker. I also worked freelance designing and illustrating ads that ran in the *Voice.* I took off my sophomore year to study art at L'Accademia di Belle Arti in Rome. It was *fantastico!* When I returned to New York I began a free-lance association with Leslie Tillett via an introduction from my brother Michael. I worked with Leslie on a wide variety of design projects: film strips, jewelry designs, and craft kits. I was also selling a few fabric designs, but I wasn't very good at that.

JOAN ELIZABETH GOODMAN

Then Papa built a plane.... ■ (From *Good Night, Pippin* by Joan Elizabeth Goodman. Illustrated by the author.)

"Meanwhile, at Pratt I was taking a wonderful design course with Werner Pfeiffer. We had to design, illustrate, print and bind our own books. Well that was *it* for me. Nothing I was doing for Leslie, for fabric designs or for fashion ads could compete with the great satisfaction of making my own books. I decided then on a career as a children's book illustrator.

(Deciding on a career and having it are two separate things. On my way to having it, I worked for Hallmark Cards in Kansas City, Missouri. I have also supported my 'career' by working in book stores.) It made great sense. I have always loved books: *Babar* by Jean de Brunhoff, first of all, *Mary Poppins* by P. L. Travers, the 'Narnia' books by C. S. Lewis and many, many others. Books have enlightened me, comforted me, and taught me the value of humor.

"I had early delusions about BEING A WRITER, but my initial attempts at fiction were too pitiful to pursue. However, I had a fine teacher in the ninth grade, Mrs. Demers, who got me started keeping a journal, which I'm still keeping. Even though I was writing drivel, at least I was in the habit of writing. And I read copiously and enthusiastically.

"As soon as I began focusing on a future as an illustrator, I began trying to write my own children's books. Trying does *not* mean succeeding. But I did keep trying. Then a few years ago I started attending a writing workshop run by Margret Gabel at the New School. It's been wonderful. My classmates are some of the best writers of children's literature currently being published. By paying attention to what they do, and taking to heart their sensitive and sensible editorial direction, I have been learning to write. And, best of all, I've had the help and encouragement of my friend and agent, Paige Gillies."

HOBBIES AND OTHER INTERESTS: Tennis, bridge, medieval history.

GUYMER, (Wilhelmina) Mary 1909-

PERSONAL: Born May 4, 1909, in Lowestoft, Suffolk, England; married James Agnew, March 25, 1972. *Education:* Attended Wimbledon College of Art, 1921-29. *Home:* 29 Edward Pinner Ct., Hook Rd., Surbiton, Surrey KT6 5DF, England.

CAREER: Has worked as a fashion artist, 1929-39, technical illustrator, 1944-70, and part time teacher. Free-lance illustrator, 1970—. *Exhibitions:* Institute of Water Colour Painters, Piccadilly, England, 1970; various galleries in East Anglia, 1970-77. *Military service:* British Red Cross, artist, 1939-44; received war medal, 1945; Imperial Service medal from Ministry of Defence, 1971. *Member:* Admiralty Art Club, World Wildlife Association, Thames Valley Art Club.

ILLUSTRATOR: M. Black and J. Edelman, *Plant Growth,* Heinemann, 1969; Arnold Darlington, *Ecology of Refuse Tips,* Heinemann, 1969; A. Darlington, *The World of a Tree,* Faber, 1972; A. Darlington, *Pollution and Life,* Blandford, 1974; William Condry, *The World of a Mountain,* Faber, 1977; Terry Jennings, *The World of a Hedge,* Faber, 1978; M. V. Brian, *The World of an Anthill,* Faber, 1979; John Powell, *The World of a Beehive* (also illustrated with photographs by J. Powell), Faber, 1979; Jill Eddison, *The World of the Changing Coastline,* Faber, 1979; Noel Blatchford, *Your Book of Forestry,* Faber, 1980. Also illustrator of Harry Jones' *Sign Language* and John Mathews' *Log Sculpture.* Contributor of illustrations to *Everymans Encyclopedia,* and *Cybernetics Simplified.*

SIDELIGHTS: "I started drawing at the age of three when living in Yorkshire with my parents. After being orphaned at four years, I was brought to London to live with an aunt and uncle. At school my talents became noticed and I excelled in English composition and art. I won a free scholarship to art school when the head of an art school visited on an open day and saw my work. Progress at art college led to preparation for entry to the Royal Academy Schools, but I had to leave as a necessity to earn my own living (I cried for a whole week!!).

"I found a position in a fashion studio and progressed through several others until war broke out. I enrolled in the Red Cross,

where I did much work on posters in aid of the prisoners of war. After the cessation of war in Europe, there was no work of artistic nature available other than engineering. So into that I went designing aircraft controls until that wound up after 'V. J.' Day.

"All labour at that time was 'directed' by order, so I was pushed into the 'Ministry of Defence.' After many efforts to 'escape,' I gave in and did very well, getting promoted and leaving eventually to join the Imperial Service Order.

"During this time however, I acquired a teaching post at Wandsworth Technical College and taught technical illustration part time for seven years.

"I also renewed my contacts for free-lance work, specializing in biological subjects and never looked back.

"The study of wildlife is my greatest joy and in all the research connected with the various subjects I have illustrated, I have learned *so* much. No one would dream that so much life went on inside a rubbish tip! Who could guess that minutiae such as a gall wasp, no bigger than a pin head when seen under a microscope could prove to be such a glorious glittering bronze in colour?

"In this work one never knows what subject may turn up next and as the books illustrated are written by authors who are specialists in their own fields, it is a constant source of inspiration to the illustrator. 'The World of' series, five of which I have illustrated are examples of this and each subject takes the artist on a new tour of discovery.

MARY GUYMER

"I worked only in black and white for these books, using pen and ink and all available mechanical tints and half tones. I have also worked in other media, including water colour, gouache, and pastel, and hope the other work may return soon.

"I have travelled widely in Europe, Austria, Italy, Switzerland, and Balearic Islands. I lived for four years in East Anglia, next door to the famous Minsurene Bird Reserve, whose friendly warden gave me carte blanche to work whenever I liked. This was a treasure house of material."

HAHN, Mary Downing   1937-

PERSONAL: Born December 9, 1937, in Washington, D.C.; daughter of Kenneth Ernest (an automobile mechanic) and Anna Elisabeth (a teacher; maiden name, Sherwood) Downing; married William E. Hahn, Jr., October 7, 1961 (divorced, 1976); married Norman Pearce Jacob (a librarian), April 23, 1982; children: (first marriage) Katherine Sherwood, Margaret Elizabeth. *Education:* University of Maryland—College Park, B.A., 1960, M.A., 1969, graduate study, 1970-74. *Politics:* Democrat. *Home:* 9746 Basket Ring Rd., Columbia, Md. 21045. *Office:* Prince George's County Memorial Library System, Laurel Branch, 507 Seventh St., Laurel, Md. 20707.

CAREER: Writer, artist, librarian. Greenbelt Junior High School, Greenbelt, Md., art teacher, 1960-61; University of Maryland—College Park, graduate assistant, 1961-63, part-time instructor, 1970-74; WETA public television, Washington D.C., free-lance artist for "Cover to Cover" (children's reading program), 1973-75; Prince George's County Memorial Library System, Laurel Branch, Laurel, Md., children's librarian, 1975—. *Member:* Washington Children's Book Guild, Society of Children's Book Writers. *Awards, honors: Daphne's Book* was a Reviewers' Choice from the American Library Association, one of Library of Congress' Children's Books, and one of *School Library Journal*'s Best Books, all 1983, one of Child Study Association of America's Children's Books of the Year and Teacher's Choice from the National Council of Teachers of English, both 1984, and received the William Allen White Children's Choice Award from the William Allen White Library, 1986.

WRITINGS—Juvenile novels; all published by Clarion Books: *The Sara Summer*, 1979; *The Time of the Witch*, 1982; *Daphne's Book*, 1983; *The Jellyfish Season*, 1985; *Wait Till Helen Comes: A Ghost Story*, 1986; *Tallahassee Higgins*, 1987.

WORK IN PROGRESS: Following the Mystery Man, the story of a girl named Madigan who finds herself in danger when she becomes involved with a stranger whom she believes is her father; a novel about the plight of a homeless Vietnam veteran and his effect upon a teenage girl, tentatively titled *December Stillness*; a picture book fantasy about a wizard and his cat, *The Wizard and Me*; and a number of picture book ideas.

SIDELIGHTS: "Ever since I was old enough to hold a crayon or a pencil, I have loved to draw. In fact, my first literary efforts were long picture stories drawn on thick newsprint pads. While I drew, I told myself the story, but, since I never wrote the words down, the drawings are a mystery to me now. Most of them seem to deal with orphans who suffer at the hands of cruel guardians, come perilously close to dying, but recover in time to be rescued by a wealthy grandfather—the result, no doubt, of my reading novels like *Oliver Twist*.

"When I wasn't drawing, I was reading, and it wasn't long before I tried writing stories—illustrated, of course. I still have

a book begun when I was in the seventh grade; called 'Small Town Life,' its heroine, Susan Dervish, fixes breakfast, goes on Girl Scout camping trips, gets a dog, quarrels with her younger siblings, and—in general—lives a life very much like my own.

"By the time I entered Northwestern High School, I was sure that I wanted to write and illustrate children's books when I grew up. I still loved to draw, and I always looked forward to embellishing my book reports and term papers with illustrations—they were my sure A's, the projects that made up for the grades I was getting in geometry, chemistry, and Latin (all the nicely-drawn, toga-clad Romans in the world couldn't make up for my failure to learn my irregular verbs and other such things).

"At the University of Maryland, I majored in fine art and English, which gave me the delightful opportunity to combine my favorite pastimes: reading, writing, and drawing. I had a wonderful time and never thought about what sort of job I would find to support myself while I pursued my hobbies.

"As a result, I have had a variety of jobs—an art teacher, a bookstore sales person, an information specialist at the phone company, a correspondence clerk at the Navy Federal Credit Union, an English teacher, a free-lance artist, and, at present, a children's associate librarian in Prince George's County, Maryland. And, of course, in my spare time, I've been writing and drawing all along.

MARY DOWNING HAHN

After an hour or so, Hope came scrambling up to join Daphne and me.... ■ (Jacket illustration
by Diane de Groat from *Daphne's Book* by Mary Downing Hahn.)

''My first serious efforts at becoming an author began when
my daughters were small and I was reading them an endless
series of picture books. Re-inspired, I wrote and illustrated
several stories and mailed them off to publishers. Although
some of the replies were polite and even encouraging, no one
made an offer.

''Still unpublished, I went back to graduate school and began
studying for a Ph.D. in English literature; I wrote dozens of
seminar papers, but I no longer enhanced my interpretations
of John Donne's poetry with pictures of lords and ladies of
the seventeenth century. I did, however, have an idea for a
dissertation: an illustrated edition of Coleridge's unfinished
poem 'Christabel,' complete with footnotes, a scholarly introduction and an epilogue exploring possible endings. Although
one of my professors was quite enthusiastic about my pro-
posal, it was rejected on the grounds that it sounded like 'too
much fun.'

''In that I never came up with any other idea for a dissertation,
I left graduate school without getting my Ph.D. and worked
instead as a free-lance artist for a children's reading program,
'Cover to Cover.'

''From there, I found my way into the public library system.
My reading of innumerable children's books prompted me to
try writing a novel for nine- to twelve-year-olds.

''That book, *The Sara Summer,* was published in 1979 after
three years of writing and re-writing. Like 'Small Town Life,'
it is set in a suburb of Washington, D.C. and draws upon my
memories of what it was like to be twelve years old, the tallest
girl in school, shy and unsure of what to do or say, and easily

influenced by others. Much of the story, of course, is made
up and changed, which is one of the nicest things about writing. You can make your life more exciting, you can change
sad endings to happy ones, you can meet all sorts of interesting
people, go places you've never been, have adventures without
leaving home or even packing a suitcase.

''My second book, *The Time of the Witch,* combines realism
and fantasy in the mountains of West Virginia. Laura—like
my own daughters—has trouble accepting her parents' divorce. When she turns to a witch for help, she discovers that
having a wish granted can be a terrifying experience. Although
some readers have trouble accepting the witch, her power is
essential to the story. As a child, I was always terribly dis-
appointed in stories whose endings explained away the magic:
it was all a dream, the ghost was just a sheet on the clothesline,
the witch was really an eccentric old lady with problems. Like
the witch in *Hansel and Gretel,* Maude is a malevolent being,
and the spell she casts is just as dangerous as Hansel's captivity.

''If *The Time of the Witch* had its roots in the fairy tales I
loved as a child, *Daphne's Book* grew out of my observations
of my own daughters and my life in Columbia, a new town
which sprang into existence in rural Howard County about
twenty years ago complete with shopping malls, man-made
lakes, footpaths, and all the conveniences of suburban living.
The plot came to me when I served as a judge in a write-a-
book contest; I was reviewing books created by two or more
students, and I found myself wondering if the joint authors
were friends or enemies. Using the write-a-book contest as a
method of getting Jessica and Daphne together, I then explored
the issue of peer pressure, hoping to give readers of the book
some insights into why girls like Daphne need acceptance. It

always surprises me when people complain about the sad ending—I truly thought I might be making it too happy to be credible. After spending over a year worrying about Daphne and Hope, I wanted the very best for them. For me, that would be going to Maine to live.

"The *Jellyfish Season,* my fourth novel, is set in an imaginary community on the Chesapeake Bay, one of my favorite summer-time places. It was truly a joy to re-visit the beach in my imagination, to remember the sunburn and jellyfish and the taste of brackish saltwater. Like Kathleen, I was our family's 'Gloomy Gus,' I had a cousin who was far more sophisticated than I, our family once had to spend a couple of months with relatives, and at the age of sixteen I had a crush on a sailor a bit like Joe. Those are the bare bones of reality upon which I draped the novel.

"In my novels, I strive to re-create real life. Like the people I know, I want my characters to be a mixture of strengths and weaknesses, to have good and bad qualities, to be a little confused and unsure of themselves. This is why Jessica never quite stands up for Daphne—she wants to, but she is afraid of being laughed at. It also explains Emily's problems in dealing with Sara and Laura's acceptance of Maude's offer to grant her wish. Kathleen's lack of self-assurance gets her into trouble with Fay who also has little confidence despite her tough exterior.

"Since happy endings and easy answers are hard to come by, I try to avoid them in my novels. At the same time, however, I make an effort to leave room for hope. Emily learns to speak up to Sara, Laura accepts her parents' divorce, Jessica maintains her friendship with Daphne, and Kathleen's family manages to pull itself together.

"Although my work as a children's librarian cuts into my writing time, it keeps me in touch with my readers and the sorts of books they enjoy. I visit schools regularly, sometimes as a writer to talk about my own books, sometimes as a librarian to talk about other writers' books, sometimes as a storyteller, and sometimes as a puppeteer. I enjoy all of these roles. Writing, as everyone knows, is a very solitary occupation, and the opportunity of meeting new people almost every day is one of the nicest things about being a librarian. To make it even better, what other job pays you to read and gives you the opportunity to tell stories and make puppets?

"When I'm not at the Laurel Public Library or curled up with my word processor, you might find me bent over my drawing board. One of my hobbies is painting pictures of wizards, dragons, unicorns, elves, and other magical creatures. I sell these at science fiction and fantasy conventions, such as Balticon and Unicon. I hope to present my wizard (who has already made a minor debut as the hero of the Summer Quest Reading Club in the Washington, D.C. metropolitan area) to a larger public when I finish my first fantasy novel, *The Wizard and Me.*

"I am also thinking about writing a non-fiction book on puppet making. So far, I've created puppets for library presentations of *Dracula, Cinderella, Punch and Judy, Who's in Rabbit's House?,* and an assortment of dwarves for an excerpt from *The Hobbit.*

"I married for a second time in 1982 when my daughters were fourteen and sixteen; Kate and Beth are now in college, and my husband and I spend our spare time exploring the footpaths that wind through Columbia. We especially enjoy the lakes and their population of ducks, swans, and wild geese—once

in a while we spot a visiting heron or glimpse a hawk soaring overhead.

"We love to poke around in flea markets and antique shops; while I examine toys and dolls, Norm pokes about in the cameras and tools. We don't buy much, but we enjoy ourselves.

"After a long walk or a busy day of junk shopping, we treat ourselves to ice cream at Friendly's or a feast at a salad bar. We also love Chinese and Mexican food, the spicier the better, and the wonderful fresh seafood available in Baltimore.

"We visit the museums in Baltimore and Washington frequently, go to the Kennedy Center for concerts and ballets, and daydream—especially when we're stuck in rush hour traffic on the Beltway—of moving to a little village on the Maine coast or spending a year or two in Great Britain exploring all the ruins we can find or setting ourselves up in a modest R.V. and traveling the craft fair circuit selling puppets.

"For now, I suppose we'll stay here in Columbia—at least till the girls finish college."

HANNAM, Charles 1925-

PERSONAL: Born July 26, 1925, in Essen, Germany; son of Max Hirschland and Gertrud (maiden name, Freudenberg) Hannam; married Sue Dowling; children: three sons, one daughter. *Education:* Cambridge University, B.A., 1951, M.A., 1961. *Home:* 28 Kingston Parade, Bristol BS6 5UF, England. *Office:* School of Education, University of Bristol, Bristol BS8 1JA, England.

CAREER: Teacher in secondary schools in England, 1951-59; University of Bristol, Bristol, England, member of faculty, 1959—, senior lecturer in education, 1973—, professor, 1973—. *Military service:* British Army, 1943-47; served in India and Burma.

WRITINGS: (Contributor) M. Ballard, editor, *New Movements in the Study and Teaching of History,* Temple Smith, 1970; (with Pat Smyth and Norman Stephenson) *Young Teachers and Reluctant Learners,* Penguin, 1971; *Parents and Mentally Handicapped Children,* Penguin, 1974, 2nd edition, 1980; (with P. Smyth and N. Stephenson) *The First Year of Teaching,* Penguin, 1975; *A Boy in That Situation: An Autobiography,* Harper, 1977; *Almost an Englishman,* Deutsch, 1979. Contributor to periodicals, including *Times Educational Supplement, Guardian, Teaching History,* and *Times Higher Educational Supplement.*

WORK IN PROGRESS: A study of childhood; working with children who have difficulty in adjusting to schools; another autobiography.

SIDELIGHTS: Hannam was born in Essen, Germany, and attended the Goethe Gymnasium there. "The *difference* between my family and so many others was that we were Jewish—trying to go on living in Germany in the 1930's when Hitler and the Nazis were coming to power. At the time I barely understood what was happening. Awareness that our religion was hateful to the government and to some of the German people only came to me gradually. I have since learnt a great deal about religious and racial persecution: It not only damages and blights the persecuted, it harms those who persecute—the persecutors lose their sense of humanity and justice, while the victims learn to hate themselves. At that time many of us

German Jews began to believe some of the Nazi propaganda and to think of ourselves as ugly and unworthy. We would make jokes about our appearance and our occupations even though we had previously thought of ourselves as German more than Jewish. Now, this self-hate is not unique to Jews. There have been black children who suffered from discrimination and persecution and who began to believe that they were not beautiful and talented, and I am told that some Navaho

CHARLES HANNAM

youngsters watching a Western film cheered the cowboys rather than their own people, who were being slaughtered. At any rate, the Nazi myth of racial purity was accepted by some German Jews to an extent, and we would comment on hooked noses and black, curly hair with the same sort of disparagement as the Nazis did.

"I suspect that most children are teased; it may be because they are thin or fat, clever or stupid, fair or redhaired. They hate it but in time the teasing stops, leaving some secret wound. But being teased for being Jewish was physically dangerous in the Germany of the 1930's. If I had not caught the train to England in May 1939, I would have been on one going to the Nazi death camps with millions of other Jews. Several members of my family perished, and I know now that for me it was a near thing. So what appeared at the start as malicious teasing by some boys and a few teachers ended in a deadly serious way. It was a preparation for their indifference to the fate of the Jews, and it laid the foundation for genocide. I have learnt since that unreasoning prejudice against *any* minority group can lead to such death and destruction.

"The world I grew up in seems so remote now. It is so far away that it seems unreal. But it was real, and as I sat down to write . . . [*A Boy in That Situation: An Autobiography*] it all came back. I had to face up to some personal facts: I had not been a very nice boy—though I suspect very few boys really are. I stole, I lied and I tried to forge my father's signature on a school report—not very skilfully, but I tried hard!

"By sitting down and remembering my childhood I have learnt many other things about myself: that I had suppressed a deep grief when my mother died and that she must have been a very spirited and humourous woman; that my father was a very calm and brave man who protected me from being afraid as much as he could; also that many of the non-Jewish people of Germany were good and decent—not all of them approved of the brutality and misery which in the end they were unable to stop. . . . Big events have small beginnings; what happened to me is a small detail of the great catastrophe which in the end wiped out most of German and European Jewry." [Charles Hannam, "Growing Up in Nazi Germany," *A Boy in That Situation: An Autobiography,* Harper, 1977.[1]]

In England, Hannam lived in a hostel for refugee boys for a year until he was sent to a camp where he was trained as a farm worker. His sister, however, was able to get him into a boarding school where he stayed until he was eighteen years old.

After serving in the British Army from 1943 to 1947, Hannam attended Cambridge University where he received his B.A. in 1951 and his M.A. in 1961. Today he is a professor at the University of Bristol in England, where he lives with his wife, daughter, and three sons. "*A Boy in That Situation* was written for my sons. I have always missed not knowing much about my own parents. They are shadowy figures and I have tried very hard to understand them better. As it happens I also lived through an extraordinary period of history and sometimes I wonder why I should have been lucky enough to survive when so many died. So I hope the book is an account of a childhood as well as a description of what it was like to live in Nazi Germany before the Second World War broke out.

"In some way all my books are autobiographical; the ones about teaching and education face the problems I had when I began my career as a teacher. We hope we are able to train teachers a bit better as the result of our efforts. *Parents and Mentally Handicapped Children* began when my first son David was born. It was a painful and difficult experience and gradually I realised that our problems could not be seen in isolation but should be shared with others.''

A Boy in That Situation has been translated into German, Dutch, Danish and Braille. *Parents and Mentally Handicapped Children* has been translated into eight languages.

HOBBIES AND OTHER INTERESTS: Modern art, collecting paintings and other works of art, cooking.

HARGROVE, James   1947-
(Jim Hargrove)

BRIEF ENTRY: Born May 7, 1947, in New York, N.Y. After receiving his bachelor's degree from the University of Illinois in Chicago, Hargrove worked at publishing companies as managing editor and editorial director before founding Book Productions Ltd. in 1979. The author of more than a dozen informative books for children and adults, Hargrove won the Best of 1975-76 Award from *Learning* for a filmstrip series he produced entitled "Math Mystery Theatre." His interest in computers and outdoor sports is evident in his children's books. *Microcomputers at Work* (Childrens Press, 1984) introduces children to the basic functions of computers; *Mountain Climbing* (Lerner, 1982), written with S. A. Johnson, combines color photographs with a primer on the various techniques of mountain climbing and the necessary equipment for a safe trip. Since the mid-1980s, Hargrove has turned his attention toward biographies for children, all published by Childrens Press, including *Mark Twain: The Story of Samuel Clemens* (1984), *The Story of the Black Hawk War* (1986), and *The Statue of Liberty* (1986). He is presently working on a travel guide to high-tech attractions in the United States. *Office:* Book Productions Ltd., 519 Greenwood Dr., Round Lake Park, Ill. 60073.

FOR MORE INFORMATION SEE: Contemporary Authors, Volume 120, Gale, 1987.

HAYES, Sheila   1937-

BRIEF ENTRY: Born June 16, 1937, in New York City. "To write for children you must *be* a child, remembering how it feels to be low man on the totem pole in this adult world," Hayes said about the skill of writing for juveniles. This philosophy is exemplified in works like *The Carousel Horse* (Thomas Nelson, 1978), and its sequel *You've Been Away All Summer* (Dutton/Lodestar, 1986), about friendships and growing up. Other novels geared toward adolescent girls are *No Autographs, Please* (Dutton, 1984), and *Speaking of Snapdragons* (Lodestar, 1982), whose protagonists confront, and eventually accept, the adult world. Hayes worked as a receptionist, an assistant, and as assistant to the director in public relations from 1957 to 1962. She began writing in 1969. *The Carousel Horse* was adapted into a segment of "Afterschool Special" by American Broadcasting Co. (ABC-TV) during the 1982-83 season.

FOR MORE INFORMATION SEE: Contemporary Authors, Volume 106, Gale, 1982.

> Learn to live, and live to learn,
> Ignorance like a fire doth burn,
> Little tasks make large return.
>
> —Bayard Taylor

HEILMAN, Joan Rattner

PERSONAL: Born in New York, N.Y.; daughter of Louis (an automobile salesman) and Erna (a housewife; maiden name, Schneider) Rattner; married Morton Heilman (an engineer), August 12, 1956; children: Katherine, Julia, David. *Education:* Smith College, B.A., 1944. *Home and office:* 812 Stuart Ave., Mamaroneck, N.Y. 10543. *Agent:* Connie Clausen, 250 East 87th St., New York, N.Y. 10128.

CAREER: This Week (magazine), New York, N.Y., women's editor, 1954-69; free-lance writer, 1969—. *Member:* American Society of Journalists and Authors, Authors League. *Awards, honors: Bluebird Rescue* was selected one of Child Study Association of America's Children's Books of the Year, 1983.

WRITINGS—Juvenile: *Bluebird Rescue,* Lothrop, 1982.

Other: (With Jean Nidetch) *The Story of Weight Watchers,* World Publications, 1970; *Kenneth's Complete Book on Hair,* Doubleday, 1972; *Growing Up Thin,* McKay, 1975; *The Lila Nachtigall Report on Menopause,* Putnam, 1977; *The Complete Book of Midwifery,* Dutton, 1977; *Having a Cesarean Baby,* Dutton, 1978; *Diabetes: Controlling It the Easy Way,* Random House, 1982; *The Complete University Medical Diet,* Rawson, 1983; *Ford Models' Crash Course in Looking Great,* Simon & Schuster, 1985; *Estrogen: The Facts Can Change Your Life,* Harper, 1986.

Contributor of non-fiction articles to numerous periodicals, including *Redbook, Family Circle, Parade,* and *Travel and Leisure.*

JOAN RATTNER HEILMAN

WORK IN PROGRESS: A juvenile book about bats; magazine articles; a travel book for adults.

SIDELIGHTS: "*Bluebird Rescue* was my first children's book. I wrote it when I realized why I hadn't seen a bluebird in many years, although I remember them flying through the fields when I was a child and I was always looking for them. Although they were once as common as robins, now their numbers have seriously diminished and they are in grave danger of extinction. I discovered that there were efforts going on throughout the country to try to save them, and I decided children would love to help if they knew how. *Bluebird Rescue* tells them just what to do."

HOBBIES AND OTHER INTERESTS: Birdwatching, tennis, wildlife, hiking, skiing.

HELWEG, Hans H.   1917-

PERSONAL: Born February 21, 1917, in Denmark; came to the United States in 1939; became naturalized citizen; son of a university lecturer and a painter; married Jane Barrett (an actress). *Education:* Attended Hornsey Art School, Heatherley School of Art, and Royal Academy of Art, Oslo, Norway.

CAREER: Author and illustrator of children's books. *Military service:* U.S. Army, 1942; U.S. Air Force until 1946, served in Europe as a war artist. *Awards, honors: The Tales of Olga da Polga* was selected one of Child Study Association of America's Children's Books of the Year, 1973.

WRITINGS—All juvenile: *Farm Animals,* Random House, 1978; *Animal Babies,* Collins, 1981; *Caring for Your Pet,* Collins, 1981; *Dogs and Puppies,* Collins, 1981; *Animals on the Farm,* Collins, 1981.

Illustrator; all juvenile: (With Mel Crawford) A. N. Bedford (pseudonym of Jane Werner Watson), *Roy Rogers and the New Cowboy,* Simon & Schuster, 1953; Eric M. Knight, *Lassie Come-Home,* abridged by Felix Sutton, Grosset, 1954; Mark Twain (pseudonym of Samuel L. Clemens), *The Adventures of Tom Sawyer,* edited and abridged by Anne Terry White, Simon & Schuster, 1956; (with Frank Bolle) Frank Sayers, *Cowboys,* Simon & Schuster, 1956; M. A. Jagendorf and C. H. Tillhagen, *The Gypsies' Fiddle, and Other Gypsy Tales,* Vanguard Press, 1956; Borghild M. Dahl, *The Daughter,* Dutton, 1956; John M. Schealer, *Zip-Zip and His Flying Saucer,* Dutton, 1956; Philip D. Jordan, *Fiddlefoot Jones of the North Woods,* Vanguard Press, 1957; B. M. Dahl, *The Cloud Shoes,* Dutton, 1957; J. M. Schealer, *Zip-Zip Goes to Venus,* Dutton, 1958; (with others) Bryna Untermeyer and Louis Untermeyer,

Olga da Polga was suffering from "mixed feelings." ■ (From *Olga Carries On* by Michael Bond. Illustrated by Hans Helweg.)

She would miss her children—there was no denying the fact—but they had to go out into the world on their own at sometime.... ■ (From *Olga Carries On* by Michael Bond. Illustrated by Hans Helweg.)

editors, *Unfamiliar Marvels,* Golden Press, 1962; Charles Dickens, *A Christmas Carol,* Golden Press, 1969; Hans Christian Andersen, *The Emperor's New Clothes,* Golden Press, 1970; L. A. Hill, reteller, *The Old Woman and Her Pig,* Oxford University Press (London), 1971; Ann Lawrence, *The Travels of Oggy,* Gollancz, 1973; A. Lawrence, *Oggy at Home,* Gollancz, 1977; A. Lawrence, *Oggy and the Holiday,* Gollancz, 1979.

All written by Michael Bond; all juvenile fiction: *The Tales of Olga da Polga* (ALA Notable Book), Penguin, 1971, Macmillan, 1973, published as *Olga da Polga,* Puffin, 1975, Volume I: *Olga Makes a Wish,* Volume II: *Olga's New Home,* Volume III: *Olga Counts Her Blessings,* Volume IV: *Olga Makes Her Mark,* Volume V: *Olga Takes a Bite,* Volume VI: *Olga's Second House,* Volume VII: *Olga Makes a Friend,* Volume VIII: *Olga's Special Day* (volumes published separately in the United States, EMC Corp., 1977), also published as *The First Big Olga da Polga Book,* Longman, 1983, and *The Second Big Olga da Polga Book,* Longman, 1983; *Olga Meets Her Match,* Longman Young Books, 1973, Hastings House, 1975; *Olga Carries On,* Kestrel Books, 1976, Hastings House, 1977; *Olga Takes Charge,* Kestrel Books, 1982; *The Complete Adventures of Olga da Polga* (contains *The Tales of Olga da Polga, Olga Meets Her Match, Olga Carries On,* and *Olga Takes Charge*), Delacorte, 1983.

SIDELIGHTS: "My childhood and youth were spent mostly in England, where my father lectured in Danish at University College, but with frequent visits to Denmark and France. My mother was a painter and our home in London was a haven for artists, writers and musicians, which probably explains my early preoccupation with drawing and illustrating.

"In 1939 I came to the United States for a six months visit which, in view of circumstances, I decided to extend indefinitely. Despite, or more likely because of a 'fine arts' background, I was sadly unprepared for a career in the commercial field, but managed somehow to exist until 1942 when the United States Army sent me greetings. After basic training with the ski troops and a six months stint in the hospital resulting from double pneumonia, I was transferred to the Air Force and sent to Europe as a war artist to do picture stories.

''On being discharged in 1946 I went to live in London where I married British actress Jane Barrett. We spent some time in Australia but mostly we have divided our time between London, New York and Vermont.

''Though there are many more profitable ways of making a living than drawing for children's books, I have never found one I like better. You immerse yourself for several weeks in a different world, often in a different period, and if the story is a good one, I am often tempted to spend more time on it than either good sense or the publisher dictate.'' [B. M. Miller and others, compilers, *Illustrators of Children's Books: 1946-1956,* Horn Book, 1958.]

FOR MORE INFORMATION SEE: B. M. Miller and others, compilers, *Illustrators of Children's Books: 1946-1956,* Horn Book, 1958; Lee Kingman and others, compilers, *Illustrators of Children's Books: 1957-1966,* Horn Book, 1968; L. Kingman and others, compilers, *Illustrators of Children's Books: 1967-1976,* Horn Book, 1978.

HESSE, Hermann 1877-1962
(Hermann Lauscher, Emil Sinclair)

PERSONAL: Born July 2, 1877, in Calw, Wuerttemberg, Germany; died August 9, 1962; Swiss citizen, 1924-62; son of Johannes (a journalist, publisher, and missionary) and Marie (Gundert) Hesse; married Maria Bernoulli, 1904 (divorced, 1923); married Ruth Wenger, January, 1924 (divorced, 1927); married Ninon Auslaender Dolbin, November, 1931 (died September 22, 1966); children: (first marriage) Bruno, Heiner, Martin. *Education:* Attended preparatory Latin school of Rector Otto Bauer, Goeppingen, Germany, 1890-91; studied the-

Hesse family, 1889. Left to right: Hermann, Johannes (father), Marulla, Marie (mother), Adele and Hans.

ology at Seminar Maulbronn, 1891-92; attended Gymnasium at Cannstadt. *Home:* Montagnola, near Lugano, Switzerland.

CAREER: Apprenticed to a bookseller in Esslingen, Germany; worked in Calw, Germany for six months as assistant to his father at Calwer Verlagsverein, a publishing association; apprentice in the clock factory of Heinrich Perrot, in Calw, 1894; Heckenhauer bookshop in Tuebingen, Germany, apprentice, 1895-98, assistant, 1898-99; worked with a bookdealer in Basel, Switzerland, 1899-1901; author, 1903-62; *Maerz* (periodical), editor, 1907-12; during World War I he edited the periodical for prisoners of war, *Sonntagsbote fuer deutsche Kriegsgefangene;* co-editor of *Deutsche Internierten-Zeitung,* 1916-17, and of *Vivos Voco,* 1919-20. *Military service:* Served as a volunteer worker through the German consulate in Bern, Switzerland, on behalf of the German prisoners of war (1914-18).

MEMBER: Prussian Academy of Poets (resigned in 1926 when he lost faith in German politics), Schweizerischer Schriftstellerverein (''Swiss Writers Club''; Zuerich). *Awards, honors:* Wiener Bauernfeldpreis, 1904; Fontanepreis, 1920, for *Demian* (Hesse declined this award as it was intended for new writers); Gottfried-Keller Prize for literature (Zuerich), 1936; Nobel Prize for Literature, 1946; Goethe-Preis (Frankfurt), 1946; honorary doctorate, University of Bern, 1947; Wilhelm Raabe-Preis, 1950; Peace Prize of the German Book Trade, 1955; Knight of the Order Pour le Merite (Friedensklasse), 1955.

WRITINGS—Works translated into English: Peter Camenzind (novel), S. Fischer, 1904, translation by Walter J. Strachan, P. Owen, 1961, translation by Michael Roloff, Farrar, Straus, 1969; *Unterm Rad* (novel), S. Fischer, 1906, translation by W. J. Strachan published as *The Prodigy,* Vision Press, 1957, translation by M. Roloff published as *Beneath the Wheel,* Farrar, Straus, 1969; *Gertrud* (novel), A. Langen, 1910, translation by Hilda Rosner published as *Gertrude,* Vision Press, 1955, revised translation, Farrar, Straus, 1969; *Rosshalde,* S. Fischer, 1914, translation by Ralph Manheim, Farrar, Straus, 1970.

Knulp: Drei Geschichten aus dem Leben Knulps (short fiction; published in part in 1908), S. Fischer, 1915, new edition with introduction, notes, and vocabulary by William Diamond and Christel B. Schomaker, Oxford University Press, 1932, translation by R. Manheim published as *Knulp: Three Tales from the Life of Knulp,* Farrar, Straus, 1971; *Maerchen,* S. Fischer, 1919, translation by Denver Lindley published as *Strange News from Another Star and Other Tales,* Farrar, Straus, 1972; (under pseudonym Emil Sinclair) *Demian: Die Geschichte von Emil Sinclairs Jugend* (novel), S. Fischer, 1919, translation by N. H. Friday published as *Demian,* Boni & Liveright, 1923, new edition with foreword by Thomas Mann published as *Demian: The Story of a Youth,* Holt, 1948, new translation by M. Roloff and Michael Lebeck, with introduction by T. Mann, published as *Demian: The Story of Emil Sinclair's Youth,* Harper, 1965.

Wanderung, Aufzeichnungen: Mit farbigen Bildern vom Verfasser (nonfiction), S. Fischer, 1920, translation by James Wright published as *Wandering: Notes and Sketches,* Farrar, Straus, 1972; *Blick ins Chaos* (three essays), Verlag Seldwyla, 1920, translation by Stephen Hudson published as *In Sight of Chaos,* Verlag Seldwyla, 1923; *Klingsors letzter Sommer* (three tales), S. Fischer, 1920, translation by Richard Winston and Clara Winston published as *Klingsor's Last Summer,* Farrar, Straus, 1970; *Siddhartha: Eine indische Dichtung* (novel), S. Fischer, 1922, translation by H. Rosner published as *Siddhartha,* New Directions, 1951; *Der Steppenwolf,* S. Fischer, 1927, translation by Basil Creighton published as *Steppenwolf,* Holt, 1929, revised edition, 1963.

Hesse in 1926. (Photograph by Gret Widmann.)

Narziss und Goldmund, S. Fischer, 1930, translation by Geoffrey Dunlop published as *Death and the Lover*, Dodd, 1932 (later published in England by P. Owen as *Goldmund*, 1959, and as *Narziss and Goldmund*, 1965), new translation by Ursule Molinaro published as *Narcissus and Goldmund*, Farrar, Straus, 1968; *Die Morgenlandfahrt: Eine Erzaehlung*, S. Fischer, 1932, translation by H. Rosner published as *The Journey to the East*, Vision Press, 1956, Noonday, 1957.

Das Glasperlenspiel: Versuch einer Lebensbeschreibung des Magister Ludi Josef Knecht samt Knechts hintelassenen Schriften, two volumes, Fretz & Wasmuth, 1943, translation by Mervyn Savill published as *Magister Ludi*, Holt, 1949, 2nd edition, Aldus, 1957, new translation by R. Winston and C. Winston published as *The Glass Bead Game (Magister Ludi)*, Holt, 1969, and as *Magister Ludi (The Glass Bead Game)*, Bantam, 1970; *Krieg und Frieden: Betrachtungen zu Krieg und Politik seit dem Jahre 1914* (twenty-nine essays; nonfiction), Fretz & Wasmuth, 1946, supplemented edition, [Berlin], 1949, translation by R. Manheim published as *If the War Goes On: Reflections on War and Politics*, Farrar, Straus, 1971; *Kinderseele und Ladidel* (two tales), edited, with introduction, notes, and vocabulary by W. M. Dutton, Harrap, 1948, Heath, 1952; *Zwei Erzaehlungen: Der Novalis [und] Der Zwerg*, edited with introduction, notes, and vocabulary by Anna Jacobson and Anita Asher, Appleton, 1948, 2nd edition, 1950.

Drei Erzaehlungen (three tales), edited by Waldo C. Peebles, American Book Co., 1950; *Spaete Prosa* (collected tales, 1944-50), Suhrkamp, 2nd edition, 1967, American text edition edited by Theodore Ziolkowski, Harcourt, 1966; *Der Briefwech-*

sel: Hermann Hesse-Thomas Mann, edited by Anni Carlsson, Suhrkamp, 1968, translated by R. Manheim, published as *The Hesse/Mann Letters: The Correspondence of Hermann Hesse and Thomas Mann 1910-1955*, Harper, 1975.

Poems, selected and translated by James Wright, Farrar, Straus, 1970; *Stories of Five Decades*, edited with introduction by T. Ziolkowski, translated by R. Manheim and Denver Lindley, Farrar, Straus, 1972; *Autobiographical Writings*, edited wth introduction by T. Ziolkowski, translated by D. Lindley, Farrar, Straus, 1972; *Eigensinn: Autobiographische Schriften*, compiled with afterword by Siegfried Unseld, Suhrkamp, 1972; *Poems*, translated by James Wright, Bantam, 1974; *My Belief: Essays on Life and Art*, edited with introduction by T. Ziolkowski, translated by D. Lindley and R. Manheim, Farrar, Straus, 1974; *Reflections: Selections from His Books and Letters*, compiled by Volker Michels, translated by R. Manheim, Farrar, Straus, 1974; *Tales of Student Life*, edited with introduction by T. Ziolkowski, translated by R. Manheim, Farrar, Straus, 1975.

For a complete bibliography see *Contemporary Authors, Permanent Series*, Volume 2, Gale, 1965.

ADAPTATIONS: ''Siddhartha,'' Lotus Films, 1972, (cassette), Newman Communications, 1986; ''Steppenwolf,'' D/R Films, Inc., 1974, (cassette), Caedmon; ''Beneath the Wheel'' (cassette), G. K. Hall, 1985; ''Hesse between Music'' (cassette), Caedmon.

SIDELIGHTS: Born **July 2, 1877** in Calw, Germany. ''I was born toward the end of modern times, shortly before the return of the Middle Ages, with the sign of the Archer on the ascendant and Jupiter in favorable aspect. My birth took place at an early hour of the evening on a warm day in July, and it is the temperature of that hour that I have unconsciously loved and sought throughout my life; when it was lacking I have sorely missed it. I could never live in cold countries and all the voluntary journeys of my life have been directed toward the south. I was the child of pious parents, whom I loved tenderly and would have loved even more tenderly if I had not

Hesse's birthplace in Calw.

very early been introduced to the Fourth Commandment. Unfortunately, commandments have always had a disastrous effect on me, however right and well meant they may be—though by nature a lamb and docile as a soap bubble, I have always behaved rebelliously toward commandments of every sort, especially during my youth. All I needed was to hear 'thou shalt' and everything in me rose up and I became obdurate. As can be imagined, this peculiarity had a far-reaching and unfortunate effect during my school years.

''I was an active and happy boy, playing with the beautiful, many-colored world, at home everywhere, not less with animals and plants than in the primeval forest of my own fantasies and dreams, happy in my powers and abilities, more delighted than consumed by my burning desires. I exercised many magic powers at that time without knowing it, much more completely than I was ever able to do later on. It was easy for me to win love, easy to exercise influence over others, I had no trouble playing the role of ringleader or of the admired one or the man of mystery. For years at a time I kept my younger friends and

Hesse, the painter.

relations respectfully convinced of my literally magic powers, of my mastery over demons, of my title to crowns and buried treasures. For a long time I lived in paradise, although my parents early made me acquainted with the serpent. Long enduring was my childish dream that the world belonged to me, that only the present existed, that everything was disposed about me to be a beautiful game.

''Not by parents and teachers alone was I educated, but by higher, more arcane and mysterious powers as well, among them the god Pan, who stood in my grandfather's glass cabinet in the guise of a little dancing Hindu idol. This deity, and others too, took an interest in me during my childhood years, and long before I could read and write they so filled me with age-old Eastern images and ideas that later, whenever I met a Hindu or Chinese sage, it was like a reunion, a homecoming. And yet I am a European . . . and all my life have zealously practiced the Western virtues of impetuosity, greed and unquenchable curiosity. Fortunately, like most children, I had learned what is most valuable, most indispensable for life before my school years began, taught by apple trees, by rain and sun, river and woods, bees and beetles, taught by the god Pan, taught by the dancing idol in my grandfather's treasure room. I knew my way around in the world, I associated fearlessly with animals and stars. I was at home in orchards and with fishes in the water, and I could already sing a good number of songs. I could do magic too, a skill that I unfortunately soon forgot and had to relearn at a very advanced age—and I possessed all the legendary wisdom of childhood.

''To this, formal schooling was now added, and it came easy to me, was amusing. The school prudently did not concern

The face struck me at that moment as neither masculine nor childlike, neither old nor young, but somehow a thousand years old.... ■ (Jacket illustration from *Demian* by Hermann Hesse.)

itself with those important accomplishments that are indispensable to life, but chiefly with frivolous and attractive entertainments, in which I often took pleasure, and with bits of information, many that have remained loyally with me all my life; for instance, today I still know beautiful, witty Latin sayings, verses, and maxims and the number of inhabitants in many cities in all quarters of the globe, not as they are today, of course, but as they were in the 1880's.

"Up to my thirteenth year I never seriously considered what I should one day become or what profession I should choose. Like all boys, I loved and envied many callings: the hunter, the raftsman, the railroad conductor, the high-wire performer, the Arctic explorer. My greatest preference by far, however, would have been to be a magician. This was the deepest, most profoundly felt direction of my impulses, springing from a certain dissatisfaction with what people call 'reality' and what seemed to me at times simply a silly conspiracy of the grown-ups; very early I felt a definite rejection of this reality, at times timorous, at times scornful, and the burning wish to change it by magic, to transform it, to heighten it.

"... From my thirteenth year on, it was clear to me that I wanted to be either a poet or nothing at all. To this realization, however, was gradually added a further, painful insight. One could become a teacher, minister, doctor, mechanic, merchant, post-office employee, or a musician, painter, architect;

there was a path to every profession in the world, there were prerequisites, a school, a course of instruction for the beginner. Only for the poet there was nothing of the sort! It was permissible and even considered an honor to be a poet; that is, to be successful and famous as a poet—unfortunately by that time one was usually dead. But to become a poet was impossible, and to want to become one was ridiculous and shameful, as I very soon found out. I had quickly learned what there was to be learned from the situation: a poet was simply something you were allowed to be but not to become. Further: native poetic talent and interest in poetry were suspect in teachers' eyes; you were either distrusted for it or ridiculed, often indeed subjected to deadly insults. With the poet it was exactly the same as with the hero, and with all strong, handsome, high-spirited, non-commonplace figures and enterprises: in the past they were magnificent, every school book was filled with their praises; in the present, in real life, people hated them, and presumably teachers were especially selected and trained to prevent as far as possible the rise of magnificent, free human beings and the accomplishment of great and splendid deeds.

"... This conflict had just begun, my conduct in my parents' house as well as in school left so much to be desired that I was banished to a Latin school in another city. A year later I became a pupil in a theological seminary, learned to write the Hebrew alphabet, and was already on the point of grasping what a *dagesh forte implicitum* is, when suddenly from inside

(From the movie "Steppenwolf," starring Max von Sydow. Copyright © 1974 by D/R Films, Inc.)

Then they sailed across, were driven far out, but directed the raft upstream to the other bank. ■ (From *Siddhartha* by Hermann Hesse. Photograph from the movie adaptation. Produced by Lotus Films, 1972.)

me storms arose that led to flight from the monastery school, punishment by strict imprisonment, and dismissal from the seminary.

"Then for a while I struggled to advance my studies at a *gymnasium;* however, the lock-up and expulsion were the end there too. After that, for three days I was a merchant's apprentice, ran away again and for several days and nights, to the great distress of my parents, disappeared. For a period of six months I was my father's assistant, for a year and a half I was an employee in a mechanical workshop and tower-clock factory.

"In short, for more than four years everything that was attempted with me went wrong; no school would keep me, in no course of instruction did I last for long. Every attempt to make a useful human being out of me ended in failure, several times in shame and scandal, in flight or expulsion, and yet everywhere they admitted that I had ability and even a reasonable amount of determination! Also I was nothing if not industrious—the high virtue of idleness I have always regarded with awe, but I have never mastered it. In my sixteenth year, after my school career had ended in failure, I consciously and energetically began my own education, and it was my good fortune and delight that in my father's house was my grand-

father's huge library, a whole hall full of old books, which contained among other things all of eighteenth-century German literature and philosophy with a persistence that would have abundantly sufficed for any normal college career.

"Then I became a bookseller in order finally to earn my own bread. I had always been on better terms with books than with the vises and cogwheels with which I had tortured myself as a mechanic. At first, swimming in modern, indeed the most modern, literature and in fact being overwhelmed by it was an almost intoxicating joy. But after a while I noticed that in matters of the spirit, a life simply in the present, in the modern and most modern, is unbearable and meaningless, that the life of the spirit is made possible only by constant reference to what is past, to history, to the ancient and primeval. And so after that first joy was exhausted it became a necessity for me to return from my submersion in novelties to what is old; this I accomplished by moving from the bookshop to an antique shop. . . ." [Hermann Hesse, *Autobiographical Writings,* edited by Theodore Ziolkowski, Farrar, Straus, 1972.[1]]

1904. *Peter Camenzind* brought Hesse immediate fame and marked the beginning of his reputation as a great writer. "My intention [with *Camenzind*], as is now known, was to familiarize modern man with the overflowing and silent life of nature. I wanted to teach him to listen to the earth's heartbeat, to participate in the life of nature, and not to overlook in the press of his own little destiny that we are not gods, not creatures of our own making, but children, parts of the earth and of the cosmic whole. I wanted to remind people that, like the songs of the poet and our night-time dreams, rivers, seas, drifting clouds, and storms are symbols and bearers of our yearnings, yearnings that embrace the earth and the heavens and whose object is the undiluted certainty of citizenship and the immortality of all living things. . . . '' [Bernhard Zeller, *Portrait of Hesse: An Illustrated Biography,* translated by Mark Hollebone, Herder & Herder, 1971.[2]]

Summer, 1904. Married Maria Bernoulli. Three sons were born to this union.

With the royalties received from the sale of *Peter Camenzind,* Hesse was now able to give up his job and pursue a full-time literary career. "Thus, amid so many storms and sacrifices, my goal had now been reached: however impossible it may have appeared, I had become a poet and had, it would seem, won the long stubborn battle with the world. The bitterness of my years of schooling and preparation, during which I had often been very close to ruin, was now forgotten or laughed at—even my relations and friends, who had previously been in despair about me, now smiled encouragingly. I had triumphed, and now if I did the silliest or most trivial thing it was thought charming, just as I was greatly charmed by myself. Now for

the first time I realized in what dreadful isolation, asceticism, and danger I had lived year after year; the warm breeze of recognition did me good and I began to be a contented man.''[1]

1912. Family moved from Gaienhofen to Bern. "Southwestern Germany and northern Switzerland are home to me, and that the area is crossed by various national borders is something that I have often enough been made aware of, in small and in big things, but deep down I have never been able to regard these borders as natural things. Home for me lay to either side of the Upper Rhine, no matter whether the area was known as Switzerland, Baden, or Wuerttemberg.''[2]

Demian was Hesse's attempt toward self interpretation. "The Life of every man is a way to himself, an attempt at a way, the suggestion of a path. No man has ever been utterly himself, yet every man strives to be so. . . . There are many who never become human. . . . Yet each one represents an attempt on the part of nature to create a human being. We enjoy a common origin in our mothers; we all come from the same pit. But each individual, who is·himself an experimental throw from the depths, strives towards his own goal. We can understand each other; but each person is able to interpret himself to himself alone.''[2]

1918. Hesse's household collapsed; his wife was in a mental institution. Any attempt to reconcile the marriage after her release was out of the question. His three sons were boarded

(From the movie "Siddhartha." Produced by Lotus Films, 1972.)

out with friends or in schools. Hesse moved to Casa Camuzzi, Montagnola. The marriage was dissolved four years later.

Beginning in **1923** Hesse began his annual visits to Baden, a health resort, to manage bouts of serious rheumatism. ''Inspired partially by the unaccustomed leisure of health resort and hotel life, and partially by a few fresh acquaintanceships with people and books, I experienced in those summer months a mood of introspection and self-examination midway between *Siddhartha* and *Steppenwolf*, a mood in which I could play the spectator both of myself and of my immediate environment, an ironic and playful desire to inspect and analyze the fleeting moment, a period of suspense between sluggish indolence and intensive work.''[2]

January, 1924. Married Ruth Wenger, daughter of Swiss writer Lisa Wenger. ''. . . I neither want marriage particularly nor am I well suited to it, but in this connection life and destiny are more powerful than my thoughts and wishes.''[2] His second marriage did not last long and was officially dissolved in 1927.

1931. Married Austrian art historian Ninon Auslaender Dolbin with whom he lived for the rest of his life. Moved out of Casa Camuzzi. ''In this house I enjoyed and suffered from the most intense loneliness, gained comfort from writing and painting much, and became more fondly familiar with the place than with any other since childhood. In my painting and my writing I have frequently expressed the gratitude I owe this house.''[2]

Hesse with his wife, Ninon.

Dr. H. C. Bodmer built a house according to Hesse's own design and presented it to him for his lifetime—''Casa Hesse'' in the village of Montagnola. ''To be fully at home somewhere, to love a particular piece of land, and to build on it rather than merely observe and paint it, to participate in the unassuming joy of the farmers and shepherds, in the exuberance of the pastoral scene, in the two-thousand-year-old rhythm of the rural calendar, struck me as a fine and enviable lot, even though, having once tried it myself, I had discovered it was not enough to bring happiness. But once more the opportunity had arisen, had fallen into my lap like a ripe chestnut falls from the tree onto the hat of a passer by: one had only to open the fruit and eat it. Contrary to all expectations, I was once again a settled man and held a piece of land if not as my own at least as a lifelong tenant. No sooner was our house built and we in proud possession of it than another stretch of peasant life began, so familiar to me from previous memories . . . [a] feeling of kinship with flowers, trees, earth, source, the feeling of responsibility for a small piece of land, for fifty trees, for a few flower beds, for fig and peach trees.''[2]

Hesse's library contained several thousand books on world literature. It was his feeling that studying literature was a way of ''giving life meaning, interpreting the past and preparing oneself to meet the future without fear. . . . Familiarizing oneself gradually with the massive treasury of thoughts, experiences, symbols, fantasies, and utopian dreams that the past has bequeathed to us in the works of writers and thinkers of many nations. It is an endless journey . . . its goal is not merely to read and know as much as possible but to acquire some inkling of the breadth and richness of what man has conceived and striven for by studying a personal selection of his greatest books.''[2] The true reader, Hesse believed, will approach his study with love: ''Reading without love, knowledge without respect, formation without deep personal involvement, are some of the most deadly sins against the spirit.''[2]

(Cover photograph by A. K. Coomaraswamy from *Siddhartha* by Hermann Hesse.)

''I set no store by contemporary literature. I appreciate of course that every period must have its own literature, just as it will have its own politics, ideals, and fashions. But I cannot rid myself of the conviction that contemporary writing is something insubstantial and sorry, a seed grown on poor soil, doubtless interesting and full of problems worthy of pursuit, but hardly something that can mature or that is capable of producing long-term results. Consequently, I can only consider the work of contemporary German writers (my own included) to be in some way inadequate and derivative; I detect everywhere a suspicion of routine, lifeless models of what things should be. On the other hand, a transitional literature, writing that has become problematical and uncertain, can perform the useful function of confessing with maximum honesty its own poverty and the poverty of its times. There are, therefore, many fine well-structured books by contemporary writers that I can no longer enjoy or welcome, whereas I can feel sympathy for several crudely written books by our youngest writers because of their attempt at unreserved sincerity. . . . This is the tension that goes right through my own little world and my writing. . . .''[2]

1942. *Das Glasperlenspiel (The Glass Bead Game)* was published in Switzerland. ''The idea that originally fired me was the notion of reincarnation as the vehicle through which to express stability in change, the continuity in tradition, and the life of the spirit generally. And then one day, many years before I actually started writing, I visualized a particular but supratemporal life history: I imagined a man who in several incarnations experiences the great epochs of human history.''[2] The book was published in Germany after World War II.

One of Hesse's last poems written in the spring of 1961 ends with the lines:

> ''What you loved and what you strove for
> What you dreamed and what you lived through,
> Do you know if it was joy or suffering?
> G sharp and A flat, E flat or D sharp—
> Are they distinguishable to the ear?''[2]

Hesse at his desk. (Photograph by Martin Hesse.)

On **August 9, 1962** Hesse died at the age of eighty-five of complications of leukemia. He reflected toward the end of his life that the three most powerful and constant influences on him had been "the Christian and almost totally un-nationalistic spirit [of his paternal home], reading of the great Chinese writers [and] the influence of the only historian I was ever devoted to and whom I could feel trust and respect for: Jacob Burckhardt [intellectual mentor and cultural arbiter of Basel's learned society]."[2]

The sixties enjoyed a revival of the works of Hermann Hesse in the United States with the suggestion of Henry Miller to his followers of Hesse's novel *Siddhartha,* which subsequently enjoyed a greater readership than it had in its original during its thirty years of existence. *Steppenwolf,* however, became a significant book for America. It reflected the attitudes of the new Beat Generation and was described by its guru Timothy Leary as a psychedelic journey. The interest in Hesse was not limited to the hippie culture alone, but spread throughout the U.S. to conventional students in secondary schools and universities as well. A wave of commercialism produced such articles as T-shirts carrying the motif of Hesse's novels, his stories were reduced to comic book form, a night club and a rock group adopted the name "Steppenwolf" and other commercial ventures of a mass culture Hesse so despised followed.

HOBBIES AND OTHER INTERESTS: Watercolor painting, music.

FOR MORE INFORMATION SEE: Stanley J. Kunitz and Howard Haycraft, editors, *Twentieth Century Authors,* H. W. Wilson, 1942; Gustav Emil Mueller, *Philosophy of Literature,* Philosophical Library, 1948; S. J. Kunitz, editor, *Twentieth Century Authors,* first supplement, H. W. Wilson, 1955; Henry Stuart Hughes, *Consciousness and Society: The Reorientation of European Social Thought, 1890-1930,* Knopf, 1958; Joseph Mileck, *Hermann Hesse and His Critics,* University of North Carolina Press, 1958.

Oskar Seidlin, *Essays in German and Comparative Literature,* University of North Carolina Press, 1961; *Current Biography,* H. W. Wilson, 1962; Alex Natan, editor, *German Men of Letters, Volume II,* Oswald Wolff, 1963; Ralph Freedman, *The Lyrical Novel: Studies in Hermann Hesse, Andre Gide, and Virginia Woolf,* Princeton University Press, 1963; Ernst Rose, *Faith from the Abyss,* New York University Press, 1965; Mark Boulby, *Hermann Hesse: His Mind and Art,* Cornell University Press, 1967; Theodore Ziolkowski, *The Novels of Hermann Hesse: A Study in Theme and Structure,* Princeton University Press, 1967; F. Baumer, *Hermann Hesse,* Ungar, 1969.

G. W. Field, *Hermann Hesse,* Twayne, 1970; B. Zeller, *Portrait of Hesse: An Illustrated Biography,* translation by Mark Hollebone, McGraw, 1971; M. Serrano, *C. G. Jung and Hermann Hesse,* Routledge & Kegan Paul, 1971; T. Ziolkowski, editor, *Hesse,* Prentice-Hall, 1973; R. H. Farquharson, *An Outline of the Works of Hermann Hesse,* Forum House, 1973; Carolyn Riley, editor, *Contemporary Literary Criticism,* Gale, Volume I, 1973, Volume II, 1974, Volume III, 1975, Volume VI, 1976.

Grown-ups never understand anything for themselves, and it is tiresome for children to be always and forever explaining things to them.

—Antoine de Saint-Exupéry

HICKS, Clifford B. 1920-

PERSONAL: Born August 10, 1920, in Marshalltown, Iowa; son of Nathan LeRoy and Kathryn Marie (Carson) Hicks; married Rachel G. Reimer, May 12, 1945; children: David, Douglas, Gary. *Education:* Northwestern University, B.A. (cum laude), 1942.

CAREER: Popular Mechanics, Lombard, Ill., member of editorial staff, 1945-60, editor, 1960-63, special projects editor, 1963-68, editor of *Popular Mechanics Do-It-Yourself Encyclopedia,* 1968-85. *Military service:* U.S. Marine Corps Reserve, 1942-45, became major, received Silver Star. *Member:* Sigma Delta Chi. *Awards, honors: First Boy on the Moon* was named Best Juvenile Book of the Year by Friends of American Writers, 1960; *Alvin Fernald, Superweasel* was chosen as a Children's Book of the Year, 1974, by the Child Study Association of America; Charlie May Simon Award, 1979, for *Alvin's Swap Shop.*

WRITINGS—Published by Holt, except as indicated: *Do-It-Yourself Materials Guide,* Popular Mechanics Press, 1955; *First Boy on the Moon* (illustrated by George Wilde), Winston, 1959; *The Marvelous Inventions of Alvin Fernald,* 1960; *Alvin's Secret Code* (illustrated by Bill Sokol), 1963; *The World Above,* 1965; *Alvin Fernald, Foreign Trader* (illustrated by B. Sokol), 1966; *Alvin Fernald, Mayor for a Day* (illustrated by Leonard Shortall), 1970; *Peter Potts,* Dutton, 1971; *Alvin Fernald, Superweasel* (illustrated by B. Sokol), 1974; *Alvin's Swap Shop* (illustrated by B. Sokol), 1976, new edition (illustrated by Lisl

Prince was the sorriest, skinniest, ugliest lion I ever did see. ■ (From *Pop and Peter Potts* by Clifford B. Hicks. Illustrated by Jim Spence.)

Weil), Scholastic, 1979; *Alvin Fernald, TV Anchorman* (illustrated by Laura Hartman), 1980; *The Wacky World of Alvin Fernald* (illustrated by L. Hartman), 1981; *Pop and Peter Potts* (illustrated by Jim Spence), Holt, 1984; *Alvin Fernald, Master of a Thousand Disguises* (illustrated by Eileen Christelow), Holt, 1986.

Editor of *Popular Mechanics Do-It-Yourself Encyclopedia,* 1968-85. Contributor of fiction and nonfiction to magazines.

ADAPTATIONS: "Marvelous Inventions of Alvin Fernald" presented on "The Wonderful World of Disney," NBC-TV, 1974, Disney Cable, 1985; "Alvin Fernald, Mayor for a Day," presented on "The Wonderful World of Disney," NBC-TV, 1974, Disney Cable, 1985.

FOR MORE INFORMATION SEE: Dorothy A. Marquardt and Martha E. Ward, *Authors of Books for Young People,* 2nd edition, Scarecrow, 1971.

HIGHAM, David (Michael) 1949-

PERSONAL: Born August 16, 1949, in Barking, Essex, England; son of Robert Walter (a handyman) and Heather (a homemaker; maiden name, Garmen) Higham; married Viktoria Johnson (a graphic designer), August 13, 1979; children: Ignatz. *Education:* Attended Thurrock Technical College, 1965-67, and Central School of Art, London, 1967-70. *Home:* 27 Ryedale, East Dulwich, London SE22 OQW, England. *Agent:*

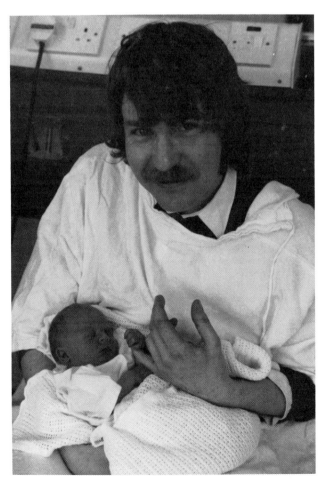

DAVID HIGHAM

Margaret Hanbury, 27 Walcot Square, London SE11 4UB, England.

CAREER: Carpenter, 1972-82; free-lance illustrator, 1976—.

WRITINGS—Self-illustrated: G. Was a Giant, Methuen, 1981.

Illustrator: Dorothy Edwards, *Here's Sam,* Methuen, 1979; Rayner Sussex, *The Magic Apple,* Methuen, 1979; Ian Fennell, *Robottom the Robot,* Methuen, 1980; Olive Jones, *The Tom and Sandy Book* (four books), Methuen, 1980; R. Sussex, *King Otto's Apprentice,* Methuen, 1983; Carol Watson, *Opposites,* Usborne, 1983; C. Watson, *Shapes,* EDC, 1983; C. Watson, *Sizes,* EDC, 1983; C. Watson, *Simple Sums,* Usborne, 1984; C. Watson, *1.2.3.,* Usborne, 1984; C. Watson, *Colours,* Usborne, 1984; C. Watson, *Telling the Time,* Usborne, 1984; Lee Pressman, *Muckfield's Midnight Monster Match,* Deutsch, 1985; Alison Prince, *A Job for Merv,* Belitha Press, 1986; L. Pressman, *Muckfield and the Muckold Menace,* Deutsch, 1987; L. Pressman, *Muckfield Marooned on Muckatoa,* Deutsch, 1988. Illustrator of fifteen Rainbow programmes for Thames' Television. Contributor of illustrations to periodicals, including *Home Computer Course.*

WORK IN PROGRESS: Illustrating Anne Fine's *Crummy Mummy and Me,* for Deutsch.

SIDELIGHTS: "Until the age of nine I lived in Dagenham on the banks (or mud flats) of the Thames. Dagenham to an English person means one thing, Ford's car plant. Dagenham is dull and uniform, all the houses look the same for miles around, the streets are lined with the same mutilated trees and the same tarmac pavements and privet hedges.

"I owe everything to Dagenham. Sensory deprivation drove me indoors where I began to draw and build my own world. I am what you might call a Cockney, that is, I have an East End London accent and working class origins.

"I lived above an electrical shop and next door was a newspaper shop. These provided all my early influences as well as comics and television. Every now and then I would see some countryside. I like the countryside, but I always feel slightly uneasy in it. We had a weekend shack, in a field but it wasn't of interest to me.

"My Aunt Greta had a beautiful house and a big garden with a pond in it (with a small island and a boat). It was contained nature, controlled, contrived, and neat with some wild corners. It could be a description of the sort of country that appears in my drawings.

"When I was twelve, I went on a school trip to Greece. We had to travel across Europe to Genoa to catch the boat. The whole trip was fantastic. There was a sense of amazement that I doubt I will ever recapture. But the most amazing experience was the first. The channel crossing was rough and we boarded the train in Calais at night in the dark. I went to sleep on the train, but I awoke and it was still dark. I pulled back the blind to look out and saw Switzerland in moonlight. We passed frozen waterfalls the height of skyscrapers and mountains and villages and pine forests. I watched until it was light. I couldn't sleep, I couldn't get enough. I have never lost my love of such countryside.

"My real love has always been industrial dereliction—disused factories, dumps, derelict buildings, old clay pits. This may sound strange, but you must realise that in the south of England where I live there is very little wild country. For hundreds

Self-portrait of David Higham with his cat, Putzi.

of years, right back to the Doomsday Book, every hedge, tree, hut, and field has been mapped out. The only forgotten places are the old industrial sights that nature is slowly claiming back. They will disappear, of course, but for the moment there's a magic about them.

"My wife is half Austrian and we go [to Austria] as often as we can afford. I always thought I could live nowhere but England, but now I admit I would love to live there.

"I now live in London. I like London, I suppose, because I know it, yet there are always little corners of it to discover, funny old shops or parks, or derelict sights. In front of our house is a typical suburban London street, but when you go through to the back, you think you're in the country. It's actually a vast disused Victorian graveyard. Ideal for me . . . forgotten nature, wild and derelict.

"My secondary education was a nightmare, I hated it. For two years at technical college I thought I had found something worthwhile, people who cared. I was doing the art course. I was going to be a fine artist, a painter. I began reading properly and collecting books. Before this time I didn't read books at all. If it didn't have pictures, I wasn't interested.

"At Central School of Art I wanted to make films. I did animation which wasn't part of the official course. I spent all my time doing this and for this reason I failed my diploma. On leaving I suddenly lost my desire to make films. I wanted to write. I tried writing children's stories. After three or four years I realised that I was not a writer. I then decided I should concentrate on illustration. This was the first good idea I had had in years.

"I made my living doing various silly jobs. But eventually I became a carpenter. I was a very good carpenter, self-taught but conscientious. I could have earned better or easier money

in an office, but I didn't like that sort of work. I needed to make something with my hands and something that would survive.

"After several years of struggle (gentle struggle) I had my first book accepted. I slowly phased out the carpentry work and today I am doing illustration full time.

"As for my 'technique,' I'm not sure I have one. To tell the truth I am a mediocre artist. I have to struggle to achieve what better craftsmen find easy. I still enjoy succeeding, making a little progress, [creating] something 'like' what I see in my mind's eye, but, in fact, the results rarely come close. That is what keeps me going, and, of course, it is the only thing I can do, so you could say I have little choice.

"I spend a lot of time 'roughing out' an illustration on layout paper. I make several versions—redrawing, tracing from other roughs via a light box, sliding in characters and props until I am reasonably satisfied with the result. This is the hardest part, the drawing. The rest of the process is positively therapeutic.

"The drawing is then 'burnished' onto a piece of watercolour board. Last minute alterations are made in faint pencil. The picture is built up slowly in watercolour, some parts may be outlined in coloured ink. Often I dab at what I have just filled in with blotting paper—its a way of half changing your mind.

"These days I sometimes use an airbrush for certain things: large areas, backgrounds, skies, etc. I hate it. It's a beast; it retires the therapy, and I get the process over with as soon as possible.

"While doing all this I'm cocooned in headphones, listening to either BBC-Radio 4 or BBC world service.

"I could give you a list as long as your arm of influences . . . artists, writers, illustrators. I will try and keep the list short— Chinese landscapes of the northern Sung period, Japanese woodblock prints, Da Vinci, Dürer, Breughel, R. Crumb, Heath Robinson, Edmund Dulac, Norman Rockwell, Frank Bellemy (an illustrator of the 'Eagle' Boys comics), Bill Elder of *Mad* magazine, Hogarth, Bosch, Walt Disney, Mervyn Peake, William Faulkner, Tolkien, Hesse, Jorge Luis Borges, Vonnegut, etc.''

HURWOOD, Bernhardt J.   1926-1987 (Father Xavier, Mallory T. Knight, D. Gunther Wilde)

OBITUARY NOTICE—See sketch in *SATA* Volume 12: Born July 22, 1926, in New York, N.Y.; died of cancer January 23, 1987, in New York, N.Y. Translator, editor, and author. Hurwood worked as a film editor for companies in Chicago, New York, and Berkeley, California between 1949 and 1952, and subsequently held odd jobs before turning to writing full-time in 1962. He wrote more than sixty books, often focusing on the supernatural. Among his books for juveniles are *Ghosts, Ghouls, and Other Horrors, Vampires, Werewolves, and Other Demons, Haunted Houses, Chilling Ghost Stories,* and *Eerie Tales of Terror and Dread.* Under the name Mallory T. Knight, he wrote the "Man from T.O.M.C.A.T." book series, as well as *Casebook: Exorcism and Possession,* under the name Father Xavier, and *Deviation,* under the name D. Gunther Wilde. Other writings include *My Savage Muse, The Whole Sex Catalogue, Writing Becomes Electronic: Successful Authors Tell How They Write in the Age of the Computer,* translations of medieval stories, and nearly two hundred scripts for animated cartoons.

FOR MORE INFORMATION SEE: Contemporary Authors, Volumes 25-28, revised edition, Gale, 1971; *Science Fiction and Fantasy Literature,* Volume 2: *Contemporary Science Fiction Authors II,* Gale, 1979. Obituaries: *New York Times,* January 26, 1987; *New York Daily News,* January 27, 1987.

JAMES, Robin (Irene) 1953-

PERSONAL: Born September 24, 1953, in Seattle, Wash.; daughter of Robert Leroy (an artist) and Irene Elizabeth (an artist; maiden name, Weinberger) James; married Michael George Cosgrove (president of Mechanical Corporation), July 1, 1980. *Home:* Snohomish, Wash.

CAREER: Free-lance artist, 1971—. *Member:* American Humane Association, Animal Protection Institute, National Wildlife Federation, International Wildlife Federation.

WRITINGS—"Baby Animal" series; all self-illustrated; all published by Price Stern: *Baby Pets,* 1984; *Baby Forest Animals,* 1984; *Baby Zoo Animals,* 1984; *Baby Farm Animals,* 1984; *Baby Puppies,* 1985; *Baby Kittens,* 1985; *Baby Horses,* 1986; *Baby Unicorns,* 1986.

Illustrator; all written by Stephen Cosgrove; all published by Price Stern: *Tale of Three Tails,* 1974; *Wheedle on the Needle,*

ROBIN JAMES

1974; *Serendipity,* 1974; *Muffin Muncher,* 1974; *The Dream Tree,* 1974; *Little Mouse on the Prairie,* 1975; *Cap'n Smudge,* 1975; *The Gnome from Nome,* 1975; *In Search of the Saveopotomas,* 1975; *Morgan and Me,* 1975; *Bangalee,* 1976; *Creole,* 1976; *Kartusch,* 1976; *Jake O'Shawnasey,* 1976; *Hucklebug,* 1976; *Gabby,* 1977; *Leo the Lop,* 1977; *Leo the Lop: Tail Two,* 1977; *Leo the Lop: Tail Three,* 1977; *Snaffles,* 1978; *Flutterby,* 1978; *Catundra,* 1978; *Feather Fin,* 1978; *Grampa-Lop,* 1979; *Shimmeree,* 1979.

Nitter Pitter, 1980; *Raz-Ma-Taz,* 1980; *Trafalgar True,* 1980; *Trapper,* 1980; *Maui-Maui,* 1981; *Ming Ling,* 1981; *Tee-Tee,* 1981; *Morgan and Yew,* 1982; *Morgan Mine,* 1982; *Morgan Morning,* 1983; *Flutterby Fly,* 1983; *Kiyomi,* 1983; *Minikin,* 1984; *Dragolin,* 1984; *Squeakers,* 1985; *Glitterby Baby,* 1985; *Jingle Bear,* 1985; *Crabby Gabby,* 1985; *Buttermilk,* 1986; *Fanny,* 1986; *Pish Posh,* 1986; *Mumkin,* 1986; *Misty Morgan,* 1987; *Buttermilk-Bear,* 1987; *Memily,* 1987; *Crickle-Crack,* 1987.

ADAPTATIONS: "Catundra" (cassette), Society for Visual Education, 1979; "Kartusch" (cassette), Society for Visual Education, 1979; "Little Mouse on the Prairie" (cassette), Society for Visual Education, 1979; "Nitter Pitter" (cassette), Society for Visual Education, 1980; "Baby Horses and Unicorns in Rhyme and Song" (filmstrips with cassettes), Society for Visual Education, 1986.

Cassettes; all produced by Price Stern: "Flutterby," 1984; "Gabby," 1984; "Grampa-Lop," 1984; "Leo the Lop," 1984; "Leo the Lop: Tail Two," 1984; "Little Mouse on the Prairie," 1984; "Ming Ling," 1984; "Morgan and Me," 1984; "Morgan and Yew," 1984; "Morgan Mine," 1984; "Morgan Morning," 1984; "Baby Farm Animals," 1985; "Baby Forest Animals"; "Baby Pets"; "Baby Zoo Animals"; "Kittens"; "Puppies"; "Baby Horses," 1986; "Baby Unicorns," 1986; "Bangalee"; "Cap'n Smudge"; "Creole"; "The Dream Tree"; "Feather Fin"; "Flutterby Fly"; "Gnome from Nome"; "Hucklebug"; "In Search of Saveopotomas"; "Jake O'Shawnasey"; "Leo the Lop Tail Three"; "Maui Maui"; "Muffin Muncher"; "Nitter Pitter"; "Raz Ma Taz"; "Serendipity"; "Shimmeree"; "Snaffles"; "Trafalgar True"; "Trapper"; "Wheedle on the Needle."

SIDELIGHTS: "I grew up in a house full of art and art projects. My parents are the main reason I am doing what I am doing. They never stopped encouraging me as I was growing up. My mother has always told me, 'you were drawing as soon as you could hold a pencil in your hand, and your first word was not "mommy," it was "horsey."' I can remember sitting on life-sized animals carved out of styrofoam in our living room, and beautiful papier maché carousel horses and mermaids hanging out in the trees to dry in our yard. I have a brother, Jim, and a sister, Wendy, who are both artists in their own right, too.

"I've always loved animals, and when I was little I dreamed of seeing a real-life sea serpent or having a little white-winged horse flutter down to land on my bedroom windowsill. I had a special dragon friend I used to draw all the time. When I started illustrating children's books, these long time friends became the characters in the books: *Serendipity, Flutterby,* and *Muffin Muncher.* It was like I had known them all my life and was giving them to the world when I put them in the books.

"I work in my studio built on the upper floor of our farmhouse which overlooks our pastures full of horses. I hope someday to expand 'MorningStar Ranch' into 'EveningStar Farm,' a retirement stable for aged horses. (One of my own was 'Mor-

She looked at the parrot. The parrot looked at her. Neither spoke a word. ■ (From *Ming Ling* by Stephen Cosgrove. Illustrated by Robin James.)

gan,' with whom I grew up and who lived to the age of thirty-two, the inspiration for a series of books.) I am an advocate of animal protection organizations: 'Pain is no less pain when suffered by an animal.'

"I enjoy a simple life and the things most important to me are my family, our home and our animals. Traveling is minimal, however, I did enjoy seeing wildlife on a few trips to Canada's National Parks we have taken."

JANCE, Judith A(nn) 1944-
(J. A. Jance)

BRIEF ENTRY: Born October 27, 1944, in Watertown, S.D. "Writing has provided a means of rewriting my own history," Jance said about her work. Her books for children reflect her concern with difficult issues facing today's youth. *It's Not Your Fault* (Charles Franklin, 1985) deals with child molestation, and *Dial Zero for Help* (Charles Franklin, 1985) concerns parental kidnapping. Under the name J. A. Jance, she has written a series of adult murder thrillers published by Avon, *Until Proven Guilty* (1985) and *Injustice for All* (1986), which

Jance describes as "escapist fare with no redeeming social value." Before becoming a professional writer in 1985, Jance was a public school teacher, an elementary school librarian, and an insurance salesperson for eleven years at Equitable Life Assurance in New York City. *Home:* 2821 Second, Seattle, Wash. 98121.

FOR MORE INFORMATION SEE: Contemporary Authors, Volume 118, Gale, 1986.

JANES, J(oseph) Robert 1935-

BRIEF ENTRY: Born May 23, 1935, in Toronto, Ontario, Canada. Janes graduated from the University of Toronto with a bachelor's degree in mining engineering and a master of engineering in geology. He became a full-time writer in 1970, after twelve years as a laboratory assistant, scientist, and geology instructor. He has written three books in his "Danger on the River" children's detective series, including *Danger on the River* (Clarke, 1982), in which five children track down the people responsible for dumping hazardous waste into a river; *Spies for Dinner* (Collins of Canada, 1984); and *Murder in the Market* (Collins of Canada, 1984). He is working on the fourth book in that series. His other children's books are *The Tree-Fort War* (Scholastic-Tab, 1976), and *Theft of Gold* (Scholastic-Tab, 1980). Janes has continued his interest in geology and the preservation of Canada. "I am very involved with environmental issues, farmlands, and trying to preserve peace and beauty of this old town of Niagara-on-the-Lake," he said. He has written a television script for "Geology" (Metro Educational Television Authority, 1966), as well as numerous teaching guides and textbooks explaining geography and geology. Janes has also written novels for adults, published by General Publishing, including *The Toy Shop* (1981), *The Watcher* (1982), and *The Hiding Place* (1984). He has received writing grants from the J. P. Bickell Foundation, Canada Council, and Ontario Arts Council, and is a member of P.E.N. International and the Association of Professional Engineers of Ontario. *Agent:* Stan Colbert, 303 Davenport Rd., Toronto, Ontario, Canada M5R 1K5.

FOR MORE INFORMATION SEE: Who's Who in Canadian Literature: 1985-1986, Reference Press, 1985.

JONAS, Ann 1932-

PERSONAL: Born January 28, 1932, in Flushing, N.Y.; daughter of Herbert (a mechanical engineer) and Dorothy (a housewife and artist; maiden name, Ireland) Jonas; married Donald Crews (an author and illustrator of children's books), January 28, 1963; children: Nina, Amy. *Education:* Cooper Union for the Advancement of Science and Art, art certificate, 1959. *Home and office:* Brooklyn, N.Y.

CAREER: Rudolph de Harak, Inc. (design company), New York, N.Y., designer, 1959-62; Advertis, Inc. (advertising agency), Frankfurt, Germany, designer, 1962-63; Donald & Ann Crews (design company), Brooklyn, N.Y., designer, 1964—; author and illustrator of children's books, 1981—. *Awards, honors: Round Trip* was chosen one of *New York Times* Best Illustrated Books of the Year, and one of *Booklist's* Children's Editors' Choice, both 1983, included in American Institute of Graphic Arts Book Show, 1984, and received Golden Sower Book Award from Nebraska Library Association, 1985; *Holes and Peeks* and *The Quilt* were both chosen a Notable

Children's Book by the Association of Library Service to Children; *Holes and Peeks* was chosen one of *School Library Journal*'s Best Books, 1984; *The Trek* was chosen one of *School Library Journal*'s Best Books, and one of Child Study Association of America's Children's Books of the Year, both 1985, and was a *Boston Globe-Horn Book* Award honor book, 1986.

WRITINGS—Picture books; all self-illustrated; all published by Greenwillow: *When You Were a Baby,* 1982; *Two Bear Cubs,* 1982; *Round Trip* (ALA Notable Book; *Horn Book* honor list; Junior Literary Guild selection), 1983; *Holes and Peeks* (ALA Notable Book), 1984; *The Quilt* (ALA Notable Book), 1984; *The Trek* (ALA Notable Book), 1985; *Now We Can Go,* 1986; *Where Can It Be?,* 1986; *Reflections,* 1987.

SIDELIGHTS: "I grew up on Long Island, in a suburban, semi-rural area. There were open fields and things to be discovered everywhere. It seems that my brother and I spent all of our free time out of doors. We did all the usual things: building tree houses in the summer and ice houses in the winter, adopting injured animals, bicycling as far from home as we dared, and playing endless ball games.

"My family attached great importance to knowing how to do as many things as possible, from skiing to cabinetmaking to repairing the family car. Everyone always had several projects going at once, and drawing was considered an incidental skill, a tool for planning a project rather than an end in itself. I still cling to my family's rather pioneer attitudes about trying to make or do things for oneself before resorting to buying them, and I enjoy designing and making objects and clothing. However, since we bought a brownstone in Brooklyn several years ago, restoration of it has consumed all the time that I might have devoted to more delicate crafts in the past. With a house comes a garden, and that has been a great pleasure. It was a weedy, neglected backyard when we bought the house, and transforming it—learning about plants and finding those that will flourish in rather difficult city conditions—has been an interesting, if occasionally frustrating experience.

ANN JONAS

"I went to work after high school, without seriously considering college. After a few years, while working in the advertising department of a department store, I realized how much I needed to know if I was to build a career in art. I attended Cooper Union, learned a lot, and, during summers and after graduation, worked in the design office of my former graphic design instructor.

or plugged,

(From *Holes and Peeks* by Ann Jonas. Illustrated by the author.)

"I met my husband, Donald Crews, at Cooper Union. He was inducted into the army a few years after graduation and subsequently sent to Germany. I followed, and after trying rather unsuccessfully to freelance, took a job with a German advertising agency. We lived in Germany for eighteen months, sharing a large apartment with a German couple, friends of friends in the United States. Our first daughter, Nina, was born there. When we returned to the United States we decided to try to build our own free-lance business. Our second daughter, Amy, was born and I was able, since our office was in our apartment, to take care of our children and still work a bit in between.

"Since that initial long stay abroad, we have made two other major trips. We went to Japan, Hong Kong, and Taiwan in 1970 during Japan's Expo 70 with a group of designers. In 1976 we took our daughters on a tour of France and England. In recent years we have been seeing quite a lot of this country, both through work-related trips and for pleasure.

"Don had been doing children's books for quite a while, whenever he had the time between other projects. Through him I met and got to know his publisher, Susan Hirschman. They both urged me to try my hand at a book. The result was *When You Were a Baby,* which Susan liked and published. Since then, writing and illustrating children's books seems to have become a full-time occupation.

"My background is that of a designer, and I find that I approach each book quite differently. Each idea seems to need a specific technique and style to most clearly illustrate the point that I'm trying to make. Since I'm not really an illustrator and don't have a style as such, I feel free to let each book look as different from the next as is necessary.

"The books that have been the most fun to do are the ones that involve some sort of visual game, as do *Round Trip, The Quilt,* and *The Trek.* Children are so inundated with images that require nothing of them that it is a pleasure to do some-

thing that demands their involvement, that makes them work a little. I hope that they can then get the satisfaction of solving it, of mastering it.''

In her 1983 book, *Round Trip,* Jonas created a book for young people that could be read forwards and then read upside down and backwards. "I had been thinking that it would be wonderful to do a book that went from beginning to end and then back to the beginning again, if I could find the way to do it. I finally realized that if I created pictures that formed a different image when turned upside down, there would then be a reason for the return trip. I drew on my graphic design experience to stylize the images sufficiently to make this reversal possible. For instance, I had always noticed that the shapes between skyscrapers mimicked the shapes of the buildings themselves. I took some pictures of the Manhattan skyline from the Brooklyn Bridge. The drawing that resulted had possibilities. I looked at a lot of landscape books, too, even upside down, to try to get my mind to see things fresh enough to find related forms. I did thumbnail sketches. Many of them I had to discard because when I enlarged them, they didn't have enough content. I made a lot of mistakes, too. I was so convinced that I could do telephone poles and have them turn into a bridge that I just worked away at it without checking on the progress of the upside-down bridge I was creating. Then when I turned the drawing over, I was shocked at what I'd done. I had to make many changes before it worked." [Sylvia and Kenneth Marantz, "Interview with Ann Jonas," *Horn Book,* May/June, 1987.[1]]

Jonas created another "visual game" for young children in her book, *The Quilt,* which was written for her daughter Nina. "My other books had used simple, flat color or had been done in black and white. This book was clearly going to need a more realistic approach. I experimented with many techniques: collage, watercolor paintings, and a combination of both. It was only after having collected many patterned papers and assembling them into quilts that I came to the decision to do

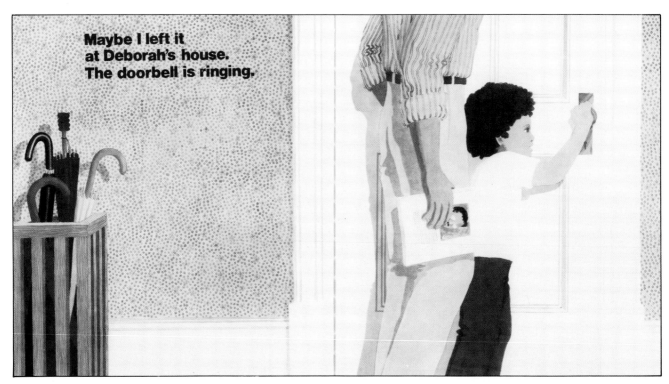

(From *Where Can It Be?* by Ann Jonas. Illustrated by the author.)

(From *The Quilt* by Ann Jonas. Illustrated by the author.)

the art as paintings. It was the only way I could get a satisfactory transition from the patterns in the quilt to their transformation in the dream sequence."[1]

About her picture book, *The Trek*, Jonas remarked: "I used to love the pictures in children's magazines that contained hidden animals. It seemed possible to combine that idea with the game that we have all played, that of seeing animals or objects in other objects. To make it work as the book I envisioned, I would have to hide animals among things that resembled them in form or color or pattern. I looked through many nature books, took photos at the zoo, and built up a collection of sketches from which to develop a story line. I think the hardest part of the book was to judge how difficult it would be for others to see the animals. In retrospect, I think I could have made them somewhat more difficult to find.

"The books that are most satisfying for me are the ones in which I can help a child to use his or her own imagination or the ones in which I can get in some reassurance about a problem or concern children have. But I don't want the message to get the upper hand. I want to entertain, not preach. When I have been able to combine both those aims, that is when the book is the most satisfying."[1]

"I try to play visual games against the background of a believable situation, to involve the child on an emotional level as well. The prime purpose of the book should be to entertain, but if it can also reassure the child a bit in the process, that's even better.

"The many photographs that my husband has taken of our children over the years, especially when they were young, help to keep me on track. Flipping through contact sheets is a great way for me to remind myself of what kids actually do, as well as how they look doing it. Our daughters have also been helpful. Now that they are grown, their memories have been the source for several of my books."

Jonas has also been influenced by many artists. "Over the years I have grown to prefer most artists' drawings and graphics to their paintings. I enjoy the work of graphic designers and illustrators such as Milton Glaser, Paul Rand, Seymour Chwast, and Leo Lionni. I am also a fan of nineteenth-century architectural renderings."[1]

About her work habits, Jonas remarked: "Two walls of my studio are covered with bulletin board. As I start to work on a book, I pin up assorted clippings, photos, scraps of fabric, anything that seems to be relevant. My finished drawings will gradually replace them. First I make tissues from the rough sketch, refining them until I'm satisfied. I transfer the tissue to watercolor paper and start building up the color. When I'm working with watercolor, the strongest colors must be saved until last, since they tend to run. So I start gradually with the lightest shades and work up to the reds, which are the trickiest of all. I usually complete each illustration before moving on to the next, so I mix large quantities of the colors I'm using and save every intermediate color I've mixed until I'm finished. This allows me to go back and make adjustments later on."[1]

FOR MORE INFORMATION SEE: Sylvia and Kenneth Marantz, "Interview with Ann Jonas," *Horn Book,* May/June, 1987.

JOYCE, J(ames) Avery 1902-1987

OBITUARY NOTICE—See sketch in *SATA* Volume 11: Born May 24, 1902, in London, England; died February 13, 1987. Educator, lawyer, editor, and author. Joyce was considered an expert on constitutional and international law and was an avid campaigner for international peace since the 1930s. A barrister in England and Switzerland at the outset of his career, he lectured widely and taught at universities and colleges in the United States and abroad. He also worked with a number of world peace organizations and in 1939 founded the World Unity Movement, which later became known as the World Citizenship Movement. For many years, Joyce was a consultant to agencies within the United Nations. Among his writings for children are *Youth Faces the New World* and *Peacemaking for Beginners*. He also wrote *The Story of International Cooperation*, *The New Politics of Human Rights*, *World Labour Rights and Their Protection*, *The War Machine: The Case Against the Arms Race*, and *One Increasing Purpose*. He edited many books, including *Three Peace Classics: Erasmus, Sully, Grotius* and World Unity booklets.

FOR MORE INFORMATION SEE: Contemporary Authors, New Revision Series, Volume 10, Gale, 1983; *Who's Who in the World,* 7th edition, Marquis, 1984. Obituaries: *Times* (London), February 16, 1987.

KAYE, Danny 1913-1987

OBITUARY NOTICE: Name originally David Daniel Kominski (some sources transliterate surname as Kaminski, Kaminsky, Karminsky, or Kominsky); born January 18, 1913, in New York, N.Y.; died of a heart attack resulting from internal bleeding and hepatitis, March 3, 1987, in Los Angeles, Calif. Entertainer, humanitarian, baseball executive, and editor of children's books, Kaye worked in show business for fifty years. Called by some "the greatest comedian of his time," Kaye's first big break came in 1933 when he joined a vaudeville dance team. The group first toured the United States and then performed in the Orient. Kaye subsequently performed in a variety of roles before making his Broadway debut in "Straw Hat Revue" in 1939. The next year, his delivery of "Stravinsky," a comical song from Broadway's "Lady in the Dark," made him a star. During the novelty number, he rattled off the names of fifty Russian composers in just thirty-eight seconds.

Kaye made his movie debut in the 1940's feature film "Up in Arms" and became one of the top comics on screen, acting in such films as "The Secret Life of Walter Mitty," "Hans Christian Andersen," and "White Christmas." His performances earned him a special Academy Award "for his unique talents, his service to the academy, the motion picture industry, and the American people" in 1954. In addition, he had a hit radio show, first broadcast in 1945, and a television variety program which ran from 1963 to 1967. "The Danny Kaye Show" won four Emmy Awards and a George Foster Peabody Broadcasting Award.

Kaye adored children and in 1950 began performing and raising money for them through the United Nations International Children's Emergency Relief Fund (UNICEF). He received the Nobel Peace Prize on behalf of UNICEF, and the Jean Hersholt Humanitarian Award in 1981 (some sources say 1982) and 1983. He was knighted by Denmark's Queen Margrethe in honor of his role as "Pied Piper to the children of the world." He edited three collections of children's stories: *Around the World Story Book, Danny Kaye's Stories from Many Lands,*

and *Stories from Faraway Places*. A frequent guest conductor with orchestras, Kaye was also a founder of, and a limited partner in, the Seattle Mariners professional baseball team.

FOR MORE INFORMATION SEE: Current Biography, H. W. Wilson, 1952; Leonard Maltin, *Great Movie Comedians,* Crown, 1978; *Who's Who in the Theatre: A Biographical Record of the Contemporary Stage,* 17th edition, Gale, 1981; *Who's Who,* 139th edition, St. Martin's, 1987. Obituaries: *Chicago Tribune,* March 4, 1987; *Detroit Free Press,* March 4, 1987; *Detroit News,* March 4, 1987; *Los Angeles Times,* March 4, 1987; *New York Times,* March 4, 1987; *Times* (London), March 4, 1987; *Washington Post,* March 4, 1987; *Maclean's,* March 16, 1987; *Newsweek,* March 16, 1987; *Sporting News,* March 16, 1987; *Time,* March 16, 1987.

KELLER, Mollie

BRIEF ENTRY: Born in Brooklyn, N.Y., Keller lives in Connecticut with her husband and two daughters. She received her bachelor's degree from Mount Holyoke College in Massachusetts, her master's from the University of Bridgeport, and has studied public history at New York University. Keller has written three biographies for children in the Franklin Watts "Impact Biography" series. In *Winston Churchill* (1984), "Keller does an excellent job of keeping readers' interest in her biography . . . which describes his unhappy childhood, school days and careers in the military, writing and politics," observed *School Library Journal*. In a review of *Golda Meir* (1983), the same magazine said, "Keller captures the spirit, the dedication and the indomitable nature of Golda Meir." Keller's other book in the series is *Marie Curie* (1982). In addition, Keller wrote *Alexander Hamilton* (1986), a biography about the Revolutionary war hero who was an advisor to George Washington and a framer of the Constitution, as part of the Franklin Watts "First Books" series. She also acts as curator for the museum of the Trumbull Historical Society in Connecticut.

KNIGGE, Robert (R.) 1921(?)-1987

OBITUARY NOTICE: Born about 1921; died of cancer, January 4, 1987, in St. Louis, Mo.; buried in Fort Snelling National Cemetery, Minneapolis, Minn. Businessman, publisher, and author of a Christmas book for children. "Silver Spurs," Knigge's story about Santa's smallest elf, first appeared in a Willmar, Minnesota newspaper and was later carried by the Associated Press. In 1974 Knigge formed Knollwood Publishing to publish his Christmas tale in book form. Selling more than 135,000 copies, *Silver Spurs* has inspired a record, T-shirts, and other merchandise. Knigge also operated a tire retreading firm in South Dakota as well as roofing and sheet metal companies in Minnesota and South Dakota.

FOR MORE INFORMATION SEE—Obituaries: *St. Paul Pioneer Press-Dispatch,* January 7, 1987; *USA Today,* January 7, 1987.

KOGAN, Deborah 1940-
(Deborah Ray; Deborah Kogan Ray)

PERSONAL: Surname legally changed to Kogan in 1981; born August 31, 1940, in Philadelphia, Pa.; daughter of Louis X. and Hildegarde (Wimenitz) Cohen; married Christopher Ray (a sculptor), July 8, 1960 (divorced, 1981); children: Karen,

DEBORAH KOGAN

Nicole. *Education:* Attended Philadelphia College of Art, 1958-59, University of Pennsylvania, 1959-61, Pennsylvania Academy of Fine Arts, 1959-62, and Albert C. Barnes Foundation, 1962-64. *Home:* 223 East Gowen Ave., Philadelphia, Pa. 19119.

CAREER: Artist. *Exhibitions:* Twenty-five one-woman shows nationally. Group shows: American Institute of Graphic Arts, New York, N.Y., 1970; Pennsylvania Academy of the Fine Arts, Philadelphia, 1975, 1982; Hibaya Library, Tokyo, Japan, 1976; Rutgers University, New Brunswick, N.J., 1978; Kikar Malkaei, Tel Aviv, Israel, 1980; Philadelphia Art Alliance, Pa., 1982; Fifth International Exhibition of Botanical Art and Illustration, Hunt Institute of Carnegie-Mellon University, Pittsburg, Pa., 1983 (as traveling exhibition), 1984-87; Philadelphia Museum of Arts, Pa., 1985; and others. Work is represented in collections of Chase Manhattan Bank (graphic mural), New York, N.Y.; Free Library of Philadelphia, Pa.; University of Minnesota, Minneapolis; Library of Congress, Washington, D.C.; Drexel University, Philadelphia; Fidelity Bank, Philadelphia; First Pennsylvania Bank, Philadelphia; Ecolaire, Inc., Great Valley, Pa.; Philadelphia Museum of Art. Pa.; Smithsonian Institute, Washington, D.C.; Philadelphia Electric Co., Pa.; Smith, Kline & French, Philadelphia; and Delaware Art Museum, Wilmington, Del.

MEMBER: Artists Equity Association, Authors Guild. *Awards, honors:* Louis Comfort Tiffany Foundation fellowship in painting, 1968; Mabel Rush Homer Award, 1968, for a painting; Philadelphia Art Directors Award for design and book illustration, 1970; *The Winter Picnic* was chosen one of American Institute of Graphic Arts Children's Books, 1970; Award

from Woodmere Art Museum, 1973, for a painting; *The Winter Wedding* and *Hubknuckles* were selected one of Child Study Association of America's Children's Books of the Year, 1975 and 1985, respectively; Purchase Award from Millersville College, 1979, for a painting; Drexel Citation from Drexel University School of Library and Information Science and the Free Library of Philadelphia, 1987, for her work in children's literature.

WRITINGS—Self-illustrated books for children: (Adapter under name Deborah Ray) *The Fair at Sorochintsi: A Nikolai Gogol Story Retold,* Macrae, 1969; (adapter under name Deborah Ray) *Abdul Abul-Bul Amir and Ivan Skavinsky Skavar,* Macrae, 1969; (under name Deborah Ray) *Sunday Morning We Went to the Zoo,* Harper, 1981; (under name Deborah Kogan Ray) *Fog Drift Morning,* Harper, 1983; (under name Deborah Kogan Ray) *The Cloud,* Harper, 1984; *My Dog, Trip,* Holiday House, 1987.

Illustrator; under name Deborah Ray, except as indicated: Robert Welber, *The Winter Picnic,* Pantheon, 1970; R. Welber, *Frog, Frog, Frog,* Pantheon, 1971; Zdenka Quinn and John P. Quinn, *Water Sprite of the Golden Town: Folk Tales of Bohemia,* Macrae, 1971; R. Welber, *The Train,* Pantheon, 1972; R. Welber, *Song of the Seasons,* Pantheon, 1973; R. Welber, *The Winter Wedding,* Pantheon, 1975; Jeanne Whitehouse Peterson, *I Have a Sister, My Sister Is Deaf,* Harper, 1977; J. W. Peterson, *That Is That,* Harper, 1979.

Patricia MacLachlan, *Through Grandpa's Eyes,* Harper, 1980; (under name Deborah Kogan Ray) Charlotte Zolotow, *The White Marble,* Crowell, 1982; (under name Deborah Kogan Ray) Danita Ross Haller, *Not Just Any Ring,* Knopf, 1982; (under name Deborah Kogan Ray) Carol A. Marron and Phyllis Root, *Gretchen's Grandma,* Carnival Press, 1983; (under name Deborah Kogan Ray) C. A. Marron, *Last Look from the Mountain,* Carnival Press, 1983; (under name Deborah Kogan Ray) Esther Hautzig, adapter and translator, *The Seven Good Years and Other Stories of I. L. Peretz,* Jewish Publication Society, 1984; (under name Deborah Kogan Ray) Emily Herman, *Hubknuckles,* Crown, 1985; (under name Deborah Kogan Ray) Brett Harvey, *My Prairie Year: Based on the Diary of Eleanore Plaisted,* Holiday House, 1986; B. Harvey, *Immigrant Girl, Becky of Eldridge Street,* Holiday House, 1987; Crescent Dragonwagon, *Diana, Maybe,* Macmillan, 1987; (under name Deborah Kogan Ray) e. e. cummings, *Little Tree,* Crown, 1987.

ADAPTATIONS: "I Have a Sister, My Sister Is Deaf," Reading Rainbow, PBS-TV, 1983; "Through Grandpa's Eyes," Reading Rainbow, PBS-TV, 1984; "The Winter Picnic" (filmstrip), Random House.

WORK IN PROGRESS: Illustrations for Eleanor Coerr's *Chang's Paper Pony,* an "I Can Read" book to be published by Harper; several manuscripts, one about watching stars, another about a character named "Small Sara."

SIDELIGHTS: "I grew up in the city. I moved four times to different houses on the same block. People stayed to their own streets in my neighborhood. Children played on the front steps and in the alleys behind the long rows of houses. In summer, when adults washed cars and gossiped in the back alley and teenagers gathered on the front steps, we children moved out into the street to play.

"Our favorite game was stick ball. It required no expensive equipment. A halved pimpleball or a cut section of garden hose and a broom stick were all that were needed.

"The girls played hopscotch. Games could last for hours. No one was allowed to touch the games once they were drawn. Taking over an unoccupied game was forbidden, too. A new one was drawn, instead. Once a week the games were washed away by the streetcleaners' sprinkler truck. They were replaced as soon as the street was dry. I was a very small, shy, bookish child. I pushed myself to mastery of the street games and I did very well in school, but I was an outsider.

"At eight, I discovered the park a couple of blocks away. The park became my refuge. There were tall trees. High hills descended to a creek. I sat by the creek for hours. I followed it's path beyond the park to where the city ended. Old farm-

houses stood in overgrown meadows. When I was older, I rode my bike up the backroads into the marshlands, where egrets and herons lived in the reedy grass. In that city park, I first learned to love the natural world. Things of nature have remained a focus of my work.

"Since I loved to draw, when I was twelve I decided I would be an artist. It filled the need of a lonely child to know that she was choosing to be different. When I graduated from high school, I was awarded an art scholarship. I enrolled in a commercial art school because I had vague thoughts of studying fabric design. I knew I had to earn a living. Within a few months, I knew this was not what I wanted to do. The next

His mother looked tired. His father looked tired. But the hot city night seemed beautiful to John Henry. ■ (From *The White Marble* by Charlotte Zolotow. Illustrated by Deborah Kogan Ray.)

I saw a man selling balloons, and I asked if I could buy one. But my mother said we should go to see the monkeys. ■ (From _Sunday Morning We Went to the Zoo_ by Deborah Kogan Ray. Illustrated by the author.)

year, I transferred to the Pennsylvania Academy of Fine Arts to study painting. I supported myself waiting on tables in a coffee house, modelling for art classes, and fitting corsets in a lingerie store. I finished art school with my infant daughter attending classes with me. She was without doubt, the youngest class member in the long history of the Academy.

"I have painted and exhibited my work in galleries since leaving art school. My paintings are of moving water, leaves and plants. They tell of the seasons and of growth and change. I paint in watercolor and acrylics. I draw and make prints.

"I adapted and illustrated a story by Nikolai Gogol that was published in 1969. This led to illustrating many other books. In illustrating children's books I have found another audience to communicate with. My aim is to create good art for children in books. My belief is that children respond to the nuance and look beyond what many adults miss. My first books were flamboyant and colorful. I used folktales for sources. I painted imagined places. My later books are about the world children know in their day to day lives. Some of my recent books have historical settings.

"Over the years my illustration has become more and more involved in presenting the real world of children. Whether the stories are about times past or now, the stories are about people and how they live. I often use pencil as my medium because it allows an intimacy and closeness of detail that is hard to find with paint.

"My transition to writing as well as illustrating books was slow. My first story was published in 1981. What I write is taken from experience. My stories are about what happens inside us. These are the things that are important to me."

Kogan's works are included in the Kerlan Collection at the University of Minnesota, the Free Library of Philadelphia, Pa., and the School of Library Science at Drexel University.

HOBBIES AND OTHER INTERESTS: "I enjoy the things of the outdoors. I love to walk in the woods or on the shore. I run. I bike. I dance."

FOR MORE INFORMATION SEE: Donnarae MacCann and Olga Richard, _The Child's First Books,_ H. W. Wilson, 1973; Martha E. Ward and Dorothy A. Marquardt, _Illustrators of Books for Young People,_ Scarecrow, 1975.

Tan Koide with wife, Yasuko Koide.

(From *May We Sleep Here Tonight?* by Tan Koide. Illustrated by Yasuko Koide.)

KOIDE, Tan 1938-1986

PERSONAL: Born June 21, 1938, in Tokyo, Japan; died February 11, 1986; son of Haku (a professor) and Yaeko (a homemaker; maiden name, Noda) Koide; married Yasuko Hashimoto (an illustrator), October 29, 1965. *Education:* Waseda University, B.A., 1961. *Home:* 3-6-1-305, Sodegaura, Narashino-shi, Chiba-prefecture, Japan.

CAREER: Nigen-sha, Tokyo, Japan, editor, 1963-68; author of children's books, 1969—. *Awards, honors:* Newcomer prize from Japanese Association of Writers for Children, 1977, for *Ground Cherry Fest;* Silver Slate Pencil from Commissie vor Collectieve Propoganda van het Nederlandse Boek in the Netherlands, 1986, for *Klop, klop, wie is daar? (May We Sleep Here Tonight?).*

WRITINGS: Ground Cherry Fest, Alice-kan (Japan), 1977; *May We Sleep Here Tonight?* (illustrated by wife, Yasuko Koide), Fukuinkan (Japan), 1981, Atheneum, 1983; *I Don't Like a Wolf,* Yugakusha, 1983, Faber, 1984; *Chobi, the Kitten,* Fukuinkan, 1984; *Dr. Janjaka and the Tiny Dinosaur,* Komine Shoten (Japan), 1985; *Put You a Riddle,* Komine Shoten, 1985.

SIDELIGHTS: "In my childhood there were fields and butterflies and dragonflies even in the big city of Tokyo. Although B-29's flew over us, I did nothing but play during the war, much the same as children during peace time. There was light and there was darkness, childish dreams and hopes, and pleasure and grief. There were air raids, hunger, and ruins. And there were no stories to tell children. Who on earth could ask their father or mother to tell stories in air raid shelters? I believe that it may have been the lack of 'stories' in my childhood that urged me to the world of picture books and juvenile literature.

"Isaac B. Singer dedicated *Zlateh the Goat* to 'many children who had no chance to grow up because of stupid wars and cruel persecutions that devastated cities and destroyed innocent families.' Singer's dedication is to the children who died during war, and I found, in a sense, I had missed some chance to grow up as well.

"If Dr. Dolittle's circus should visit my town, I would go there by any means possible to meet with pushmi-pullyu, because during my childhood Dr. Dolittle's circus did not come to my town. If there was a country in the world like Dr. Dolittle's, I should gladly bear any hardship to live there, though I no longer have the energy of a child, I would still be very eager to explore every corner.

"When I come back from that country, I may write some adventures I experienced. I am sure that I will start writing with words like Singer's, 'I dedicate this book to many children who will inevitably grow up some day.'"

Before his death on February 11, 1986, Koide was working on a sequel to *May We Sleep Here Tonight?,* writing three stories in all, which his wife, Yasuko, is completing for publication by Fukuinkan.

KYTE, Kathy S. 1946-

PERSONAL: Born June 5, 1946, in Reno, Nev.; daughter of Lafe and Shirley (Allen) Sharar; children: Brendan, Brooke. *Education:* Lewis & Clark College, B.S., 1981; University of Iowa, M.F.A., 1984. *Home and office:* 1820 16th Ave., #303, Seattle, Wash. 98122.

CAREER: Writer, 1981—. *Member:* Society of Children's Book Writers, Authors Guild.

WRITINGS—All published by Knopf: *In Charge: A Complete Handbook for Kids with Working Parents* (illustrated by Susan Detrich), 1983; *Play It Safe: The Kids' Guide to Personal*

KATHY S. KYTE

Safety and Crime Prevention (illustrated by Richard Brown), 1983; *The Kids' Complete Guide to Money* (illustrated by R. Brown), 1984; *The Writing Game*, David S. Lake/Fearon Educational Aids, in press.

WORK IN PROGRESS: An adult novel.

SIDELIGHTS: "While I was preparing a paper for college, I came across an article on America's 'latchkey children' (children who live in families where both parents work outside the home or who live in a single-parent family where the parent works outside the home). I was astonished to find that there were millions of these children—and the number was growing rapidly. I was even more astonished to find that (at that time) there were no books, self-help guides or anything similar for these kids. After my semester was over, I got busy writing just such a book and was fortunate enough to sell it to Alfred A. Knopf. My research for the first book led to my second and third books. All are concerned with giving kids more control over their lives in a world that is increasingly confusing and complex."

HOBBIES AND OTHER INTERESTS: Traveling, reading, and photography.

LANDON, Margaret (Dorothea Mortenson) 1903-

PERSONAL: Born September 7, 1903, in Somers, Wis.; daughter of Annenus Duabus (in the business department of *Saturday Evening Post*) and Adelle Johanne (Estberg) Mortenson; married Kenneth Perry Landon (retired associate dean of area and language studies, U.S. Department of State Foreign Service Institute), June 16, 1926; children: Margaret Dorothea (Mrs. Charles W. Schoenherr), William Bradley II, Carol Elizabeth (Mrs. Lennart Pearson), Kenneth Perry, Jr. *Education:* Wheaton College, Wheaton, Ill., A.B., 1925; also studied journalism at Northwestern University, 1937-38. *Religion:* Protestant. *Home:* 4711 Fulton St., N.W., Washington, D.C. 20007. *Agent:* William Morris Agency, 1350 Avenue of the Americas, New York, N.Y. 10019.

CAREER: Taught English and Latin in Bear Lake, Mich., 1925-26; author, 1939—.

WRITINGS: Anna and the King of Siam (illustrated by M. Ayer), Day, 1944, version for young people, Day, 1947, abridged edition, Square Press, 1963; *Never Dies the Dream* (novel), Doubleday, 1949.

ADAPTATIONS: "Anna and the King" (motion picture; based on *Anna and the King of Siam*), starring Irene Dunne and Rex Harrison, Twentieth Century-Fox, 1946, (television series) starring Samantha Eggar and Yul Brynner, CBS-TV, 1972; "The King and I" (musical play; based on *Anna and the King of Siam*), starring Gertrude Lawrence and Yul Brynner, St. James Theatre, New York City, March 29, 1951, (motion picture), starring Deborah Kerr and Yul Brynner, Twentieth Century-Fox, 1956; "Anna and the King of Siam" (recorded book), Recordings for the Blind, 1953, (cassette), performed by Rita Moreno, Caedmon, (cassette), performed by Rex Harrison and Irene Dunn, AVC Corp.

SIDELIGHTS: "I grew up in Evanston, Illinois, which had excellent schools. My great interest from fourth grade on was sports: softball, volleyball, tennis, basketball, canoeing. My grades were good but I did not aspire to lead my class scholastically. I had an especially brilliant English teacher in my junior year of high school, Miss Effie Wambaugh. She compelled her pupils to think. One day she came up behind me in the hall and put her hand on my shoulder, turning me around. 'Margaret,' she said, 'you have the gift of words. Do something with it!' This so startled me that I never forgot it. I finished high school, went on to Wheaton College, was married and found myself unexpectedly slated to go to Siam. That is I knew before our marriage that my fiancé had changed his plans and had chosen to serve the Presbyterian Church abroad rather than at home.

MARGARET LANDON

(From the first stage production of "The King and I," starring Gertrude Lawrence and Yul Brynner. Opened at the St. James Theatre, March 29, 1951.)

(From the movie "The King and I," starring Deborah Kerr and Yul Brynner, for which Brynner won an Academy Award for Best Actor. Produced by Twentieth Century-Fox Pictures, 1956.)

(From the movie "Anna and the King of Siam," starring Irene Dunne. Produced by Twentieth Century-Fox, 1946.)

(From the musical stage production of "The King and I," starring Constance Towers and Michael Kermoyan. Produced by the New York City Center Light Opera Company, it opened at New York City Center Theatre, May 23, 1968.)

(One of Jo Mielziner's Tony award-winning set designs for the musical production of "The King and I." Presented at the St. James Theatre, 1951.)

(Scene from Jerome Robbins' memorable staging of "The Little House of Uncle Thomas" [a Siamese version of *Uncle Tom's Cabin*]. From the musical "The King and I," which opened at the St. James Theatre, March 29, 1951.)

"I hadn't forgotten Miss Wambaugh's words, but in Siam there was no time for writing, other than my letters home. When we returned to the United States in 1937, I enrolled in two evening courses at the Medill School of Journalism, one in the writing of short stories, one in the writing of articles. The latter was taught by Elmo Scott Watson, who was editor of a syndicate. There were fifty pupils in his class, and each of us was to write three articles. Mr. Watson read two of mine to the class, to my pleasure of course. And at the end of the course he said flatly, 'There are three of you who can write.' He named a man already a newspaper reporter, a woman who wrote publicity for one of the big stores, and me. And he helped me rewrite an article I had called 'Hollywood Invades Siam.' It was my first professional sale, and was later included in a book, *Essays for Discussion,* under the changed title 'Celluloid Heroes Capture Siam.'

"In 1939 I started to write *Anna,* as we always refer to the book. I had planned to write a biography of an early missionary to Siam, Edna S. Cole, a fascinating woman who was still living, and who had great influence on the education of girls and women at a time when there was a common saying, 'Educate a buffalo before a woman.' Miss Cole told me this herself and let me read a file of letters she had written from Siam to her two sisters. She was understandably unwilling to let me use her letters unless I did so in St. Joseph, Missouri, where she lived. That was impossible for me. I had a husband, and three children, and they were my principal responsibility.

"Then at a lunch for ministers in Evanston, Dean of St. Luke's Cathedral, the Very Reverend Gerald G. Moore, leaned across the table and asked my husband, who had been the speaker, 'My mother had a cousin who went to Siam years ago. I don't suppose you ever heard of our Aunt Annie?' Kenneth couldn't think of any 'Annie,' then suddenly answered, 'You don't mean Anna Leonowens, do you? My wife is interested in writing an article about her.' Dean Moore was astounded and took Kenneth home to meet his mother, who was in her nineties and remembered the day in 1867 when Anna Leonowens came to their family home in Enniscorthy, Ireland. Through the Moores I met Miss Avis Fyshe, the only one of Anna's descendants interested in having her grandmother's story told. She supplied me with the family material and authorized me to use it as I pleased, and I was on my way.

"I am amused and pleased when I see what *Anna . . .* has done. I had hoped while writing it that two or three thousand people might buy it. One of the leading editors in New York had told a friend who was acting as my agent that 'this book will have no interest for the American public.'"

Anna and the King of Siam has had numerous printings all over the world, including Sweden, Canada, Denmark, Norway, Portugal, Spain, Finland, Italy, France, Germany, Hungary, Czechoslovakia, and Siam.

"Why haven't I written more? My mind teemed with ideas, but it was a case of family comes first, for one thing; the fact

(Thirty-four years after his first appearance as "The King," Yul Brynner returned in a farewell engagement in "The King and I." Opened at the Broadway Theatre, 1985.)

that I had rheumatic fever two years after finishing *Anna* . . . when I was well into my second book; and the many social calls on my time and efforts once my husband became the first officer on Southeast Asia in the Department of State.

"I have not been able to write for nine years because of a series of iatrogenic illnesses. I've reached the age now when I realize that I have neither the strength nor the years needed to complete another book. This is a disappointment, of course. I am a very slow writer, often rewriting a chapter ten, twelve, twenty times."

In 1951 *Anna and the King of Siam* was adapted into a musical play starring Gertrude Lawrence and Yul Brynner, who was virtually an unknown actor until his debut in "The King and I." The play achieved the status of a classic in musical theater and Brynner made a career with his role as King of Siam. Originally, the musical ran for four years on Broadway. In 1956, Brynner and Deborah Kerr starred in the movie version of the musical. "The life expectancy of a book is not long under modern conditions. I had thought *Anna's* cycle complete when, in December, 1949, Helen Strauss, of the William Morris Agency, wrote that there was a possibility of the book's becoming a musical play.

The strange scenes of the day chased each other in confusion across her mind. ■ (From *Anna and the King of Siam* by Margaret Landon. Illustrated by Margaret Ayer.)

"Helen had sold *A Tree Grows in Brooklyn* to George Abbot and Robert Fryer for a musical comedy, and the casting department of the agency suggested Gertrude Lawrence for its star. Helen thought this poor casting, and 'suddenly out of nowhere, I seemed to put Miss Lawrence and Anna together, and I called Miss Holtzman, who is Miss Lawrence's attorney,' Helen wrote. Miss Lawrence liked the suggestion. Rodgers and Hammerstein were persuaded to write and produce the play. And, on March 29, 1951, Anna Leonowens made her Broadway debut.

"One of my friends, commenting on the unexpected tenacity of the book, remarked that it almost made one believe in mortmain, in the medieval sense that a hand beyond the grave could, under some circumstances, direct a hand on this side of it. 'The boys had better look out,' she said, referring thus irreverently to Mr. Rodgers and Mr. Hammerstein, 'for the one sure thing is that Anna will be right there on the stage of the St. James, marching triumphantly along.'

"And perhaps she is. Certainly the widening audience that has come to know her through the book, the movie and the play, is a fitting memorial to a gallant and courageous woman.

"Anna Leonowens never had a memorial in Siam. There is no statue of bronze or stone erected to her there, no school named for her, not so much as a library or a street. But in another sense she has had a memorial in reverse. It is built of the hatred and vilification that have been heaped upon her memory. Those whose privileges were curtailed, whose power to control the lives of others for gain, limited by the reforms of the young king who was her pupil, have never forgiven her, nor have their descendants. And this, in itself, is a formidable tribute." [Margaret Landon, "Anna and I," *Town and Country*, December, 1952.']

The twenty-fifth anniversary of "The King and I" was celebrated with a new Broadway production starring Yul Brynner in his original role and Constance Towers as "Anna." It subsequently went on a road tour with Brynner who gave more than 4,000 performances over the years. "I have had one pleasant surprise in the unbelievable successful tour of the 'The King and I' with Yul Brynner. On Broadway it broke the all-time record for box office receipts in a single week, a week later broke that record, and has since broken even that second record. What is gratifying about this besides the royalty involved is the fact that the play has given such a great amount of pleasure to young and old. The credit for the play belongs to Rodgers and Hammerstein, of course, but it is based on my book *Anna and the King of Siam*, as my book is based on Anna's books, plus several hundred Thai documents and books dealing with the history and culture of Anna's time. As always, Anna marches gallantly and triumphantly along."

FOR MORE INFORMATION SEE: New York Herald Tribune, June 29, 1944, October 25, 1944; *New York World-Telegram,* June 29, 1944; *Current Biography,* H. W. Wilson, 1945; *Town and Country,* December, 1952; Stanley J. Kunitz, *Twentieth Century Authors,* first supplement, H. W. Wilson, 1955; Sidney Gordon "27th Anniversary of 'The King and I,'" *Hollywood Studio,* November, 1976; Richard Philp, "'The King and I' Revival: Is Not a Puzzlement," *After Dark,* September, 1977; Jack Pitman, "'King and I,' with Yul Brynner, to Set $15 Top, London Record," *Variety,* January 24, 1979; "Brynner to Tour in 'King and I'; Leigh Forms Producing Firm," *Legitimate,* August 13, 1980; *New York Times,* August 29, 1980, March 23, 1984; Don Nelsen, "Grrrr! Notes from a Theatergoer," *Daily News,* January 15, 1985.

(From the movie "Anna and the King of Siam," starring Rex Harrison. Released by Twentieth Century-Fox, 1946.)

LAURÉ, Jason   1940-

PERSONAL: Born October 15, 1940, in Chehalis, Wash.; son of James and Lisa (Lawry) Braly; married Ettagale Blauer, May 5, 1974 (divorced, January 16, 1984). *Education:* Attended Los Angeles City College, Columbia University, and Sorbonne, University of Paris. *Home:* 8 West 13th St., New York, N.Y. 10011.

CAREER: Copywriter for *New York Times*, New York, N.Y.; free-lance photojournalist, 1968—. Photographer for presidential mission of Nelson Rockefeller to Latin America, 1969; accompanied UNICEF's mission among the nomads of the African Sahara, 1970-71, official correspondent in Bangladesh; work exhibited in one-man shows, including Institute of Contemporary Art, London, England, and group shows, including Baxter Gallery, Cape Town, South Africa, 1979. *Military service:* U.S. Army. *Member:* African-American Institute.

AWARDS, HONORS: Grant from International Center of Photography, 1972; nominated for Pulitzer Prize for photography, c. 1972, and nominated for award from Overseas Press Club of America, c. 1972, both for pictures of Bangladesh published in *New York Times;* award from National Educational Association, 1973, for filmstrip, "Bangladesh: Birth of a Nation"; best of the year awards for filmstrips from National Educational Association, 1973, for "Shifting Sands of the Sahel," and 1975, for "Zero Population Growth," and "The Dogon of Mali"; National Book Award finalist, 1975, and selected as a Notable Book in the Field of Social Studies by

Whether she is rich or poor, marriage is her destiny. ■ (From *Joi Bangla! The Children of Bangladesh* by Jason Lauré and Ettagale Lauré. Photograph by Jason Lauré.)

the joint committee of the National Council of Social Studies and Children's Book Council, both for *Joi Bangla! The Children of Bangladesh; Joi Bangla! The Children of Bangladesh* and *Jovem Portugal: After the Revolution* were both chosen one of New York Public Library's Books for the Teen Age, 1980, 1981, and 1982, and *South Africa: Coming of Age under Apartheid*, 1981, and 1982.

WRITINGS—All with Ettagale Lauré; with own photographs: *Joi Bangla! The Children of Bangladesh* (young adult), Farrar, Straus, 1974; *Jovem Portugal: After the Revolution* (young adult), Farrar, Straus, 1977; *South Africa: Coming of Age under Apartheid* (young adult; ALA Notable Book), Farrar, Straus, 1980.

Filmstrips: "Bangladesh: Birth of a Nation," Current Affairs Filmstrips, c. 1973; "Shifting Sands of the Sahel," Current Affairs Filmstrips, 1975. Also "Zero Population Growth," for Current Affairs Filmstrips, "The Dogon of Mali," for Current Affairs Filmstrips, and "White Roots." Correspondent for *Pace*. Contributor to magazines, including *National Geographic*, *Newsweek*, *Time*, *Africa Report*, and *Junior Scholastic*, and newspapers.

WORK IN PROGRESS: Africatrek, a photographic odyssey ("This work portrays the vast continent of Africa as I have seen it during my ten years of working and traveling there as a photojournalist and author.")

SIDELIGHTS: "I like to say that I specialize in new countries. I was in Bangladesh when it became a new nation and participated in the excitement. When I was in Angola to work on a book, I witnessed that country's change from colonial status, tied to Portugal, to independence. I also saw the civil war that was going on in the country and knew that true independence would be slow in coming. In Portugal I witnessed demonstra-

JASON LAURÉ

tions in the street as people tried to find a new kind of government.

"The most difficult aspect of my work is finding the subjects, finding someone whose story I want to tell and then convincing him that he should become part of my work. We can spend so much time with subjects, and at the end find they have changed their minds. This occurs with people at both ends of the financial spectrum, the very poor and the very rich. In Portugal it resulted in having my interview tapes confiscated one time."

FOR MORE INFORMATION SEE: Los Angeles Times Book Review, August 3, 1980; *Washington Post Book World*, September 7, 1980; *Chicago Tribune Book World*, November 9, 1980.

LAURENCE, (Jean) Margaret (Wemyss) 1926-1987

OBITUARY NOTICE: Some sources spell maiden name Wemys; born July 18 (one source says July 19), 1926, in Neepawa, Manitoba, Canada; died of cancer, January 6, 1987, in Lakefield, Ontario, Canada. Journalist, editor, translator, and author. Laurence was considered one of Canada's most successful and influential novelists. After a stint as a reporter for the *Winnipeg Citizen*, she published her first novel, *This Side Jordan*, in 1960, and in subsequent years continued producing highly regarded fiction. She wrote a number of books for children, including *Jason's Quest, Six Darn Cows, The Olden-Days Coat*, and *The Christmas Birthday Story*. Among her best-known works is the series of novels set in the fictional town of Manawaka, which Laurence reportedly modeled after Neepawa, where she grew up. This series includes *The Stone Angel, A Jest of God*, which was adapted for the film "Rachel, Rachel," and *The Diviners*, which aroused controversy because of its explicit accounts of an abortion and a sexual encounter. Laurence also set the stories in *A Bird in the House* in the same fictional town. Her other works include the autobiographical novel *New Wind on a Dry Land*, as well as short stories, some of which were published in periodicals like, *Queen's Quarterly* and the *Saturday Evening Post*. She also edited and translated *A Tree for Poverty: Somali Poetry and Prose*, and, soon before her death, wrote a memoir in collaboration with her daughter.

FOR MORE INFORMATION SEE: Contemporary Authors, Volumes 7-8, revised edition, Gale, 1963; Clara Thomas, *Margaret Laurence*, McClelland & Stewart, 1969; Joan Hind-Smith, *Three Voices: The Lives of Margaret Laurence, Gabrielle Roy, Frederick Philip Grove*, Clark, Irwin, 1975; Patricia Morley, *Margaret Laurence*, Twayne, 1981; George Woodcock, editor, *A Place to Stand On: Essays by and about Margaret Laurence*, Newest Press, 1983. Obituaries: *New York Times*, January 7, 1987; *Times* (London), January 7, 1987; *Washington Post*, January 7, 1987; *Globe and Mail* (Toronto), January 10, 1987; *Maclean's*, January 19, 1987; *Publishers Weekly*, February 20, 1987.

LEEDY, Loreen (Janelle)   1959-

BRIEF ENTRY: Born June 15, 1959, in Wilmington, Del. Leedy graduated cum laude with a B.A. in art from the University of Delaware. A full-time craftsperson from 1982 to 1984, she sold original jewelry at craft shows before publishing her first picture book in 1985. "Writing and illustrating picture books for children allows me to share my abilities in an inspiring way,'' Leedy said. Her books, all published by Holiday House, include a series about Ma Dragon and her ten brightly-colored offspring. The first, *A Number of Dragons,* ''is a knockout attraction with a counting lesson encapsulated in a giddy tale of a big day for baby dragons,'' wrote a reviewer in *Publishers Weekly. The Dragon ABC Hunt* (1986) is an alphabet scavenger hunt for the ten bored dragons, while *The Dragon Halloween Party* (1986) includes instructions for how to prepare for a party and design costumes—including one for a dragon. *Publishers Weekly* wrote: ''This is a book to be relished, long after the last popcorn ball has been devoured.'' Leedy also produced *Big, Small, Short, Tall* (1987), a book of opposites. She is currently working on *The Bunny Play,* an introduction to the theater for young children, as well as *A Dragon Christmas,* another book in the ''Dragon'' series. *Home:* 2016 Crescent Blvd., Orlando, Fla. 32817.

FOR MORE INFORMATION SEE: Delaware Today, October, 1986.

God be thanked for books. They are the voices of the distant and the dead, and make us heirs of the spiritual life of past ages.
                                   —William Ellery Channing

LESTER, Alison   1952-

PERSONAL: Born November 17, 1952, in Foster, Australia; daughter of Donald R. (a grazier) and Jean (a nurse; maiden name, Billings) Lester; married Edwin Hume (a solicitor), January 22, 1977; children: William, Clair, Lachlan. *Education:* State College, Melbourne, Australia, higher diploma of teaching, 1975. *Politics:* Labour. *Home and office:* Dore Rd., Nar Nar Goon North, Victoria, 3812, Australia.

CAREER: Alexandra High School, Alexandra, Victoria, Australia, art teacher, 1976; Victorian Education Correspondence School, Victoria, Australia, art teacher, 1977. *Exhibitions:* Post Office Gallery, Mornington, Victoria, Australia, 1984; Seasons Gallery, Sydney, Australia, 1985, 1986; Gallery Art Navie, Melbourne, Australia, 1985. *Awards, honors:* Children's Book Council of Australia, Junior Book of the Year, 1983, for *Thing,* high commendation for picture book of the year, 1986, for *Clive Eats Alligators.*

WRITINGS—Self-illustrated: *Clive Eats Alligators,* Houghton, 1985; *Ruby,* Oxford University Press, 1987.

Illustrator; published by Oxford University Press, except as noted: June Epstein, *Big Dipper,* 1980; J. Epstein, *Big Dipper*

"I'll call it Thing," said Emily. ■ (From *Thing* by Robin Klein. Illustrated by Alison Lester.)

ALISON LESTER

Rides Again, 1982; Robin Klein, *Thing,* 1983; R. Klein, *Thingnapped!,* 1984; J. Epstein, *Big Dipper Returns,* 1985; J. Epstein, *Big Dipper Songs,* 1985; R. Klein, *Ratbags and Rascals,* 1985; Morris Lurie, *Night! Night!,* 1986; June Factor, *Summer,* Penguin, 1987. Also illustrator of *Taught Not Caught* by the Clanty Collective, Spiral, 1983.

"Augustus" books; all written by J. Epstein; all published by T. Nelson, 1984: *Augustus; . . . Conducts the Band; . . . Teaches the Children; . . . Flies a Plane; . . . Works in a Factory; . . . Plays Football; . . . the King; . . . the Painter.*

WORK IN PROGRESS: "I'm working on a series of four baby books for Penguin and the illustrations for *Berk the Berserker,* a Robin Klein story for Omnibus Books. Life is certainly busy. I have about three books of my own worked out that I just have to wait to get time to do, including a follow-up to *Clive Eats Alligators.* I just need more hours in the day!"

SIDELIGHTS: "I'd always been fairly unambitious and lazy, I guess, until I was expecting my first child and saw a life as a housewife stretching out before me. I'd been illustrating class books at the correspondence school and loving it, so I took a folio to Oxford University Press and met Rosalind Price, then the children's editor at Oxford. My illustrating career took off from there. It was a great start working with Rosalind and later Rita Scharf at Oxford, both have an excellent idea of just what is right in children's books. My first self-illustrated book, *Clive Eats Alligators,* was published in 1985, and was a big thrill.

"I grew up on a beef farm in Southern Victoria—an area of hot summers, but blasting cold wet winters. It is beautiful farming country rolling from windswept hills down to great sandy beaches and sparkling sea. Life *was* the farm and as kids we were constantly riding after cattle (we loved it), or doing some other project on the farm.

"I went to boarding school for four years, then to University for a year of reveling. After failing two out of four subjects (to no one's surprise), I went to train as an art teacher for four

years. It was a good course with a very wide range of subjects, but little depth in anything. After this course I taught for one year, then I was married and went to South America for a year of travel (seems a long way away now). On returning, we had our first baby and settled on a piece of land just south of Melbourne. We live here now, in this quiet place, surrounded by a beautiful, wild and rambling garden, with the kids, dog, cat, and horses.

"Concerning my work, I always feel that I haven't 'made it,' even when a book is successful. I guess most people are full of self doubt in regards to their work. It's such a personal thing and can give pleasure, as well as pain. I almost find it depressing to enter a children's bookshop and see hundreds of exquisite books—all such labours of love. Oh well, it's still not a bad life."

HOBBIES AND OTHER INTERESTS: Riding horses, photography, camping, the beach, singing, "rock and roll," basketball, and good conversation.

LITTLE, Lessie Jones   1906-1986

OBITUARY NOTICE: Born October 1, 1906, in Parmele, N.C.; died of cancer, November 4, 1986, in Washington, D.C. Educator, clerical worker, and author. Little began writing as a sixty-seven-year-old great-grandmother, and with her daughter, Eloise Greenfield, published two books for children. The first of these, *I Can Do It by Myself,* aimed at instilling more self-confidence into young children. The second, *Childtimes: A Three Generation Memoir,* detailed experiences of Little's own family. Prior to becoming an author, Little worked in rural North Carolina as an elementary-school teacher, and in Washington, D.C. as a clerk in the Office of the Surgeon General.

FOR MORE INFORMATION SEE: Contemporary Authors, Volume 101, Gale, 1981. Obituaries: *Washington Post,* November 13, 1986.

LONG, Earlene (Roberta)   1938-

PERSONAL: Born October 4, 1938, in Ford County, Ill.; daughter of Earl Robert (a farmer) and Estella Mary (a director of Christian education; maiden name, Rollins) Ketchum; married Richard Guy Long, Jr. (a parts counterman), September 3, 1965; children: Mary Catherine, Richard Vincent. *Education:* Purdue University, B.S., 1963. *Address:* P.O. Box 1712, Cheyenne, Wyo. 82003. *Office:* Needs, Inc., P.O. Box 404, Cheyenne, Wyo. 82003.

CAREER: Author, 1954—; Needs, Inc. (a non-profit, short-term emergency help agency), Cheyenne, Wyo., director, 1982—.

WRITINGS—Picture books: *Johnny's Egg* (illustrated by Neal Slavin and Charles Mikolaycak), Addison-Wesley, 1980; *Gone Fishing* (illustrated by Richard Brown), Houghton, 1984. Contributor to magazines including *Family Circle, Woman's Day,* and *Good Housekeeping.*

WORK IN PROGRESS: Several children's books; an adult horror novel; an adult nonfiction on "how to make it on almost nothing." "There are all sorts of books and articles dashing madly around my head, some of which I am fortunate enough to trap at least somewhat on paper for 'future' use. Some

EARLENE LONG

things are there very strongly, but I do not feel 'ready' to tackle them with the finesse that is essential.''

SIDELIGHTS: ''I was an only child and the second oldest of many cousins. None of them lived in the same small town as I did, but we got together frequently and I felt very close to them because they were my 'brothers and sisters.'

''I believe that the major portion of everyone's life philosophy is set by the age of eight. (Of course, it is modified and clarified by further maturity and nurturing.) Because of this belief, I spend the majority of my writing time writing books for children of this age—hoping I can add subtly to their own self-image.

''I've always had an interest in writing but understood I was not the kind of creator who could live in an attic and starve to achieve my ideals. Thus I went to college to learn a profession that would allow me to have time and money to continue on with my writing.

''The main reason I write for very young people is because I believe there really is not enough variety of interesting books on the market for them. How are they going to want to learn to read if something does not interest them?

''As a writer I observe people of all ages, sizes, colors, and ethnic backgrounds. Isn't it absolutely marvelous that everyone, and I do mean _every one_ of us, is unique? I glory in this and hope to ensure that each and every child has a chance to experience this pleasure of knowing.''

HOBBIES AND OTHER INTERESTS: ''Vital interest in land reclamation; earthworms; organic gardening; reading ability of any one any age. These are my passions ongoing at all times. Communication and motivation are two other high interest areas.''

MacEWEN, Gwendolyn 1941-

PERSONAL: Born September 1, 1941, in Toronto, Ontario, Canada; daughter of Alick James (a photographer) and Elsie (a housewife; maiden name, Mitchell) MacEwen; married Nikos Tsingos (a singer), 1971 (divorced, 1978). _Education:_ Attended schools in Toronto and Winnipeg. _Residence:_ Toronto, Ontario, Canada. _Address:_ c/o The Writers' Union, 24 Ryerson Ave., Toronto, Ontario M5T 2P3, Canada.

CAREER: Writer. Left school at eighteen to concentrate on writing poetry and fiction. Writer-in-Residence, University of West Ontario, 1984-85, University of Toronto, 1986-87. Has given numerous poetry readings across Canada. _Awards, honors:_ First prize, New Canadian Writing Contest of the Canadian Broadcasting Company (CBC), 1965, for poetry; Governor General's Literary Award for poetry, 1970, for _The Shadow-Maker;_ A.J.M. Smith Poetry Award from Michigan State University, 1973, for _The Armies of the Moon;_ first prize, CBC Radio Literary Competition V, 1983, for short story ''Loneliest Country in the World''; Gold and Silver du Maurier Awards for poetry from Canadian Periodical Publishers Association, 1983, for poetry.

WRITINGS—Poetry, except as indicated: _Selah,_ Aleph, 1961; _The Drunken Clock,_ Aleph, 1961; _The Rising Fire,_ Contact Press, 1963; _Julian the Magician_ (novel), Cornith Books, 1964; _A Breakfast for Barbarians,_ Ryerson, 1966; _The Shadow-Maker,_ Macmillan, 1969.

King of Egypt, King of Dreams (novel), Macmillan (Toronto), 1971; _The Armies of the Moon,_ Macmillan (Toronto), 1972;

GWENDOLYN MacEWEN

Once upon a time in a land to the north, there lived a moose called Martin. ■ (From *The Chocolate Moose* by Gwendolyn MacEwen. Illustrated by Barry Zaid.)

Noman (short stories), Oberon, 1972; *Magic Animals: Selected Poems Old and New,* Macmillan, 1974, published as *Magic Animals: Selected Poetry of Gwendolyn MacEwen,* Stoddart, 1984; *The Fire-Eaters,* Oberon, 1976; *Mermaids and Ikons: A Greek Summer* (travel), House of Anansi, 1978; *The Trojan Women* (play), Playwrights Co-Op, 1979, new edition, Exile Editions, 1981; *The Chocolate Moose* (juvenile; illustrated by Barry Zaid), NC Press, 1979.

Earthlight: Selected Poetry of Gwendolyn MacEwen, General, 1982; *The T. E. Lawrence Poems,* Mosaic Press, 1982; *The Honey Drum: Seven Tales from Arab Lands* (juvenile), Mosaic Press, 1983; *Noman's Land* (short stories), Coach House, 1985; *Afterworlds,* McClelland & Stewart, 1987.

Also author of radio plays for Canadian Broadcasting Company, including "Terror and Erebus," 1965, "Tesla," 1966, "The World of Neshiah," 1967, "A Celebration of Evil," 1968, and "The Last Night of James Pike," 1976. Translator of some of Greek poet Yannis Ritsos' work. Work is represented in numerous anthologies and magazines.

ADAPTATIONS—Poetry: "Canadian Poets on Tape" (cassette), Ontario Institute Studies in Education, 1969; "Open Secrets" (record), CBC, 1972; "Canadian Poets 1" (record), CBC, 1972; "Gwendolyn MacEwen" (cassette), High Barnet, 1976.

WORK IN PROGRESS: A novel; a new book of poems.

SIDELIGHTS: "I have been writing seriously since I was about eighteen and had some poems published in *The Canadian Forum* when I was younger. It was always natural for me. I realized that writing was what I could do and do well. That's why I didn't go on to university. Everyone thought that I would, that it would be an obvious step. But I didn't want to spend a whole lot of time having to learn what literature was all *about*. I simply wanted to make it myself, and I knew that it would take years of work before I'd get anywhere at all." [Patricia Keeney Smith, "WQ Interview with Gwendolyn MacEwen," *Cross Canada Writers Quarterly*, Volume 5, number 1, 1983.[1]]

One of the differences between writing prose and poetry is that "the sheer effort of *memory* in prose is enormous—simply remembering from day to day what one has written the day before, whereas with poetry, you can often see the whole poem at a glance. [In writing prose] I can usually hang onto a thread for about a hundred pages or so, but then I have to stop and back track, especially as I often do a lot of research. The Egyptian novel, for instance, *King of Egypt, King of Dreams* took me five years to complete, but I loved every minute of it. Keeping track of all the names and details was a tremendous effort, though. . . . I enjoy writing when there's an *intellectual* challenge in front of me all the time. I could write an awful lot more poetry than I do—you know, mood poetry, descriptive poetry. But I don't feel this challenges me enough intellectually. The Lawrence poems did, though, because I had to work with historical facts and philosophical paradoxes."[1]

MacEwen's poems were published during the early sixties. "It seems there was a real poetry explosion then. Suddenly people were talking about poetry; poets were reading and getting audiences out to hear them. It was all very exciting."[1]

"I write in order to make sense of the chaotic nature of experience, of reality—and also to create a bridge between the inner world of the *psyche* and the 'outer' world of things. For me, language has enormous, almost magical power, and I tend to regard poetry in much the same way as the ancients regarded the chants or hymns used in holy festivals: as a means of invoking the mysterious forces which move the world and shape our destinies.

"I write to communicate joy, mystery, passion—not the joy that naively exists without knowledge of pain, but that joy which arises out of and conquers pain. I want to construct a myth."

HOBBIES AND OTHER INTERESTS: Swimming and nonfiction reading (history and science).

FOR MORE INFORMATION SEE: Canadian Literature, summer, 1970, summer, 1977; *Saturday Night*, January, 1972; Frank Davey, "Gwendolyn MacEwen: The Secret of Alchemy," *Open Letter*, spring, 1973; *Dalhousie Review*, winter, 1975-76; Gary Geddes, "Now You See It . . . ," *Books in Canada*, July, 1976; *Contemporary Literary Criticism*, Volume XIII, Gale, 1980; Patricia Keeney Smith, "WQ Interview with Gwendolyn MacEwen," *Cross Canada Writers Quarterly*, Volume 5, number 1, 1983; Jan Bartley, *Invocations: The Poetry and Prose of Gwendolyn MacEwen*, University of British Columbia Press, 1983; Margaret Atwood, "MacEwen's Muse," *Second Words*, Anasi, 1984.

How long a time lies in one little word!
Four lagging winters and four wanton springs
End in a word. . . .

          —William Shakespeare
      (From *King Richard the Second*)

MacLEAN, Alistair (Stuart) 1922(?)-1987 (Ian Stuart)

OBITUARY NOTICE—See sketch in *SATA* Volume 23: Born April 28, 1922 (one source says 1923), in Glasgow (some sources say Daviot), Scotland; died of heart failure following a stroke, February 2, 1987, in Munich, West Germany. Educator and author. One of Britain's most popular novelists, MacLean is best remembered for his war adventures, including *The Guns of Navarone*, which was adapted as a motion picture starring Gregory Peck. Of his thirty books, very popular among young adults, twenty-seven were best-sellers and many became films. MacLean began his career during the 1950s in Scotland, where he worked as a teacher of English and history and wrote short stories in his spare time. One story, submitted for a newspaper competition, attracted the attention of the William Collins & Sons publishing company, who encouraged MacLean to write a book. He completed his first novel, *H.M.S. Ulysses*, in just three months, and Collins published it in 1955. The book proved immensely successful, selling 250,000 hardcover copies in its first six months. Subsequent novels by MacLean include *Ice Station Zebra* and *Breakheart Pass*. His first original screenplay was "Where Eagles Dare," which he rewrote and published as a novel under the same title. MacLean also wrote mystery novels, also popular with young adults, under the name Ian Stuart. These include *The Snow on the Ben* and *The Satan Bug*.

FOR MORE INFORMATION SEE: Contemporary Authors, Volume 57, Gale, 1976; Martha E. Ward and Dorothy A. Marquardt, *Authors of Books for Young People*, supplement to the second edition, Scarecrow, 1979; *Who's Who in the World*, 8th edition, Marquis, 1987. Obituaries: *Chicago Tribune*, February 3, 1987; *Detroit Free Press*, February 3, 1987; *Los Angeles Times*, February 3, 1987; *Modesto Bee*, February 3, 1987; *New York Times*, February 3, 1987; *Times* (London), February 3, 1987; *Washington Post*, February 3, 1987; *AB Bookman's Weekly*, February 23, 1987; *School Library Journal*, March, 1987.

MICHAEL MARTCHENKO

MARTCHENKO, Michael 1942-

PERSONAL: Born August 1, 1942, in Carcassone, France; son of John (employed by a mining company) and Mary (a seamstress; maiden name, Jurczak) Martchenko; married Patricia Kerr (a director of sales and marketing), May 28, 1983; children: Holly Michelle. *Education:* Ontario College of Art, Toronto, A.O.C.A. (Associate of the Ontario College of Art), 1966. *Home:* 100 Airdrie Rd., Toronto, Ontario M4G 1M3, Canada. *Office:* TDF Artists Ltd., 980 Yonge St., Toronto, Ontario, Canada.

CAREER: Spitzer, Mills & Bates, Toronto, Canada, art director, 1966-69; Needham, Harper & Steers, Toronto, art direc-tor, 1969-70; Art Associates, Toronto, designer/illustrator, 1970-72; TDF Artists Ltd., Toronto, creative art director, 1972—. *Exhibitions:* Harbourfront Gallery, Toronto, 1983; travelling children's book illustration show, cross-Canada, 1983; (one-man show) Latcham Gallery, Stouffville, Ontario, 1987. *Member:* Art Directors Club of Toronto. *Awards, honors:* Ad Club of Toronto, award of merit, 1974, three awards of merit, 1977; *Graphica Show*, two awards of merit, 1976; *Mortimer* was exhibited at the Bologna International Children's Book Fair, 1985; Ruth Schwartz Award from the Ontario Arts Council for *Thomas' Snowsuit,* 1986.

ILLUSTRATOR—All written by Robert Munsch, except as noted; all published by Annick Press, except as noted: Dorothy

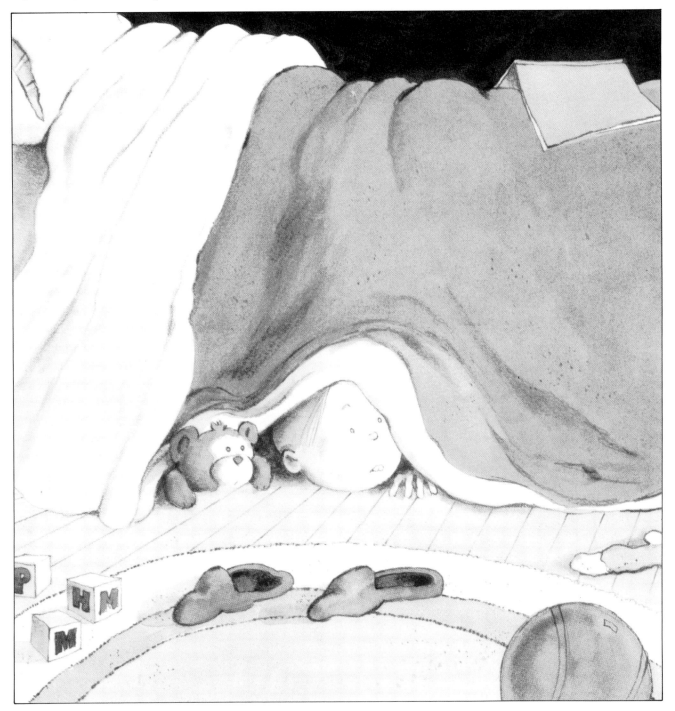

(From *Mortimer* by Robert Munsch. Illustrated by Michael Martchenko.)

Jane Goulding, *Margaret*, McGraw, 1966; *The Paper Bag Princess*, 1980, Scholastic, 1982; *Jonathan Cleaned Up, Then He Heard a Sound; or, Blackberry Subway Jam*, 1981; *Murmel Murmel Murmel*, 1982; *The Boy in the Drawer*, 1982; *David's Father*, 1983; *Angela's Airplane*, 1983; *The Fire Station*, 1983; *Mortimer*, 1983, large print edition, 1985; Allen Morgan, *Matthew and the Midnight Tow Truck*, 1984; *Thomas' Snowsuit*, 1985; A. Morgan, *Matthew and the Midnight Turkey Trap*, 1985; *50 Below Zero*, 1986; *I Have to Go!*, 1986; Anne Fotheringham, *Hurrah for the Dorchester*, Conceptus Renaissance (Montreal), 1986; A. Morgan, *Matthew and the Midnight Money Van*, 1987.

WORK IN PROGRESS: Illustrating Judy Owen's *One Sock, Two Socks* for Gage Press in Toronto.

SIDELIGHTS: "Art has always played an important role in my life. As a child, I loved comic books and picture books. I would fill notebooks full of the most dreadful little drawings as I listened to 'The Shadow' or 'Inner Sanctum' on the radio. It was a great exercise for the imagination.

"All through my school years, I would use just about any excuse to illustrate my notes. Math got it's own special style of uncomplimentary drawings. Throughout high school I knew that I wanted to make art my career.

"I studied at the Ontario College of Art in Toronto and just loved it! It was my first exposure to formal art training and I got into it with a vengeance. It was also my first experience of the 'big city.' It's amazing that I managed to graduate and have a great time as well.

"After graduation I became an agency art director for five years and then I went on to become a studio designer. Presently I am the creative director of TDF Artists in Toronto. Throughout my advertising and graphics career, I have always illustrated children's stories, books and educational material.

"My association with Annick Press began when the publishers and the author saw one of my illustrations hanging in a show several years ago. It was a drawing of a flock of seagulls doing a formation landing in a park, beside a rather nonplussed gent trying to read his newspaper. Robert Munsch, the author, felt that anyone with such a bizarre imagination should illustrate his next book. That was the beginning of a long association which has resulted in our collaboration on eleven books to date.

"When I illustrate a book, I try to imagine what a child would like to see as he reads the story. I try to make the illustrations fun and lively with likeable characters. I also like to add little touches to a drawing—things tucked away in corners or placed on someone, something that kids can spot. I also like to add mine or my family's names, or initials in the drawings. Even the family cat has appeared in several books.

"My favourite technique is pencil and wash. Watercolours are very bright and reproduce well. Pencil, very soft or charcoal, strengthens the shapes and shading.

"My studio is a converted sunroom at the back of the house. This works out very well when I work late. I don't disturb anyone and they don't disturb me. The studio is full of books, old art, lots of paint and junk scattered all around. My wife doesn't dare go in there. I have my collection of hats hanging on the walls and balanced on styrofoam heads for company.

"I get my ideas for situations, characters and locations from the things around me or from magazines, but more often than

not, I make them up. If I need detailed reference on particular objects such as buildings or airplanes, I look through books, magazines and art reference files at work.

"While illustrating children's books is hard work, it's also great fun, with the added advantage of having little interference and few restrictions placed upon you, such as you may have in the commercial art field.

"I'm sure that everyone visualizes pictures when reading a story. I feel very fortunate that in illustrating children's stories, I can put my mental pictures down on board. I hope that I do it in such a way, that children can not only identify with the story, but can use their own imaginations to bring the characters to life."

HOBBIES AND OTHER INTERESTS: Aviation art and history, books on art and military history, movies.

FOR MORE INFORMATION SEE: Quill & Quire, October, 1985.

McKINLEY, (Jennifer Carolyn) Robin 1952-

PERSONAL: Born November 16, 1952, in Warren, Ohio; daughter of William (an officer in the U.S. Navy and Merchant Marines) and Jeanne Carolyn (a teacher; maiden name, Turrell) McKinley. *Education:* Attended Dickinson College, 1970-

ROBIN McKINLEY

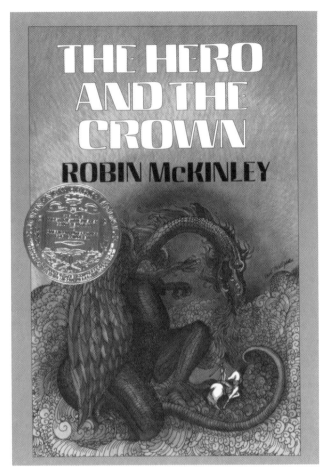

(Jacket illustration by David McCall Johnston from *The Hero and the Crown* by Robin McKinley.)

72; Bowdoin College, B.A. (summa cum laude), 1975. *Politics:* "Few affiliations, although I belong to MADD and NOW, and have strong feelings pro-ERA and pro-freedom—and anti-big-business and anti-big-government." *Religion:* "You could call me a lapsed Protestant." *Home and office:* Maine and New York City. *Agent:* Merrilee Heifetz, Writers House, Inc., 21 West 26th St., New York, N.Y. 10010.

CAREER: Ward & Paul (stenographic reporting firm), Washington, D.C., editor and transcriber, 1972-73; Research Associates, Brunswick, Me., research assistant, 1976-77; clerk in bookstore in Maine, 1978; teacher and counselor at private secondary school in Natick, Mass., 1978-79; Little, Brown, Inc., Boston, Mass., editorial assistant, 1979-81; barn manager on horse farm, Holliston, Mass., 1981-82; Books of Wonder, New York, N.Y., clerk, 1983; free-lance reader, copy and line-editor, general all-purpose publishing dogsbody, 1983—. *Awards, honors: Beauty: A Retelling of the Story of Beauty and the Beast* was selected one of New York Public Library's Books for the Teen Age, 1980, 1981, and 1982; *The Blue Sword* was chosen one of the American Library Association's Best Young Adult Books, 1982; Newbery Honor Book, 1983, for *The Blue Sword; The Hero and the Crown* was chosen a Notable Book by the Association for Library Service to Children of the American Library Association, 1984; Newbery Medal, 1985, for *The Hero and the Crown;* "Best Anthology," World Fantasy Awards, 1986, for *Imaginary Lands;* honorary Doctor of Letters, 1986, from Bowdoin College.

WRITINGS: Beauty: A Retelling of the Story of Beauty and the Beast (novel; ALA Notable Book; *Horn Book* honor list),

Harper, 1978; *The Door in the Hedge* (short stories), Greenwillow, 1981; *The Blue Sword* (novel; ALA Notable Book), Greenwillow, 1982; (contributor) Terri Windling and Mark Arnold, editors, *Elsewhere II,* Ace, 1982; *The Hero and the Crown* (novel; ALA Notable Book), Greenwillow, 1984; (contributor) T. Windling and M. Arnold, editors, *Elsewhere III,* Ace, 1984; (editor) *Imaginary Lands,* Greenwillow, 1985; adapter, *Jungle Book Tales,* Random House, 1985; (contributor) T. Windling, editor, *Faery,* Ace, 1985; (adapter) Anna Sewell, *Black Beauty* (illustrated by Susan Jeffers), Random House, 1986.

WORK IN PROGRESS: A retelling of *Robin Hood;* a book laid in a different part of *Sword* and *Hero*'s world; an adult fantasy; other miscellaneous bits and pieces.

ADAPTATIONS: "The Blue Sword" (listening cassette), Random House; "The Hero and the Crown" (listening cassette), Random House, 1986.

SIDELIGHTS: "One of my first memories is of being read aloud to. My mother would prop me in a corner of the sofa and read to me before I was old enough to sit up by myself. But my parents were determined that I *not* learn to read before I went to school; they were afraid I might then start school disliking it and finding it boring. So I went to first grade very eager: I already knew that books were the best things going,

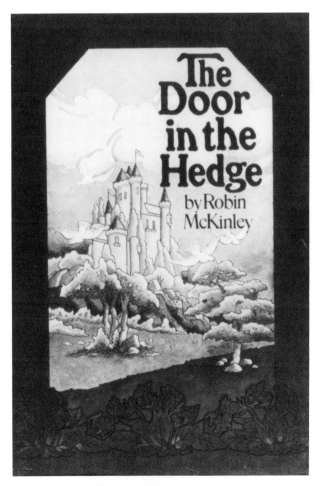

Perhaps they did not think of what that open door in the hedge would bring about, or perhaps they put it deliberately out of their minds.... ■ (Jacket illustration by Ted Bernstein from *The Door in the Hedge* by Robin McKinley.)

and school was going to give them to me. My mother tells the story that I came home from my first day in a rage: 'I haven't learned to read yet!' I think it took about six more weeks.

"My father was in the Navy and came back from his long overseas trips with his suitcases full of books and rolls of film. Wherever we moved, my mother borrowed books by the shelf from the local library, working tirelessly through the fiction racks from A to Z. We moved so often and therefore had to start a new library so often that she sometimes brought the same book home twice. 'Have I read this before?' she'd say, handing me a book across the breakfast table: I was allowed to read at table only at breakfast.

"My earliest childhood was in Arlington, Virginia and Washington, D.C. I attended kindergarten in Long Beach, California, the first place I clearly remember. (I did think kindergarten was pretty boring.) First, second and third grade were spent in upstate New York, and by the end of second grade I was reading sixth grade books. Books were my best friends; people, after all, were pretty insubstantial since we moved so often. I am an only child and 'a solitary' by nature; the world of books was much more satisfactory than the so-called real world. Frances Hodgson Burnett's *A Little Princess,* about a little girl all alone in a strange land who told stories so wonderful that she believed them herself, fascinated me. I never quite lived up to Sara Crewe's standard, but I tried awfully hard.

"After New York we lived in Japan for almost five years. I took my first horseback riding lessons in Japan; I was ten years old. I've been horse-crazy since second grade—I can even tell you the book that began it all: *Dixie Dobie, a Sable Island Pony,* by two people named Johnson. I first read it sitting cross-legged on the floor of the Watertown Public Library, and I haven't been the same since; I've never grown out of being horse-mad, the way girls are supposed to.

"In Fuchinobe, near Tokyo, where we lived, two Japanese ex-cavalrymen operated a riding school for the American military. My mother took lessons for a little while, but it didn't really appeal to her. My father took to it with almost as much enthusiasm as I did, and we rode faithfully every weekend till we left Japan—in spite of the fact that it was a two-hour drive to the stables each way, and back roads in Japan twenty years ago were seriously harrowing. My mother came along, and cheered us from the bleachers, although I think she closed her eyes when I fell off, and made me always wear my hard hat. Our instructors' method of teaching us riding was to set up jumps higher and higher and make you go over them till the horse refused or you fell off or both. I was not a natural rider— I didn't have that beautiful balance and adaptability you see in natural athletes—and I was scared to death half the time, but anything was worth it to ride.

"We returned to the States, to Rhode Island, in the middle of eighth grade for me. It was a pretty rough adjustment, in spite

The first place I remember is a large pleasant meadow, where I lived with my mother. ■ (From *Black Beauty* by Anna Sewell, adapted by Robin McKinley. Illustrated by Susan Jeffers.)

of the stable just a few steps from our house, where I worked, eagerly if not tirelessly, every day after school and every weekend.

"The States was home, of course. I knew that. I'd known it all the four and a half years we lived overseas; and however much I grew to love Japan and the Japanese countryside, one look at my blond hair and green eyes made me a foreigner, a foreigner inescapably and forever. But when I got back to the States I found that it wasn't home any more—Japan, where I was a foreigner, had become home. The States was strange, the houses were big and sprawly and careless—although the roads were sure a lot better. I had come home too with an abiding love for Oriental art, though it took me a few years to realize this; I hadn't paid that much attention to it while I lived with it. There's an aphorism here, although I'm not quite sure how it goes: you find out what you can't give up when you can't give it up.

"My father retired from the Navy when I was in my mid-teens. We moved to Vinalhaven, Maine, which became a very grim two and a half years for me. Vinalhaven is a tiny island off the coast with at that time a year-round population of about one thousand, and it was not a good place to be in if you are an introverted teen-ager who doesn't do a whole lot very well except read. My last year of high school was spent at a prep school, Gould Academy, in western Maine. That was the beginning of sorting myself out into the adult I would eventually become. Gould was wonderful to me. I had two extremely good teachers who believed in me—for some reason. They saw within this overweight weird teenager someone who might grow up into an interesting human being. I seem to have out-grown being fat and come into my own as weird, but it can only be prescience that let them see it back then.

"I went to Dickinson College in Carlisle, Pennsylvania, the fall of '70. It had a good reputation as an intellectual school; I thought it was a country club, although whether that was my fault or the school's I'm no longer sure. I dropped out after a year and a half (on my way giving the poor Dean of Women a terribly high-minded little essay on how Dickinson was failing to meet my scholastic needs) and went to Washington, D.C. where I eventually married a boy who had been commuting down to Dickinson to see me on weekends. I became a motorcycle messenger and a transcriber for a stenographic reporting firm—one that covered a lot of Watergate, by the way. My husband and I lived around the corner from the police station that first discovered the break-in, too. We lived across the street from a hospital, had the police station around one corner and a fire station around the other, and the George Washington University hospital emergency room about a block and a half away. It was interesting but it was not peaceful. My husband went into public relations when he got out of the Army. We would walk down the streets together, me in my motorcycle leathers and he in his three-piece suit, holding hands. I was nineteen and he was twenty-one and we knew we were hot stuff.

"We decided to go back to school, and I applied to Bowdoin College, in Brunswick, Maine, which my husband had left to join the Army. Bowdoin was very hard to get into in those days and they must have caught my folder when they threw all the transfer applications up in the air and grabbed the first six coming down—my grades from Dickinson were okay but nothing spectacular. I graduated Phi Beta Kappa and summa cum laude, so they didn't choose so badly. I majored in English lit, though, still the kid who didn't do anything too well except read—it was also a good indication of my fine bold disdain for anything so trivial as earning a living. Two years in D.C. should have taught me better.

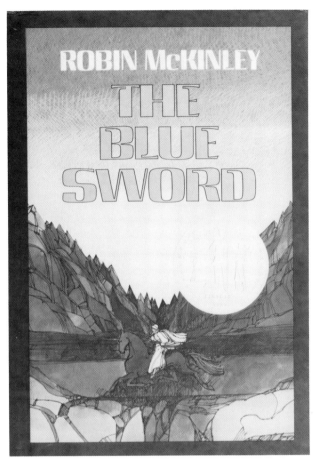

The far sides of the mountains were less steep, but no less forbidding. Broken foothills extended a long way, into the hazy distance.... ■ (Jacket illustration by David McCall Johnston from *The Blue Sword* by Robin McKinley.)

"After graduation I settled down to write; my husband joined the police department. I worked part-time to help keep the rent paid, and in all honesty I spent more time sharpening pencils and reading the *New York Times Book Review* than I did writing. But it was during this period that I finally wrote *Beauty*.

"Writing has always been the other side of reading for me; it never occurred to me not to make up stories. Once I became old enough to realize that authorship existed as a thing one might aspire to, I knew it was for me. But I was also secretly determined to follow in seven-league-boot-sized footsteps like Dickens' and George Eliot's and Hardy's and Conrad's and Kipling's—and J.R.R. Tolkien's. I never will resign myself to the fact that I am not going to write *Tess of the D'Urbervilles* or *Rewards and Fairies*. I don't entirely blame my younger self for spending a lot of time sharpening pencils. I still sharpen a lot of pencils.

"I had been working on the stories that would eventually become the Damarian cycle, which so far is only two books: *The Blue Sword* and *The Hero and the Crown*. I had begun—this would be about '76—to realize that there was more than one story to tell about Damar, that in fact it seemed to be a whole history, volumes and volumes of the stuff, and this terrified me. I had plots and characters multiplying like mice and running in all directions—and I had never even written a short story I was completely happy with.

We could just see at the bank that the water was very high. ■ (From *Black Beauty* by Anna Sewell, adapted by Robin McKinley. Illustrated by Susan Jeffers.)

"Then a friend of mine called me with the news that the Hallmark Hall of Fame was going to present 'Beauty and the Beast' on television, starring George C. Scott. I had seen Scott in 'Jane Eyre' with Susannah York several years before and loved it and was very anxious to see this. My husband kindly borrowed a tiny black-and-white set from his great-aunt for me (we did not stoop to owning a television; or you could say it was the exigencies of keeping the rent paid) and I sat down on the appointed evening with my heart in my mouth—and hated it. They did everything wrong. About halfway through the show, I was feeling so sour, I started wondering nastily how they were going to turn George C. Scott into a handsome young prince at the end. They didn't, of course. The Beast turns into a middle-aged George C. Scott, with his big nose and bandy legs, although he still had his beautiful voice.

"This was the one thing that hung over me: I had never quite come to terms with how the prince in the fairy tale turns back into this smooth-faced young man at the end after long sad lonely years as the Beast. It didn't fit. So, without a whole lot more in mind than just that, I sat down at my desk that same night to write what I intended to be a short story—and a brief break from Damar, which was driving me nuts—my version of my favorite fairy tale, *Beauty and the Beast*. For five months I sat down at my desk every evening and said, 'Tonight I finish it.'

"To my surprise and uncertain pride I found I had a novel on my hands—but I was at least half embarrassed by it. What a silly thing to have done, to put so much time and energy and heart's blood into retelling a fairy tale. Everybody already knows how it ends; nobody would care, and certainly nobody would publish it. I dithered about this for months and finally sent it to Harper & Row—who, I thought, looking at the science-fiction-and-fantasy section in the town library, seemed to publish the sort of thing I thought I might have written. And they took it.

"I left my husband the spring of '78; *Beauty* came out that fall, and I left Maine shortly thereafter. I first worked at a small prep school in eastern Massachusetts. I was one of those pathetic creatures known as a dorm counselor: it meant you lived there with the kids and at three a.m. dragged yourself out of bed to find out what the row in the hall was about. I hated it: I don't like that kind of authority, and I'm not good at it. I wrote a couple of the short stories that would eventually go into *The Door in the Hedge*, but that's about all; while I know the adolescent years are supposed to be spent testing your boundaries, I felt like a fence that was falling down.

"I was lucky enough to be in the right place at the right time in Boston, and was hired by John Keller to be the new reader for the children's department at Little, Brown. Boston publishing is so small I'm still a little in awe of this stroke of luck. I moved to Boston the spring of '79, and worked two years at Little, Brown; *Door* was published by Greenwillow Books while I was there. I enjoyed the work but it was soon leaving me too little time to write; after I was promoted to editorial assistant, there was simply always too much to do, till *Sword* began to turn into something resembling a permanent migraine headache. I'll always owe John—who has little use for fantasy himself—a debt of gratitude, however, for suggesting I try Susan Hirschman at Greenwillow after I left Harper & Row.

"I met a woman, another writer, owner of a horse farm not far outside Boston, who was looking for someone to live in her farmhouse apartment in return for working part-time in the barn—a very appealing arrangement. As I was casting about

for the courage to take such a leap into the unknown, Greenwillow offered me an advance against *Sword* without having seen so much as one word of outline for the book. I lived on tuna fish and hot dogs for a year, worked in the stable, and wrote *Sword*.

"I've said I was never much of a rider. It's hard to explain how serious this was to me when I was a teenager. I was an awkward and self-conscious kid who viewed her body as an essentially alien creation that had, somehow, to be managed. I still feel that way but I've gotten better at the managing. While I was living on the horse farm I started taking dressage lessons. Dressage is something like gymnastics for a human being: the point is to make your horse more supple and balanced, a better athlete. A horse is not necessarily well-coordinated, any more than a person may be; some horses are natural athletes. Most aren't. Once I began to study dressage I realized that lacking a natural gift wasn't a death knell for either you or the horse, if you're willing to put a lot of labor and sweat into learning what is easy for some people. One of my riding teachers turned out to be just what I needed—Kathy is now also one of my closest friends. I can't begin to describe how those two years of dressage lessons justified my pains as a teenager. Some of this is reflected in the way Aerin in *Hero* learns to wield a sword; she had to learn it by rote, too, because she wasn't getting any discernable help from talent.

"Some things you never learn though. Harry's vaulting into the saddle in *Sword* is the same sort of blatant wish-fulfillment as Beauty's being skinny and undersized (although at least I permitted her a few spots) is. One thing I will probably always do badly is mount. The horse staggers off as I drag myself aboard, relocating our balance. The mare I ride most often now is pretty used to me, and I can see her spread her feet when I approach her near side.

"After almost two years at the horse farm, however, I was spending more time in the barn than at my typewriter; and however close a second horses run in my life, the writing still comes first. I left Massachusetts and moved to New York City; friends of mine living on Staten Island had rented half a large house and they, like me, were among the motley crowd of publishing free-lancers, which meant they didn't have much money. I moved into their spare room on Halloween of '82, just in time to help pay the winter heating bills. And started writing *The Hero and the Crown*.

"Damar has never been a trilogy—although fantasies are half expected to be trilogies these days: a rather ironic heritage of *Lord of the Rings*, perhaps, which would embarrass Tolkien, who fought against having his story chopped up in three volumes. I've called Damar 'a series of indefinite length' since I began to realize how much of it there is. *Sword* as *Sword* was a late addition—even the name Damar was—to a cacophony of stories rattling around in my brain demanding space and attention. I've said I was taking time out from the tumult to write *Beauty*. But the first disentangled thread of story was Aerin's—or rather the thread of story that led me to the tangle was Aerin's. The first real spark of her story is from my many passionate rereadings of *Lord of the Rings* in junior high, and there's been a lot of brooding, plotting and wondering time between then and now.

"I recognized that there were specific connections between Harry and Aerin, and I deliberately wrote their stories in reverse chronological order, because one of the things I'm fooling around with is the idea of heroes: real heroes as opposed to the legends that are told of them afterwards. Aerin is one of her country's greatest heroes, and by the time Harry comes along, Harry is expected—or Harry thinks she is—to live up to her. When you go back and find out about Aerin in *Hero,* you discover that she wasn't this mighty invincible figure with a cult of acolytes; she had a very hard and solitary time of her early fate.

"As a compulsive reader myself, I believe that you are what you read. I despised myself for being a girl, and ipso facto being someone who stayed at home and was boring, and started trying to tell myself stories about girls who did things and had adventures, to cheer myself up after *The Count of Monte Cristo* and *The Four Feathers*—and 'The Jungle Books' and *Lord of the Rings*. To a great extent I am now merely writing down slightly more coherent versions of the stories I was telling myself twenty and more years ago.

"My books are also about hope—I hope. Much of modern literature has given up hope and deals with anti-heroes and despair. It seems to me that human beings by their very natures need heroes, real heroes, and are happier with them. I see no point in talking about how life is over and it never mattered anyway. I don't believe it. I like getting out of bed in the morning. Or, no—I like having gotten out. The getting is often disagreeable.

"It is of course significant that Beauty's real name is Honour. Authors—this one anyway—are rarely too bright about what their books 'mean,' but I know that I am preoccupied with honor and duty. I will fight to the death over whether or not my books really 'mean' anything beyond being stories as lively as I can make them (usually about girls who do things), but part of that liveliness comes, I think, from the conflict of honor with inclination, and with fate. It's the way the characters who present themselves to me to be written about behave.

"*Beauty*'s derivation is a fairy tale, however, and I cold-bloodedly named her Honour, and her sisters Grace and Hope. I chose, or was chosen by, the name Angharad for the protagonist in *The Blue Sword* at least partly because I liked calling her 'Harry.' The nickname arrived more or less simultaneously with the name, although it took me a little time to realize they were the same person. But I consciously wanted a name that either was androgynous to begin with or that could be shortened to something confusing. It's all part of my feeling that the gender wars are so bitter because the areas of rightness and propriety for each side are too absolutely defined; anything that muddies the line that society has drawn in the dirt and dared us to step over, is to the good, in fiction or in life. I also think that girls who want to do things are going to have a slightly easier time if they aren't frightened with a silly girly name. Just wanting to do things is enough of a burden. In a story I'm working on now, however, the protagonist's name is Elly. I don't know if she's going to have a harder time than if she were named Jim or Frank or not.

"As an important adjunct to hope and honor, I am obsessed with the idea of freedom, especially because I'm a WASP female of limited imagination. I'm preoccupied with the notion of woman's ability, or inability, to move within her society. I am not so purblind as to think that the only thing seriously wrong with our civilization is that men have more freedom of choice than women: but I strongly believe that that is one important thing wrong, and that it must be changed. Nor will I give up the idea that men and women can cope with each other in some relaxed and affectionate fashion—under this crabby exterior there beats the squashy heart of a romantic. (One of my guiltiest guilty pleasures is rereading Georgette Heyer's frivolous historical novels: I know *Friday's Child* and *These Old Shades* virtually by heart). Some weeks, when the

Dewar's ads of successful people all seem to be interesting women and *Ms.* magazine has just arrived, I think we're getting somewhere; other weeks, when I've been watching too much MTV and reading too many *New Yorker* stories about passive angst, I think we aren't. But meanwhile there are no princesses who wring their hands and stand around in ivory towers waiting for princes to return from the wars in my stories. Aerin wanted to grow up to be a hero because her mother had died of despair upon learning she had borne a daughter and not a son. The Blue Sword herself is a woman's sword, to be wielded by a woman; as Corlath tells Harry, it will betray any man, come to his full growth, who carries it.

"One of the things I am constantly asked about is my style, which people tell me I have a great deal of. This is pretty amusing, or dismaying, depending on the mood I'm in, because I have almost no control over it. It's the way the stories tell themselves. I write by ear, I hear the rhythm of the story—of the characters talking, of the pace of the plot. While I try my best to get this rhythm down on paper, I don't do much besides hold my heart in my mouth while I listen, and hope that what I catch at as it rushes by doesn't go down too raggedly on the paper. When people ask me about my style, I mumble a little and change the subject.

"My first draft is in longhand. I try to translate the story in my head into words: It's a process of turning what I see and hear into a story that will look and feel like a story to other people. Since I write by ear, I don't rewrite well. It has to go down more or less right, or at least recognizable, the first time or I have to throw it out. If there's a spot where it's starting to go seriously wrong on me, I stop. I have several half-finished things in drawers waiting to be sorted out; it's often years later that it occurs to me what to do, and then I sometimes have to start over from scratch. This is depressing—I don't like hard work so awfully well that I want to do any more of it than I have to—and I try urgently to avoid it.

"But sometimes during a rough draft I have to be careful that I'm not just stopping at a minor trouble spot; if I stopped every time I knew that I was writing badly I would never get through the first chapter. (The humiliating thing is how little difference there is, when I look back, between the bits I think are inspired and the bits I knew were garbage). So I go on, and trust that the story will get itself better put together as I go on. In the second draft, which is the first typed draft, the story gets longer, often a lot longer. I start putting in what people who don't know the story as well as I do need to make connections. I also put in the bits that I forgot the first time—getting the story down that first time is the most terrifically hard work I know (worse than posting to the trot without stirrups) and I get sort of glazed over with exhaustion sometimes, and leave out important things.

"In the third and final draft I tinker with the punctuation and try to get the words, both English and Damarian, spelled right, and make sure that character 'A' has the same color hair on page 261 that she did on page twelve. Language, like style, is something I can't say much about. Most of the words come as part of the storytelling. As the story grows, I hear people talking to each other and I hear the names they call each other, the unfamiliar words they use.

"You see, the stories come from somewhere; I don't feel that I make them up. They are certainly very colored by their vehicle—me. But I'm not their place of origin. I say sometimes that there's a crack in my skull, and the stories come through, like sunlight in a cave. It bothers me that I know how much purer the stories were before I started meddling with them.

BEAUTY

A RETELLING OF THE STORY OF

Beauty & the Beast

by Robin McKinley

The wall was waist-high, and covered with the largest and most beautiful climbing roses that he had ever seen. ■ (Jacket illustration by David Palladini from *Beauty: A Retelling of the Story of Beauty and the Beast* by Robin McKinley.)

Just the fact that the stories must come through me must change them in some way; and then I am far too opinionated and overbearing to make an ideal medium. One of the things that I'm curious about myself is whether the stories I tell come to me because I am who I am with my set of preoccupations, or if I have become who I am and built up these preoccupations because of the stories that come to me.

"When I'm deeply into a story I begin dreaming it at night, but I very rarely find my way out of any corners I've written myself into while I'm asleep; mostly what I get is a much stronger sense of background, like closing the other eye when you focus through a camera lens. I look for ways out on my long walks. I walk a lot; my daily circle, when I'm home, is about eight miles. It gets the blood flowing again after I've gotten all jammed up at the typewriter—and I get terminally restive and cranky if the weather forces me to stay indoors more than a day or two in a row. I don't begin anywhere so specific as 'I have to get my characters from point A to point B. How am I going to do it?' I start telling the story to myself—mostly I can control what place in the story I want to think about—and watch and listen, like a movie, maybe, except it feels three-dimensional. Sometimes one of the characters is telling the story—to me or someone; sometimes the story itself happens. I forget sometimes where I am, and stop, or turn my head to listen better, forgetting that's not how I'm listening.

"I know the story very well when I start writing it down. As I said, I write by ear, I can't do a lot of heavy revision. It's getting to be time to try it out on paper when I can begin to organize it—still in my head—into sentences that I can write down, with my this-world hand, on a sheet of this-world paper. I know it's time to start writing when I can see the first sentence of the story, literally, the first sentence, black print on a white page—which won't in fact exist yet till the second draft.

"The writing always has it surprises, however, which is just as well; it's such hard work that if it weren't also astonishing and exhilarating, I could never stick with it. But I do know the characters so well by the time I come to write about them, how they behave and who they are, that when they meet up with something that surprises all of us, I'm right there. We see each other through.

"For example, at the end of *Sword*, Mathin was supposed to die. I kept putting off writing that scene, putting it off and putting it off, because I couldn't bear it. I finally gritted my teeth and sat down to it, and to my amazement, Harry went into this flame-blinded trance and healed him. I was *so glad*.

"I thought I knew how *Hero* was going to end, too; after the battle on the plain in front of the City. And then there was all this business with Tor and Aerin and Maur's head. I went on writing, thinking, well, this is very interesting, what next? And I went on, and on, and then it occurred to me that I'd passed the end of the book I was writing, and was into another book. Whereupon I stopped and went back and tidied off, and that's the first I knew that there would be another book about Aerin.

"One of the reasons I know the Damar stories originate somewhere other than in my mind is because of this kind of lack of 'control' over my 'material.' Another example of what is virtually automatic writing is Aerin's dragon-killing. I've certainly never killed a dragon. When I wrote the first dragon scene in *Hero* I was shocked by how graphic it was. I didn't know, for example, that there was going to be the second

dragon, any more than Aerin did. My hand kept moving across the page—my handwritten drafts, by the way, are appalling; they look like they were written while hanging upside-down from the rigging of a small boat in high seas. Occasionally a word or a paragraph will be so bad *I* can't read it—and I was just following along, with my mouth a little open, wishing I could write faster, because I wanted to know how it was going to end. I barely changed a word for the final copy. When I got to the scene where Aerin encounters the huge Black Dragon, Maur, I was dreading it; I knew something of how this was going to go, and I didn't really want to know more. I don't know where it all came from, but they sure know about dragons there. I went around the house for weeks after Aerin kills Maur with my left arm cradled next to my body, and dragging my right foot a little—yes, I do tend to identify with the heroes.

"*The Hero and the Crown* won the 1985 John Newbery Medal. The Newbery award is supposed to be the peak of your career as a writer for children or young adults. I was rather young to receive it; and it is a little disconcerting to feel—okay; you've done it; that's it, you should retire now. And I was informed that I would give a thirty-minute speech of acceptance to maybe 2000 people—a speech by which, by the bye, I am going to be remembered forever. There will be people who know nothing about me except that Newbery speech—it's recorded on tape, and published in several places—which is something I prefer not to think about. Composing that damn speech is the hardest bit of writing I have ever had to do. (The second worst was an essay I was asked to write about Tolkien. Stories are *nothing* in comparison.) I don't like public performances, and I feel that the books are what matter anyway; all us authors are secondary, and, to a very great extent, irrelevent.

"I dislike giving speeches, but I rather like giving informal talks to smaller groups—much smaller groups—at schools and libraries, which give readers an opportunity to meet the author as a human being, a chance to talk back, a chance to ask questions. I also remember very vividly how much it would have meant to me to meet an author—a Real Author—when I was a kid. There's almost always someone like me then in my audiences now: someone who really wants to know about writing, about how it works, about how you live with it.

"I'm almost always asked, too, what my advice is to aspiring writers—young or old; it's not always the kids who ask, and since I get published in paperback as 'adult fantasy' I sometimes draw mixed crowds. My advice is that there's no one right way to do it. But you read as much as you can, and you write as much as you can. You don't have to be organized about it, and you don't have to have a wonderful liberal arts education. I am afraid I take great delight in tweaking teachers who ask me solemnly, 'How has your education helped your career as a writer?' The answer is, 'It hasn't.' I didn't like school; I am so much happier now it is easy to see just how miserable I was for most of my school life. I had a few good teachers, and I owe them a great deal; but I owe them more the debt of inspiration by enthusiasm than anything more formal; as I owe my parents being bitten by the book bug so early.

"Simply read what you like, read what makes you happy, read what makes you enthusiastic. Follow your nose through the library; talk to anyone who will talk to you about what they've read, and learn whose advice to take. And write, and keep writing. Keep a journal; write fragments of stories if you can't write complete stories; but write. Reading feeds your writing, and writing, like anything worthy of being done well, takes practice. When that story you simply must write happens to you, you will be well-exercised in the craft of writing, and ready to take it on. Find out—by practicing—how *you* write. Feel free to plagiarize favorite writers when you're first learning how to put a story together; it will teach you a lot about plot and pacing and development and use of the language. Find out if you're happier writing outlines or not; if you need to go through dozens of revisions or not; if you take notes as you work a story up or if you're better off keeping it in your head till almost the last minute.

"I'm working on several things at once right now, which is something I don't do because I confuse easily; perhaps my muse is trying to teach me something new—or maybe my usual state of disorganization is reaching the terminal. I know that some of this is issue-skirting: after *Sword* was a Newbery honor book, I was afraid that the reaction to *Hero*—even though I'd planned to write it next since before I'd written *Sword*—was that I was cashing in on a good thing. Then *Hero* won the Medal itself and now I'm terrified. I have too many tales left to tell about Damar to have any thoughts about giving it up, but the next thing I finish won't be about Damar, and maybe the one after that as well. I'm not entirely sorry for the delay, however (although I'm already getting restive fan mail from readers of *Sword* and *Hero* who demand to know when the next one is coming out). When I wrote *Beauty* I found that the novel, even though it was not the same place in my head where my favorite fairy tale had lived, somehow exorcised the tale from my mind: Beauty and the Beast, which was a place I used to go often, is barred to me now. I've never quite gotten over this; and I couldn't bear it if it happened to me with Damar as well. If I ever find myself running to the end of the Damarian stories, I will stop writing them down, because *I* want to be able to keep on going there.

"But as I began, so I go on. I still read compulsively, and I still travel a lot, although my life is complicated by the possession of several thousand books, about half that many records and tapes, and a baby grand piano, which I play extremely badly. I am very grateful I was born in the era of stereo equipment; I have music going fourteen or sixteen hours a day. (Indeed it's hard to get around in my workroom, with its four doors, two desks, three filing cabinets, a woodstove, a baby xerox machine, stereo gear, and heaps of books, records, and manuscripts-in-process on the floor. No computer—my IBM selectric isn't a lot younger than I am). I used to sing around the house a lot when I was a kid, but my father—from whom I get my love of opera—couldn't stand it. Without records I might have had to get used to the way I play and sing. A dreadful fate. My latest self-indulgence is a VCR, and I'm busy collecting old 'Star Trek' episodes—speaking of guilty pleasures. I've just about worn out my copy of John Huston's movie of Kipling's story 'The Man Who Would Be King,' the poster from which has hung over my desk—wherever my desk was—for ten years.

"A little over two years ago I bought a little house in a village about two-thirds of the way up the Maine coast—twelve miles from where my parents now live. (For the first time since I left home to go to boarding school I can call my mother any time I like, without worrying about long-distance rates). I had not considered becoming a property owner until I saw my house, which I recognized immediately. Fortunately there was a FOR SALE sign nailed to the maple tree in the front garden.

"Even though I claim to live in Maine now, I keep going back to New York City, but sleeping in friends' living rooms gets old quickly—and not every living room has a good place for setting up a typewriter. Being a property owner has proved so compellingly interesting that I recently bought a co-op there—it's so small it makes my tiny house look large—in an attempt

to regularize my improbable commute. (I still go for long walks, even in New York City, although it's a little more challenging. I put tapes of my loudest, meanest rock music in my Walkman when I'm there, to get myself in the mood.) I shuttle cheerfully, if slightly manically, between the two, when I'm not flying to Seattle or London or plotting to get to Australia or back to the Far East. And while my lilac-covered cottage is the light of my life, I still want a castle in Scotland."

FOR MORE INFORMATION SEE: Kirkus Reviews, December 1, 1978; *Washington Post Book World,* December 3, 1978, April 12, 1981; *Newsweek,* December 18, 1978; *Horn Book,* April, 1979, August, 1981, July/August, 1985; Lee Kingman, editor, *Newbery and Caldecott Medal Books: 1976-1985,* Horn Book, 1986.

MELTZER, Milton 1915-

PERSONAL: Born May 8, 1915, in Worcester, Mass.; son of Benjamin (a window cleaner) and Mary (a factory worker; maiden name, Richter) Meltzer; married Hilda Balinky (a college counsellor), June 22, 1941; children: Jane, Amy. *Education:* Attended Columbia University, 1932-36. *Politics:* Independent. *Religion:* Jewish. *Home:* 263 West End Ave., New York, N.Y. 10023. *Agent:* Harold Ober Associates, 40 East 49th St., New York, N.Y. 10017.

CAREER: Historian, biographer, and author of books for young people. Federal Theatre Project of the Works Projects Administration, New York, N.Y., staff writer, 1936-39; CBS Radio, New York, N.Y., researcher and writer, 1946; Public Relations Staff of Henry A. Wallace for President, 1947-49; Medical and Pharmaceutical Information Bureau, New York, N.Y, account executive, 1950-55; Pfizer, Inc., New York, N.Y., assistant director of public relations, 1955-60; Science & Medicine Publishing Co., Inc., New York, N.Y., editor, 1960-68; University of Massachusetts, Amherst, adjunct professor, 1977-80. Consulting editor for Thomas Y. Crowell Co., Doubleday & Co., Inc., and Scholastic Book Services; lecturer at universities in U.S. and England, and at professional meetings and seminars. Producer of films and filmstrips. *Military service:* U.S. Army Air Force, 1942-46; became sergeant. *Member:* Authors Guild (member of national council), P.E.N., Organization of American Historians.

AWARDS, HONORS: Thomas Alva Edison Mass Media Award for special excellence in portraying America's past, 1966, for *In Their Own Words: A History of the American Negro,* Volume 2, *1865-1916;* Children's Literature Award of the National Book Award, finalist, 1969, for *Langston Hughes: A Biography,* 1975, for *Remember the Days: A Short History of the Jewish American* and *World of Our Fathers: The Jews of Eastern Europe,* and 1977, for *Never to Forget: The Jews of the Holocaust;* Christopher Award, 1969, for *Brother, Can You Spare a Dime? The Great Depression, 1929-1933,* and 1980, for *All Times, All Peoples: A World History of Slavery.*

Slavery: From the Rise of Western Civilization to the Renaissance was selected one of *School Library Journal's* Best Books, 1971; Charles Tebeau Award from the Florida Historical Society, 1973, for *Hunted Like a Wolf: The Story of the Seminole War;* Jane Addams Peace Association Children's Book Award Honor Book, 1975, for *The Eye of Conscience: Photographers and Social Change; Boston Globe-Horn Book* Nonfiction Honor Book, 1976, for *Never to Forget: The Jews of the Holocaust,* and 1983, for *The Jewish Americans: A History in Their Own Words, 1650-1950;* Association of Jewish Libraries Book

MILTON MELTZER

Award, 1976, Jane Addams Peace Association Children's Book Award, 1977, Charles and Bertie G. Schwartz Award for Jewish Juvenile Literature from the National Jewish Book Awards, 1978, Hans Christian Andersen Honor List, 1979, and selected by the American Library Association as a "Best of the Best Books 1970-1983," all for *Never to Forget: The Jews of the Holocaust; Dorothea Lange: A Photographer's Life* was selected one of *New York Times* Best Adult Books of the Year, 1978; Washington Children's Book Guild Honorable Mention, 1978, and 1979, and Nonfiction Award, 1981, all for his total body of work.

American Book Award finalist, 1981, for *All Times, All Peoples: A World History of Slavery;* Carter G. Woodson Book Award from the National Council for Social Studies, 1981, for *The Chinese Americans;* Jefferson Cup Award from the Virginia State Library Association, 1983, for *The Jewish Americans: A History in Their Own Words, 1650-1950;* Children's Book Award special citation from the Child Study Children's Book Committee, one of *School Library Journal*'s Best Books for Young Adults, both 1985, and Olive Branch Award from the Writers' and Publishers' Alliance for Nuclear Disarmament, Jane Addams Peace Association Children's Book Award, and New York University Center for War, Peace, and the News Media, all 1986, all for *Ain't Gonna Study War No More: The Story of America's Peaceseekers;* John Brubaker Memorial Award from the Catholic Library Association, 1986; Golden Kite Award for nonfiction from the Society of Children's Book Writers, 1987, for *Poverty in America.* Several of Meltzer's books have been selected as Library of Congress' Best Children's Books of the Year, Notable Children's Trade Book in Social Studies from the National Council for Social Studies, and *New York Times* Outstanding Children's Books of the Year.

WRITINGS—For young people, except as noted; all nonfiction, except as noted: (With Langston Hughes) *A Pictorial History of the Negro in America* (adult), Crown, 1956, 5th revised edition, with C. Eric Lincoln, published as *A Pictorial History of Black Americans*, 1983.

Mark Twain Himself (adult), Crowell, 1960; *A Light in the Dark: The Life of Samuel Gridley Howe* (ALA Notable Book),

Crowell, 1964; *In Their Own Words: A History of the American Negro,* Crowell, Volume I, *1619-1865* (ALA Notable Book), 1964, Volume II, *1865-1916* (ALA Notable Book), 1965, Volume III, *1916-1966* (ALA Notable Book), 1967, abridged edition published as *The Black Americans: A History in Their Own Words, 1619-1983,* Crowell, 1984.

Tongue of Flame: The Life of Lydia Maria Child, Crowell, 1965; (with August Meier) *Time of Trial, Time of Hope: The Negro in America, 1919-1941* (with teacher's guide; illustrated by Moneta Barnett), Doubleday, 1966; *Thaddeus Stevens and the Fight for Negro Rights,* Crowell, 1967; (with L. Hughes) *Black Magic: A Pictorial History of the Negro in American Entertainment,* Prentice-Hall, 1967; *Bread—and Roses: The Struggle of American Labor, 1865-1915,* Knopf, 1967; *Langston Hughes: A Biography* (ALA Notable Book), Crowell, 1968; *Brother, Can You Spare a Dime? The Great Depression, 1929-1933* (ALA Notable Book), Knopf, 1969; (with Lawrence Lader) *Margaret Sanger: Pioneer of Birth Control,* Crowell, 1969.

Freedom Comes to Mississippi: The Story of Reconstruction, Follett, 1970; *Slavery: From the Rise of Western Civilization to the Renaissance,* Cowles, 1971, Volume 2, *Slavery: From the Renaissance to Today,* Cowles, 1972; *To Change the World: A Picture History of Reconstruction,* Scholastic Book Services, 1971; *Underground Man* (novel), Bradbury Press, 1972; *Hunted Like a Wolf: The Story of the Seminole War,* Farrar, Straus, 1972; *The Right to Remain Silent,* Harcourt, 1972; (with Bernard Cole) *The Eye of Conscience: Photographers and Social Change,* Follett, 1974; *World of Our Fathers: The Jews of Eastern Europe,* Farrar, Straus, 1974; *Remember the Days: A Short History of the Jewish American* (illustrated by Harvey Dinnerstein), Doubleday, 1974; *Bound for the Rio*

Migrant Mother. Nipomo, California, 1936. ■ (From *Dorothea Lange: Life through the Camera* by Milton Meltzer. Photograph by Dorothea Lange.)

Old and young were befriended by the Hebrew Immigrant Aid Society upon their arrival in America. ■ (From *The Jews in America: A Picture Album* by Milton Meltzer. Photograph by Stephen Epstein.)

Grande: The Mexican Struggle 1845-1850, Knopf, 1974; *Taking Root: Jewish Immigrants in America,* Farrar, Straus, 1974.

Violins and Shovels: The WPA Arts Projects, Delacorte, 1976; *Never to Forget: The Jews of the Holocaust* (*Horn Book* honor list; with teacher's guide), Harper, 1976; *Dorothea Lange: A Photographer's Life* (adult), Farrar, Straus, 1978; *The Human Rights Book,* Farrar, Straus, 1979.

All Times, All Peoples: A World History of Slavery (illustrated by Leonard Everett Fisher; *Horn Book* honor list), Harper, 1980; *The Chinese Americans,* Crowell, 1980; *The Truth about the Ku Klux Klan,* F. Watts, 1982; *The Hispanic Americans* (illustrated with photographs by Morrie Camhi and Catherine Noren), Crowell, 1982; *The Jewish Americans: A History in Their Own Words, 1650-1950* (ALA Notable Book), Crowell, 1982; *The Terrorists,* Harper, 1983; *A Book about Names* (illustrated by Mischa Richter), Crowell, 1984.

Ain't Gonna Study War No More: The Story of America's Peaceseekers, Harper, 1985; *Mark Twain: A Writer's Life,* F. Watts, 1985; *Betty Friedan: A Voice for Women's Rights* (illustrated by Stephen Marchesi), Viking, 1985; *Dorothea Lange: Life through the Camera* (illustrated by Donna Diamond and with photographs by Dorothea Lange), Viking, 1985; *The Jews in America: A Picture Album,* Jewish Publication Society, 1985; *Poverty in America,* Morrow, 1986; *Winnie Mandela: The Soul of South Africa* (illustrated by S. Marchesi), Viking, 1986; *George Washington and the Birth of Our Nation,* F. Watts,

1986; *Mary McLeod Bethune: Voice of Black Hope,* Viking, 1987; *The Landscape of Memory,* Viking, 1987; *The American Revolutionaries: A History in Their Own Words, 1750-1800,* Crowell, 1987.

Other: *Milestones to American Liberty: The Foundations of the Republic,* Crowell, 1961, revised edition, 1965; (with Walter Harding) *A Thoreau Profile,* Crowell, 1962, reissued, Thoreau Lyceum, 1970; *Thoreau: People, Principles and Politics,* Hill & Wang, 1963; (editor with Patricia G. Holland and Francine Krasno) *The Collected Correspondence of Lydia Maria Child, 1817-1880: Guide and Index to the Microfiche Edition,* Kraus Microform, 1980; (editor with P. G. Holland) *Lydia Maria Child: Selected Letters, 1817-1880,* University of Massachusetts Press, 1982.

Editor of "Women of America" series, Crowell, 1962-74, "Zenith Books" series, Doubleday, 1963-73, and "Firebird Books" series, Scholastic Book Services, 1968-72.

Films; documentaries: "History of the American Negro" (series of three half-hour films), Niagara Films, 1965; "Five," Silvermine Films, 1971; "The Bread and Roses Strike: Lawrence, 1912" (filmstrip), District 1199 Cultural Center, 1980; "The Camera of My Family," Anti-Defamation League, 1981; "American Family: The Merlins," Anti-Defamation League, 1982.

Author of scripts for radio and television. Contributor to periodicals, including *Virginia Quarterly Review, New York Times*

Magazine, New York Times Book Review, English Journal, Library Journal, Wilson Library Bulletin, School Library Journal, Microform Review, Horn Book, Children's Literature in Education, Lion and the Unicorn, and *Children's Literature Association Quarterly.* Member of U.S. editorial board of *Children's Literature in Education,* 1973—, and of *Lion and the Unicorn,* 1980—.

WORK IN PROGRESS: Benjamin Franklin, for F. Watts; *American Politics: How It Really Works,* for Morrow; *A Childhood Memoir,* for Viking.

SIDELIGHTS: **May 8, 1915.** Born in Worcester, Massachusetts. Meltzer was the son of a hard-working immigrant who supported his wife and three sons as a window-washer. "When I was growing up in Worcester, Massachusetts, I had little sense of being a Jew. We lived in a mixed neighborhood of three-decker houses. There were other Jewish families on Union Hill, but there were many more who were Irish, Polish, Lithuanian, Swedish, German, Italian, Armenian in origin. Some

were Protestant, more were Catholic. We played prisoner's base together and king of the mountain, and baseball and football and hockey. And we went to the same school. Many of their parents, like mine, had come from Europe to the Promised Land, so most of us were the first generation to be born in America.

"My mother and father had met in New York, after emigrating from Europe. All I knew about their origins was that both came from what was then Austro-Hungary. The old maps showed it to have been a large, pasted-together empire, of many nationalities. It sprawled over much of Eastern Europe. Just which part, which town or village they were born in, I never learned until long after childhood. (And discovered only recently that my impression had been wrong.) Not that it was a secret. My mother and father simply did not talk about their life in the old country. And all wrapped up in myself, I never thought to ask. They were here, in Worcester, this was now, and I had no time for anything else. The past didn't interest me then (who would have thought I'd write history one day?)

Picketing and parading, the Lawrence textile workers clashed often with the Massachusetts state militia. ■ (From *Bread—and Roses: The Struggle of American Labor, 1865-1915* by Milton Meltzer.)

and the future stretched only as far as tomorrow morning. My mother and father had had a little schooling in Europe, I knew, but nothing that prepared them for anything but unskilled labor. Both had worked in factories before coming to Worcester. Now my mother was staying at home to raise a family of three sons. And my father tried to support us by washing windows.

"I remember that they spoke only English. It was no doubt a faulty and accented English. They rarely used Yiddish. That must have been because they wanted us to grow up 'American.' And the faster we learned the American language, the better.

"My father was not a believer. He did not go to the synagogue on the other side of the hill. I vaguely remember going wth my mother once or twice on a high holiday. Still, I was prepared briefly for a *bar mitzvah,* the ceremony for boys reaching the age of thirteen. But it only meant that for several months a bearded old man came to our house after I came home from school, hammered a bit of Hebrew into my reluctant ears, and listened to me memorizing a set speech. As soon as that Saturday's ordeal passed, the lessons ended. I think now I was put through it because my mother was concerned with what her mother and father might think (they lived in far-

off New York) if we hadn't done it. By the time my younger brother reached thirteen, she didn't even bother.

"There were no books about Jewish life or history in our house (or about any other subject, for that matter). And being Jewish was never discussed. Until, that is, a neighbor told my mother that I was seen 'fooling around' with the daughter of an Irish cop on the next block. Then my mother let me know (with a slap in the face) that this was a bad thing. Jew and non-Jew couldn't mix. 'It never works out.'" [Milton Meltzer, *World of Our Fathers: The Jews of Eastern Europe,* Farrar, Straus, 1974.[1]]

1920. Although he cried on his first day at public school, Meltzer soon adjusted to school, enjoying all his subjects, especially reading. "The first reading I can remember enjoying was 'Gasoline Alley.' It was a comic strip in the local paper, the only thing to read in our house. [There was] . . . no time or money for books. As soon as I was big enough to carry a paper route I bought dime serials at the candy store and followed the doings of Frank Merriwell; the eternal student at Yale, and Nick Carter, snooping on the sinful streets of New York.

"Then I found out about the public library, a jumble of old red brick downtown, full of hardcovers you could take out for nothing. Saturday became a double delight. Mornings I'd spend at the library, yanking books off the shelves at random, sampling everything. Afternoons I'd drag the borrowed load over to the movie theater we called The Dump, where I'd see the latest Charlie Chaplin, Tarzan and Pearl White while I ate a hot dog. Then home to read myself into a daze.

"What I liked most were adventure stories that took me out of my skin. And biographies. I was always trying on a new hero for size—explorer, tennis star, reporter, detective. One day I looked up from a book and realized that what I was feeling inside, in my own private world, was astonishingly like what people everywhere felt—whether they lived yesterday or a hundred or a thousand years ago. This fear, hope, shame, love, it wasn't happening only to me. Maybe there was something of me in everyone, and something of everyone in me." [Milton Meltzer, "American Bicentennial Reading," *Children's Book Council,* 1975.[2]]

1927. Entered Grafton Junior High School in Worcester. Besides school, Meltzer was expected to work and help the family. His life at this time revolved around school, work, girls, and reading books. ". . . My parents were . . . intensely interested in education, and delighted when I early became a slave to the printed word, devouring library shelves from one end to the other. I saw less of my father because of his terribly, hard physical labor and long hours. We all went to work early to help the family. I worked as milkman, newsboy, warehouse worker, and shoe clerk among other things. But I had lots of fun at outdoor sports—swimming, skating, coasting, tennis. I attended good local schools, and I enjoyed going to them." [Lee Bennett Hopkins, "Milton Meltzer," *More Books by More People,* Citation Press, 1974. Amended by Milton Meltzer.[3]]

1929. Entered Classical High School, a public college prep school of Worcester. Although there was no money in the family for a college education, Meltzer expected to somehow go on to college. ". . . As the decade of the Great Depression opened, I had entered my second year in high school. Worcester, Massachusetts, an industrial town, was about to suffer hard times. But at the age of fifteen it took me a while to feel the impact the Depression would have on the lives of friends and neighbors.

For four years Dorothea carried on her work in the field. She covered much of the vast American continent. ▪ (From *Dorothea Lange: Life through the Camera* by Milton Meltzer. Illustrated by Donna Diamond.)

Josh dug his pole deep to move the raft faster. ■ (Jacket illustration by Ann Grifalconi from *Underground Man* by Milton Meltzer.)

"The stock market crash in the fall of 1929 was no signal of disaster to the family of a window cleaner. My father washed the windows of factories, stores, offices, and homes. Their owners held some of the stocks that tumbled so disastrously— $26 billion—in the first month of the Depression. But we owned no stocks and didn't even know what they were. All we owned were our clothes and the furniture of the tenement we lived in.

"Our family did not 'go broke' in the Depression. We started broke. . . ." [Milton Meltzer, *Violins and Shovels: The WPA Arts Projects,* Delacorte, 1976.⁴]

1932. "It was our senior year in high school. Some of the kids joked about whether the school would last long enough to let us graduate. After all, Chicago, an infinitely bigger city, had just shut down its schools because of lack of funds. Their teachers had not been paid for months.

"A new mayor took office in Worcester. The Honorable John C. Mahoney said in his inaugural address that the biggest task he faced was relief. The city was now spending more for that than on its fire and police departments.

"The next day a sixty-five-year-old man, a retired broker now penniless, shot himself. The mayor's own staff took a 10 percent cut. Needy men were put to work cleaning out the Quinapoxet reservoir basin.

"By the middle of January, the governor of Massachusetts was warning the cities that funds were so low they must cut

down on relief. Our mayor slashed relief costs by 10 percent. He said he would no longer pay rent for jobless families unless landlords issued eviction notices and people were about to be put out on the street.

"In February, a young, university-trained actress who had gone to Broadway full of hope and ambition, came back to Worcester. She had failed to find even a walk-on role in a starving theater. She sat silently at home for a few weeks, then took a trolley car out to Lake Quinsigamond, chopped a hole in the ice, and drowned herself.

"The last story of that winter I care to remember is that of Albert Fortin and Pasquale Furtaldo. Albert, twenty-three, had not eaten for several days. He saw Pasquale, fifteen, leave a grocery store carrying a loaf of bread and a bottle of milk. He followed the boy home and as Pasquale was about to enter his house, seized an ax and struck him on the head. Frightened by his own violence, he dragged the boy to the rear of the house, and then fled, without the bread and milk. A few hours later he surrendered to the police.

"In March, Detroit, Michigan, which seemed so remote from New England in those days, suddenly was as close as the day's headline. Unemployed auto workers marched on Henry Ford's factory, and four men were murdered in a volley of police bullets. Throughout the Midwest, farmers were banding together. They threatened to shoot anyone who would foreclose their mortgages. In Iowa, angry farmers had dragged a foreclosing judge off the bench and beat him unconscious. Right here at home, Arthur Thornby, the owner of a downtown restaurant, had disappeared. He left a note for his wife, saying his debts had piled so high he couldn't go on.

"Our mayor ordered streetlights to be dimmed to save money on power. As the lights went down, a shock ran through our neighborhood. The motorman on a trolley line we all used was held up by two boys. They had boarded the trolley and sat quietly in the rear until the end of the run. After all the other passengers got off, they pulled out a gun and took $8 in fares from the motorman. Everybody knew Paul and Leo. No one had ever expected they would do something like that. What would happen to them now?

"At school, the senior year rolled on, and we ignored the world outside. A class dance, the basketball and hockey games, electioneering for office. No athlete, but a 'word man,' I made the debating team and the yearbook board, and wound up elected class prophet. Old and wise as I felt at seventeen, I never could have prophesied what was about to happen.''[4]

June, 1932. Graduating from high school, Meltzer was accepted on a full scholarship to New College at Columbia University in New York City. New College was an experimental college that trained teachers. "The biggest thing in my life then was the chance to go to college. A New York school had accepted me, and by combining a scholarship, job, loan, and a few dollars a week from my father's meager earnings, it looked like I might at least make a start. I sweated through that summer in New York, earning money as an unskilled worker in an uncle's garment shop. Riding the bus to work each morning, I saw strung along the Hudson River shore hundreds of shacks made of tin cans, packing crates, cardboard, and old tar paper. They were no bigger than chicken coops, these rent-free homes, and their tenants had named them Hoovervilles in honor of the President.

"Soon after classes started in the fall, Roosevelt was elected. In those days presidents didn't take office until the following March. While FDR and the country waited for inauguration day, 'that Austrian corporal,' Adolf Hitler, took over in Germany. I remember a cold January night at a professor's house when we students hung over his shortwave radio, unable to believe the hysteria vomiting from Hitler's throat and the roar of his audience's response.

"On the eve of Roosevelt's taking office, we dropped into the bottommost pit of the Depression. Losing all confidence in banks, people made a panicky rush to withdraw their money. The banking system of the whole country collapsed overnight. That was where we stood the day FDR took up his duties. For three years we had suffered a tragedy even more bitter than war. In war the enemy was visible, knowable. The anguish and frustration of the Depression came from forces we could not identify, could not fight. Millions had lost material possessions and had forgotten the skills necessary to work. Their health suffered, and worst of all, their pride and self-respect.

"Almost frantic with despair, we waited to hear the President's inaugural address. In ringing words he said, 'The only thing we have to fear is fear itself.' He promised 'action and action now' and a 'New Deal' for all Americans. And at once he moved so powerfully that it was possible to hope again. In the first hundred days of his administration, more major measures were signed into law than in any comparable period in our history. From the universities, from the schools of law, engineering, and social work, FDR drew hundreds of advisers to Washington to take part in the stupendous task of saving a

Constant oppression meant constant migration. ■ (From *Remember the Days: A Short History of the Jewish American* by Milton Meltzer. Illustrated by Harvey Dinnerstein.)

nation. My campus was but one of many that saw dozens of the best brains disappear into New Deal agencies.

"I did not follow every move the President made. I was on my own for the first time in my seventeen years, and that was troublesome enough. Everyone in my class was a stranger to me, and I did not make friends easily. Then there was New York itself, a monstrous city to a boy from a New England town. The college I was in was experimental—part of its program called for students to spend a year working in industry or on a farm. I went back to Worcester for my second year, living again at home. Somehow I found a miserable job in a factory, painting women's shoes with a spray gun. On Saturdays I sold shoes to workers and farmers in a cheap store that paid me $2 for the twelve-hour day. And evenings I read voraciously, keeping careful notes to show my instructors.

"In the fall of **1934,** I returned to school, which was now swept by fevered discussions. Many of my professors were either deeply committed to the New Deal or radical critics of its shortcomings. And so I became more sensitive to what was going on in the larger world. The New Deal was in trouble because it had not brought about economic recovery. So far it had failed to improve the lot of workers, tenant farmers, old people, or small business. Above all, there was still an enormously large number of unemployed. What FDR had done was to pump relief funds into the states and to stimulate the construction industry with a federal public works program. By these means, he hoped to take the federal government out of the relief business altogether. He had also tried direct work relief. One such agency was the Civilian Conservation Corps (CCC), which enrolled some 300,000 young men throughout the country. As part of FDR's ardent conservation program, they did reforestation and other work in the national parks.

"As I began my last year in college, private employment was still hard to find. It was 1935, the fifth year of the Depression. Eight million Americans still had no jobs. Nearly 3 million youths between sixteen and twenty-four years of age were on relief. The surface signs of the Depression had almost disappeared, however: no apple sellers on the streets, breadlines gone, the Hoovervilles vanished. But I knew many young men and women who had finished college and had failed to find work. Some had gone back home to live with their families. Some were bumming around the country. And a few, the lucky ones, had landed jobs on the WPA.

"I began to feel it was no use going on with my studies. In the papers I read that one-third of the previous year's graduating class had been unable to find any work at all, and another third had gotten jobs for which they had no interest, talent, or training. Going the rounds of the campus was an 'Ode to Higher Education':

> "I sing in praise of college,
>   of MAs and PhDs,
> But in pursuit of knowledge
>   We are starving by degrees.

"Toward the end of my senior year, I dropped out of college. My father had cancer, and died that fall. I found a place on the West Side of New York City, in the Chelsea neighborhood. The rent was $3 a week. Stepping through the front door of the brownstone was like entering a public urinal. At the top of five flights of stairs was a room almost narrow enough for me to touch the walls with outstretched arms. There was an iron cot, no sheets, a frayed army blanket, a rocklike pillow, a wooden folding chair, a rickety wardrobe that leaned menacingly over me, and a single window through whose smeary glass I could barely see the brick walls of the tenement opposite.

Those first days in prison were the worst in her life. ■
(From *Winnie Mandela: The Soul of South Africa* by Milton Meltzer. Illustrated by Stephen Marchesi.)

"I applied for help at the city's relief bureau. I cannot remember how many days I waited before an investigator came. It felt terribly long because I was so nervous. But at last I qualified, and the relief began coming. The city paid my rent, and every other Friday gave me $5.50. That was what I lived on. Dinner was a cheese sandwich and a cup of coffee. Price—20 cents. When rain or snow began squishing up through the holes in my shoes, I couldn't afford to repair them. My brother showed me how to take the pulpy separators out of egg cartons and stuff them into my shoes for protection. A few months later my luck changed. The Federal Theatre Project gave me a job."[4]

1936-39. Worked as a writer in the press department of the Federal Theatre Project. "In my own case, I had only the flimsiest claim to professionalism as a writer. I was simply too young then to have gathered the necessary experience or recognition. The same was true of many needy young people who were taken on the projects to work side by side with far more experienced talent. I know we youthful apprentices learned from our elders, and perhaps our elders also acquired something from our innocence and eagerness to try the unknown.

Railroad tracks through gates of Auschwitz, where Nazis killed more than one million Jews. ■
(From *The Jews in America: A Picture Album* by Milton Meltzer. Photograph by Stephen Epstein.)

"'Is this social work or theatre?' one director moaned in a letter to project headquarters. He was wrestling with this mixture of 'capables' and 'incapables.' When payroll cuts had to be made, it was often the less capable who went first. But those who remained were retrained. . . .

"To encourage the writing of drama, the Federal Theatre Project started a playwrights' unit in New York. Into it went about a dozen young men and women, all on relief and eager to learn to write plays.

"I reported for work at a beat-up Greek temple on Eighth Avenue near Forty-fourth Street. The building had once been the home of the Bank of the United States. It had failed late in 1930, to the despair of nearly half a million depositors—many of them immigrants. Because of its name, they had thought it was the government's own bank, and as safe as America herself. Now it was the headquarters of the Federal Theatre of New York. The dismal rooms swarmed with people of incredible variety—actors, directors, stagehands, vaudevillians, puppeteers, dancers, circus performers, scene painters, costumers, makeup artists, technicians, clerks, accountants—and writers.

"Which is where I came in. When I applied for home relief, I listed myself as an unemployed writer. It was a bold claim to make on the basis of a few pieces published in the college press and in some magazines of limited circulation. I had to put something down, however, and I wanted very much to become a professional writer. My older brother had had some experience as a publicity writer in New York, had gone on relief, and had then been given a Federal Theatre job in the press department. His function was to help provide information about the project to the media.

"One corner of the press department housed a tiny group of writers who wrote stories explaining the project to teachers and students. Many Federal Theatre productions were performed in the schools and pupils often came in organized groups to attend the performances in our theaters. Perhaps because I had some writing samples to show, the head of this division asked for me. (He may have been prodded a bit by my brother.)

"My pay was $23.86 a week. It was the salary everyone got who came from the relief rolls and could qualify as a 'senior research worker.' It was called a 'security wage.' This meant we were paid *more* than the sum doled out for direct relief, but *less* than the prevailing union wage—to encourage us to return to private jobs as soon as we could find them. The projects adjusted the number of hours people worked to satisfy the unions, which did not like to see their wage structure undercut.

"What's important to remember about the $23.86 salary is that on an annual basis, most actors earned more than they ever did in the commercial theater. And they knew they would work every week. It was a job security they had never before enjoyed.

"Job security was just one of the goals of the WPA. . . .''⁴

June 22, 1941. Married Hilda Balinky.

1942. Drafted into the Army Air Force.

1946. Worked as a researcher-writer for CBS-radio network in New York.

1947-1948. Worked as a publicist for Henry Wallace's presidential campaign.

1956. Wrote his first book with Langston Hughes, *A Pictorial History of the Negro in America*. "I met Langston in 1955 when we began a collaboration that resulted in two big history books (*A Pictorial History of the Negro in America*, Crown, 1956, and *Black Magic: A Pictorial History of the Negro in American Entertainment*, Prentice-Hall, 1967). I also wrote his biography for young adults. Published in 1968, the book was nominated for the National Book Award."

1968. Quit his job as an editor to work full time as a writer. An historian and biographer, Meltzer has written more than sixty books reflecting his interest in the contemporary struggle for freedom and justice. "In those first years I wrote books without any great self-consciousness about the subjects I chose. Then one day a reviewer described me as a writer known for his interest in the underdog. A pattern had become obvious. It was not a choice deliberately made. But that is how it has gone, books about human aspiration and struggle—the Black American's struggle to organize for freedom and equality; the worker's struggle to organize and improve his living standards; the struggle of the hungry and dispossessed in the Great Depression for bread and a job; the struggle of various racial or ethnic groups—Native Americans, Black Americans, Jewish Americans, Hispanic Americans, Asian Americans—to live and grow and work in security and freedom.

"As for my biographies, they deal with the lives of people who appeal to me for many different reasons. But what links them all is the fact that each one has fought for unpopular causes. . . .

"All these people share one quality: they never say there is nothing they can do about an injustice or a wrong they encounter. They are not victims of apathy, that state people get themselves into when they believe there's no way to change things. My subjects choose action. They show the will to do something about what troubles them. Action takes commitment, the commitment of dedicated, optimistic individuals. Our American past is full of examples of people like these who tried to shape their own lives. Of people who sometimes understood that they could not manage their own life without seeking to change society, without trying to reshape the world they lived in."

The author writes in his booklined New York City apartment on the West Side. "How do I write? By sitting down with pen and pad every day for many hours at a stretch, until what I'm after becomes clear and sounds right in my ear. This, of course, after an intense period of research—a process that is hard work but great fun at the same time, and which almost always leads to ideas for still other books. After working and reworking the manuscript, I type it out and rework it once more. Then the last clear copy for the publisher. But everyone has his own way of working; what is effective for me might not be for another."

Meltzer prefers to write his nonfiction books for young people because ". . . I felt the need to do more substantial and hopefully more lasting work. I've written for both adults and young people, and find the latter more satisfying as an audience. They care more, respond more quickly, are more open to new ideas."

1977. Awarded the Jane Addams Children's Book Award and the Charles and Bertie G. Schwartz Award for Jewish Juvenile Literature from the National Jewish Book Awards for his book for children on the Holocaust, *Never to Forget*. "Why did I want to write it? The impulse came from a pamphlet reporting a study of American high school textbooks. 'Their treatment

Slavery started a long time ago, in the early history of mankind. It was not the invention of any one mind.... ■ (From *All Times, All People: A World History of Slavery* by Milton Meltzer. Illustrated by Leonard Everett Fisher.)

of Nazism was brief, bland, superficial, and misleading,' said the author of the study. Racism, anti-Semitism, and the Holocaust were either ignored or dismissed in a few lines. Nor were college textbooks much better. As far as young people were concerned, 'darkness hid the vilest crime ever perpetrated by man against man.'

"By one of those remarkable coincidences, an editor at Harper and Row had read the same pamphlet at about the same moment, and concluded Harper's must try to fill that hole. Knowing my other books on Jewish history, she approached me just as I was about to look for a publisher.

"This was to be a book for young readers. I assumed they would know little or nothing about the Holocaust and what gave rise to it. . . . I knew the book couldn't be for Jews alone. It had to be a book for non-Jews too.

"The work of scholar-specialists on the Holocaust is enormous. They have been digging deep for the facts and publishing their monographs in the academic journals or in volumes few adults and even fewer young people would ever read. So too with the Holocaust studies of the philosophers and theologians. They have been trying for decades to grapple with the meaning of this cataclysmic event. Then there are the memoirs of survivors of the Holocaust—men and women whose bodies and spirit bear the scars of that racial fury.

"I read for a long time in the forbidding masses of source material. To include everything was manifestly impossible. I had to be concerned with selection, deletion, emphasis, proportion. I had to find a form and a voice that would enlarge the reader's experience, deepen it, intensify it.

"With young readers as my primary audience, I wanted much of the testimony to come from boys and girls, or to be about them. There are 27 such documentary passages fitted into the narrative. . . .

"In writing true history you are dealing not simply with the what and when of events but with the why and how. If you do not always have an easy time determining what happened and when, you are sure to have a much harder time finding out why and how it happened. For it brings you to the heart of what history is about—human behavior. This is the subject novelists deal with; it is just as much the subject for historians.

"It is arguable whether history is any kind of guide, whether we have any lessons to learn from it. But even those who deny that the function of history is to be useful in a practical sense must accept the fact that it throws valuable light on human behavior—so illogical, so erratic, so unpredictable, and therefore so endlessly fascinating.

"Studying the Holocaust and the behavior of human beings in that time we can detect a kind of logic in what happened. This is, of course, hindsight. Could we learn enough from it to be able to predict its repetition in the future? Not, I think, where it might happen, or when, or to whom, but only that it *could* happen again. And, I am afraid I have to say, that it is all the more likely to happen again because it has *already* happened.

"Here I would like to single out one idea which runs throughout *Never to Forget*. It is that we should not see the destructive process of the Holocaust as the work of a small band of arch-criminals led by a Svengali who took control of the minds of the German people and forced them to carry out an insane policy. On the contrary, the Holocaust can be better understood if we regard it as the expression of profound tendencies of modern civilization. Central among these tendencies is the bureaucratization of power. Mankind has known oppression through millennia of enforced servitude, from the ancient world down through American slavery. But it was modern methods of bureaucratization that made possible the expenditure of human life on such a scale and with such absolute ruthlessness as Auschwitz testifies to.

"The greatest sin is indifference. It is a sign of how dehumanized we have become. It is what can make us cogs in the machinery of destruction.

"Now I come back to where I started—the possibilities of nonfiction writing for young readers. Does it have to be nothing but a pastiche of facts? Is there a function for the imagination? Is there room for ideas? for exercise of judgment? for the portrayal of character? for the illumination of human behavior? for the play of craftsmanship?

"Of course there is. And teachers, librarians, reviewers, all of us simply as readers, must look for it, ask for it, point out where we find it, and where we miss it.

"And, as writers, we must demand it of ourselves every time we sit down to the job." [Milton Meltzer, "Beyond Fact," *Beyond Fact: Nonfiction for Children and Young People,* compiled by Jo Carr, American Library Association, 1982.[5]]

FOR MORE INFORMATION SEE: Milton Meltzer, "The Fractured Image: Distortions in Children's History Books," *School Library Journal,* October, 1968; M. Meltzer, "Hughes, Twain, Child and Sanger: Four Who Locked Horns with the Censors," *Wilson Library Journal,* November, 1969; Doris de Montreville and Donna Hill, editors, *Third Book of Junior Authors,* H. W. Wilson, 1972; *Children's Literature in Education,* number 14, 1974, Volume II, number 3, 1980; M. Meltzer, *World of Our Fathers: The Jews of Eastern Europe,* Farrar, Straus, 1974; Lee Bennett Hopkins, *More Books by More People,* Citation Press, 1974; M. Meltzer, "American Bicentennial Reading," *Children's Book Council,* 1975; M. Meltzer, "Where Do All the Prizes Go? The Case for Nonfiction," *Horn Book,* February, 1976; M. Meltzer, *Violins and Shovels: The WPA Arts Projects,* Delacorte, 1976; Paul Heins, editor, *Crosscurrents of Criticism: Horn Book Essays, 1968-1977,* Horn Book, 1977; Betsy Hearne and Marilyn Kaye, editors, *Celebrating Children's Books: Essays on Children's Literature in Honor of Zena Sutherland,* Lothrop, 1981; Jo Carr, compiler, *Beyond Fact: Nonfiction for Children and Young People,* American Library Association, 1982; *Innocence and Experience: Essays and Conversations on Children's Literature,* Lothrop, 1987.

MORTON, (Eva) Jane   1931-

PERSONAL: Born November 13, 1931, in Colorado Springs, Colo.; daughter of William Earnest (a rancher) and Eva (Wolowsky) Ambrose; married Richard John Morton (an elementary school principal), June 7, 1953; children: John, Lizabeth Morton Duckworth, Mary Morton Crawford. *Education:* Attended Colorado State University, 1949-50; University of Northern Colorado, B.A., 1952. *Politics:* Democrat. *Religion:* Methodist. *Home and office:* 205 Briar Rose La., P.O. Box 270, Breckenridge, Colo. 80424. *Agent:* Gloria R. Mosesson, 290 West End Ave., New York, N.Y. 10023.

CAREER: Flood Junior High School, Englewood, Colo., English teacher, 1952-53; Seaside High School, Seaside, Ore.,

JANE MORTON

journalism teacher, 1955-56, Twin Falls High School, Twin Falls, Idaho, journalism teacher, 1956-57; Denver, Colorado public schools, teacher and substitute teacher, 1961-78; Denver District Attorney's Crime Advisory Commission, Denver, Colo., office manager of Whistlestop Crime Prevention Program, 1978-79; free-lance writer, 1979—. *Member:* Colorado Authors League, Society of Children's Book Writers.

WRITINGS: (With husband, Richard J. Morton) *Innovation without Renovation in the Elementary School,* Citation Press, 1974; *Running Scared* (juvenile), Elsevier/Nelson, 1979; *I Am Rubber, You Are Glue,* Beaufort Books, 1981. Contributor to juvenile magazines, including *Wee Wisdom, Working for Boys, Friend, Child Life,* and *American Girl.*

WORK IN PROGRESS: Mellow Like Me; a junior novel about a boy, a ghost, and a bully, tentatively titled, *The Ghost, the Bully and the Chicken Feather.*

SIDELIGHTS: "When I was in high school I won two cans of peanuts for my last line in a jingle contest. It was years before I could see myself writing for anything more than that.

"I entered every contest that came along. I completed sentences in twenty-five words or less, wrote jingle last lines, and named everything from Kool-Aid pitchers to race horses. Prizes ranged from refrigerators to vibrating bar bells, and my winnings almost furnished our house.

"But I tired of praising soaps and toothpastes and cooking oils about the same time my family tired of eating from cans with-

out labels, boxes without tops, and using the same brand of soap for months on end. So I took a juvenile writing course at the University of Colorado, Denver Center, and shortly after published my first story for young people.

"While I was working on *Running Scared,* I read a chapter about juvenile hall to a high school class I was teaching. After I'd finished, one of the boys said, 'He didn't get beat up.'

"I realized then that when I visited the halls, those in charge didn't tell me everything. I talked to the students, and they filled me in, so I think my book is realistic about the way it is.

"I have to write from experience. If I write about a school, I have to visualize a school that I know. If I write of a park, it has to be a park that I've seen. My characters are composites of people I know. No one person would recognize himself in my stories, because I've taken a little here and a little there until I've created a fictional being who is real to me and I hope to my readers.

"I have the most trouble with my plots. I wish I could outline and know from the beginning where the story is going, but I can't. I have to know what my main character wants, I know how the story will begin, and I have a vague idea of how it will end, but getting from one point to the other is a matter of going from chapter to chapter and deciding at the end of each one what will come next.

"I love to write, and nothing equals the feeling I have when I finish a book and I am satisfied that I've done what I set out to do."

HOBBIES AND OTHER INTERESTS: Running a mile a day, hiking, skiing.

MUNSCH, Robert N. 1945-

PERSONAL: Born June 11, 1945, in Pittsburg, Pa.; son of Thomas John (a lawyer) and Margaret (a homemaker; maiden name, McKeon) Munsch; married Ann Beeler (a university educator), January 22, 1973; children: Julie, Andrew. *Education:* Fordham University, B.A., 1969; Boston University, M.A. (anthropology), 1971; Tufts University, M.A. (early childhood education), 1973. *Residence:* Guelph, Ontario, Canada. *Office:* c/o Writers Union of Canada, 24 Ryerson Ave., Toronto, Ontario, Canada M5T 2P3.

CAREER: Storyteller and author of books for children. Employed at a day care center in Coos Bay, Ore., part-time, 1973-75; University of Guelph, Guelph, Ontario, Canada, assistant professor of family studies and head teacher at Family Studies Laboratory Preschool, part-time, 1976-84; writer and house-husband, 1984—. *Member:* Association of Canadian Television and Radio Artists (ACTRA); Canadian Association of Children's Authors, Illustrators, and Performers; Writers Union of Canada. *Awards, honors:* Recipient of grant from Canada Council, 1982; Juno Award for Best Canadian Children's Record, 1985, for "Murmel Murmel Munsch"; (with Michael Martchenko) Ruth Schwartz Children's Book Award, 1986, for *Thomas' Snowsuit.*

WRITINGS—Juvenile; illustrated by Michael Martchenko, except as noted; published by Annick Press: *The Dark* (illustrated by Sami Suomalainen), 1979; *The Mud Puddle* (illustrated by S. Suomalainen), 1979, revised editon, 1982; *The Paper Bag*

ROBERT N. MUNSCH

Princess, 1980; *Jonathan Cleaned Up, Then He Heard a Sound; or, Blackberry Subway Jam,* 1981; *The Boy in the Drawer,* 1982; *Murmel, Murmel, Murmel,* 1982; *Angela's Airplane,* 1983; *David's Father,* 1983; *Fire Station,* 1983; *Mortimer,* 1983; *Millicent and the Wind* (illustrated by Suzanne Duranceau), 1984; *Thomas' Snowsuit,* 1985; *50 Below Zero,* 1986; *I Have to Go,* 1987; *Love You Forever* (illustrated by Sheila McGraw), Firefly Books (Canada), 1987.

Contributor to periodicals, including *Journal of the Canadian Association for the Education of Young Children.*

ADAPTATIONS—Recordings, except as noted: "Munsch: Favourite Stories" (includes published and unpublished works), narrated by the author, Kids Records (Toronto), 1983; "Jonathan Cleaned Up" (animated film), National Film Board of Canada, 1984; "Murmel, Murmel, Munsch," Kids Records, 1985; "Love You Forever," Kids Records, 1987.

WORK IN PROGRESS: Birthday, a story about Moira who invites her whole school to her birthday party.

SIDELIGHTS: **June 11, 1945.** Born in Pittsburgh, Pennsylvania. A storyteller and author, Munsch first studied for seven years to become a Jewish priest and anthropological missionary. "I started out studying to be an anthropologist, but made the mistake of taking a part-time job in a day care centre. I liked the kids better than anthropology. Maybe that was because I came from a family of nine children. I went through a series of jobs with young children (daycare, infant daycare, nursery school and an orphanage). Along the way I picked up a degree in early childhood education."

1972. ". . . I was a student teacher at a nursery school near Boston. On the day when I was supposed to do my first circle time I came with a lot of small containers full of corn. They made a lot of noise when rattled. I gave them to the kids and then told a sort of story-song that I made up the night before. It was about a little boy named Mortimer who did not want to go to bed. He kept singing:

"Clang, clang, rattle bing bang,

Gonna make my noise all day.

Clang, clang, rattle bing bang,

Gonna make my noise all day.

"I had made up the song the night before and was quite proud of it. Every time I sang it the kids would shake their containers and a nice loud time was had by all. The story went over so well that the children kept asking for it. I even told it to my sister's children the next time I visited her. When I called her later she said that her children had taught it to the whole neighborhood and even made a play out of it. 'You should get it published,' she said.

"At the time, my wife and I were living in a tent looking for the perfect place to live or else just waiting for our money to run out. Publishing was an alien idea and besides I found it more threatening than evading scorpions in Arizona. Also, *Mortimer* was not even written down and I hated to write. I had always hated to write because I could not spell. (Maybe I should have listened to my sister. When *Mortimer* was finally published ten years later I dedicated it to her children.)

"So *Mortimer* was the first story I made up even though it was not the first to be published. Its structure grew out of the simple fact that three- and four-year-olds do not like to be lectured at. As nursery school teachers soon find out, the best way to keep a group of them interested is to let them participate in some way. *Mortimer* is, in fact, half way between a story and a song. Like a lot of my stories, it spread by word of mouth and by the time it was published there were lots of daycares in Ontario using it as an oral story.

"*Mortimer* went over so well that I continued to storytell whenever I worked with young children. I soon noticed that while I made up lots of stories, there were only a few that the

Angela had never been in an airplane before, so she decided to look around. ■ (From *Angela's Airplane* by Robert N. Munsch. Illustrated by Michael Martchenko.)

children kept requesting to hear again and again. They were the good ones. For most of this time I was working in daycare centres or nursery schools and usually making up a story every day. I figured out once that the stories the children kept requesting came to 2% of my total output.

"When the children kept requesting a story, it went through rapid evolution in plot and structure as I told it day after day. Often a good story would start out with an idea that they liked (getting jumped on by a mud puddle was one) which was not backed up by much of anything. As the story evolved, it developed the structure and style of presentation that made it into an inter-active participation sequence with the children. The more the children yelled out predictable repetition elements or imitated sound effects and gestures, the more they stayed put.

"Note that at this period of my life I did not think of stories as things in themselves, but rather as little machines that kept kids happy and occupied. They existed only in interaction with the audience, were not written down and did not even have titles. Children requested stories by content or else they asked by the names of the children in the story. The names were especially meaningful because I used the names of the children I was working with at the time. So, 'Tell Shelley' referred to a particular story.

"When I got a job at the University of Guelph laboratory nursery school, I suddenly found myself in an environment where people got raises and kept their jobs by publishing. The laboratory school director, Bruce Ryan, and his wife, Nancy (a children's librarian!), both urged me to do something about my stories. So I started writing them down. At first I made the mistake of attempting to change my stories into what I considered good writing. They were terrible. Finally I tried keeping the text as close as possible to the oral version and that worked.

"I think it worked because children's books are read aloud. It so happened that the oral version read quite well as long as I stuck to the oral version. In fact, the written text tended to lead to the same type of interactive participation that children liked in the oral version." [Robert Munsch, "Whatever You Make of It," *Canadian Children's Literature,* number 43, 1986.[1]]

1978. Mailed a selection of his stories to various publishers. The following year, two of them, *The Dark* and *The Mud Puddle* were published by Annick Press. "For me, writing often consists in coming up with a good oral story and then dictating it to myself as I type. Getting a good oral story takes at least three years of telling. The basic plot settles quite soon but the vital word changes that make a participation story work come very slowly. Often it is a case of finding the exact words that the kids expect will come next. Here is an example of what I mean from a later story:

"That is the ugliest thing I have seen in my life. If you think that I am going to put on that ugly snowsuit, you are CRAZY.

(From the animated film "Blackberry Subway Jam," based on the book *Jonathan Cleaned Up, Then He Heard a Sound; or, Blackberry Subway Jam.* Produced by National Film Board of Canada, 1984.)

"Burble, burble, glug-glug," said the cat. ■ (From *The Boy in the Drawer* by Robert N. Munsch. Illustrated by Michael Martchenko.)

''This simple fragment is a storyteller's dream, a perfect sentence; because if I say it in a certain way an audience of young children will join in on the word 'crazy' even though they have never heard the story before. Actually, they don't join in on the whole word. They join in on the 'z.'

''I rate choral response elements in stories according to how many times I have to say them before the kids *spontaneously* join in. Thus in the *Mud Puddle* story 'Mommy, mommy, mommy! A mud puddle jumped on me' has a rating of three because I have to say it at least three times before kids will join in on their own when they are hearing the story for the first time. 'Crazy' in the above example has a rating of one half because the kids join in (sometimes) when I am only half

of the way through the word. It is very difficult to come up with that kind of wording. The above example did not appear in the story until I had been telling it for two years.

''I think that 'crazy' works there because it is the exact word that kids expect based on context and delivery. If I were to say 'strange' or 'dumb as a lobotomized dodo' the kids would not join in.

''Now the link between a text that tells well and a text that reads well is not self evident. It took me a while to figure out that the books that were selling best were often the ones that were best developed orally. Once I figured that out, my writing of my oral stories became a lot easier. Munsch the writer simply wrote what Munsch the storyteller dictated.''[1]

1981-1983. Continued to record his oral stories for publication and to work as a head teacher at the Family Studies Laboratory Preschool at the University of Guelph in Ontario. Munsch received a grant in 1982 from the Canada Council for his efforts. When asked to explain the meaning of his stories, Munsch commented: ''. . . Some of my stories are not oral stories and one is half and half. The half and half one is *Jonathan Cleaned Up*. It was a little story fragment that I used to tell about a boy whose house got turned into a subway station. Ann Millyard and Rick Wilks, from Annick Press, heard me tell it at a Toronto bookstore. They decided to publish it so I wrote the story and added an ending. The first part of the story is a simple oral participation story. The whole city

hall part is written text. The two parts are really quite different. That second part of *Jonathan* was my first bit of regular written English. The book sold and I decided to try it again.

''*Murmel, Murmel, Murmel* isn't an oral story at all. This led to an interesting problem when school audiences requested the story. If there were too many kids (say 400) it didn't work to read the book, as most of the people could not see the pictures. So I ended up developing an oral version of the story that works for storytelling.

''I wrote *Murmel* just after we adopted our first child and it was, for me, a statement about adoption. Now it is not a very

They had an enormous fight and when it was done Thomas was in his snowsuit. ■ (From *Thomas' Snowsuit* by Robert Munsch. Illustrated by Michael Martchenko.)

Mortimer, be quiet. ■ (From *Mortimer* by Robert Munsch. Illustrated by Michael Martchenko.)

clear statement about adoption. I hate clear statements because they only mean what they mean. Unclear statements have the nice effect of meaning whatever they mean to whomever they mean it to and if various meanings appeal to various groups then the book sells more. Unfortunately, the one group that *Murmel* sometimes does not appeal to is adoptive parents, who are the one group I had especially in mind. They get upset because the book is about rejection as well as acceptance.

''While I am on the topic of adoption, *David's Father* is about adoption. More specifically it is about interracial adoption and the group I wrote it for was my family because nobody else ever gets that out of it. This brings up the problem of multi-

level meanings. *David's Father* means a lot of different things to different people and to lots of people it is a funny story that does not mean anything at all.

''One child wrote me and said, 'I like *David's Father* because my father is just like David's father only smaller.' For this child, *David's Father* functioned like a traditional giant story.

''Is the child correct?

''Yes, the child is correct; because I want my stories to mean different things to different people. I spend time getting them to do that. So the correct answer to, 'What does a Munsch story mean?' is, 'To whom?' If you are the reader then you are the arbiter of the meaning. I set it up that way. Besides, I have probably changed my mind several times about what the story meant since I wrote it down. So your own meaning is yours. You as the reader own the story. Have fun.''[1]

When asked how he decides which of his stories gets published, Munsch responded: "A lot of stories I tell just drop out. Finally, some get to the point where I think that they're acceptable. The question then of what story becomes a book is a discussion with my publisher. . . .''[1]

Since Munsch's stories are for young children, they are heavily illustrated, and one of the major illustrators of Munsch's books has been Michael Martchenko. Martchenko had not illustrated a children's book where he had to develop the characters himself before illustrating Munsch's books. ''. . . With Michael Martchenko, . . . I find that I just like what he does and I trust him to come up with neat ideas. Still, compared to a lot of writers, I have a lot of input. Michael will do pencil roughs of major characters, and I'll look at them and say, 'That's what Shelley really looks like' or 'No, that's too old or too young.' Then he comes with the sketchboard of the whole thing, and we go over it. Then he does a colour picture, and then he does them all in colour. There's lots of room for give and take. There was one major disaster, however. For *David's Father*, the distributor called up six months before we thought we needed anything and said, 'We need the cover illustration to put into the catalogue.' It was a rush job. Michael had to do the cover, but the publisher, who gave him the text, didn't tell him that the girl in the story, Julie (Julie is my daughter), is half Jamaican, and has curly hair and brown skin. So he comes back on the day for the cover to be photographed with this picture of a blond-haired, blue-eyed, Caucasian kid. He had varnished the picture, so he couldn't add any colour to it. I was just freaking out. This was Julie's story; it was dedicated to her. Finally, he taped over Julie with scotch tape and coloured the scotch tape with magic marker. They photographed the cover like that. But the problem was that he could change her colour but he couldn't curl her hair. When Julie first saw it, she said, 'What's the matter with my hair?'''[1]

1984. *Millicent and the Wind* published. ''. . . *Millicent* is one of my oldest stories. That's one of the original daycare, naptime stories. It's a quiet-them-down naptime story, so it's much more laid back than the kind I do now in front of an audience, where the idea is to whoop them up. There's a difference in tone and a difference in purpose.

"When I first sent stories to Annick, I sent them *Mud Puddle* and *Millicent*. So *Millicent* was one of the first stories they got, and they really liked it but they didn't think they had an illustrator for it. They were sitting on it for five years and then, all of a sudden, they called me up. I had a contract on another story signed and delivered, and they said, 'We've changed our minds. We've found an illustrator for *Millicent*!' They showed me some proofs, and I said, 'Well, that looks like it will float.'''[1]

In 1984 Munsch became an adjunct professor. "At first royalties were not enough to support my family and I relied on storytelling to make up the difference. This rapidly grew into a second career. Once word got around that my performances always sold out in advance, various promoters got interested and there followed a bit of performing to very large groups (1,000 to 3,000). This sort of thing was great for income and a disorganized lifestyle; but it was bad for writing.

"In 1987 I dropped my agent, cut back paid performances to one a month and began once again to do free storytellings in local schools, daycare centers, nursery schools and libraries." Much to the dismay of teachers and librarians, who have tried booking him in advance, he does his free storytellings with little or no advance notice; often simply showing up at the front door and asking to tell stories (he has yet to be refused!).

"On my occasional government sponsored tour of remote areas (Baffin Island, Yukon Territory, etc.) I always stay with families with children. It is often these children who end up being the source for new stories. While telling stories in Hay River, Northwest Territory, I stayed with Moira's family. She had a birthday while I was there and *Birthday,* a story about Moira who invites her whole school to her birthday party, is the story I made up for her.''

"Of the new stories I tell, one in twenty-five is a really good story that will last. The others will hold the kids for the moment. The acid test of a good story is when the same kids request it again and again." [Ann Vanderhoff, "The Weird and Wonderful Whimsy of Robert Munsch," *Quill & Quire,* May, 1982.[2]]

Munsch's works have been translated into seven languages, including Spanish, French, German, and Swedish.

HOBBIES AND OTHER INTERESTS: Cycling, geology.

FOR MORE INFORMATION SEE: Irma McDonough, editor, *Profiles 2,* Canadian Library Association, 1982; Anne Vanderhoff, "The Weird and Wonderful Whimsy of Robert Munsch," *Quill & Quire,* May, 1982; D. L. Kirkpatrick, editor, *Twentieth Century Children's Writers,* St. Martin's, 1983; *Canadian Children's Literature,* number 43, 1986.

OPGENOORTH, Winfried 1939-

BRIEF ENTRY: Born June 20, 1939, in Düsseldorf, Germany (now West Germany). After graduating from art school, Opgenoorth worked as a professional graphic artist in West Germany, Switzerland, and Austria until 1979, when he became a full-time children's book illustrator at his home in Austria. "The priority in my work is to entertain children, to make them happy, to make them laugh at this or that," he said. Opgenoorth has illustrated about twenty children's books, a number of which have been translated from their original German into English. Describing his illustrations in Wolf Harranth's *Isn't It a Beautiful Meadow?, Book World* wrote: "The brightly contrasting colors and what seems like hundreds of different people doing hundreds of different things all in one picture imply a delight in complexity and confusion. . . ." Opgenoorth won awards for two of his books: the Austrian Illustrators' Prize in 1982, for *Valerie and the Good-Night Swing,* written by Austrian author Mira Lobe; and the Illustrators' Prize of the City of Vienna in 1985, for *Christopher Wants a Party,* also written by Lobe. His other collaborations with Lobe include *Hocus-Pocus, The Snowman Who Went for a Walk, Pig in a Muddle,* and *Pig on the Run. Home:* Zeltgasse 1/4/15, A-1080 Vienna, Austria.

PALTROWITZ, Donna (Milman) 1950-

BRIEF ENTRY: Born April 12, 1950, in Brooklyn, N.Y. After receiving her B.A. from Hofstra University in 1971, Paltrowitz established Paltrowitz Productions with her husband Stuart, also a writer. This writing team has produced more than fifty books as well as computer software programs for children. In 1974 Paltrowitz received her M.A. from Hofstra, and one year later produced *Crime and the Sweets* (1975), the first of twenty-four books in the "I Hate to Read" series co-written with her husband and published by Educational Activities. The other titles include *Kate You're Late* (1975), *Nervous Jervis* (1975), *Chicken Delight* (1977), and *Bits and Pizzas* (1979). The Paltrowitzes have also written a number of books about computers, including *Robotics* (Messner, 1983), which introduces children to the world of automated workers, *The Mystery and Adventure Computer Storybook* (Tribeca Communications, 1983), *The Science Fiction Computer Storybook* (Tribeca Communications, 1983), and *Turtle Soup: LOGO for Children* (Dilithium, 1984). Their interest in computers also extends to programs like the "Mystery Mazes" computer reading series produced by Educational Activities, and the "Phonics" software series produced by Media Materials. *Home and office:* 2971 Lee Pl., Bellmore, N.Y. 11710.

FOR MORE INFORMATION SEE: Contemporary Authors, Volume 119, Gale, 1987.

PALTROWITZ, Stuart 1946-

BRIEF ENTRY: Born January 31, 1946, in Brooklyn, N.Y. Paltrowitz received his B.A. from Hofstra University in 1967 and M.S. from Long Island University in 1975. He established Paltrowitz Productions with his wife, Donna, also a writer, in 1971; together they produced their first book, *Crime and the Sweets* (Educational Activities) in 1975. Their subsequent collaborations include eight titles for Educational Activities' "Work World" series, including *Workout* (1977), *Job Jive* (1977), *No Way to Fly* (1980), and *More than Money* (1980), and "Springboard" series of curriculum minitexts. The Paltrowitzs' interest in computers has led to the "Mystery Mazes" computer reading series produced by Educational Activities, including *The Carnival Caper* (1985), *Houseboat Hideaway* (1985), and *Castle Clues* (1986); and the "Phonics" computer software series produced by Media Materials, which presents keys to sounds and vowels in programs such as *Key to Consonant Sounds* (1984), *Key to Vowel Digraphs* (1984), and *Key to Word Recognition* (1984). Additional books by the husband-and-wife team include *Animal Soup* (National Educators for Creative Instruction, 1980), and *Do You Know Your Boss?* (Price, Stern, 1983). *Home and office:* 2971 Lee Pl., Bellmore, N.Y. 11710.

FOR MORE INFORMATION SEE: Contemporary Authors, Volume 119, Gale, 1987.

PAPAS, William 1927-

PERSONAL: Born July 15, 1927, in South Africa; British national; son of Kostas (property owner) and Laura (Vollmer) Papas; married second wife, Theresa Pares (an artist/writer) February 16, 1970; children: (first marriage) Peta, Warren, Vollmer. *Education:* Attended art school in Cape Town, South Africa, and Beckenham Art School, England, 1947. *Address:* 1306 NW Hoyt St., Portland, Ore. 97209.

CAREER: Abandoned formal studies to hitchhike around Europe, sketching and working as a dishwasher in Sweden, a walking billboard advertising schnapps in Germany, and a riveter's helper in England; *Cape Times,* Cape Town, South Africa, artist and illustrator, 1951; *Drum* (magazine), Cape Town, artist and illustrator, beginning 1951; farmer, 1954-56; *Sunday Times,* London, England, author of cartoon strip "Bella and Lujah," and editorial cartoonist, 1959-66; *Guardian,* London, feature artist and political cartoonist, 1959-69; writer and il-

WILLIAM PAPAS

lustrator of children's books, 1964—; *Punch,* London, political cartoonist, 1966-70. *Exhibitions*—One-man: Greek Centre, London, England, 1966; Indian Tea Centre, London, 1968; British Council, Athens, Greece, 1975; Dowmunt Gallery, London, 1980; Old City Museum, Jerusalem, 1981; Gallerie Kourd, Athens, 1983; Galerie Weber, Geneva, Switzerland, 1983; O'Grady Galleries, Chicago, Ill., 1984; O'Grady Galleries, Scottsdale, Arizona, 1984; Attic Gallery, Portland, Ore., 1984; Arttee Gallery, Peoria, 1986; Allards Gallery, Fresno, Calif., 1986; Senate Office Building, Washington, D.C., 1986; Gusman Cultural Center, Miami, Fla., 1987. *Military service:* South African Air Force; became flight sergeant. *Awards, honors:* Greenaway Medal commendation from the British Library Association, 1965, for his body of work; Carnegie Medal from the British Library Association, 1966, for *The Grange at High Force;* Greenaway Medal commendation, 1968, for *The Church and No Mules;* Greenaway Medal honor, 1969, for *Taresh the Tea Planter, A Letter from India,* and *A Letter from Israel.*

WRITINGS—Juvenile; all self-illustrated; all published by Oxford University Press, except as noted: *The Press,* 1964; *Tasso,* Coward, 1967; *No Mules,* 1967, Coward, 1968; *Taresh the Tea Planter,* 1968, World Publishing, 1969; *A Letter from India,* 1968, F. Watts, 1969; *A Letter from Israel,* 1968, F. Watts, 1969; *Theodore; or, the Mouse Who Wanted to Fly,* 1969; *Elias the Fisherman,* 1970; *Theodore; or, the Mouse Who Wanted to Own a Frying Pan,* 1970; *The Monk and the Goat,* 1971; *The Long Haired Donkey,* 1972; *Instant Greek,* privately printed, 1972; *The Most Beautiful Child,* 1973; *The Zoo,* 1974; *Yes, Yes, Yes,* privately printed, 1974; *Instant Hebrew,* privately printed, 1979.

Captain Pamphile had his methods. ■ (From *Captain Pamphile's Adventures* by Alexandre Dumas. Illustrated by William Papas.)

Adult books: *People of Old Jerusalem*, Holt, 1980; *Papas' America*, Papas' Studio, 1986.

Illustrator: Frederick Grice, *A Severnside Story*, Oxford University Press, 1964; Charles Downing, *Tales of the Hodja*, Oxford University Press, 1964, Walck, 1965; George Mikes, *Jamaica*, Deutsch, 1965; Philip Turner, *The Grange at High Force*, Oxford University Press, 1965; Rene Guillot, *Guillot's African Folk Tales*, F. Watts, 1965; Ruth Manning-Saunders, *Damien and the Dragon*, Roy, 1965; P. Turner, *The Grange at High Force*, Oxford University Press, 1965; Theodore Papas, *The Story of Mr. Nero*, 1965, Coward, 1966; Jonathan Stone, *The Law*, Oxford University Press, 1966; P. Walsh, *Freddy the Fell Engine*, Oxford University Press, 1966; G. Mikes, *How to be Affluent*, Deutsch, 1966; N. Shrapnel, *The Parliament*, Oxford University Press, 1966; Geoffrey Moorhouse, *The Church*, Oxford University Press, 1967; H. M. Namad, *The Peasant and the Donkey: Tales of the Near and Middle East*, Oxford University Press, 1967, Walck, 1968; H. F. Brinsmead, *Beat of the City*, Coward, 1968; Andrew Salkey, *Riot*, F. Watts, 1969; Paul Ries Collin, *Parcel for Henry*, Oxford University Press, 1970; Alexander Dumas, *Captain Pamphiles Adventures*, Oxford University Press, 1971; Charles Downing, translator, *Armenian Folk-Tales and Fables*, Oxford University Press, 1972; Fynn, *Mister God, This Is Anna*, Collins, 1974; W. H. Nelson, *The Londoners*, Random House, 1974; Skurzynski, *Two Fools and a Faker*, Lothrop, 1977; Malcolm Muggeridge, *In the Valley of This Restless Mind*, Collins, 1977; Pope John Paul I, *Illustrimi*, Collins, 1978; C. S. Lewis, *The Screwtape Letters*, new edition, Collins & World, 1979; *World Folk Tales*, Holp Shuppan, 1979; Amos Oz, *Soumchi*, Chatto & Windus, 1980, Harper, 1981; Bruce Lansdale, *Metamorphosis*, Westview Press, 1985; Fynn, *Anna's Book*, Holt, 1986.

WORK IN PROGRESS: Portfolio of ten images of San Francisco and a companion book.

SIDELIGHTS: Papas started his career as artist/reporter for the *Cape Times* before moving to London in 1959 to become a political cartoonist for the *Manchester Guardian, Sunday Times* and *Punch* magazine. His cartoons were syndicated worldwide. He retired to Greece in 1970 to concentrate on large paintings, drawings, printmaking and illustrating and writing books. He and his wife now live in Oregon where they have established a studio in Portland.

Papas considers his book illustrating a form of "elongated cartooning," especially when children's books are on social and political themes.

FOR MORE INFORMATION SEE: Young Readers' Review, March, 1967; *New Statesman*, November, 1968; Lee Kingman and others, compilers, *Illustrators of Children's Books: 1957-1966*, Horn Book, 1968; L. Kingman and others, compilers, *Illustrators of Children's Books: 1967-1976*, Horn Book, 1978; *Chicago Tribune Book World*, December 7, 1980.

PAULSEN, Gary   1939-

PERSONAL: Born May 17, 1939, in Minneapolis, Minn.; son of Oscar (an army officer) and Eunice Paulsen; married second wife, Ruth Ellen Wright (an artist), May 5, 1971; children: (second marriage) James Wright. *Education:* Attended Bemidji College, 1957-58, and University of Colorado, 1976. *Politics:* "As Solzhenitsyn has said, 'If we limit ourselves to political structures we are not artists.'" *Religion:* "I believe in spiritual progress." *Residence:* Leonard, Mich. *Agent:* Ray Peekner Literary Agency, 2625 North 36th St., Milwaukee, Wis. 53210.

CAREER: Writer. Has also worked variously as a teacher, field engineer, editor, soldier, actor, director, farmer, rancher, truck driver, trapper, professional archer, migrant farm worker, singer, and sailor. *Military service:* U.S. Army, 1959-62; became sergeant. *Awards, honors:* Central Missouri Award for Children's Literature, 1976; *The Green Recruit* was chosen one of New York Public Library's Books for the Teen Age, 1980, 1981 and 1982, and *Sailing: From Jibs to Jibing*, 1982; *Dancing Carl* was selected one of American Library Association's Best Young Adult Books, 1983, *Tracker*, 1984; *Dogsong* was chosen one of Child Study Association of America's Children's Books of the Year, and was a Newbery Honor Book, 1986; Society of Midland Authors Award, 1985, for *Tracker*.

WRITINGS—Juvenile books: *Mr. Tucket*, Funk & Wagnalls, 1968; (with Dan Theis) *Martin Luther King: The Man Who Climbed the Mountain*, Raintree, 1976; *The Small Ones* (illustrated by K. Goff and with photographs by Wilford Miller), Raintree, 1976; *The Grass-Eaters: Real Animals* (illustrated by K. Goff and with photographs by W. Miller), Raintree, 1976; *Dribbling, Shooting, and Scoring Sometimes*, Raintree, 1976; *Hitting, Pitching, and Running Maybe*, Raintree, 1976; *Tackling, Running, and Kicking—Now and Again*, Raintree, 1977; *Riding, Roping, and Bulldogging—Almost*, Raintree, 1977; *Careers in an Airport* (illustrated with photographs by Roger Nye), Raintree, 1977; *The CB Radio Caper* (illustrated by John Asquith), Raintree, 1977; *The Curse of the Cobra* (illustrated by J. Asquith), Raintree, 1977; *The Golden Stick*, Raintree, 1977.

Running, Jumping, and Throwing—If You Can (illustrated by Heinz Kluetmeier), Raintree, 1978; *Forehanding and Back-*

handing—If You're Lucky (illustrated with photographs by H. Kluetmeier), Raintree, 1978; _Downhill, Hotdogging and Cross-Country—If the Snow Isn't Sticky_ (illustrated with photographs by Willis Wood and H. Kluetmeier), Raintree, 1979; _Facing Off, Checking and Goaltending—Perhaps_ (illustrated with photographs by Melchior DiGiacomo and H. Kluetmeier), Raintree, 1979; _Going Very Fast in a Circle—If You Don't Run Out of Gas_ (illustrated with photographs by H. Kluetmeier and Bob D'Olivo), Raintree, 1979; _Launching, Floating High and Landing—If Your Pilot Light Doesn't Go Out_ (illustrated with photographs by H. Kluetmeier), Raintree, 1979; _Pummeling, Falling and Getting Up—Sometimes_ (illustrated with photographs by H. Kluetmeier and Joe DiMaggio), Raintree, 1979; _Track, Enduro and Motocross—Unless You Fall Over_ (illustrated with photographs by H. Kluetmeier and others), Raintree, 1979; (with Art Browne, Jr.) _TV and Movie Animals_, Messner, 1980; _Sailing: From Jibs to Jibing_ (illustrated by wife, Ruth W. Paulsen), Messner, 1981.

Novels: _The Implosion Effect_, Major Books, 1976; _The Death Specialists_, Major Books, 1976; _Winterkill_, T. Nelson, 1977; _The Foxman_, T. Nelson, 1977; _Tiltawhirl John_, T. Nelson, 1977; _C. B. Jockey_, Major Books, 1977; _The Night the White Deer Died_, T. Nelson, 1978; _Hope and a Hatchet_, T. Nelson, 1978; (with Ray Peekner) _The Green Recruit_, Independence Press, 1978; _The Spitball Gang_, Elsevier/Nelson, 1980; _Campkill_, Pinnacle Books, 1981; _The Sweeper_, Harlequin, 1981; _Clutterkill_, Harlequin, 1982; _Popcorn Days and Buttermilk Nights_, Lodestar Books, 1983; _Dancing Carl_, Bradbury, 1983; _Tracker_, Bradbury, 1984; _Dogsong_, Bradbury, 1985; _Sentries_, Bradbury, 1986; _Murphy_, Walker, 1987.

Nonfiction: _The Special War_, Sirkay, 1966; _Some Birds Don't Fly_, Rand McNally, 1969; _The Building a New, Buying an Old, Remodeling a Used Comprehensive Home and Shelter Book_, Prentice-Hall, 1976; _Farm: A History and Celebration of the American Farmer_, Prentice-Hall, 1977; (with John Morris) _Hiking and Backpacking_ (illustrated by Ruth Wright), Simon & Schuster, 1978; (with J. Morris) _Canoeing, Kayaking and Rafting_ (illustrated by John Peterson and Jack Storholm), Simon & Schuster, 1979; _Beat the System: A Survival Guide_, Pinnacle Books, 1983.

Plays: "Communications" (one-act), first produced in New Mexico at a local group theatre, 1974; "Together-Apart" (one-act), first produced in Denver at Changing Scene Theatre, 1976.

Also author of _Meteor_, and more than 200 short stories and articles.

WORK IN PROGRESS: Madonna, a collection of stories; collaborating on a book with a Soviet writer.

SIDELIGHTS: Born **May 17, 1939,** in Minneapolis, Minnesota. "I'm only a second-generation American. My father's family came to this country from Denmark; my mother's people emigrated from Norway and Sweden. My father was a career military man who served as an officer on General Patton's staff during World War II. He spent most of my childhood years fighting the Germans, and my mother spent the war years working in a munitions plant in Chicago—'Rosie the Riveter' type stuff. I was reared by my grandmother and several aunts. I first saw my father when I was seven in the Philippines where my parents and I lived from 1946 until 1949.

"After we returned to the States, we moved around constantly. I lived in every state. The longest time I spent in one school

GARY PAULSEN

was about five months. I was an 'Army brat,' and it was a miserable life. School was a nightmare because I was unbelievably shy, and terrible at sports. I had no friends, and teachers ridiculed me. I wound up skipping most of the ninth grade and had to make it up during the tenth grade so I could graduate on time. As it was, I squeezed through with 'C's and 'D's. And there were family problems. Again, I was sent to live with relatives. In order to buy clothes and have some spending money, I sold *The Grand Forks Herald* in hospitals and bars; during junior high school I set up pins every night in a bowling alley. Had teen suicide been a topic in the news as it is today, had it in any way suggested a way out, I know I would have seriously considered the possibility.

"But I did have 'safety nets'—all of them women. My grandmother and aunts were terribly important to me. And there was someone else. One day as I was walking past the public library in twenty below temperatures, I could see the reading room bathed in a beautiful golden light. I went in to get warm and to my absolute astonishment the librarian walked up to me and asked if I wanted a library card. She didn't care if I looked right, wore the right clothes, dated the right girls, was popular at sports—none of those prejudices existed in the public library. When she handed me the card, she handed me the world. I can't even describe how liberating it was. She recommended westerns and science fiction, but every now and then would slip in a classic. I roared through everything she gave me, and in the summer read a book a day. It was as though I had been dying of thirst and the librarian had handed me a five-gallon bucket of water. I drank and drank."

(Jacket illustration by Jon Weiman from *Tracker* by Gary Paulsen.)

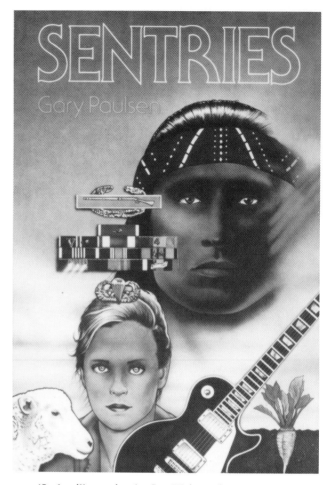

(Jacket illustration by Jon Weiman from *Sentries* by Gary Paulsen.)

1957-1958. Attended Bemidji College. "As I'd grown up hunting and trapping, I was able to pay my way through the first year by laying trap lines for the State of Minnesota."

1959-1962. Served in the U.S. Army; attained rank of sergeant. "I worked with missiles. When I got out of the service, I took extension courses and accrued enough credits to become a field engineer."

1962-1966. Worked as a field engineer in the aerospace departments of Bendix and Lockheed. "I worked on the Gemini shots, the Mariner probes and on designing the guidance section for the Shrike, an anti-radar missile. I was good at my work, but didn't like it."

"I was sitting in a satellite tracking station in California in front of a massive console and related computers . . . I'd finished reading a magazine article on flight-testing a new airplane during an inactive period, and thought, *God,* what a way to make a living—writing about something you like and getting paid for it! I remembered writing some of my past reports, some fictionalized versions I'd included. And I thought: What the hell, I *am* an engineering writer.

"But, conversely, I also realized I didn't know a thing about writing professionally. After several hours of hard thinking, a way to earn came to me. All I had to do was go to work editing a magazine." [Franz Serdahely, "Prolific Paulsen," *Writer's Digest,* January, 1980.¹]

The dogs had run for Oogruk but that was more than two years earlier. They had not run since for anybody.
■ (Jacket illustration by Neil Waldman from *Dogsong* by Gary Paulsen.)

"I wrote a totally fictitious resume which landed me an associate editorship on a men's magazine in Hollywood, California. It took them about two days to find out that I knew nothing about publishing. I didn't know what a lay-out sheet was, let alone how to do one. My secretary—who was all of nineteen years old—edited my first three issues. They could see I was serious about wanting to learn, and they were willing to teach me. We published some excellent writers—Steinbeck, Bradbury, Ellison—which was great training and exposure for me."

"I was there for about a year, and it was the best of all possible ways to learn about writing. It probably did more to improve my craft and ability than any other single event in my life."[1]

While living in California, Paulsen did a considerable amount of work as a film extra. "Once I played a reporter in a movie called *Flap* starring Anthony Quinn. I was onscreen for about thirty-five seconds." Paulsen also took up sculpting, and won 'Best in Show' at an exhibit in Santa Barbara. "I worked mostly at wood carving, which I love. But by then I knew I wanted to be writing, and backed away from sculpture. I didn't feel I could do justice to both."

His first book, *The Special War,* was based on interviews he did with servicemen returning from Viet Nam. "The other war story I covered was the Watts riot. And let me tell you, the racial 'disturbances,' as they were sometimes referred to then, were out-and-out battles."

After twelve years as a writer, Paulsen had become one of the most prolific authors in the country, having published nearly 40 books, over 200 magazine articles and short stories, and two plays. He wrote nonfiction on hunting, trapping, farming, animals, medicine and outdoor life, as well as juvenile and adult fiction. On a bet with a friend, he once wrote eleven articles and short stories inside four days and sold all of them. To burn off tension, he was given to long walks around his Minnesota farm during which he would "blow the hell out of a hillside"[1] with a rifle.

Paulsen's life was changed radically and abruptly after the 1977 publication of his novel *Winterkill;* he was sued for libel. It seemed that some people thought they saw themselves as characters in the book. "My attorney, Margaret Truer, is now a reservation magistrate. The brief was presented to the Minnesota Supreme Court, where we finally won. It was a good fight, and I'd do it all over again, but it brought me to the edge of bankruptcy. And I didn't get the support I'd expected from my publisher. In fact, the whole situation was so nasty and ugly that I stopped writing. I wanted nothing more to do with publishing, and burned my bridges, so to speak.

"So there I was, living deep in the country in northern Minnesota with no way to earn a living. Having no choice in the matter, I went back to trapping for the state. It was predator control work, aimed at coyotes and beavers. The traps we used

Even now with the tracks gone, there is a line of gravel and skunkweed where there used to be ties and steel. ■
(Jacket illustration by Andrew Rhodes from *Popcorn Days and Buttermilk Nights* by Gary Paulsen.)

(Jacket illustration by Richard Cuffari from *The Foxman* by Gary Paulsen.)

were snares, which kill the animals right away. It's not pleasant, but it's humane, if death can be humane. I was working a 60-mile line mostly on foot, sometimes on skis, going out in the early morning and heading home at night. Very slow work.

"One day a man named Bob McWilliams came to my house saying he had four dogs—a sprint team used to doing 12-mile races—he couldn't keep. As we were so broke we didn't even have a car, the prospect of *any* sort of transportation was very inviting. And besides, the dogs were free. This team was real slow, but they did make my work much easier. One day about midnight we were crossing Clear Water Lake, which is about three miles long. There was a full moon shining so brightly on the snow you could read by it. There was no one around, and all I could hear was the rhythm of the dogs' breathing as they pulled the sled. We came to the top of a hill, the steam from the dogs' breath all but hid their bodies—the entire world, seemed to glisten. It almost stopped my heart; I'd never seen anything so beautiful. I stayed out with the dogs for seven days. I didn't go home—my wife was frantic,—I didn't check line, I just ran the dogs, sixty to seventy miles a day. We covered a lot of northern Minnesota. For food, we had a few beaver carcasses. You know, you don't train these northern breeds to pull sleds. It's part of their genetic make-up. When a puppy gets to be seven months old, you put a harness on him and he'll pull a sled. I was initiated into this incredibly ancient and very beautiful bond, and it was as if everything

that had happened to me before ceased to exist. When I came off that seven-day run, I pulled all my traps, having resolved never again to kill.

"Shortly afterward, McWilliams told me about the Iditarod, a 1200-mile dog sled race that runs through Iditarod, an old mining town in the middle of Alaska, to Nome. On the spur of the moment, I announced, 'Sure, I'll run.' I had no idea what I was in for. And I certainly never figured I could raise the money it takes to get a team together and so on. It was getting down to the wire when Richard Jackson, the publisher of Bradbury Press, called wanting to know what I was writing. Now I had never met or worked with Jackson. 'I'm not writing! I'm running dogs!' I told him. I was hard up for the upcoming Iditarod. 'I'll send you the money,' he said, 'and when you get around to writing something, let me be the first to see it.'

"So I ran the Iditarod—a mind-boggling experience. You don't sleep for seventeen days. You begin to hallucinate. You are not allowed any outside assistance. If you make a mistake, you are left to die. Even the CBS helicopters covering the event can't intervene. You have no physical contact with your dogs—it's all voice commands given from where you stand on the back of the sled. If your lead dog doesn't like and respect you, the odds are good that you will get in trouble. If the dogs sense that you are losing your nerve, they may simply stop, make craters in the snow, roll up in a ball and sleep for days. That's called 'cratering' and once they start, there's absolutely nothing you can do to stop it. The dogs may also go berserk and trash the sled. And there you are, all alone in the middle of Alaska. The dogs are deeply intuitive and incredibly smart, far more intelligent than most people.

When you first start the race, you feel great, exhilarated by the unbelievable beauty of your surroundings. After about eight miles of moving through mountains, you start to feel scared. After twelve miles, you realize that you are nothing and the dogs are everything. To survive, you must be in deep harmony with your team. The Iditarod may sound like a macho thrill, but it's the opposite. You go where death goes, and death doesn't give a damn about macho. Besides, the last three races were won by women.

"Here's something that was brought home to me: macho is a lie. It's testicular garbage. Core toughness and compassion are the opposite of macho. The absence of fear comes with knowledge, not strength or bravura. More people should be telling this to young people, instead of 'climb the highest mountain and kill something.'"

Paulsen's experiences with the dogs motivated him to continue with his writing. *Dancing Carl* was published in 1983 by Richard Jackson's Bradbury Press and had its first beginnings as a dance. "I began it when I was trapping beaver. It was a narrative ballet for two dancers with original music by John Collins and choreography by Nancy Keller. A seven-minute version of this piece was aired on Minnesota Public Television."

Tracker, brought out a year later, deals with the metaphysics of tracking an animal. John, the thirteen-year-old protagonist, faces his first season of hunting alone, while his grandfather lay dying of cancer. Said Paulsen, "They're a farm family in northern Minnesota; they have always hunted their meat. 'We take meat with a gun,' John's grandfather tells him. 'It doesn't make you a man. It doesn't make you anything to kill.' What I'm exploring is the almost mystical relationship that develops between the hunter and the hunted. It's a relationship with its own integrity, not to be violated. There is, in the book, the

Maybe Carl wasn't dancing but just being and they didn't know how to do that. ■ (Jacket illustration by Jon Weiman from *Dancing Carl* by Gary Paulsen.)

concept of 'giving death' to the deer. I've seen this. At a certain point, the animal senses death coming and accepts it. This acceptance of death is something I was trying to write about in *Tracker*.''

Dogsong also deals with an adolescent boy struggling to become deeply humane. Russell, a fourteen-year-old Eskimo, has sought guidance from Oogruk, a tribal wise man, who counsels him to take his dog team across Alaska and back. En route, Russell finds a pregnant girl about his age, dying of exposure. Helping her to give birth, he does his best to save her life. ''I wrote *Dogsong* in camp while I was training my team for the Iditarod. It'd be twenty below, and there I'd sit by the fire writing longhand in my notebook. You know, I miss *Dogsong*. I wish I could keep writing it. It's like a friend who's gone away.'' The book was named a Newbery Honor Book in 1986. ''It's like things have come full circle. I felt like nothing the first time I walked into a library, and now library associations are giving me awards. It means a lot to me.''

Paulsen is currently working on *Madonna*, a collection of stories intended as a tribute to women who, by virtue of what he calls ''core toughness,'' have deeply impressed him. ''It started with Gloria, a friend of mine, whose two sons (out of a total of five kids) were born with spina bifida. Not only has she kept her family together for twenty-five years, but she's recently gone to college for a nursing degree and has consistently been at the top of her class. That got me started looking at the ladies in my family. They amaze me. Women are inevitably emotionally tougher than men. I want to understand their kind of toughness, and so feel that I must write about it.''

''I don't think there's any attempt on the part of men (writers) to understand what women are or the influence they have on our lives. Incidentally, my grandmother taught me how to crochet. When I was fighting or doing some of the other hard things in life, I found I had a tempering, a soft influence that I could use. It saved me many hours of agony. The male thing is to have an objective and go out and get it done. You can't stop. . . . And when you try one of these things and fail, you have this feminine influence to fall back on. You can lean back and say, all right, maybe the male side is crushed because I didn't make it, but I can also have compassion. I can try to understand my failure and I can try to learn from it.'' [Maryann N. Weidt, ''Gary Paulsen: A Sentry for Peace,'' *Voice of Youth Advocates*, August/October, 1986.[2]]

''I have about seven stories so far for *Madonna*. I've been doing performances of them with John Collins who has composed music. Some of the pieces are read, others sung. I don't know if they'll eventually find their form in a book, or if they are meant to be sung, painted, or danced.

''I write because it's all I can do,'' admits Paulsen. ''Every time I've tried to do something else I cannot, and have to come back to writing, though often I hate it—hate it and love it. It's much like being a slave, I suppose, and in slavery there is a kind of freedom that I find in writing: a perverse thing. I'm not 'motivated,' as you put it. Nor am I particularly driven. I write because it's all there is.''

Paulsen writes for a youth market because for his part he feels that it's ''artistically fruitless to write for adults. Adults created the mess which we are struggling to outlive. Adults have their minds set. Art reaches out for newness, and adults aren't new. And adults aren't truthful. The concept behind my last book, *Sentries*, is that young people know the score. *Sentries* is mostly a lot of questions, and I'm betting that young people have the answers.''

His work habits have changed considerably over the years. He now does most of his writing on computer. ''I even have a portable Radio Shack model I can take camping with me. When I was training dogs, we would run six hours on, four off. During my 'down time' in camp, I'd write. But these days, I'm camping less and less, and hardly running dogs at all. I'm building an office on my property with more advanced computers, modem links and the like. I find I do a lot more revision now that I work on computer. Diskettes are perfect for raw research. It's a new form and perfect for experimentation.''

Paulsen gives public readings, performances, and storytelling in small towns near his Minnesota farm. ''It's real nice. Generally, it takes place in a town hall. People bring coffee, bake cakes and pies. There's a wood stove. Everyone sits around listening and swapping tales.

''I'm also building a garden. The first thing I do every day is go into my garden and meditate. I try to become serene and write from whatever reservoir of serenity I find within myself.''

Paulsen also devotes a good deal of his time to nuclear disarmament causes. ''I believe that governments are standing in the way of solving this thing. It's up to private citizens. We cannot let our children grow up terrified of being blown apart by a thermonuclear device. Last spring, my sixteen-year-old son and I sat down and wrote a letter to the Soviet Writers Union. A simple letter to let them know we have no desire to blow them up, that we do not consider them the 'Evil Empire' (as does our President). Everyone should write letters—it makes a difference.'' In response to the letter Paulsen was invited to discuss his work with a delegation of Russian writers who met in Minneapolis. Furthermore, one of the Soviet writers and Paulsen plan to collaborate on a book in an effort to break down barriers between our two nations.

—Based on an interview by Marguerite Feitlowitz

FOR MORE INFORMATION SEE: Franz Serdahely, ''Prolific Paulsen,'' *Writer's Digest,* January, 1980; Maryann N. Weidt, ''Gary Paulsen: A Sentry for Peace,'' *Voice of Youth Advocates,* August/October, 1986.

RACHLIS, Eugene (Jacob)   1920-1986

OBITUARY NOTICE: Born February 5, 1920, in Boston, Mass.; died of cardiac arrest, November 10, 1986, in New York, N.Y. Publisher, journalist, editor, and author. Rachlis was a correspondent for the *Chicago Sun* in the 1940s, then commenced editorial work for publications such as *Changing Times* and the *New York Star* until 1957 when he began writing full time. He later became a writer, then editor in chief at Prentice-Hall publishers, and editor in chief and publisher of Bobbs-Merrill. His children's books include *Indians of the Plains, Story of the United States Coast Guard,* and *The Voyages of Henry Hudson.* He also wrote novels for adults, including *Peter Stuyvesant and His New York,* written with Henry J. Kessler, and *They Came to Kill.*

FOR MORE INFORMATION SEE: Contemporary Authors, Volumes 5-8, revised, Gale, 1969. Obituaries: *New York Times,* November 12, 1986; *Publishers Weekly,* November 28, 1986.

My Book and Heart, Shall never part.
                                        —New England Primer

REYHER, Rebecca Hourwich 1897-1987
(Becky Reyher)

OBITUARY NOTICE—See sketch in *SATA* Volume 18: Born January 21, 1897, in New York, N.Y.; died of pneumonia January 10, 1987, in St. Inigoes. Women's suffragist, educator, and author. Reyher's works for children included *My Mother Is the Most Beautiful Woman in the World,* a Russian folk tale she retold under the name Becky Reyher. She also wrote *Babies and Puppies Are Fun!,* and edited *The Stork Run: A Collection of Baby Cartoons,* which portrays many antics of babies and young children as well as their parents. During her crusade for women's voting rights, Reyher was active in the National Woman's Party in Boston, New York, and Washington, D.C. She later supported the passage of the Equal Rights Amendment and worked for the Institute of Women's Studies in Washington, D.C. Reyher taught at the New School for Social Research and at New York University, and lectured about her travels in Asia and Africa. She wrote several books based on the years she spent abroad, including *Zulu Woman: The Autobiography of Christina Sibiya,* and *The Fon and His Hundred Wives,* a report of the polygamy of one African tribesman. During the 1920s, Reyher wrote articles for *Hearst's International* magazine and was an associate editor for *Equal Rights* magazine.

FOR MORE INFORMATION SEE: Who's Who of American Women, 15th edition, Marquis, 1986. Obituaries: *Portland Evening Express,* January 11, 1987; *Washington Post,* January 11, 1987; *New York Times,* January 13, 1987.

RILEY, Jocelyn (Carol) 1949-

BRIEF ENTRY: Born March 6, 1949, in Minneapolis, Minn. After graduating from Carleton College in 1971, Riley became managing editor of the *Carleton Miscellany* and then held the position of marketing assistant for Beacon Press in Boston. She began free-lance writing and editing in 1973. In 1982 Riley received the Arthur Tofte Memorial Award from the Council for Wisconsin Writers for her young adult novel entitled *Only My Mouth Is Smiling* (Morrow, 1982), also named a "best book for young adults" by the American Library Association. Her award-winning novel centers around thirteen-year-old Merle and her struggle to deal with her mother's increasing mental illness. "The situation in the book is serious but not macabre, handled with sympathy and insight, psychologically sound and written with depth, candor, and skill," wrote a reviewer for the *Bulletin of the Center for Children's Books.* In the sequel, *Crazy Quilt* (Morrow, 1984), Merle comes to terms with her mother's illness. "Riley has an instinctive understanding of the vulnerability of adolescence," observed *School Library Journal,* "yet she makes it clear . . . individuals are responsible for how they live their lives." Riley also wrote "The Brass Ring," a television film based on *Only My Mouth Is Smiling* that was first broadcast by Showtime-TV in 1985. Among her other writings are a book of essays for adults and several novels. A contributor of numerous articles to periodicals, Riley's memberships include Women in Communication, Authors Guild, Society of Children's Book Writers, Association for Multi-Image, and Council for Wisconsin Writers. *Agent:* Jane Gelfman, John Farquharson Ltd., 250 West 57th St., New York, N.Y. 10107.

FOR MORE INFORMATION SEE: Who's Who of American Women, 14th edition, Marquis, 1984; *Contemporary Authors,* Volume 115, Gale, 1985; *International Authors and Writer's Who's Who,* 10th edition, International Biographical Centre, 1986.

RINALDI, Ann 1934-

BRIEF ENTRY: Born August 27, 1934, in New York, N.Y. Rinaldi first worked as a columnist for the *Somerset Messenger Gazette* in New Jersey from 1969 to 1970. Since then, she has written a column and feature stories for the *Trentonian* newspaper, also in New Jersey, as well as books for young adults. "Real life, as I know it, as I've learned it to be from my newspaper experience and own past, goes into my books," Rinaldi observed. In a review of *Term Paper* (Walker & Co., 1980), her first published book, *Bulletin of the Center for Children's Books* wrote: "The characterization and dialogue are strong, the writing style and plot development consistently structured and paced." *Term Paper* is about an orphaned teenager, Nicki DeBonis, and her confrontations with her older brother, who is also her guardian. In the sequel, *Promises Are for Keeping* (Walker & Co., 1982), Nicki learns responsibility and begins to understand the complexities of relationships. "Rinaldi is extremely skilled at depicting a much more typical kid than many in teen novels," noted *Voice of Youth Advocates.* Rinaldi's other books for teens are *But in the Fall I'm Leaving* (Holiday House, 1985), *Time Enough for Drums* (Holiday House, 1986), and *The Good Side of My Heart* (Holiday House, 1987). She is the recipient of the 1978 New Jersey Press Association's first place and second place awards for newspaper columns. *Home:* 302 Miller Ave., Somerville, N.J. 08876.

FOR MORE INFORMATION SEE: Contemporary Authors, Volume 111, Gale, 1984.

ROOSEVELT, (Anna) Eleanor 1884-1962

PERSONAL: Surname is pronounced *Roe*-ze-velt; born October 11, 1884, in New York, N.Y.; died November 7, 1962, in New York, N.Y.; daughter of Elliott (a businessman) and Anna (Hall) Roosevelt; niece of Theodore Roosevelt (26th President of the United States); married Franklin Delano Roosevelt (32nd President of the United States), March 17, 1905 (died April 12, 1945); children: Anna Eleanor (Mrs. James A. Halsted), James, Franklin Delano, Jr. (died November 1, 1909), Elliott, Franklin Delano, Jr., John Apsonwall. *Education:* Educated privately in the United States and in England. *Politics:* Democrat. *Religion:* Episcopalian. *Residence:* Hyde Park, Dutchess County, N.Y.

CAREER: Humanitarian, writer, educator. Teacher, Rivington Street Settlement House, c. 1902-05; New York Democratic State Committee, women's division, finance chairman, 1924-28; co-owner, vice-principal, instructor in sociology, economics, and government, Todhunter School, 1927-33; Democratic National Campaign Committee, member of advisory committee in charge of women's activities, 1928; First Lady of the United States, 1933-45; United Feature Syndicate, author of column, "My Day," c. 1936-39; Office of Civilian Defense, Washington, D.C., assistant director, 1941-42; *Ladies' Home Journal,* author of "If You Ask Me" (question and answer page), 1941-?; U.S. representative to the General Assembly of the United Nations, 1946-52, chairman of Commission on Human Rights, 1947-52; participant in radio discussion program, "Eleanor and Anna Roosevelt," 1948-?; partner, Val-Kill Inn (hotel and restaurant), Val-Kill Farms, Hyde Park.

MEMBER: American Newspaper Guild, Women's National Press Club, American Association for the United Nations, New York State League of Women Voters (vice-president), Phi Beta Kappa (honorary member), New York Woman's City Club, Cosmopolitan Club, 100,000 Mile Club, Altrusa Club. *Awards, honors:* Recipient of Humanitarian award, 1939; first annual award for distinguished service in the cause of American social progress from *Nation,* 1940; Franklin Delano Roosevelt Brotherhood Award, 1946; voted "most admired woman living today in any part of the world" by American Institute of Public Opinion, 1948; First American Award in Human Relations, 1949; nominated to "Honor Roll of Democracy" by *Chicago Defender,* 1949; Four Freedoms Award from Four Freedoms Foundation, 1950, as "the individual who best exemplifies the ideals of the late President Franklin D. Roosevelt"; Prince Carl Medal, Sweden, 1950; Irving Geist Foundation Award, 1950; highest honor award from National Society for Crippled Children and Adults, 1950; award of merit from New York City Federation of Women's Clubs; voted most popular living American by *Woman's Home Companion;* Wel-Met Children's Book Award from Child Study Association, 1950, for *The United Nations and Youth;* Constance Lindsay Skinner Award from Women's National Book Association, 1961, for "outstanding contribution to the world of books"; D.H.L., Russell Sage College, 1929; LL.D., John Marshall College of Law; honorary degrees from the universities of Oxford (England) and Lyons (France).

WRITINGS: (Editor) Elliott Roosevelt, *Hunting Big Game in the Eighties: The Letters of Elliott Roosevelt, Sportsman,* Scribner, 1932; *When You Grow Up to Vote* (juvenile; illustrated by Manning de V. Lee), Houghton, 1932; *It's Up to the Women,* Federick A. Stokes, 1933; *A Trip to Washington with Bobby and Betty* (juvenile), Dodge Publishing, 1935; *This Is My Story* (autobiography), Harper & Brothers, 1937, published in England as *The Lady of the White House: An Auto-*

Eleanor with her father and brother Hall. (Photograph courtesy of Franklin D. Roosevelt Library.)

biography, Hutchinson, 1938; *My Days* (autobiography), Dodge Publishing, 1938; *This Troubled World,* H. C. Kinsey, 1938; *Christmas* (juvenile; illustrated by Fritz Kredel), Knopf, 1940, republished in *Eleanor Roosevelt's Christmas Book,* Dodd, 1963; *The Moral Basis of Democracy,* Howell, Soskin, 1940; (with Frances Cook MacGregor) *This Is America,* Putnam, 1942.

If You Ask Me, Appleton-Century, 1946; *This I Remember* (autobiography), Harper, 1949, reprinted, Greenwood Press, 1975; (with Helen Ferris) *Partners: The United Nations and Youth* (juvenile), Dutton, 1950; *India and the Awakening East,* Harper, 1953; (with William De Witt) *UN: Today and Tomorrow,* Harper, 1953; *It Seems to Me,* W. W. Norton, 1954; (with Lorena A. Hickok) *Ladies of Courage,* Putnam, 1954; *On My Own* (autobiography), Harper, 1958; (with Regina Tor) *Growing Toward Peace* (juvenile), Random House, 1960; *You Learn by Living,* Harper, 1960; *Autobiography,* Harper, 1961, published as *The Autobiography of Eleanor Roosevelt,* Barnes & Noble, 1978; (with H. Ferris), *Your Teens and Mine,* Doubleday, 1961; *Book of Common Sense Etiquette,* Macmillan, 1962; *Tomorrow Is Now,* Harper, 1963.

SIDELIGHTS: **October 11, 1884.** Born into New York's "high society," the eldest child and only daughter of Elliott and Anna Hall Roosevelt, young Eleanor was reared in accordance with the conventions of the wealthy class. "I was a shy, solemn child even at the age of two, and I am sure that even when I danced, which I did frequently, I never smiled.

"My earliest recollections are of being dressed up and allowed to come down into what must have been a dining room and dance for a group of gentlemen who applauded and laughed as I pirouetted before them. Finally, my father would pick me up and hold me high in the air. All this is rather vague to me, but my father was never vague. He dominated my life as long as he lived, and was the love of my life for many years after he died.

"We had a country house at Hempstead, Long Island, so that he could hunt and play polo. He loved horses and dogs, and we always had both. During this time he was in business, and with this, added to the work and the sports, the gay and popular young couple lived a busy, social life. Some of the older members of my father's family have told me since that they thought the strain on his health was very great, but my mother and he himself probably never realized this. I knew only that he was the center of my world, and that all around him loved him." [Eleanor Roosevelt, *This Is My Story,* Harper & Brothers, 1937.[1]]

Roosevelt was in awe of her mother's beauty. Not personally blessed with beauty, she felt inadequate next to her mother, who nicknamed her "Granny" because of her serious demeanor.

December 7, 1892. Mother died of diphtheria. Within months, the disease claimed the life of Roosevelt's little brother. The remaining children were sent to live with their maternal grandmother. ". . . It was arranged that we three children were to go and live with my Grandmother Hall. I realize now what that must have meant in dislocation of her household, and I marvel at the sweetness of my two uncles and the two aunts who were still at home, for never by word or deed did any of them make us feel that we were not in our own house.

"After we were installed, my father came to see me, and I remember going down into the high ceilinged, dim library on the first floor of the house in west 37th Street. He sat in a big chair. He was dressed all in black, looking very sad. He held out his arms and gathered me to him. In a little while he began to talk, to explain to me that my mother was gone, that she had been all the world to him, and now he only had my brothers and myself, that my brothers were very young, and that he and I must keep close together. Some day I would make a home for him again, we would travel together and do many things which he painted as interesting and pleasant, to be looked forward to in the future together.

"Somehow it was always he and I. I did not understand whether my brothers were to be our children or whether he felt that they would be at school and college and later independent.

"There started that day a feeling which never left me—that he and I were very close together, and some day would have a life of our own together. He told me to write to him often, to be a good girl, not to give any trouble, to study hard, to grow up into a woman he could be proud of, and he would come to see me whenever it was possible.

"When he left, I was all alone to keep our secret of mutual understanding and to adjust myself to my new existence.

"Though he was so little with us, my father dominated all this period of my life. Subconsciously I must have been waiting always for his visits. They were irregular, and he rarely sent word before he arrived. . . .

"One more sorrow came to my father the winter that my mother died. My little brother, Ellie, was simply too good for this world, and he never seemed to thrive after my mother's death. Both he and the baby, Josh, got scarlet fever, and I was returned to my Cousin Susie, and, of course, quarantined.

"The baby got well without any complications, but Ellie developed diphtheria and died. My father came to take me out occasionally, but the anxiety over the little boys was too great for him to give me a great deal of his time."[1]

August 14, 1894. ". . . Just before I was ten years old, word came that my father had died. My aunts told me, but I simply refused to believe it, and while I wept long and went to bed still weeping, I finally went to sleep and began the next day living in my dream world as usual.

"My grandmother decided that we children should not go to the funeral, and so I had no tangible thing to make death real to me. From that time on I knew in my mind that my father was dead, and yet I lived with him more closely, probably, than I had when he was alive."[1]

1894-1899. "During the years from ten to fifteen I became an omnivorous reader for I had no playmates near by. . . . My aunts were often away, but even when they were home we loved to be alone except for the young friends whom they asked to visit them. This solitude encouraged my habit of taking a book out into the fields or in the woods and sitting in a tree or lying under it, completely forgetting the passage of time. No one tried to censor my reading, though occasionally when I happened on a book that I could not understand and asked too many difficult questions before people, the book would disappear. I remember this happened to Dickens' *Bleak House,* and I spent days hunting for it and wondering where I could have left it!

"My grandmother, after my father's death, allowed me less and less contact with his family. Never have I quite understood the reason unless it was that she felt I would grow up too quickly or become accustomed to things of which she disap-

proved. In any case, I saw very little of my Roosevelt cousins. I did, however, pay one or two short visits to Aunt Edith and Uncle Ted in summer."[1]

1899. Sent to London to Mlle. Souvestre's School, "Allenswood." "I did not know that my grandmother and my aunts had written about me before I arrived, so I felt that I was starting a new life, free from all my former sins and traditions. I am not sure that I would not recommend this for any child who has been somewhat fearful of authority in her early youth, for this was the first time in all my life that all my fears left me. If I lived up to the rules and told the truth, there was nothing to fear.

"School life itself was fairly uneventful, but in the world outside great excitement reigned. I had hardly been conscious of our own Spanish War in 1898, even though I had heard a great deal about the sinking of the *Maine* and about Uncle Ted and His Rough Riders; my grandmother and her family lived so completely out of the political circles of the day and took very little interest in public affairs. . . ."[1]

1902. Upon her return to the States, Roosevelt spent the year as a debutante, attending social dinners and dances. "I was tall, but I did not dance very well, nor had I had much opportunity in England, and in any case English dancing was different from ours. I had lost touch with all the girls whom I had known before I went abroad, though, of course, afterwards I picked up some of my old relationships. . . .

"I do not think I quite realized beforehand what utter agony it was going to be or I would never have had the courage to

Eleanor Roosevelt in her wedding dress. (Photograph by Pach Brothers from the Bettmann Archive, Inc.)

go. . . . By no stretch of the imagination could I fool myself into thinking that I was a popular debutante!''[1]

Began to see her cousin, Franklin Delano Roosevelt.

Autumn, 1903. ''I had a great curiosity about life and a desire to participate in every experience that might be the lot of woman. There seemed to me to be a necessity for hurry; without rhyme or reason I felt the urge to be a part of the stream of life, and so . . . when Franklin Roosevelt, my fifth cousin once removed, asked me to marry him, though I was only nineteen, it seemed an entirely natural thing and I never even thought that we were both rather young and inexperienced. I came back from Groton, where I had spent the week end, and asked Cousin Susie whether she thought I cared enough, and my grandmother, when I told her, asked me if I was sure I was really in love. I solemnly answered 'yes,' and yet I know now that it was years later before I understood what being in love was or what loving really meant.

''I had very high standards as to what a wife and mother should be and not the faintest notion of what it meant to be either a wife or a mother, and none of my elders enlightened me.

''I marvel now at my husband's patience, for I realize how trying I must have been in many ways. I can see today how funny were some of the tragedies of our early married life.

''My mother-in-law had sense enough to realize that both of us were very young and very undeveloped, and in spite of the fact that she thought I had been well brought up, she decided to try to make her son think this matter over—which at the time, of course, I resented. As he was well ahead in his studies, she took him with his friend and room-mate, Lathrop Brown, on a cruise to the West Indies that winter, while I lived in New York with Mrs. Parish.

''Franklin's feelings did not change, however.''[1]

The engagement to Franklin Delano Roosevelt was formally announced the following autumn, in 1904.

March 5, 1905. Inauguration of Uncle Teddy Roosevelt, 26th President of the United States. ''I was interested and excited, but politics still meant little to me, for though I can remember the forceful manner in which Uncle Ted delivered his speech, I have no recollection of what he said! We came back to the

Eleanor with three-year-old son Elliott at Campobello. (Photograph courtesy of Franklin D. Roosevelt Library.)

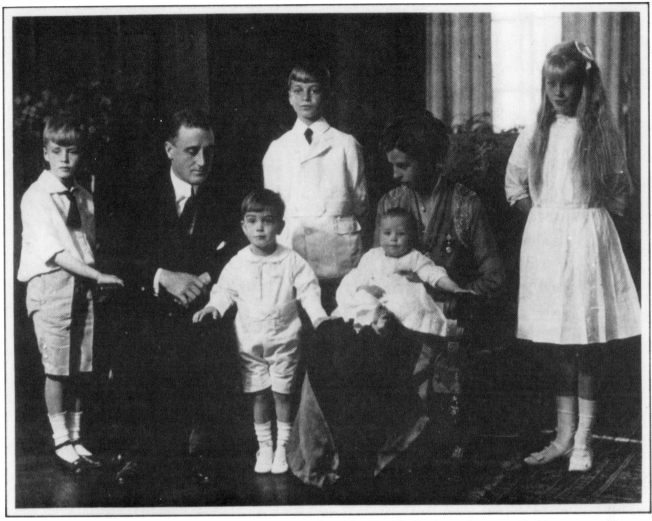

The Roosevelts in 1916. Left to right: Elliott, Franklin, Franklin Jr., James, Eleanor with John, and Anna. (Photograph by Harold L. Ritch from the Franklin D. Roosevelt Library.)

White House for lunch, and then saw the parade and back to New York. I told myself I had seen an historic event—and I never expected to see another inauguration in the family!''[1]

March 17, 1905. Married Franklin Delano Roosevelt. Many have since theorized about the attraction between the young Roosevelts. Some speculate that he already realized the ideal partner she would make in helping him toward his political goals. In a biography of his parents, their son Elliott wrote: ''He must have taken enormous pleasure in bringing her out of her shell. . . . There was a strong element of pity as well as love. Beyond that, he felt secure with a girl whose lack of worldly experience exceeded his.''[1]

The wedding took place in New York City, and President Theodore Roosevelt gave the bride away. ''. . . Those closest to us did take time to wish us well, but the great majority of the guests were far more interested in the thought of being able to see and listen to the President—and in a very short time this young married couple were standing alone! The room in which the President was holding forth was filled with people laughing gaily at his stories, which were always amusing. I do not remember being particularly surprised by this, and I cannot remember that even Franklin seemed to mind. We simply followed the crowd and listened with the rest. Later we gathered together enough ushers and bridesmaids to cut the

wedding cake, and I imagine we made Uncle Ted attend this ceremony. . . .

''We left amidst the usual shower of rice. . . . And then took the train for Hyde Park, where we spent our first honeymoon. It is not customary to have two honeymoons, but we did, because my husband had to finish out his year at law school.

''Our first home was a small apartment in a hotel in the West Forties in New York City for the remainder of the spring while Franklin continued his study of law.''[1]

After law school was over, the couple spent the summer touring Europe on their ''second honeymoon.'' ''I was beginning to be an entirely dependent person—no tickets to buy, no plans to make, someone always to decide everything for me. A very pleasant contrast to my former life, and I slipped into it with the greatest of ease.

''The edge of my shyness was gradually wearing off through enforced contact with many people. I still suffered but not so acutely, and I was beginning to be conscious of the fact that it was rare that you could not establish some kind of a relationship with your neighbor at dinner or at any social gathering. . . . As young women go, I suppose I was fitting pretty well into the pattern of a fairly conventional, quiet, young society matron.''[1]

Eleanor Roosevelt using a voting machine, 1925.

May 3, 1906. During the first ten years of marriage, six children were born to the Roosevelts—one girl and five boys. "... Our first boy, James,... will never know with what relief and joy I welcomed him into the world, for again I had been worried for fear I would never have a son, knowing that both my mother-in-law and my husband wanted a boy to name after my husband's father. Many a time since I have wished that two girls had started our family, so that Anna might have had a sister, and in the end I reached a point where boys were almost commonplace, but my heart sang when James was safely in the world."[1]

1908. "My mother-in-law thought that our house was too small, and that year she bought a plot and built in East 65th Street two houses, Nos. 47 and 49. She and my husband entrusted the plans to Mr. Charles A. Platt, an architect of great taste who certainly did a very remarkable piece of work. The houses were narrow, but he made the most of every inch of space and built them so that the dining rooms and drawing rooms could be thrown together and make practically one big room as the doors between them were very wide doors.

"My early dislike of any kind of scolding had developed now into a dislike for any kind of discussion and so, instead of taking an interest in these houses, one of which I was to live

in, I left everything to my mother-in-law and my husband. I was growing very dependent on my mother-in-law, requiring her help on almost every subject, and never thought of asking for anything which I felt would not meet with her approval."[1]

November 8, 1909. Third baby, a boy named Franklin, died at the age of eight months. "We took him to Hyde Park to bury him, and to this day, so many years later, I can stand by his tiny little stone in the churchyard and see the little group of people gathered around his tiny coffin, and remember how cruel it seemed to leave him out there alone in the cold.

"I was young and morbid and reproached myself very bitterly for having done so little about the care of this baby. I felt he had been left too much to the nurse and I knew too little about him, and that in some way I must be to blame. I even felt that I had not cared enough about him, and I made myself and all those around me most unhappy during that winter. I was even a little bitter against my poor young husband who occasionally tried to make me see how idiotically I was behaving.

"My next child, Elliott Roosevelt, was born at 49 East 65th Street on **September 23rd, 1910.** He suffered for a great many years with a rather unhappy disposition, and I think in all probability I was partly to blame, for certainly no one could have behaved more foolishly than I did practically up to the time of Elliott's arrival, and I should have known better.''[1]

1910. Franklin Roosevelt elected to the state senate. Family moved to Albany, New York. ''Here in Albany began for the first time a dual existence for me, which was to last all the rest of my life. Public service, whether my husband was in or out of office, was to be a part of our daily life from now on. To him it was a career in which he was completely absorbed. He probably could not have formulated his political philosophy at that time as he could today, but the science of government was interesting—and people, the ability to understand them, the play of your own personality on theirs, this was a fascinating study to him.

''I still lived under the compulsion of my early training; duty was perhaps the motivating force in my life, often excluding what might have been joy or pleasure. I looked at everything from the point of view of what I ought to do, rarely from the standpoint of what I wanted to do. In fact, there were times when I think I almost forgot that there was such a thing as wanting anything. You so obviously must want that which you ought to do! So I took an interest in politics, but I don't know whether I enjoyed it! It was a wife's duty to be interested in whatever interested her husband, whether it was politics, books or a particular dish for dinner. This was the attitude with which I approached that first winter in Albany.''[1]

1913. Moved to Washington, D.C. after Franklin Roosevelt was appointed Secretary to the Navy. For the first time since her marriage, she began to develop her own independence and self-confidence, while fulfilling the obligations of a politician's wife. Most afternoons were spent calling on wives of officers, Supreme Court justices, Congressmen, Senators, and Cabinet members. ''. . . I could have learned much about pol-

Mrs. Roosevelt inspecting a slum in the Caribbean area, 1934. (Photograph courtesy of *The News.*)

When her husband was running for a second term and she had to travel around the country with him aboard his campaign train, she used the time between each stop to write a book about her own early life. ■ (From *Eleanor Roosevelt, First Lady of the World* by Doris Faber. Illustrated by Donna Ruff.)

itics and government, for I had plenty of opportunity to meet and talk with interesting men and women. As I look back upon it, however, I think the whole of my life remained centered in the family. The children were still small, two more were to be born during this period, and, outside of the exclusively personal life, there was the social aspect, which seemed to me then most important.

''. . . I was perfectly certain that I had nothing to offer of an individual nature and that my only chance of doing my duty as the wife of a public official was to do exactly as the majority of women were doing, perhaps to be a little more meticulous about it than some of the others were. Whatever I was asked to do must be done, and it was not always conducive to comfort on my part or on the part of anyone else.''[1]

1917. When the United States entered the first World War, life changed dramatically. Eleanor Roosevelt helped to organize the Navy Red Cross, and visited the Naval Hospital. ''My mother-in-law used to laugh at me and say I could provide my chauffeur with more orders to be carried out during the day than anyone else she had ever listened to, but this was just a symptom of developing executive ability. My time was now completely filled with a variety of war activities, and I was learning to have a certain confidence in myself and in my ability to meet emergencies and deal with them.''[1]

Appalled by the conditions at the Naval Hospital, Eleanor Roosevelt ordered an investigation, and as a result of her action, the hospital eventually received the necessary appropriations enabling it to become a model of its kind. She also was instrumental in starting a program of occupational work for mentally disabled men.

1920. With the war over, Franklin Roosevelt was nominated for vice-president, and the couple spent the year campaigning for his election. ''I am sure that I was glad for my husband, but it never occurred to me to be much excited. I had come to accept the fact that public service was my husband's great interest and I always tried to make the necessary family adjustments easy. I carried on the children's lives and my own as calmly as could be, and while I was always a part of the

public aspect of our lives, still I felt detached and objective, as though I were looking at someone else's life. This seems to have remained with me down to the present day. I cannot quite describe it, but it is as though you lived two lives, one of your own and the other which belonged to the circumstances that surround you.

''The election was an overwhelming defeat which was accepted very philosophically by my husband, who had been completely prepared for the result. . . .''[1]

By this time, many of the hopes held by Franklin on his wedding day were on their way to being realized. His career was progressing smoothly, and his political future seemed secure. Many of the dreams held by Eleanor back in 1905, however, had been shattered. A woman whose strongest desire had been to please her husband, she was crushed to learn of his infidelity in the autumn of 1918.

Details of the relationship between Franklin Roosevelt and Lucy Mercer, a woman originally introduced into the family

Queen Elizabeth with Eleanor enroute to the White House. (Photograph by United Press International.)

Eleanor with John F. Kennedy, hours after he announced his candidacy. (Photograph by United Press International.)

as secretary to Eleanor, are unknown. Most accounts tell of a confrontation and discussion of divorce, but the consequences of such an action on Franklin's career would have been disastrous. It is further speculated that Franklin's mother exerted her influence, threatening to cut him off financially if he did not discontinue the liaison with Lucy. Franklin and Eleanor seemed to have come to some sort of understanding, and although their relations as husband and wife may have been altered, they continued their partnership in public service.

1921. While the family vacationed at their usual summer spot on Campobello Island off the coast of New Brunswick, Franklin Roosevelt became gravely ill. Finally, he was diagnosed as a victim of infantile paralysis. ''. . . For several weeks that winter his legs were placed in plaster casts in order to stretch the muscles, and every day a little of the cast was chipped out at the back, which stretched the muscles a little bit more. This was torture and he bore it without the slightest complaint, just as he bore his illness from the very beginning. I never but once have heard him say anything bordering on discouragement or bitterness. That was some years later, when he was debating whether to do something which would cost considerable money, and he remarked that he supposed it was better to spend the money on the chance that he might not be quite such a helpless individual.''[1]

It was over a year before Franklin Roosevelt was able to resume work. Eleanor Roosevelt's activities became more political, which helped to strengthen her husband's will to carry on. During this rehabilitation period, the Roosevelts built a cottage, Val-Kill. ''Little by little, through exercise and wearing braces, he learned to walk, first with crutches and then with a cane, leaning on someone's arm. The first braces were heavy; later, lighter ones were made. However, for the rest of his life he was unable to walk or stand without the braces and some help, though he could still swim and play water polo.

''The perfect naturalness with which the children accepted his limitations, though they had always known him as an active person, helped him tremendously, I think, in his own acceptance of them. He had so many outside interests that he was always busy, and boredom was something he never experienced in his whole life.

''Two things he could still enjoy—swimming and driving his own car. His car had special hand controls, since he could not use his legs. He was as good a driver as any one I have known with this specially equipped car.

''Franklin's illness was another turning point, and proved a blessing in disguise; for it gave him strength and courage he had not had before. He had to think out the fundamentals of living and learn the greatest of all lessons—infinite patience and never-ending persistence.

"People have often asked me how I myself felt about his illness. To tell the truth, I do not think I ever stopped to analyze my feelings. There was so much to do to mangage the household and the children and to try to keep things running smoothly that I never had any time to think of my own reactions. I simply lived from day to day and got through the best I could." [Eleanor Roosevelt, *This I Remember,* Harper & Brothers, 1949.[2]]

1927. Although united politically with her husband, Roosevelt led a separate personal life, pursuing her own interests. She became co-owner and teacher of American history, English and American literature at Todhunter School, a private school for girls. She also managed a craft factory at Val-Kill with two friends, Marian Dickerman and Nancy Cook. "Readjustment is a kind of private revolution. Each time you learn something new you must readjust the whole framework of your knowledge. It seems to me that one is forced to make inner and outer readjustments all one's life. The process never ends. And yet, for a great many people, this is a continuing problem because they appear to have an innate fear of change, no matter what form it takes: changed personal relationships, changed social or financial conditions. The new or the unknown becomes in their minds something hostile, almost malignant. . . . No matter how outwardly tranquil or unchanging one's situation may appear to be, it requires constant readjustment." [Eleanor Roosevelt, *You Learn by Living,* Harper, 1960.[3]]

January, 1929. Franklin Roosevelt became governor of New York. Family moved to Albany. "In spite of my political activities and having to run the Executive Mansion in Albany, after my husband was elected governor I continued to teach for two and a half days a week, leaving Albany on Sunday evenings and returning Wednesday afternoons. It was rather strenuous when we were in Albany, but, of course, fairly easy when we were at Hyde Park, as we were there for longer periods, when the legislature was not in session. For a while, after we went to Washington, I conducted a class for graduates and their friends, first on a weekly and then on a monthly basis."[1]

1932. Developed a friendship with Lorena A. Hickok, a reporter for the Associated Press who had been assigned to report on Eleanor Roosevelt during the presidential campaign. Much has been written about their thirty-year friendship and correspondence, which consisted of more than 3,000 letters. During the twelve years that Eleanor Roosevelt lived in the White House, Hickok accompanied her on several trips and often stayed at the White House, helping the First Lady with her writing projects.

In later years, Hickok was the author of several books on Eleanor Roosevelt and collaborated with her on a 1954 book, *Ladies of Courage.* In 1958, Hickok donated her letters to the Franklin D. Roosevelt Library, with the stipulation that they remain closed for ten years after Hickok's death. In 1978, the letters became accessible to researchers. A 1980 book, *The Life of Lorena Hickok: E. R.'s Friend* by Doris Faber, detailed their thirty-year relationship with excerpts from the letters.

Eleanor Roosevelt on a balcony of the White House, March, 1940, greeting the children gathered for the annual egg-rolling. (Photograph by Acme.)

(From the movie "The Roosevelt Story." Produced by United Artists, 1947.)

1933. Became First Lady when husband Franklin was elected thirty-second President of the United States. "From the personal standpoint, I did not want my husband to be president. I realized, however, that it was impossible to keep a man out of public service when that was what he wanted and was undoubtedly well equipped for. It was pure selfishness on my part, and I never mentioned my feelings on the subject to him. I did not work directly in the campaign, because I felt that that was something better done by others, but I went on many of the trips and always did anything that Franklin felt would be helpful.

"That Election night, amidst all the rejoicing after the results were known, he came to me and said: 'I wish I knew what you are really thinking and feeling.' He showed in that question great perspicacity, for one would naturally expect the wife of a man who had just been elected President of the United States to be completely overjoyed.

"I was happy for my husband, of course, because I knew that in many ways it would make up for the blow that fate had dealt him when he was stricken with infantile paralysis; and I had implicit confidence in his ability to help the country in a crisis. Naturally he had wanted to win, and he wanted this opportunity to serve his country in public life.

"But for myself, I was probably more deeply troubled. . . . As I saw it, this meant the end of any personal life of my own. I knew what traditionally should lie before me; I had watched Mrs. Theodore Roosevelt and had seen what it meant to be the wife of the president, and I cannot say that I was pleased at the prospect. By earning my own money, I had recently enjoyed a certain amount of financial independence, and had been able to do things in which I was personally interested. The turmoil in my heart and mind was rather great that night, and the next few months were not to make any clearer what the road ahead would be.

"Life began to change immediately. As soon as my husband's election was established, the secret service assumed responsibility for his protection. Our house in 65th Street was filled with secret-service agents, and guests were scrutinized and had to be identified when Franklin was in the house.

"In the first days of his administration, my husband was much too busy finding ways and means of meeting the financial crisis in the country to be bothered with anything else, so I went to work to organize the household and the secretarial side of the office which did the work for the president's wife."[2]

Roosevelt demonstrated that a First Lady can be an independent thinker and an individual. Largely because of her example, those filling the role after her have had the freedom to, and are essentially expected to, become politically involved. Because of Franklin Roosevelt's physical limitations, he gradually became dependent on his wife to bring him first-hand

(From the movie "Sunrise at Campobello," starring Ralph Bellamy and Greer Garson. Copyright © 1960 by Warner Brothers.)

accounts of different situations around the world. A writer for *Newsweek* once compared the First Lady's role during FDR's administration to that of a lightning rod. "These trips gave me a wonderful opportunity to visit all kinds of places and to see and get to know a good cross section of people. Always during my free time I visited as many government projects as possible, often managing to arrive without advance notice so that they could not be polished up for my inspection. I began to see for myself some of the results of my husband's actions during the first hundred days of his administration, and in meeting and talking with people all over the country I got the full impact of what the new programs had meant to them. It was evident that the home and farm loans, for example, had saved many a family from outright disaster.

"Of course I always reported to Franklin upon my return, but aside from any value my reports may have been to him, I had another, more personal, reason for wanting to make these trips. All the years that I lived in Washington I was preparing for the time when we should no longer be there. I did not want to give up my interests in New York City, because I always felt that some day I would go back. I never anticipated that so many years would pass before I left Washington. There was much to do while we were there, and I had many enjoyable privileges, but I kept expecting to leave at the end of every four years and I did not want to be spoiled by enjoying the privileges too much or to lose my interest in activities that might be continued after I left the White House. This seems

to me ridiculous as I look back upon it now, but I might as well record the fact that it was one of my constant preoccupations.

"Because I was under contract for the lecture trips, I had to keep to my schedule. That meant work and discipline—and I felt I needed both. In addition, I really did enjoy getting away to less formal surroundings, though I was to find that going on lecture trips did not always mean that I succeeded in being 'unofficial.' On occasion, I was more guarded and watched over than in Washington."[2]

Roosevelt also continued writing a weekly column and a page in *Woman's Home Companion* in addition to contributing articles to periodicals and writing books for children.

1936. Signed a five-year contract with United Feature Syndicate to do a daily column in the form of a diary. "I have never known what it was to be bored or to have time hang heavily on my hands. It has always been difficult to find time to do the things I want to do. When I was young I read a great deal, but during these last years I have had to read so many things that those I should like to read are too often neglected. Sometimes I think it would be delightful if an afternoon or evening could actually be given to uninterrupted reading for pure pleasure. In the White House I often left a movie in order to work on my mail and went back just before the end, hoping that my guests did not know I had deserted them in between. I practically never found time to go to the movies outside the White House, and life is not very different even now. I never have time to listen to the radio except to news broadcasts morning and evening, and now and then to a program which holds some special interest.''[2]

December 7, 1941. Attack on Pearl Harbor. Roosevelt spent a great deal of time traveling after the bombing, and spent several weeks in England at her husband's request. She also visited Australia and New Zealand at FDR's suggestion. Both trips involved risk because the countries visited were actual war zones.

1945. Despite declining health, FDR was elected for a fourth term. ''Early in January, realizing full well this would certainly be his last inauguration, perhaps even having a premonition that he would not be with us very long, Franklin insisted that every grandchild come to the White House for a few days over the 20th. I was somewhat reluctant to have thirteen grandchildren ranging in age from three to sixteen together, for fear of an epidemic of measles or chicken pox, but he was so insistent that I agreed.

''We bulged at the corners, for it was a tremendous family to house; though it was not so bad as during one of the earlier inaugurations when I had several grandchildren with their mothers and nurses as well as several of my friends staying in the house. That time, when I came to assign beds for two

grandchildren and a nurse who were uncertain about coming until the last minute, I found I had to give up my own rooms and sleep in a room on the third floor which my maid used as a sewing and pressing room, and I had to take my mail and work on part of Miss Thompson's desk in her very small office. I was not too comfortable, nor, I fear, too sweet about it.''[2]

April 12, 1945. Husband died of a massive cerebral hemorrhage. ''. . . As always happens in life, something was coming to an end and something new was beginning. I went over many things in my mind as we traveled the familiar road back to Washington.

''It is hard for me to understand now, but at the time I had an almost impersonal feeling about everything that was happening. The only explanation I have is that during the years of the war I had schooled myself to believe that some or all of my sons might be killed and I had long faced the fact that Franklin might be killed or die at any time. This was not consciously phrased; it simply underlay all my thoughts and merged what might happen to me with what was happening to all the suffering people of the world. That does not entirely account for my feelings, however. Perhaps it was that much further back I had had to face certain difficulties until I decided to accept the fact that a man must be what he is, life must be lived as it is, circumstances force your children away from you, and you can not live at all if you do not learn to adapt yourself to your life as it happens to be.

(From the movie "The Eleanor Roosevelt Story." Narrated by Archibald Macleish, it won an Academy Award for Best Documentary. Copyright © 1965 by American International Pictures.)

(From the television movie "Eleanor and Franklin," starring Jane Alexander and Edward Herrman. Produced by Talent Associates, 1975.)

"Before we went to Washington in 1933, I had frankly faced my own personal situation. In my early married years the pattern of my life had been largely my mother-in-law's pattern. Later it was the children and Franklin who made the pattern. When the last child went to boarding school I began to want to do things on my own, to use my own mind and abilities for my own aims. When I went to Washington I felt sure that I would be able to use opportunities which came to me to help Franklin gain the objectives he cared about—but the work would be his work and the pattern his pattern. He might have been happier with a wife who was completely uncritical. That I was never able to be, and he had to find it in other people. Nevertheless, I think I sometimes acted as a spur, even though the spurring was not always wanted or welcome. I was one of those who served his purposes."[2]

1946-1952. Began her association with the United Nations General Assembly. President Truman asked her to serve as a member of the organizing delegation and the nomination was supported in the Senate.

Eleanor Roosevelt travelled so extensively that she was at home an average of only two weeks out of every month. Around the world she was welcomed by heads of state. She remained active in party politics and spoke at Democratic conventions.

1960. Developed aplastic anemia. As her health steadily declined, blood transfusions and a number of hospital stays were necessary. She did her best to ignore her physical disabilities and kept as many engagements as she could.

October, 1962. A rare bone marrow tuberculosis, triggered by the treatment for the blood disease, was diagnosed.

November 7, 1962. Died. "To me all goodbyes are poignant now. I like less and less to be long separated from those few whom I deeply love." [Bernard Asbell, editor, *Mother and Daughter: The Letters of Eleanor and Anna Roosevelt,* Coward, 1982.[4]]

FOR MORE INFORMATION SEE—Juvenile books: Sally Elizabeth Knapp, *Eleanor Roosevelt: A Biography,* Crowell, 1949; Jeanette Eaton, *Story of Eleanor Roosevelt,* Morrow, 1956; Richard Harrity and Ralph G. Martin, *Eleanor Roosevelt: Her Life in Pictures,* Duell, Sloan, 1958; Alfred Steinberg, *Eleanor Roosevelt,* Putnam, 1959; Lorena A. Hickok, *Story of Eleanor Roosevelt,* Grosset, 1959; Ann Weil, *Eleanor Roosevelt: Courageous Girl,* Bobbs-Merrill, 1965; Charles P. Graves, *Eleanor Roosevelt, First Lady of the World,* Garrard, 1965; Miriam Gilbert, *Shy Girl: The Story of Eleanor Roosevelt, First Lady of the World,* Doubleday, 1965; Wyatt Blassingame, *Eleanor Roosevelt,* Putnam, 1967; Mickie Davidson, *Story of Eleanor Roosevelt,* Four Winds Press, 1967; Jane Goodsell, *Eleanor Roosevelt,* Crowell, 1970.

Eleanor, flanked by her husband, Franklin, and her mother-in-law, Sara Delano Roosevelt. ■
(From the movie "The Roosevelt Story." Produced by United Artists, 1947.)

Books; for adults: Eleanor Roosevelt, *If You Ask Me*, Appleton-Century, 1946; Eleanor Roosevelt, *This I Remember* (autobiography), Harper, 1949; Lorena A. Hickok, *Political Profile of Mrs. Eleanor Roosevelt*, Putnam, 1954; Eleanor Roosevelt, *It Seems to Me*, Norton, 1954; Alfred Steinberg, *Mrs. R.: The Life of Eleanor Roosevelt*, Putnam, 1958; Eleanor Roosevelt, *On My Own* (autobiography), Harper, 1958; Eleanor Roosevelt, *You Learn by Living*, Harper, 1960; Eleanor Roosevelt, *Autobiography*, Harper, 1961; Eleanor Roosevelt (with Helen Ferris), *Your Teens and Mine*, Doubleday, 1961; George Johnson, *Eleanor Roosevelt: The Compelling Life Story of One of the Most Famous Women of Our Time*, Monarch, 1962; Hickok, *Reluctant First Lady*, Dodd, 1962; Joseph P. Lash, *Eleanor Roosevelt: A Friend's Memoir*, Doubleday, 1964; James R. Kearney, *Anna Eleanor Roosevelt: The Evolution of a Reformer*, Houghton, 1968; J. Lash, *Eleanor and Franklin: The Story of Their Relationship*, Norton, 1971; J. Lash, *Eleanor: The Years Alone*, Norton, 1972; Elliott Roosevelt and James Brough, *An Untold Story: The Roosevelts of Hyde Park*, Putnam, 1973; A. David Gurewitsch, *Eleanor Roosevelt: Her Day*, Quadrangle, 1974; Elliott Roosevelt and Brough, *Rendezvous with Destiny: The Roosevelts in the White House*, Putnam, 1975; James Roosevelt (with B. Libby), *My Parents: A Differing View*, Playboy Press, 1976; Elliott Roosevelt and Brough, *Mother R.: Eleanor Roosevelt's Untold Story*, Putnam, 1977; Rhoda Lerman, *Eleanor: A Novel*, Holt, 1979; Joan Marlow, "Eleanor Roosevelt (1884-1962), Humanitarian and Diplomat," *The Great Women*, Galahad, 1979; Doris Faber, *The Life of Lorena Hickok: E. R.'s Friend*, Morrow, 1980; Bernard Asbell, editor, *The Letters of Eleanor and Anna Roosevelt*, Coward, 1982.

Periodicals: *Equity*, October, 1958; *Good Housekeeping*, May, 1960, June, 1967; *McCall's*, October, 1963, May, 1965; *Reader's Digest*, October, 1963; *New York Times Magazine*, November 3, 1963; *Newsweek*, November 23, 1964, June 7, 1976, November 5, 1979; *Life*, December 3, 1965; *U.S. News and World Report*, August 22, 1966; *Time*, June 7, 1976, December 17, 1979; *People*, November 12, 1979.

Albums: "A Recorded Portrait—Eleanor Roosevelt in Conversation with Arnold Michaelis," M-G-M Records, 1958.

Movies and filmstrips: "The Roosevelt Story" (motion picture), United Artists, 1947; "Eleanor Roosevelt" (motion picture in four parts), N.E.T. Film Service, 1956; "Eleanor Roosevelt" (motion picture), Encyclopaedia Britannica Films, 1960; "Sunrise at Campobello" (motion picture; starring Greer Garson and Ralph Bellamy), Warner Brothers, 1960; "The First Lady of the World" (motion picture), BCG Films, 1962; "Eleanor Roosevelt" (motion picture), Official Films, Inc., 1963; "Eleanor Roosevelt" (film documentary), Metromedia, 1966; "Eleanor Roosevelt: Humanitarian" (filmstrip), Popular Science Audio Visuals, 1970; "The Eleanor Roosevelt Story" (motion picture), American International Pictures, 1965; "Eleanor Roosevelt: First Lady of the World" (filmstrip), Society for Visual Education, 1974; "First Lady of the World: Eleanor Roosevelt" (motion picture), ACI Films, 1974; "Eleanor and Franklin" (motion picture; starring Jane Alexander and Edward Herrman), Talent Associates, 1975; "Eleanor and Franklin—The Early Years" (motion picture), Lucerne Films, 1976; "Eleanor and Franklin—The Rise to Leadership" (motion picture), Lucerne Films, 1976; (videocassette) "Eleanor Roosevelt—First Lady of the World," National Park Service, 1985.

Obituaries: *New York Times*, November 8-18, 1962; *Life*, November 16, 1962; *Time*, November 16, 1962; *New Yorker*, November 17, 1962; *Newsweek*, November 19, 1962; *Look*,

December 18, 1962; *U.S. Department of State Bulletin*, January 14, 1963; *Current Biography Yearbook*, 1964.

RYLANT, Cynthia 1954-

PERSONAL: Second syllable of surname is pronounced "lunt"; born June 6, 1954, in Hopewell, Va.; daughter of John T. (an army sergeant) and Leatrel (a registered nurse; maiden name, Rylant) Smith; children: Nathaniel. *Education:* Morris Harvey College (now University of Charleston), B.A., 1975; Marshall University, M.A., 1976; Kent State University, M.L.S., 1982. *Politics:* Democrat. *Religion:* Christian. *Residence:* Kent, Ohio. *Office:* c/o Bradbury Press, 866 Third Ave., New York, N.Y. 10022.

CAREER: Writer, 1978—. Part-time English instructor at Marshall University, Huntington, West Va., 1976-80, Ohio University at Ironton, 1979-80, University of Akron, Akron, Ohio, 1983-84; Akron Public Library, children's librarian, 1983. *Awards, honors: Booklist* Reviewer's Choice, and finalist, American Book Award from the Association of American Publishers, both 1982, Ambassador of Honor Book Award from Books-Across-the-Sea Library, and author of Caldecott Honor Book from the American Library Association, both 1983, all for *When I Was Young in the Mountains; School Library Journal* Best Book, Association for Library Service to Children Notable Book, and National Council for Social Studies Best Book, all 1984, and Society of Midland Authors Award, 1985, all for *Waiting to Waltz: A Childhood; School Library Journal*

CYNTHIA RYLANT

Afterward we stood in front of the old black stove, shivering and giggling, while Grandmother heated cocoa on top. ■ (From *When I Was Young in the Mountains* by Cynthia Rylant. Illustrated by Diane Goode.)

Best Book, 1985, for *Every Living Thing; A Blue-Eyed Daisy* and *The Relatives Came* were each selected one of Child Study Association of America's Children's Books of the Year, 1985; *The Relatives Came* was selected one of *New York Times* Best Illustrated Children's Books of the Year, 1985, and was a Caldecott Honor Book, 1986; Newbery Honor Book from the American Library Association, 1987, for *A Fine White Dust.*

WRITINGS—Juvenile; picture books, except as noted: *When I Was Young in the Mountains* (ALA Notable Book; *Horn Book* honor list; Reading Rainbow selection; illustrated by Diane Goode), Dutton, 1982; *Miss Maggie* (illustrated by Thomas DiGrazia), Dutton, 1983; *This Year's Garden* (illustrated by Mary Szilagyi), Bradbury, 1984; *Waiting to Waltz: A Childhood* (poetry; ALA Notable Book; illustrated by Stephen Gammell), Bradbury, 1984.

A Blue-Eyed Daisy (novel), Bradbury, 1985; *Every Living Thing* (short stories; illustrated by Stephen D. Schindler), Bradbury, 1985; *The Relatives Came* (*Horn Book* honor list; illustrated by S. Gammell), Bradbury, 1985; *Night in the Country* (Junior Literary Guild selection; illustrated by M. Szilagyi), Bradbury, 1986; *A Fine White Dust* (novel; *Horn Book* honor list), Bradbury, 1986; *Birthday Presents* (illustrated by Sucie Stevenson), Orchard, 1987; *Henry and Mudge: The First Book* (illustrated by S. Stevenson), Bradbury, 1987; *Henry and Mudge in Puddle Trouble: The Second Book of Their Adventures* (illustrated by S. Stevenson), Bradbury, 1987; *Children of Christmas* (short stories; illustrated by S. D. Schindler), Orchard, 1987; *Henry and Mudge in the Green Time,* Bradbury, 1987; *Henry and Mudge under the Yellow Moon,* Bradbury, 1987; *Henry and Mudge and the Sparkle Days,* Bradbury, 1988; *Mr. Griggs' Work* (picture book), Bradbury, 1988.

ADAPTATIONS: "When I Was Young in the Mountains" (filmstrip with cassette and teacher's guide; ALA Notable filmstrip), Random House, 1983; "This Year's Garden" (filmstrip with cassette), Random House, 1986; "The Relatives Came" (filmstrip with cassette), Random House, 1986.

WORK IN PROGRESS: A young adult novel.

SIDELIGHTS: "I grew up in West Virginia and what happened to me there deeply affects what I write: the years I lived with my grandparents in Cool Ridge (ages four to eight) and those with my mother in Beaver (ages eight to eighteen). My grandfather was a coal miner, had been in the mines since he was nine. Both of my grandparents were originally from Alabama (my pen-name is my grandfather's last name) and they always seemed to me more Southern than Appalachian. With my grandparents there was some poverty but mostly a very rich existence. They both possessed a quiet dignity (I still remember how carefully they dressed to go into town, how clean my grandmother kept me) and they did not complain about life. Like most Southerners, they kept their emotions tight to themselves, neither showing great anger or great sorrow or immense joy. You had to learn the intimations of things to know what was going on. They lived life with strength, great calm, a real sense of what it means to be devoted to and responsible for other people. The tone of my work reflects the way they spoke, the simplicity of their language, and, I hope, the depth of their own hearts.

"In Beaver I lived in a three-room apartment with my mother, who was a nurse. The boy next door and I became quick friends. We knocked on the walls with certain codes, we played Beatles records in our shared basement, and I had popcorn and Kool-aid with his family on Friday nights while we watched their black-and-white TV. Beaver was full of kids and I knew them all. I seemed to make no real judgments on them—accepting the hoodlums with the Christians and somehow feeling a strong intimacy with them all. Beaver was without a doubt a small, sparkling universe that gave me a lifetime's worth of material for my writing. I couldn't wait to get out of town when I grew up, but I owe it everything.

"My mother was a constant puzzle to me and to everyone else and provided me later on with great stories for my books. *Waiting to Waltz: A Childhood* is full of her spirit: the constant fascination with small-town people, the involvement with animals, and the feeling, always, that you really are not like everyone else.

"I was popular in school—"A" student, school queen. But I always felt on the fringe of things and worried that any time I might drop off, might go to school one day and not meld.

"I had many heroes. First was a pock-faced man named Tom who visited my grandparents. Then my Uncle Joe who went to Vietnam. Then Paul McCartney. Then Bobby Kennedy. And I wanted to be famous. I wanted to be in their worlds.

"I didn't know I was a writer. I always felt inferior to friends who wrote poetry and short stories. Always felt my life had been too limited. Nothing to write about.

"I read mostly comics growing up, trading with Danny Alderman over the backyard fence. Then I moved to paperback romances. There weren't a lot of good books at hand. And little money to buy them even if there had been a bookstore, which there wasn't. And no library. And dull English textbooks.

"I went to college and sort of ignited in freshman English. I loved everything I read. I'd read anything. And I was good at it, good at reading and understanding and good at writing about it. But certainly never imagined I could be a writer.

"Two things happened when I was about twenty-two. I read bonafide children's literature for the first time and it knocked me for a loop. And I read James Agee's *A Death in the Family* and *Let Us Now Praise Famous Men.* I fell in love with a genre, and I realized that in Agee's voice was something of my own. Mine was not nearly as clean and lyrical and lush—but enough.

"So one night I sat down and wrote *When I Was Young in the Mountains.* I sent it in the mail to a New York publisher ('Dear Sir . . .'). And it sold.

"It took me about seven books to feel like a writer. But I know now that's what I am. At least right now. I don't know about tomorrow.

"I like writing about child characters because they have more possibilities. They can get away with more love, more anger, more fear than adult characters. They can be more moving. I like them more. I sympathize with them more. Especially the pre-adolescent, still some child, but more adult edging in there. I think Ellie in *A Blue-Eyed Daisy* is wonderful. I enjoy her a lot, admire her. She doesn't know, though, that she is admirable. And in the novel *A Fine White Dust,* Pete, the narrator, is fourteen and I worry about him. I see a lot of beauty in him and I hope he doesn't change too much.

So he checked out and sat beside Beaver Creek and now would never leave it. ■ (From "Brain Surgeon" in *Waiting to Waltz: A Childhood*, poems by Cynthia Rylant. Illustrated by Stephen Gammell.)

''I like writing picture books, too, because that medium gives me a chance to capture in a brief space what I consider life's profound experiences. Grandmother crying at a swimming hole baptism; a family planting a garden together; the relatives coming for a visit. There is a poignancy and beauty in these, and I don't want to write adult poetry about them because then I'll have to layer it with some adult disillusionment. So I write a picture book that speaks to any person, any age, and the experience is not corny but pure, and I've gotten away with it.

''I come from people who worked very, very hard and whose lives were never simple nor easy. In my books I try to touch on how hard life can be sometimes, but always, *always* show that for everything that we lose, we will get something back.

The relatives weren't particular about beds, which was good

since there weren't any extras, so a few squeezed in with us

and the rest slept on the floor, some with their arms

thrown over the closest person, or some with an arm across one person

and a leg across another.

And I like to show the way our lives are beautiful, breathtaking, in the smallest things: shelling beans on a porch in the evening; sitting in a run-down shoe repair shop; wanting a pretty little lamp; giving saltines to squirrels.

"So young, in my twenties, I began looking at things the way you might expect an old person to see them. I don't know why. But I hope I always dig into what I see with my heart, and then find some good words.

"In only six years I've written seventeen books. I'm proud of them, and I like that I'm versatile—writing picturebooks, poetry, short stories, novels, easy readers. But I have to wonder when it will slow down. And when it does what I'll do then.

It was different, going to sleep with all that new breathing in the house.

(From *The Relatives Came* by Cynthia Rylant. Illustrated by Stephen Gammell.)

''I'd like to be known as one of the great writers of children's books.''

HOBBIES AND OTHER INTERESTS: ''I love to see films and to watch whales, sea otters, and dolphins. I'm a fan of Woody Allen, Vincent Van Gogh, James Agee, Don McLean, and Calvin and Hobbes.''

SACHAR, Louis   1954-

BRIEF ENTRY: Born March 20, 1954, in East Meadow, N.Y. Sachar received his bachelor's degree from the University of California, Berkeley, in 1976 and returned to the San Francisco campus for a law degree which he earned in 1980. A children's author since 1977, Sachar's first book, *Sideways Stories from Wayside School* (Follett, 1978), received the Ethical Culture Book Award in 1979 for best humorous book. This award was determined by children in grades four through six at the Ethical Culture School in New York City. He is also the author of *Johnny's in the Basement* (Avon, 1981), *Someday, Angeline* (Avon, 1983), and *There's a Boy in the Girl's Bathroom* (Knopf, 1987). *Home:* 151 Henry St., San Francisco, Calif. 94114.

FOR MORE INFORMATION SEE: Contemporary Authors, New Revision Series, Volume 15, Gale, 1985.

SCHINDLER, S(tephen) D.

BRIEF ENTRY: Schindler graduated with a degree in biology from the University of Pennsylvania, and has utilized his interest in botany for many of his illustrations. *The First Tulips in Holland* (Doubleday, 1982), written by Phyllis Krasilovsky, received the 1982 Parents' Choice Award for illustration. The *New York Times Book Review* hailed the book as ''. . . a spectacular-looking production—oversized, with brilliantly colored illustrations that echo Dutch paintings and spill out to the edges of nearly every page.'' Schindler also illustrated *Every Living Thing* (Bradbury, 1985), written by Cynthia Rylant, which was listed in *School Library Journal*'s ''best books of 1985.'' His other illustrated books include *Favorite Nursery Tales* (Doubleday, 1983), retold by Morrell Gipson, and *The Golden Goose and Other Tales of Good Fortune* (Golden Books, 1986), edited by Eric Suben. In a review of Leon Garfield's *Fair's Fair* (Doubleday, 1983), *School Library Journal* wrote: ''Schindler's beautifully detailed illustrations are full of unusual perspectives of a wonderful snow-covered London and cozy interiors.'' The illustrator's work has also appeared in magazines and textbooks.

SEITZ, Jacqueline   1931-

PERSONAL: Born November 10, 1931, in Manhattan, N.Y.; daughter of John (a lawyer) and Aileen (a teacher; maiden name, Scanlon) Brandon; married Richard Seitz (a heating contractor), August 6, 1955; children: Eric, Keira. *Education:* St. Vincent's Hospital School of Nursing, New York, N.Y., R.N., 1952. *Religion:* Roman Catholic. *Home:* Oyster Bay, N.Y. 11765. *Office:* Living Flame Press, Locust Valley, N.Y. 11560.

CAREER: St. Vincent's Hospital, New York, N.Y., registered nurse, beginning 1955; Living Flame Press, Locust Valley, N.Y., assistant editor, 1982—.

ILLUSTRATOR: The Mysterious World of Honeybees, Messner, 1979; Kelly B. Kelly, *Grains of Wheat,* Living Flame Press, 1982; Kathy Thomas, *The Angel's Quest,* Living Flame Press, 1983; K. B. Kelly, *Bread for the Eating,* Living Flame Press, 1984. Illustrator of various cookbooks for charitable organizations.

WORK IN PROGRESS: ''Designing and producing my own line of greeting cards in acrylic/watercolor. Subjects run the gamut from traditional to inspirational to gently humorous cartoons.''

SIDELIGHTS: ''I always loved to draw—I began as a child and had routine school instruction, but opted to enter nursing school and actively nursed until my children arrived.

''I have painted murals on almost every wall of my home because of my need to express myself with line and color. Making greeting cards and fun collages for family members has kept me busy until the opportunity to work as an assistant editor at Living Flame Press came along.

''I have illustrated four prayer-related books in pen and ink. *The Angel's Quest* was my first children's book. I used pen and pencil. I attempted to illustrate the story completely so

JACQUELINE SEITZ

that a child could follow the pictures and enjoy the full message of the story without having to read the text.

"When illustrating for children, I allow the characters to develop with loose pencil sketches. They begin to show themselves and talk to me, and finally let me know they like themselves before I tighten them up with the pen. I've found that some characters just won't perform properly unless they like their own features, clothes, etc. It becomes a real 'getting to know you' experience for me.

"I hope to paint and draw for eons, believing that any talent that is exercised will grow and improve."

SHULEVITZ, Uri 1935-

PERSONAL: Given name pronounced *oo*-ree; born February 27, 1935, in Warsaw, Poland; came to United States in 1959; naturalized during the 1960s; son of Abraham and Szandla (Hermanstat) Shulevitz; married Helene Weiss (an artist), June 11, 1961 (divorced). *Education:* Teacher's College, Israel, teacher's degree, 1956; attended Tel-Aviv Art Institute, 1953-55, and Brooklyn Museum Art School, 1959-61. *Religion:* Jewish. *Address:* c/o Farrar, Straus & Giroux, Inc., 19 Union Sq. W., New York, N.Y. 10003.

CAREER: Kibbutz Ein Geddi (collective farm), Israel, member, 1957-58; art director of youth magazine in Israel, 1958-59; illustrator of children's books, 1961—; author of children's books, 1962—; School of Visual Arts, New York City, instructor in art, 1967-68; Pratt Institute, Brooklyn, N.Y., instructor in art, 1970-71; New School for Social Research, New York City, instructor in art and in writing and illustrating of children's books, 1970—; Hartwick College, Oneonta, N.Y., director of summer workshop in writing and illustrating children's books, 1974—. Work has been exhibited in numerous

URI SHULEVITZ

galleries and museums, including Tel Aviv Museum, A. M. Sachs Gallery, New York, N.Y., Metropolitan Museum of Art, New York, N.Y., New York Public Library. *Military service:* Israeli Army, 1956-59. *Member:* Authors Guild, Authors League of America (member of children's books committee).

AWARDS, HONORS: American Institute of Graphic Arts, Children's Book Awards, 1963-64, for *Charley Sang a Song,* 1965-66, for *The Second Witch,* 1967-68, for *One Monday Morning,* and Certificate of Excellence, 1973-74, for *The Magician* and *The Fools of Chelm and Their History,* and 1979, for *The Treasure; One Monday Morning* was chosen one of the American Institute of Graphic Arts Children's Books, 1967-68; *The Fools of Chelm and Their History* and *The Magician* were included in the American Institute of Graphic Arts Children's Books Show, 1973-74, and *The Treasure,* 1980; Certificate of Merit, Society of Illustrators (New York), 1965, for *Charley Sang a Song;* books displayed at Children's Book Exhibition, New York Public Library, 1967, 1968, 1969, 1972, 1973, and 1974, and at International Biennale of Illustrations, Bratislava, Czechoslovakia, 1969; Caldecott Medal from the American Library Association, 1969, for *The Fool of the World and the Flying Ship* and selected for inclusion in American Booksellers 1969 Gift to the Nation from the Library of the White House; *Rain Rain Rivers* was chosen one of Child Study Association of America's Children's Books of the Year, 1969, *Soldier and Tsar in the Forest: A Russian Tale,* 1972, *Dawn,* 1974, and *The Touchstone,* 1976.

Bronze Medal, Leipzig International Book Exhibition, 1970, for *Rain Rain Rivers; Book World's* Children's Spring Book Festival Picture Book honor, 1972, for *Soldier and Tsar in the Forest: A Russian Tale; The Magician* received *Book World's* Children's Spring Book Festival Award for Younger Children, and was selected one of *New York Times* Outstanding Books of the Year, both 1973, and was included in the Children's Book Showcase of the Children's Book Council, 1974; *Dawn* was selected one of *New York Times* Outstanding Books of the Year, 1974, received the Christopher Award, 1975, was included in the Children's Book Showcase of the Children's Book Council, 1975, included on the International Board of Books for Young People honor list, 1976, and received the Brooklyn Art Books for Children Citation, 1976, 1977, and 1978; *Hanukah Money* was selected one of *New York Times* Best Illustrated Books of the Year, 1978, and *The Treasure,* 1979; certificate from Graphic Arts Awards of the Printing Industries of America, 1979, for *The Treasure.*

Caldecott Honor Book, 1980, for *The Treasure; The Golem* was selected one of *New York Times* Outstanding Books of the Year, and one of *School Library Journal's* Best Children's Books, both 1982, and received the Parents' Choice Award for Literature from the Parents' Choice Foundation, 1983.

WRITINGS—All self-illustrated: *The Moon in My Room,* Harper, 1963; *One Monday Morning* (ALA Notable Book; *Horn Book* honor list), Scribner, 1967; *Rain Rain Rivers* (ALA Notable Book; *Horn Book* honor list), Farrar, Straus, 1969; (adapter) *The Magician,* Macmillan, 1973; *Dawn* (ALA Notable Book), Farrar, Straus, 1974; *The Treasure* (*Horn Book* honor list), Farrar, Straus, 1979; *Writing with Pictures: How to Write and Illustrate Children's Books,* Watson-Guptill, 1985; *The Strange and Exciting Adventures of Jeremiah Hush,* Farrar, Straus, 1986.

Illustrator: Charlotte Zolotow, *A Rose, a Bridge, and a Wild Black Horse,* Harper, 1964; Mary Stolz, *The Mystery of the Woods,* Harper, 1964; H. R. Hays and Daniel Hays, *Charley*

(Shulevitz's progression in clarifying an image. From *Writing with Pictures: How to Write and Illustrate Children's Books* by Uri Shulevitz.)

The city was deserted, as in a time of epidemic, when people shun the outdoors so as not to breathe the pestilent air. ■ (From *The Golem* by Isaac Bashevis Singer. Illustrated by Uri Shulevitz.)

Sang a Song, Harper, 1964; Sulamith Ish-Kishor, *The Carpet of Solomon,* Pantheon, 1964; Jack Sendak, *The Second Witch,* Harper, 1965; Molly Cone, *Who Knows Ten? Children's Tales of the Ten Commandments,* Union of American Hebrew Congregations, 1965; Jacob Grimm and Wilhelm Grimm, *The Twelve Dancing Princesses,* translated by Elizabeth Shub, Scribner, 1966; M. Stolz, *Maximilian's World,* Harper, 1966; Jean Russell Larson, *The Silkspinners,* Scribner, 1967; Dorothy Nathan, *The Month Brothers,* Dutton, 1967; John Smith, editor, *My Kind of Verse,* Macmillan, 1968; Jan Wahl, *Runaway Jonah and Other Tales,* Macmillan, 1968; Arthur Ransome, adapter, *The Fool of the World and the Flying Ship: A Russian Tale* (ALA Notable Book), Farrar, Straus, 1968.

J. Wahl, *The Wonderful Kite,* Delacorte, 1971; Yehoash Biber, *Treasure of the Turkish Pasha,* translated from Hebrew by Naruch Hochman, Blue Star Book Club, 1971; E. Shub, adapter, *Oh What a Noise!* (text adapted from "A Big Noise" by William Brighty Rands), Macmillan, 1971; Alexander Afanasyev, *Soldier and Tsar in the Forest: A Russian Tale,* translated by Richard Lourie, Farrar, Straus, 1972; Isaac Bashevis Singer, *The Fools of Chelm and Their History,* Farrar, Straus, 1973; Robert Louis Stevenson, *The Touchstone,* Greenwillow, 1976; Sholem Aleichem, *Hanukah Money,* Greenwillow, 1978; Richard Kennedy, *The Lost Kingdom of Karnica,* Sierra Club Books, 1979; I. B. Singer, *The Golem* (ALA Notable Book), Farrar, Straus, 1982. Contributor to *Horn Book.*

ADAPTATIONS: "One Monday Morning" (film), Weston Woods, 1972, (filmstrip), 1973; "The Fool of the World and the Flying Ship" (cassette), Weston Woods, 1980; "The Treasure," Weston Woods, 1980; "Dawn" (filmstrip with cassette), Weston Woods, 1982.

WORK IN PROGRESS: Illustrations for an adult book, *Lilith's Cave: Jewish Tales of the Supernatural,* compiled and retold by Howard Schwartz, to be published by Harper.

SIDELIGHTS: **February 27, 1935.** Born in Warsaw, Poland. "Drawing has always been with me. The encouragement of my parents, who were both talented, probably contributed to my early interest in drawing. I was born in Poland and began drawing at the age of three. The Warsaw blitz occurred when I was four. I vividly remember the streets caving in, the buildings burning, and a bomb falling into the stairwell of our apartment building one day when I was at home. I recall people carrying water from the Vistula to drink and to wash in, and the complete paralysis of most public services, including electricity."

"In **1939** we fled Warsaw, and for the next eight years we were wanderers, arriving, eventually, in Paris in 1947. Here

(From *The Magician,* adapted by Uri Shulevitz. Illustrated by the author.)

I went to a grammar school and spent many hours browsing the book stalls on the Quai de la Seine. I developed an enthusiasm for French comic books and soon I and a friend began making our own, I drew the pictures. . . .''

1947. Won first prize in a grammar school drawing contest in Paris, France. ''As a child, when I drew a picture I was aware only of its visible aspect, the objects in it. When I drew a tree, I saw the tree, but not the empty space around it and between its branches. Nor did I see exactly where in the picture the tree stood. I also packed an assortment of objects into the picture. I wasn't quite sure how to arrange them to avoid confusion and to help the picture as a whole. Gradually I learned that the invisible space, the 'nothingness' around the tree, was as important as the tree itself. And I learned that there was a hidden understructure that organized everything in the picture.

''These two hidden aspects of a picture are the *picture space* and *composition*. Picture space is the depth of space represented within the picture frame, including both objects and the space around them. Composition is the way all the elements in the picture are organized into a unified whole.

''Every element, visible or hidden, works for or against the picture. No aspect can be ignored.'' [Uri Shulevitz, *Writing with Pictures: How to Write and Illustrate Children's Books,* Watson-Guptill, 1985.[1]]

One night, he had a dream. ■ (From *The Treasure* by Uri Shulevitz. Illustrated by the author.)

For two days and two nights they traveled.... ■ (From *The Silkspinners* by Jean Russell Larson. Illustrated by Uri Shulevitz.)

1949. Settled in Israel, where he was distinguished as the youngest member to participate in a drawing exhibition at the Museum of Tel Aviv.

1953. Attended the Teachers Institute and studied at the Art Institute in Tel Aviv.

1957-1958. Joined the Ein Geddi kibbutz in Israel. ''During the Sinai War (1956), I went into basic training with the Israeli army, then joined the Ein Geddi kibbutz (collective settlement) by the Dead Sea, which was founded by a group of my friends. After a long trip by the dry, stark and hot shores of the Dead Sea, Ein Geddi unfolds like a Chinese scroll with its waterfall and rich vegetation. I lived at Ein Geddi for more than a year. There I designed a Passover Haggadah containing the narrative of the Exodus read at Seder. This was my first attempt at graphics. I was able to combine art with military service by working as art director of a magazine for teenagers. After my army service was over, I began to free-lance. . . .''

1959. ''. . . At the age of twenty-four, I came to New York City. For the next two years I studied painting at the Brooklyn

Museum Art School. I did my first illustrations for a New York publisher of Hebrew books for children. I was strictly supervised and permitted only to work from sketches given to me; still, this experience improved my pen and brush techniques. It was in 1962, while working in this regimented atmosphere, that I discovered a style which I made my own. . . .

''I developed this new, free style, and in 1963 my first book appeared. Writing, I came to realize, has less to do with language than one thinks. First, one has to have something to say. This may come in pictures or in sounds, depending on one's inclination, and not necessarily in words. . . .''

1963. Wrote and illustrated first book under the direction of two editors, Susan Carr Hirschman and Ursula Nordstrom. ''I have imagined myself in various activities, but never in my wildest dreams have I imagined myself as a writer.

''It was my luck, when I began toting my portfolio around to publishers in 1962, that Susan Carr Hirschman (then at Harper & Row) was the first editor I saw. I had come with the hope that they might have a book for me to illustrate. After looking

at my portfolio, she suggested I try writing my *own* picture book. I was horrified. My end had come, I thought, before I really had had a chance to start.

"Write my own story? Impossible. My training and orientation were in art. Writing seemed a faraway country suited to those who had mysterious ways with words. To me, using words was like taming wild tigers.

"'But that's impossible,' I said, 'I don't know how to write.'

"'Why don't you try?' she asked. It was hard to argue with that.

"'But,' I ventured—and here, I thought, was an insurmountable obstacle—'my English isn't even good.' (At the time I had been speaking English for less than four years.)

"'Don't worry,' she reassured me, 'we'll fix your English.'

"Now, there was nothing left to do but try. And try I did, many times. I went back and forth to Susan Hirschman's of-

fice, bringing my awkward writing efforts. Her criticisms and suggestions served as my apprenticeship. After many unsuccessful attempts, I finally came up with a picture book. With minor changes it became *The Moon in My Room,* my first book. If not for those many unsuccessful attempts beforehand, I don't think I could have written it. They formed the ladder that enabled me to jump over the wall.

"I eventually understood that my initial reaction, my fear that I could not write, was based on a preconception. A preconception that writing was strictly related to words and to spoken language. That it was essential to use many words in a skillful way. I was overlooking what was of primary importance—*what* I had to say; and I was caught in a secondary consideraton—*how* to say it. That secondary concern has nothing to do with writing, but I was allowing it to take over the primary one.

"I began by concentrating on what happens in the story; first I visualized the action, and then I thought of how to say it in words. I realized that all I had to do was communicate the action as simply as possible. It also dawned on me that I could

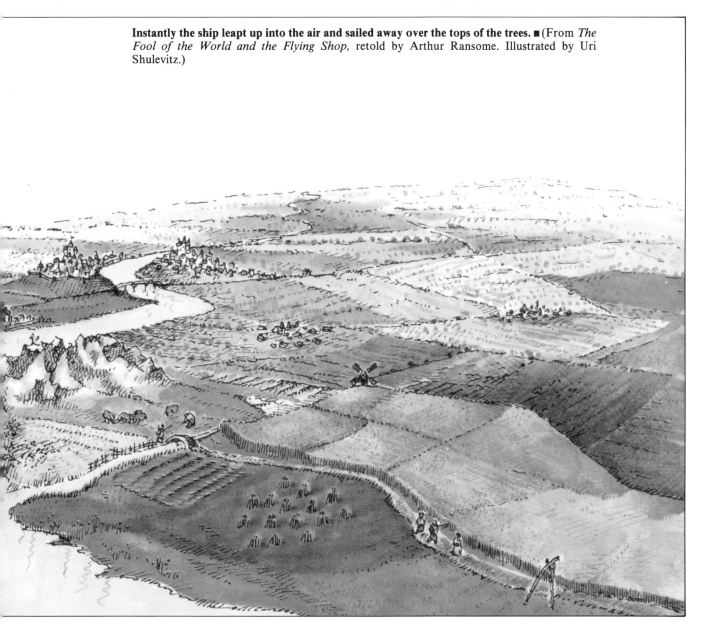

Instantly the ship leapt up into the air and sailed away over the tops of the trees. ■ (From *The Fool of the World and the Flying Shop,* retold by Arthur Ransome. Illustrated by Uri Shulevitz.)

In his victory ode, Zeckel Poet foretold that the army of Chelm would one day conquer India, Izbitza, Ethiopia, Frampol, and Madagascar. ■ (From *The Fools of Chelm and Their History* by Isaac Bashevis Singer. Illustrated by Uri Shulevitz.)

utilize my natural inclination and channel it into my writing. Assuming that each of us has a preference for one of the sense perceptions, we can capitalize on that preference in our writing. If one likes to talk and feels at ease with spoken words, one can take a conversational approach to writing. But if, like myself, one is inclined to see pictures, a visual approach makes more sense. That is how I wrote *The Moon in My Room;* the story unfolded in my head like a movie. I was the camera seeing the action conveyed by pictures. The few words necessary to communicate the story fell into place on their own. It was all so simple and natural.

"Furthermore, the use of this visual approach, with which I have always felt at ease, released a flow of images I hadn't experienced before. There was no doubt, *writing with pictures* was my way. . . .

"'Writing with pictures' proved very valuable in my work as well as in teaching others how to write. The visual thinking essential to picture-book making can be extended to writing for people in the visual arts and can increase the ability to visualize in writers without an art background. Visual thinking can also avoid excessive wordiness in writing in general. In this way my visual approach evolved—an approach, based on my writing and teaching experience, that I would like to introduce here.

"My illustrations for *The Moon in My Room* also came about in an unexpected way. One day while talking on the telephone, I noticed my doodles had a fresh and spontaneous look. The lines appeared to be taking a leisurely walk on the page—the starting point of the approach to my first book illustrations. Looking back, I have often wondered how it happened when I least expected it, for in addition to my preconception about writing, I also had a preconceived idea of how a concept of an illustration evolves. I had assumed it would be a laborious act of will requiring much effort, but the way it actually happened was quite different. While my mind was busy with the phone conversation, I forgot my preconceptions; I didn't interfere with the lines flowing effortlessly through my hand onto the paper. The lines seemed to have a life and an intelligence of their own, leading my hand by their own needs, while my hand followed without imposing my desires on those lines. True, it subsequently took considerable work and effort to develop the doodles, but that was at the secondary phase and not in the initial step." [Uri Shulevitz, "Writing with Pictures," *Horn Book*, February, 1982.[2]] The doodle eventually became the title page of *The Moon in My Room*.

1969. Won the Caldecott Medal for his illustrations in *The Fool of the World and the Flying Ship*, a Russian tale retold by Arthur Ransome. The dummy took Shulevitz six months to prepare. It was his first book done in full-color drawings. "The main function of illustration is to illuminate text, to throw light on words. In fact, illustration in medieval books is called *illumination* and the term *illustration* derives from the Latin verb meaning 'to light up,' 'to illuminate.'

"Pictures help to clarify words because they make the subject matter concrete, closer to the way we perceive the world. This clarification comes from accurately representing the literal meaning and then going beyond that by representing the mood and the feeling of the words. The picture may also provide details the reader has missed or not fully understood and in this way throw new light on the words. The range of illustration thus extends from its modest role as mere explanation of text to its highest possible achievement, when it enlightens spiritually and mentally.

"So sorry, sport," spoke the sloth slowly, interrupting his speech with several yawns. ■ (From *The Strange and Exciting Adventures of Jeremiah Hush* by Uri Shulevitz. Illustrated by the author.)

"Illustration also decorates the text. Medieval artists sometimes used gold in their pictures, literally *lighting up* the page. But neither gold nor a decorative design is necessary for a picture to adorn a text; it adorns by virtue of being visual. The mere introduction of pictures enhances the beauty of a book and provides the reader a rest from reading the words. In fact, the artist need not be concerned with decorating the text at all—it is a natural result of the process of illustration. The artist need only read the text thoroughly and concentrate on pictorially clarifying the text and on the picture's readability.

"Outstanding illustrations are effective on at least two levels. First, they tell us the story, portraying the subject matter accurately; and second, the abstract pattern of the picture is alive in its own right, with an underlying geometric structure that gives character and strength to the forms. Imagine a story in which a small boy stands before a giant oak tree. On the first level, a good illustration accurately portrays the oak tree and the boy. But an outstanding illustration also embodies the content in its design. The oak tree is not only accurately represented but also has life and substance as a form.

"Pictures that function only on the first level are acceptable illustrations, whereas those that function only on the second level are good designs but poor illustrations. It takes success on both levels to make an excellent illustration. Although, in books, it is more important that a picture be an adequate illustration than a good design, it is more rewarding when pictures satisfy on both levels."[1]

One chetvertak and one chetvertak makes two chetvertaks, and another chetvertak makes three chetvertaks.... ■ (From *Hanukah Money* by Sholem Aleichem. Illustrated by Uri Shulevitz.)

Live here? Oh, I don't know. I don't know if the room is large enough. And my mother might not.... ■ (From *The Second Witch* by Jack Sendak. Illustrated by Uri Shulevitz.)

The Fool of the World and the Flying Ship, according to Shulevitz, was basically a traditional folk tale with an implied philosophy. "Unfortunately, more often than one thinks, children are in a predicament at home similar to that of the Fool of the World. They feel hopelessly trapped, discouraged, misunderstood. Worst of all, most of the time they do not know the real reason for their misery. They are too weak to break through their prison walls. They are very vulnerable and can be easily crushed. Sometimes they play the Fool to survive. But most of them never get to marry the Czar's daughter. Instinctively knowing the danger, they eagerly seek sustenance to support their drive for life. They look for a refuge of security where they can grow and become stronger until they can stand on their own.

"A picture book is not a silly little plaything. It is much more. Sometimes it can be everything to a child. A picture book can be a messenger of hope from the outside world. Its message, written in coded language, reaches the child in his prison, is understood by him while often hidden from the adult or the parent who is unwilling to listen to its true content or is simply insensitive to it.

"It seems to me that in order to tune in on the wavelength that will penetrate prison walls and reach the child, all one has to do is tune in to a life-affirming attitude. Children are very sensitive to this, because their lives depend upon it. A destructive, life-negating attitude will not do. Neither will a saccharine approach. A picture book does not have to be deep, but it does have to be alive—whether it offers pleasure, joy, or sadness. I believe this point of view is essential to anyone interested in the field." [Lee Kingman, editor, *The Illustrator's Notebook*, Horn Book, 1978.[3]]

1970. Taught art at the Pratt Institute and the New School for Social Research in New York City. "In teaching, I observe how often students will excuse a poor illustration on an inability to draw or on a lack of artistic talent, while the real problem lies in unclear thinking. To blame it on a drawing deficiency is merely a rationalization. This misconception discourages many students without much art experience, who imagine they have to produce works of art—when all they need do is record, in the best way they can, what they are seeing. The same mistake can be made by the student with an extensive art background, who spends all his energy on putting on a good show while neglecting the more vital aspects of the illustration—coherence, readability, and its relation to the text. One of my students, who had done no drawing since childhood, only began to draw in her thirties. Now, five years later, she has completed the illustrations for her second book for a major New York publisher.

"I had thought that learning was a function of acquiring and accumulating knowledge, but I found that it could be a perfect way to cover up one's ignorance as well. Unlearning, giving up preconceptions, dropping pretense and false knowledge—'to empty the cup,' to use a Zen expression—can be by far the more practical way. Only in the secondary stage of developing and organizing material was previous knowledge or art experience helpful."[2]

Rain Rain Rivers, was awarded a Bronze Medal at the International Book Exhibition in Leipzig. "I first had the idea for my own picture book *Rain Rain Rivers* about five years before actually starting on the illustrations; it came and imposed itself on me in an unmistakable way. One evening I heard the patter of rain and simultaneously saw a series of images—impressions of which I immediately wrote down. This was the beginning. I thought that it was raining outside, since I could

actually hear it. But when I looked out of the window, there was a clear night sky over the Greenwich Village rooftops. All this happened in a flash, and it was the seed of the future book. Subsequent work on the book—the unfolding, developing, extending, and organizing of the material—took considerably more time and effort. But everything was potentially there in the initial vision. The life substance of what was to come was there, provided I kept it alive by thought and care. As I worked on the pictures and the book gradually took shape, I began to distinguish in it the existence of different levels. In addition to the rhythm of rain, I felt in it the rhythmic beat of breathing. And so accordingly, I made the pictures large and small, small and large, as if breathing in and out; the energy accumulating, building to the final climax, and giving birth to splashes of joy. Colors in a rainbow, birds in the streets, children stamping in mud, the sky reflected in street puddles—a union of sky and earth through rain. When I reached the climactic doublespread of the ocean, I felt like the ancient Greek philosopher who said: 'Everything is water,' meaning that everything in the universe consists of that substance in different states of consistency. In the ocean picture everything was brought back to its primordial state. As work was progressing, I felt that the little girl was making contact through the growth of the plant on the window sill of her room with the whole process of growth in the universe, and that in each drop of rain was contained a potential ocean, and in the child a potential of unlimited growth, energy, and freedom. All this had a definite purpose: to express what is real, to give hope, and to reinforce what is positive.

"Unless we perceive and accept the fact that everything is related in a greater or lesser degree, nothing makes much sense and we are impoverishing our own resources. When I start on a new book, I try to see the images contained in the words of the story and to 'listen' to the different pictorial elements and their impact, their orchestration, and whether they are expressing what I want them to. Although my natural way of thinking is through images, at some point there is a fusion of the different modes of expression. One 'listens' with one's eyes, and 'sees' through one's ears and fingers. For me, it is the small chaos preceding creation.

"Ideas and thoughts make up our inner landscape and extend to what surrounds us. Life-affirming thoughts emanate energy that can stimulate the child to grow, expand, and even perform wonders. A picture book, like any other art form, has a life energy of its own. Take that away, and all you have left is an empty shell. Therefore, why not treat a picture book with care in order to make it grow—like a plant or an animal? One has to heed and nurture the something-that-is-there. Force it and it will die. For the process of artistic creation is an extension of the life process itself, and life itself is the supreme master."[3]

1975. Awarded the Christopher Award for his book, *Dawn*, which was also selected to represent the United States on the International Honors List at the 1976 Congress of International Board of Books for Young People. "In *Dawn* the gradual transition to daylight comes to an expected, but still dramatic, conclusion as the heroes finally see their surroundings fully revealed in all their color by the rising sun.

"The beginning gives birth to the end, and the end remembers the beginning; none of the elements introduced at the beginning are forgotten, no loose threads are left hanging. . . . The implied promise made to the reader in the beginning has been kept.

"In my book *Dawn* . . . I used picture book and story book concepts in different parts of the same book. Early in the book

(From *One Monday Morning* by Uri Shulevitz. Illustrated by the author.)

there is a picture of a mountain by a lake before dawn. The text reads simply: 'Still.' Without the picture, you would not know what 'still' referred to. This is characteristic of the picture book concept.

"Later, however, I describe how 'Under a tree by a lake an old man and his grandson curl up in their blankets.' The picture here shows them curled up in their blankets. This approach is characteristic of the story book concept. Although the words help guide the reader to where to focus in the picture, the words could be understood without the picture."[1]

Shulevitz continually changes his methods of illustrating, which include pen and ink, watercolor, Japanese reed pen, and Chinese brush. "Creating a picture book presents the same problems as composing a painting: how to arrange the parts into a whole. The storyboard and book dummy complement each other and allow you to transform all the pages into a unified book. Different authors, however, use these tools in different ways.

"My own working procedure has changed since I first began illustrating books. For my first book I made several actual-size, finished dummies; for subsequent books I made small, rough dummies and storyboards only. Generally, I like to make as many storyboards and small, rough dummies as necessary and go back and forth from one to another as I plan the book. I prefer to start by making a storyboard, however, and I recommend that beginners start this way too.

"Sometimes, after having made a storyboard and a rough thumbnail dummy for my own use, I paste down the final

sketches (or photocopies of them) with masking tape onto an actual-size dummy to show to the editor or the designer. In any case, I find that a readable dummy is the most helpful tool for communicating how you see the book. For picture books, which rely so much on the visual aspect, some editors require it before giving you a contract. They also want to see how you are progressing. On many occasions, I show my dummies to the editor to convey how I envision the book. The editor can then give me criticism, which in turn enables me to go back and work on my book idea further."[1]

Shulevitz encourages the would-be illustrator to discard the idea of a "perfect flawless picture" and to concentrate on making the picture come alive instead. "All too often there is a loss of emotion and freshness during the progression from first rough sketch to final illustration. The finished picture may be more resolved, polished, and readable, but the spontaneity of the first sketch has almost disappeared. Readability is essential to good illustration, and some compromises to achieve it are justified. If, however, the price of readability is lifelessness, the result can be viewed as a failure.

"The problem has been of great concern to me. My first sketch is often more alive than later versions. . . . The lines no longer have the same energy.

"I've noticed that in the beginning I concentrate on capturing the subject matter of the story, which I do in one or more preliminary sketches. But during subsequent stages, when I'm busy getting rid of excess lines, clarifying, sharpening, making it more elegant and readable, the picture loses vitality. That

(From the animated filmstrip "The Treasure." Produced by Weston Woods, 1980.)

is also when thoughts that were of no concern to me in the initial stage arise. I wonder: How will the picture look? Will it be liked? That is when I gradually begin to lose sight of the primary goal—*what* I'm illustrating, the picture and its requirements, how it will best relate to the words—and shift my attention to an imaginary audience, and *how* the picture will look and be accepted. The emphasis shifts from the purpose of the picture to its outward appearance or surface look.

"In some ways the progression from rough to finished work resembles the game 'telephone relay,' in which a child whispers a sentence to another child, who then whispers it to someone else, and so on down the line. By the time the words reach the last child, they bear little or no resemblance to the original sentence."[1]

Shulevitz offers the following advice to his students. "When asked why they want to write children's books, many people reply, 'I love children.' Sentimentality, unfortunately, is no help; in fact it is a hindrance. Sentimentality does not replace the craft that is essential in making good children's books. Your first obligation is to the book, not to the audience. Only by understanding the book's stucture—including its mechanical structure—and how it functions can you make a good book.

"When working on your first book, you may ask: Am I happy with the book? Am I happy with the illustrations? These seemingly innocent questions actually shift the importance from the book and the illustrations to yourself. A happy book will inevitably make a happy author. Therefore ask: Is the book happy? Are the illustrations happy?"[1]

HOBBIES AND OTHER INTERESTS: Art, music, movies, old tales and parables of eastern traditions, yoga and tai-chi-chuan, ballroom dancing.

FOR MORE INFORMATION SEE: The Villager, October 3, 1963; *New York Herald Tribune,* October 6, 1963; *Chicago Tribune,* November 10, 1963; *Christian Science Monitor,* November 19, 1963, November 6, 1969; *Buffalo Evening News,* January 18, 1964; *Book Week* (children's section), May 7, 1967; *Graphis* (Zurich), number 131, 1967; Lee Kingman and others, compilers, *Illustrators of Children's Books: 1957-1966,* Horn Book, 1968; *Publishers Weekly,* February 17, 1969, July 26, 1985; *School Library Journal,* May, 1969; *Horn Book,* August, 1969, December, 1969, June, 1971, February, 1982; *Commonweal,* November 21, 1969; *New York Times,* December 8, 1969; *New York Times Book Review,* September 21, 1969, September 19, 1970, September 8, 1971, April 15, 1973, November 3, 1974, April 29, 1979; Lee Bennett Hopkins, *Books Are by People: Interviews with 104 Authors and Illustrators of Books for Young Children,* Citation Press, 1969.

Martha E. Ward and Dorothy A. Marquardt, *Illustrators of Books for Young People,* Scarecrow, 1970; Selma G. Lanes, *Down the Rabbit Hole,* Atheneum, 1971; *Washington Post Book World,* November 7, 1971; M. E. Ward and D. A. Marquardt, *Authors of Books for Young People,* 2nd edition, Scarecrow, 1971; *Graphis 155,* Volume 27, 1971/72; Doris de Montreville and Donna Hill, editors, *Third Book of Junior Authors,* H. W. Wilson, 1972; Donnarae MacCann and Olga Richard, *The Child's First Books,* H. W. Wilson, 1973; L. Kingman, editor, *Newbery and Caldecott Medal Books: 1966-1975,* Horn Book, 1975; *Children's Literature Association Newsletter,* spring, 1976; L. Kingman and others, compilers, *Illustrators of Children's Books: 1967-1976,* Horn Book, 1978; L. Kingman, editor, *The Illustrator's Notebook,* Horn Book, 1978; *Books of the Times,* December, 1979; *Wilson Library Bulletin,* October, 1980; *North Light,* October, 1985.

SMALL, David   1945-

PERSONAL: Born February 12, 1945, in Detroit, Mich.; son of Edward Pierce (a doctor) and Elizabeth (Murphy) small; married Sherry St. John Stewart (a writer), September, 1980; children: five (from previous marriages). *Politics:* None. *Religion:* None. *Education:* Wayne State University, B.F.A., 1968; Yale University, M.F.A., 1972. *Home:* 25626 Simpson Rd., Mendon, Mich. 49072.

CAREER: Free-lance artist; author and illustrator of children's books. State University of New York—Fredonia College, assistant professor of art, 1972-78; Kalamazoo College, Kalamazoo, Mich., assistant professor of art, 1978-83, artist-in-residence, 1983-86. *Awards, honors: Eulalie and the Hopping Head* was selected one of Library of Congress' Children's Books of the Year, one of *School Library Journal's* Best Books for Spring, and a Parents' Choice Remarkable Book from the Parents' Choice Foundation, all 1982; *Mean Chickens and Wild Cucumbers* was selected a Notable Book for Children in the Field of Social Studies by the National Council of Social Studies, 1983; *Anna and the Seven Swans* was chosen one of *School Library Journal's* and one of *Booklist's* Best Books, both 1984; *The Christmas Box* was chosen one of Child Study Association of America's Children's Books of the Year, 1985; Parents' Choice Award for literature from the Parents' Choice Foundation, 1985, for *Imogene's Antlers.*

WRITINGS—Picture books; self-illustrated: *Eulalie and the Hopping Head,* Macmillan, 1982; *Imogene's Antlers* (Reading Rainbow selection), Crown, 1985; *Paper John,* Farrar, Straus, 1987.

Illustrator: Nathan Zimelman, *Mean Chickens and Wild Cucumbers,* Macmillan, 1983; Jonathan Swift, *Gulliver's Travels,* Morrow, 1983; Burr Tillstrom, *The Kuklapolitan Players Present: The Dragon Who Lived Downstairs,* Morrow, 1984; Maida Silverman, *Anna and the Seven Swans,* translated from the Russian by Natasha Frumin, Morrow, 1984; Eve Merriam, *The Christmas Box,* Morrow, 1985; Arthur Yorinks, *Company's Coming,* Crown, 1988.

WORK IN PROGRESS: A retelling of *March Has Horse's Ears* for Simon & Schuster.

SIDELIGHTS: "I was born and raised in Detroit but spent many of my summers in rural Indiana. Therefore I have always had a taste for both the big city and the country and can live in both comfortably.

"As a child I loved books and animals. I was not healthy and spent a lot of time in bed; I believe it was this forced removal from the world that fired my imagination. From the age of two I drew pictures. My mother encouraged this and took me for lessons at the Detroit Institute of Arts. I don't recall much about the lessons, but I have never forgotten the experience of walking through the museum galleries which, to me as a child, seemed vast.

"One work in particular was a revelation to me; that was the mural room by the Mexican painter Diego Rivera. I still find it overwhelming when I visit it. It is a great work of art which tells a specific story but which is also filled with inexplicable mysteries. For me, this one monumental work legitimized the work of the artist, making it seem a noble, important profession. When, later on, I found out that Rivera had been persecuted for painting it and the mural was not shown to the public for years after it was completed, I learned what a powerful tool the visual image really is.

"Come now, dear," said Mother Lumps to the child. "You're much too big for the carriage. You'll have to walk."

The child did not move, and Mother Lumps had to drag her as she pushed Eulalie's carriage.

As they walked, Eulalie leaned over and told the child, "You really ought to stand up. You'll get your dress dirty that way."

The child said nothing, but Mrs. Shinn immediately replied, "I told you. This child makes no noise. Because of that it is better than all other children. *Your* child, Mother Lumps, would do well to follow its example!"

(From *Eulalie and the Hopping Head* by David Small. Illustrated by the author.)

"In my books I have spoken to the concerns I had as a child—those of being different from others, of being an outsider. I was a terrible student, painfully shy, much abused by the world around me and unable for many years to be comfortable in it. For all our advancements in education, I do not believe that sensitive and creative children—those whose intelligence and talents are not measured by the normal tests—are treated any better today than when I grew up. Teachers, administrators, and parents—with few exceptions—equate brilliance with good grades and social skills. In fact, the extraordinary children often do not do well in school and are so different it's hard to accept them. My books (*Eulalie and the Hopping Head, Imogene's Antlers,* and *Paper John*) speak directly to those kids.

"I think of my books as a kind of dog whistle pitched high above normal human hearing, sending their signal of acceptance to the strange ones out there, telling them to hold on.

"My wife Sherry and I live in a house that is more than 150 years old and is on the National Historic Register. It is situated on a bend of the St. Joseph River. Sherry is a wonderful gardener. I am fond of long walks, bike rides, and sketching in the out-of-doors."

STEINER, Stan(ley) 1925-1987

OBITUARY NOTICE—See sketch in *SATA* Volume 14: Born January 1, 1925, in New York, N.Y.; died of a heart attack, January 12, 1987, in Santa Fe, N.M. Historian, educator, editor, and author. Steiner was an authority on the American West, and was particularly knowledgeable about native Americans and Mexican Americans. His work was represented in more than fifty university textbooks and anthologies as well as numerous periodicals, including the *New York Times, Washington Post, Navajo Times,* and *Natural History.* He taught at several institutions, including Colorado College and the University of Wyoming. Among Steiner's writings are *The New Indians; La Raza: The Mexican Americans,* which received the Anisfield-Wolf Award from *Saturday Review* in 1971; *The Tiguas: Lost Tribe of City Indians* and *The Vanishing White Man,* both winners of the Golden Spur Award from Western Writers of America. Steiner also co-edited *The Way: An Anthology of American Indian Literature* and *Aztlan: An Anthology of Mexican American Literature.*

FOR MORE INFORMATION SEE: Contemporary Authors, New Revision Series, Volume 16, Gale, 1986; *Who's Who in America,* 44th edition, Marquis, 1986. Obituaries: *New York Times,* January 15, 1987.

SUHL, Yuri 1908-1986

OBITUARY NOTICE—See sketch in *SATA* Volume 8: Born July 30, 1908, in Podhajce, Austria-Hungary (now part of Poland); immigrated to the United States, 1923; died of a cerebral hemorrhage, November 8, 1986, in Martha's Vineyard, Mass. Historian, educator, translator, editor, and author of poetry and prose. Suhl was an expert on the Holocaust, particularly the Jewish resistance to the Nazis. He served with American forces during World War II and returned to his native Poland after the war, where he was powerfully affected by the accounts of Jewish survivors. Suhl, whose first works of poetry were published during the 1930s, devoted much of his literary career to children's books. In 1972 he received the Lewis Carroll Shelf Award for *Simon Boom Gives a Wedding;* the following year, he won the Association of Jewish Libraries

Award for *Uncle Micha's Partisans.* His other books for children include *Eloquent Crusader: Ernestine Rose,* an account of the life of an early Polish feminist; *An Album of Jews in America,* a pictorial history; *On the Other Side of the Gate,* which depicts a Jewish couple during the Holocaust; *The Man Who Made Everything Late;* and *The Purim Goat.* In the early 1950s, Suhl published his first original works in English, the autobiographical novels *One Foot in America* and *Cowboy on a Wooden Horse,* as well as *They Fought Back: The Story of Jewish Resistance in Nazi Europe,* his best-known contribution to Holocaust literature. In 1971 he taught a course at the New School for Social Research on the Jewish resistance.

FOR MORE INFORMATION SEE: Children's Literature Review, Volume 2, Gale, 1976; *Authors of Books for Young People,* supplement to the second edition, Scarecrow, 1979; *Contemporary Authors, New Revision Series,* Volume 2, Gale, 1981. Obituaries: *New York Times,* November 13, 1986; *International Herald,* November 14, 1986.

SWINDELLS, Robert E(dward) 1939-

PERSONAL: Born March 20, 1939, in Bradford, England; son of Albert Henry (in sales) and Alice (Lee) Swindells; divorced; remarried; children: Linda, Jill. *Education:* Huddersfield Polytechnic, teaching certificate, 1972. *Politics:* "Ecology." *Home and office:* 3 Upwood Park, Black Moor Rd., Oxenhope, Keighley, West Yorkshire BD22 9SS, England. *Agent:* Jennifer Luithlen, "The Rowans," 88 Holmfield Rd., Leicester LE2 1SB, England.

CAREER: Telegraph and Argus, Bradford, England, copyholder, 1954-57, advertising clerk, 1960-67; Hepworth & Grandage (turbine manufacturer), Bradford, Yorkshire, engineer, 1967-69; Undercliffe First, Bradford, teacher, 1972-77; Southmere First, Bradford, part-time teacher, 1977-80; full-time writer, 1980—. *Military service:* Royal Air Force, 1957-60. *Member:* Bradford Children's Book Group. *Awards, honors: When Darkness Comes* was chosen one of Child Study Association of America's Children's Books of the Year, 1975; National Book Award nomination, children's category, from the Arts Council of Great Britain, 1980, for *The Moonpath and Other Stories;* Other Award, 1984, and Children's Book Award from the Federation of Children's Book Groups, and Carnegie Medal runner-up from the British Library Association, both 1985, all for *Brother in the Land.*

WRITINGS—Juvenile: *When Darkness Comes* (novel; illustrated by Charles Keeping), Hodder & Stoughton, 1973, Morrow, 1975; *A Candle in the Night* (novel), David & Charles, 1974; *Voyage to Valhalla* (illustrated by Victor Ambrus), Hodder & Stoughton, 1976, Heinemann Educational (U.S.), 1977; *The Very Special Baby* (illustrated by V. Ambrus), Prentice-Hall, 1977; *The Ice-Palace* (illustrated by Jane Jackson), Hamish Hamilton, 1977; *Dragons Live Forever* (illustrated by Petula Stone), Prentice-Hall, 1978; *The Weather-Clerk* (illustrated by P. Stone), Hodder & Stoughton, 1979; *The Moonpath and Other Stories,* Wheaton, 1979, published as *The Moonpath and Other Tales of the Bizarre* (illustrated by Reg Sandland), Carolrhoda Books, 1983; *Norah's Ark* (illustrated by Avril Haynes), Wheaton, 1979; *Norah's Shark* (illustrated by A. Haynes), Wheaton, 1979.

Ghost Ship to Ganymede (illustrated by Jeff Burns), Wheaton, 1980; *Norah to the Rescue* (illustrated by A. Haynes), Wheaton, 1981; *Norah and the Whale* (illustrated by A. Haynes), Wheaton, 1981; *World Eater* (novel), Hodder & Stoughton,

ROBERT E. SWINDELLS

1981; *The Wheaton Book of Science Fiction Stories,* Wheaton, 1982; *Brother in the Land,* Oxford University Press, 1984, Holiday House, 1985; *The Thousand Eyes of Night,* Hodder & Stoughton, 1985; *The Ghost Messengers,* Hodder & Stoughton, 1986; *Staying Up,* Oxford University Press, 1986.

Translator of four juvenile books by Gunilla Bergstrom, all published by Wheaton Publishing, 1979: *Alfie and His Secret Friend; Who'll Save Alfie Atkins?; Alfie and the Monster; You're a Sly One, Alfie Atkins.*

Short story "Moths" included in anthology, *The Methuen Book of Strange Tales,* edited by Jean Russell, Methuen, 1980.

WORK IN PROGRESS: Mavis Davis, for Oxford University Press; *A Serpent's Tooth,* for Hamish Hamilton; *Night School,* for Ladybird Books.

SIDELIGHTS: "I have wanted to be a writer ever since I was thirteen. Adverse circumstances gave me no real opportunity until, in 1969, I began a three-year teacher training at Huddersfield Polytechnic. Then I wrote my first novel for children. I am now a full-time writer. I want to be loved and respected, in that order; but more, much more than this, I would like to live to see the day when every child everywhere will enjoy a childhood without hunger, anxiety, war, or any form of deprivation.

"I am in the final stages of an M.A. degree in peace studies at Bradford University, and I hope that the things I have learned during my course of study will help me write more tellingly for peace and cooperation."

HOBBIES AND OTHER INTERESTS: Reading (almost anything), walking, training with weights, watching films.

TAPP, Kathy Kennedy   1949-

BRIEF ENTRY: Born January 1, 1949, in Long Beach, Calif. Tapp is a librarian at the Janesville Public Library in Wisconsin, and an author of books for children. "My own three children have helped to keep me in tune with the current interests of young people," she said. Her first novel for children, *Moth-Kin Magic* (Atheneum, 1983), illustrated by Michele Chessare, was a Junior Literary Guild selection. The story concerns a race of little people who are scooped up with a handful of moss and trapped in a classroom terrarium until their masterful escape. "Vivid characterizations and accelerating suspense are the major attributes of this pleasing first novel," wrote *Booklist. Smoke from the Chimney* (Atheneum, 1986), deals with the emotional and financial drain an alcoholic parent has on ten-year-old Erin's family. "Tapp's writing is fresh and accessible, not maudlin or overly sentimental. . . . Readers are drawn into events and introduced to each of the skillfully drawn characters in turn," observed *School Library Journal.* Tapp's most recent book, *The Scorpio Ghosts and the Black Hole Gang* (Harper), was published in 1987. *Residence:* Janesville, Wisconsin.

FOR MORE INFORMATION SEE: Contemporary Authors, Volume 116, Gale, 1986.

Books are a guide in youth and entertainment for age.
—Jeremy Collier

TREDEZ, Denise (Laugier) 1930-
(Denise Trez)

PERSONAL: Born June 22, 1930, in Marseille, France; married Alain Tredez (an author and illustrator), 1950; children: Isabelle, Corinne, Florence. *Education:* Notre-Dame-de-France.

CAREER: Author of books for children. *Dominique* (children's magazine), Paris, France, co-editor with husband, 1952—. *Awards, honors: New York Herald Tribune*'s Children's Spring Book Festival honorable mention, 1964, for *Sophie; The Smallest Pirate* was selected one of Child Study Association of America's Children's Books of the Year, 1970.

WRITINGS—Under pseudonym Denise Trez; with Alain Trez, pseudonym of husband, Alain Tredez; published by World Publishing, except as indicated: *Circus in the Jungle*, 1958; *Fifi*, 1959; *The Butterfly Chase*, 1960; *Le Petit Chien*, 1961, translation by Douglas McKee and Donine Mouche, published as *The Little Dog*, Faber, 1962; *The Magic Paintbox*, 1962; *The Little Knight's Dragon*, 1963; *Sophie*, 1964, translated from French by D. McKee, published in England as *Sophie Runs Away*, Faber, 1964; *Le Vilain Chat*, 1965, translation by D. McKee, published as *The Mischievous Cat*, Faber, 1966; *The Royal Hiccups*, translated from French by D. McKee, Viking, 1965; *Rabbit Country*, translated from French by D. McKee, Viking, 1966; *Good Night, Veronica*, translated from French by D. McKee, Viking, 1968; *Maila and the Flying Carpet*, translated from French by D. McKee, Viking, 1969; *The Three Little Mermaids*, 1969; *The Smallest Pirate*, translated from French by D. McKee, Viking, 1970; *Pourquoi Pas?*, L'Ecole des loisirs, 1971.

ADAPTATIONS: "The Smallest Pirate," Miller-Brody.

FOR MORE INFORMATION SEE: Doris de Montreville and Donna Hill, editors, *Third Book of Junior Authors*, H. W. Wilson, 1972.

UTZ, Lois (Marie) 1932-1986

OBITUARY NOTICE—See sketch in *SATA* Volume 5: born January 4, 1932, in Paterson, N.J.; died November 12, 1986, in New York, N.Y. Secretary, business officer, counselor, artist, editor, and author of children's books. Prior to her career as an author and illustrator of children's books, Utz worked as a secretary and artist-administrative assistant. In addition, she counseled alcohol and drug addicts through an employee assistance agency and served as activities director of a day-care center. Utz's self-illustrated books include *The Pineapple Duck with the Peppermint Bill, A Delightful Day with Bella Ballet, The Simple Pink Bubble That Ended the Trouble with Jonathan Hubble*, and *The King, the Queen and the Lima Bean*. She began writing for children in the late 1960s. She also published a column in the *Paterson Morning Call* and contributed poems to various periodicals.

FOR MORE INFORMATION SEE: Contemporary Authors, Volumes 25-28, revised, Gale, 1977; *Who's Who in America*, 42nd edition, Marquis, 1982. Obituaries: *Star Ledger* (Newark), November 16, 1986.

Between the dark and the daylight,
  When the night is beginning to lower,
Comes a pause in the day's occupations,
  That is known as the Children's Hour.
—Henry Wadsworth Longfellow

von SCHMIDT, Eric 1931-

PERSONAL: Born May 28, 1931, in Bridgeport, Conn.; son of Harold (an illustrator) and Forest (Gilmore) von Schmidt; married second wife, Kuulei Kirn (a portrait artist); children: (previous marriage) Caitlin, Megan, Gigi, Kittie. *Education:* Studied at Farnsworth School of Art, 1950-51, and briefly at Art Students League, 1950. *Politics:* "Don't like them." *Religion:* "Self-taught."

CAREER: Graphic artist, 1950—, and writer with so many sidelines that he finds it hard to separate the vocations from the hobbies. Illustrator of over fifty children's books and twice as many record and book jackets. Songwriter and musician, turning out music and lyrics for more than thirty copyrighted songs; owner and operator of frame shop in Florida, 1955; taught painting, 1957; worked with disturbed children in Boston, Mass., 1958; art director for Pathways of Sound (recordings for children), Cambridge, Mass., 1959-66; began illustrating and then writing children's books in the 1960s; folksinger, appearing at New York Folk Festival in Carnegie Hall and Newport Folk Festival, 1965 and 1968. Formed Minglewood (a song publishing company affiliated with American Society of Composers, Authors, and Publishers), 1970; member of Broadcast Music, Inc. *Military service:* U.S. Army, 1952-54; became sergeant.

MEMBER: American Society of Composers, Authors, and Publishers, American Federation of Musicians, Authors Guild, Authors League of America. *Awards, honors:* Fulbright scholarship to paint in Italy, 1955-56; other awards for painting and graphic art; *New York Herald Tribune*'s Spring Book Festival Award, middle honor, 1959, for *Treasure of the High Country*, and 1962, for *Mr. Mysterious and Company;* Boys' Club Junior Book Award, Southern California Council on Literature for Children and Young People Notable Book Award, both 1964, Recognition of Merit Award from George G. Stone Center for Children's Books and Claremont Reading Conference, 1972, and Friends of Children and Literature Award from the Los Angeles Public Library, 1983, all for *By the Great Horn Spoon!; Hee Haw* was chosen one of the American Institute of Graphic Arts Children's Books, 1970; *The Gnu and the Guru Go behind the Beyond* was selected one of *New York Times* Best Illustrated Books of the Year, 1970; *Book World*'s Spring Book Festival Award, middle honor, 1971, for *Jingo Django; Mr. Mysterious's Secrets of Magic* was chosen one of the Child Study Association of America's Children's Books of the Year, 1975.

WRITINGS—Self-illustrated juveniles, except as indicated: (Compiler) *Come for to Sing*, Houghton, 1963; *The Young Man Who Wouldn't Hoe Corn*, Houghton, 1964; *The Ballad of Bad Ben Bilge*, Houghton, 1965; *Mr. Chris and the Instant Animals*, Houghton, 1967; *Feeling Circus*, United Church Press, 1970, published with teacher's guide by Hazel Schoonmaker and new introduction as *Eric von Schmidt's Feeling Circus*, 1974; (with Jim Rooney) *Baby, Let Me Follow You Down: The Illustrated Story of the Cambridge Folk Years* (adult), Doubleday-Anchor, 1979.

Record albums: *The Folk Blues of Eric von Schmidt*, Prestige Records, 1964; *Eric Sings von Schmidt*, Prestige Records, 1965; *Who Knocked the Brains Out of the Sky?*, Smash/Mercury Records, 1969; *Third Row, Second Right*, Poppy Records, 1972.

Illustrator: Edith Patterson Meyer, *Champions of Peace: Winners of the Nobel Peace Prize*, Little, Brown, 1959; Jonreed Lauritzen, *Treasure of the High Country*, Little, Brown, 1959;

(From *Humbug Mountain* by Sid Fleischman. Illustrated by Eric von Schmidt.)

Sara Weeks, *Tales of a Common Pigeon*, Houghton, 1960; J. Lauritzen, *The Glitter-Eyed Wouser*, Little, Brown, 1960; Sid Fleischman, *Mr. Mysterious and Company* (*Horn Book* honor list; Junior Literary Guild selection), Little, Brown, 1962; S. Fleischman, *By the Great Horn Spoon!* (Junior Literary Guild selection), Little, Brown, 1963; Clay Fisher, *Valley of the Bear: A Novel of the North Plains Sioux*, Houghton, 1964; S. Fleischman, *Chancy and the Grand Rascal* (*Horn Book* honor list), Little, Brown, 1966; E. P. Meyer, *Champions of the Four Freedoms*, Little, Brown, 1966; Richard O'Connor, *Sitting Bull: War Chief of the Sioux*, McGraw, 1968; Ann McGovern, *Hee Haw*, Houghton, 1969.

Janet H. Ervin, *Last Trip of the Juno*, Follett, 1970; Peggy Clifford, *The Gnu and the Guru Go behind the Beyond*, Houghton, 1970; S. Fleischman, *Jingo Django* (ALA Notable Book; Junior Literary Guild selection), Little, Brown, 1971; Anne Eve Bunting, *The Two Giants*, Ginn, 1971; Mary Main, *Take Three Witches*, Houghton, 1971; Jean Anderson, *The Haunting of America: Ghost Stories from Our Past*, Houghton, 1973; Lyn Lifshin, *Museum* (poems), Conspiracy Press, 1973; S. Fleischman, *The Ghost on Saturday Night*, Little, Brown, 1974; S. Fleischman, *Mr. Mysterious's Secrets of Magic*, Little, Brown, 1975; S. Fleischman, *Me and the Man on the Moon-Eyed Horse* (Junior Literary Guild selection), Little, Brown, 1977; S. Fleischman, *Humbug Mountain* (*Horn Book* honor list; Junior Literary Guild selection), Little, Brown, 1978; S. Fleischman, *Jim Bridger's Alarm Clock and Other Tall Tales*, Dutton, 1978.

ADAPTATIONS: "The Ballad of Bad Ben Bilge" (television film), Lilliputian Films.

WORK IN PROGRESS: More children's books; a musical play for children based on *The Young Man Who Wouldn't Hoe Corn.*

SIDELIGHTS: "My first training in illustration came very early because I grew up underfoot in my father's studio. That studio was a wonderful place. Horse skulls, Indian bonnets, flintlock

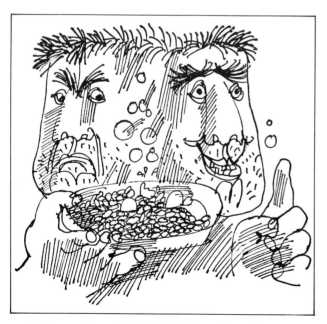

"Doggone!" snorted Potato Mike, making a face like a dried pumpkin. "These beans taste *soapy*!" ■ (From *Chancy and the Grand Rascal* by Sid Fleischman. Illustrated by Eric von Schmidt.)

rifles, books with pictures of naked ladies, good smells of turpentine and varnish. Everything a boy could ask for. When I wasn't drawing I would dress up in one of the costumes and fight imaginary battles. Chaplin, Disney, and Krazy Kat were my heroes. With the exception of Walt, they pretty much still are. I did my first professional work for the *American Magazine* and *True* when I was eighteen. Both art directors died shortly after. Work became hard to find after that, and I drifted into the streets. I got high with some companions by looking at a book of Piero reproductions and in a short time found I had become addicted to painting, a habit I haven't kicked to this day. I had some one-man shows and won some prizes. The nicest was a Fulbright Grant to study painting in Italy in 1955-56. When I came back, things were thin, so I started illustrating again. At night I played the guitar in coffee houses. At first, I illustrated other people's books and sang other people's songs. Then I got around to writing my own songs and books and even having my own children. I put my wife in my songs and my children in the books." [Lee Kingman and others, compilers, *Illustrators of Children's Books: 1957-1966*, Horn Book, 1968.]

Von Schmidt lived for a time on St. Vincent Island, British West Indies, and has traveled in Europe and Asia. He has a deepening interest in the Plains Indians and the history of the West during the nineteenth century.

His works are included in the Kerlan Collection at the University of Missouri.

FOR MORE INFORMATION SEE: St. Petersburg Times, April 17, 1966, December 17, 1972; *Tampa Tribune*, December 4, 1966; Lee Kingman and others, compilers, *Illustrators of Children's Books: 1957-1966*, Horn Book, 1968; Martha E. Ward and Dorothy A. Marquardt, *Authors of Books for Young People*, 2nd edition, Scarecrow, 1971; *The Boston Phoenix*, April 10, 1973; Eric von Schmidt, "Custer, Dying Again at That Last Stand, Is in a New Painting," *Smithsonian*, June, 1976; L. Kingman and others, *Illustrators of Children's Books: 1967-1976*, Horn Book, 1978.

WALTERS, Helen B.   (?)-1987

OBITUARY NOTICE: Born in Wisconsin; died of pneumonia, January 26, 1987. Children's author. Walters wrote biographies and historical books for children, including *No Luck for Lincoln; When John Wesley Was a Boy; Nikola Tesla, Giant of Electricity; Wernher Von Braun, Rocket Engineer; Henry Stanley and His Secret Key; Hermann Oberth: Father of Space Travel;* and *Ponies for a King.* She also contributed to periodicals.

FOR MORE INFORMATION SEE—Obituaries: Daily News (Van Nuys, Calif.), January 31, 1987.

WARTSKI, Maureen (Ann Crane)   1940-
(M. A. Crane)

PERSONAL: Born January 25, 1940, in Ashiya, Japan; naturalized U.S. citizen, 1962; daughter of Albert Edwin (in business) and Josephine (a teacher; maiden name, Wagen) Crane; married Maximilian Wartski (in business), June 1, 1962; children: Bert, Mark. *Education:* Attended University of Redlands, 1958-59; Sophia University, B.A., 1962. *Home:* 15 Francis Rd., Sharon, Mass. 02067. *Agent:* Barbara Lowenstein Associates, Inc., 250 West 57th St., New York, N.Y. 10107.

MAUREEN WARTSKI

CAREER: Free-lance writer. *English Mainichi,* Kobe, Japan, reporter, 1957-58; teacher at public schools in Sharon, Mass., 1968-69; high school history teacher in Sharon, 1978-79. Has also taught creative writing, conducted workshops and lectured on writing. *Awards, honors:* Annual Book Award of the Child Study Committee at Bank Street College of Education, for *A Boat to Nowhere,* and honor book, for *A Long Way from Home,* both 1980.

WRITINGS: My Brother Is Special (juvenile), Westminster, 1979; *A Boat to Nowhere* (illustrated by Dick Teicher), Westminster, 1980; *A Long Way from Home,* Westminster, 1980; *The Lake Is on Fire,* Westminster, 1981. Also author of juvenile plays. Contributor of articles, stories, and plays (sometimes under name M. A. Crane) to magazines, including *Highlights, Scholastic, Catholic Digest, Boys' Life, Women's Day, Writer,* and *American Girl.* Columnist for *Sharon (Mass.) Advocate.*

WORK IN PROGRESS: Short stories.

SIDELIGHTS: "All I ever wanted to do was write. My career seemed assured when I sold my first story at age fourteen, but then there were several years before I published anything else!

"*My Brother Is Special* was my first try at a young adult book. I wanted, at first, to write about the Special Olympics. The story did not come together until my husband rescued a crippled black duck and brought it home for our sons to nurse back to health. I feel that it is a worthwhile story. I have known and loved special children and have always felt that each of us has our own race to run, our own problems to overcome. Too often, young people (and older ones for that matter) feel

that courage is shown by winners, by people who are physically strong, or who get there first. I wanted to show that true courage means a great deal more.

"My second book is about Vietnamese boat people who escape the war-torn country and head out into nowhere. The fact that our family had lived in Bangkok from 1962 to 1966 was helpful as background, and I had also visited Vietnam around that time."

"Writing any story or novel consists of finding a topic that is interesting, a plot that has the necessary components of conflict and resolution, and characters that readers care about. Many years ago one of my finest teachers told me that I needed to write about characters and emotions that I knew at first hand. This seemed severely limiting, until I realized that what he meant was that I needed to write about characters and emotions that rang true. It's excellent advice, and in writing for young adults I have tried very hard to keep my books concerned with issues and characters I myself could honestly understand and appreciate.

". . . Young readers react positively to issues that move them or capture their interest. As to what those interests are, I find it's essential to be around teen-agers. I've been very lucky in this respect; the fact that I was a high school teacher for some years has helped me immensely, and my two sons have influenced my characters' concerns, dialogue and humor. All this familiarity has made me like and respect the people I write

Thay Van Chi knelt down on the beach and scooped some of the sand into the little bright bag

(From *A Boat to Nowhere* by Maureen Crane Wartski. Illustrated by Dick Teicher.)

for, which leads to the cardinal rule of writing: if you don't care for your readers, you can't write for them successfully.

"*How* one goes about writing successfully is a personal matter. Each writer has a style that is almost like a signature—a style that can be polished and strengthened but never really changed. Because of this I hesitate to give advice on the actual writing of young adult fiction except to suggest what you probably already know: never write down to your readers.

"There is another point of technique that I've learned through the years: In young adult writing especially, the first or rough draft must be done as quickly and as spontaneously as possible. Too much self-criticism, discussion, or even a rereading of the unfinished draft can often kill a good idea. I work swiftly, often blocking in scenes, sketching out characters and adding dialogue as it comes. I never reread until the draft is done, and at this stage I seldom discuss parts of the book or story with anyone. Also, in the rough draft I pay scant attention to spelling, syntax or language. There is always the second draft for all of that.

"I wonder if there's a writer alive who enjoys the second draft. To me, this is a time of travail and woe. I have burned countless pots and pans, ignored friends and even family while working on a second draft. Seasons have whirled past me while I sat mole-like in my study, researching and typing and retyping. And even when I've finished and there is a fat manuscript to show for all the effort, I often wonder if it is worth it.

"In fact, I very often ask myself *why*. Why go through all the work and discipline to write for a young adult audience? The market is competitive, and with the encroachment of censorship in the schools, the subject matter is limited. Also, young people seldom have much money, and a hardcover book is rarely their first concern.

"But there is reason to persevere. . . . I can probably write material that will sell better, make [me] richer, have a greater readership and appeal, but I doubt whether [I] will ever write for an audience that so feels with its heart. These readers are young. They are new. Their sensitivities and sensibilities have not become blunted, their experience has not been dulled. There is no mellowing, no blurring of their vision. Everything they find in a book they bring to it from their own experience. The joy, the sorrow, the hope of each new character they meet is an echo of their own emotion. Give these readers a book they love, and you may open a new world to them." [Maureen Crane Wartski, "Writing for Young Adults," *Writer*, December, 1986.]

FOR MORE INFORMATION SEE: Maureen Crane Wartski, "Writing for Young Adults," *Writer*, December, 1986.

WEISS, Leatie 1928-

BRIEF ENTRY: Born May 8, 1928, in New York. After receiving her B.A. in 1949 from Brooklyn College (now the City University of New York), and her M.A. from Columbia University in 1951, Weiss taught preschool and elementary grades in New York and New Jersey. She is the author of three books for children, all illustrated by her daughter, Ellen Weiss. Their first collaboration, for *Heather's Feathers* (F. Watts, 1976), won the Garden State Children's Book Award in 1979. "The subject is most relevant, the language is straight, and characterization is accomplished in remarkably little space and is underscored by sassy, three-color illustrations," ob-

served *Booklist*. They also worked together on *Funny Feet!* (F. Watts, 1978), about a pigeon-toed penguin, and *My Teacher Sleeps in School* (F. Watts, 1978), every child's favorite misconception—although, in this case, all the students are pachyderms.

FOR MORE INFORMATION SEE: Contemporary Authors, Volume 65, Gale, 1977; *Who's Who of American Women,* 12th edition, Marquis, 1981.

WHITE, Bessie (Felstiner) 1892(?)-1986

OBITUARY NOTICE: Born about 1892 in Buchach, Austria-Hungary (now U.S.S.R.); immigrated to United States, 1896; died of cardiopulmonary arrest, December 30, 1986, in Rockville, Md. Social worker, translator, editor, and children's author. Prior to her marriage in 1915, White worked as a children's social worker. As a writer, she translated Yiddish plays in the 1920s and 1930s, published as *Nine One-Act Plays from the Yiddish,* and wrote children's books during the 1940s and 1950s. All set in nineteenth-century Scandinavia, her works include *A Bear Named Grumms,* a Spring Book Festival Honor Book in 1953, *The Strange Man and the Storks, On Your Own Two Feet,* and *Carry On Grumms.* White also edited *One-Act Plays for Stage and Study.*

FOR MORE INFORMATION SEE: Who's Who of American Women, 2nd edition, Marquis, 1961; *Authors of Books for Young People,* Scarecrow, 1964. Obituaries: *Boston Globe,* January 2, 1987; *Washington Post,* January 2, 1987.

BARRY WILKINSON

At last the sailors saw that they would never be able to reach land. So they picked up Jonah and threw him into the great waves. ■ (From *Jonah and the Great Fish,* retold by Ella K. Lindvall. Illustrated by Barry Wilkinson.)

WILKINSON, (Thomas) Barry 1923-

PERSONAL: Born April 29, 1923, in Dewsbury, Yorkshire, England; son of B. C. (a police inspector) and Janet (a housewife; maiden name, Boyd) Wilkinson; married Pam Harding (an artist and teacher), 1950; children: Joanna, Tom. *Education:* Royal College of Art, London, diploma, 1949. *Home:* 18 Compton Ave., Brighton, East Sussex BN1 3PN, England. *Agent:* B. L. Keanley Ltd., 16 Chiltern St., London, England.

CAREER: Following college, worked in a stained-glass studio; Wimbledon College of Art, Wimbledon, London, England, instructor in stained-glass, 1952-54, head of graphics department, 1954-59; free-lance artist, 1962—; commissioned to design the Regent Street Christmas Lights of London, England, 1962; author and illustrator of books for children, 1963—. *Military service:* Royal Air Force, 1942-47. *Awards, honors:* Work selected for inclusion in *Graphis* children's issue, 1967; *The Diverting Adventures of Tom Thumb* and *Puss in Boots; or, The Master Cat* were each selected one of Child Study Association of America's Children's Books of the Year, 1969, and *Agib and the Honey Cakes,* 1972.

WRITINGS—All picturebooks; all self-illustrated: *The Diverting Adventures of Tom Thumb,* Bodley Head, 1967, Harcourt, 1969; *Jonathan Just,* Bodley Head, 1971; *What Can You Do with a Dithery-Doo?,* Bodley Head, 1971.

Illustrator: Griselda Gifford, *The Mystery of the Wooden Legs,* Bodley Head, 1964, new edition (bound with *Seven White Pebbles* by Helen Clare), 1975; William MacKellar, *Davie's Wee Dog,* Bodley Head, 1965, new edition (bound with *Rory the Roebuck* by David Stephen), 1975; Roger Collinson, *A*

Boat and Bax, Oliver & Boyd, 1967; Paul Berna, *The Secret of the Missing Boat,* translated from the French by John Buchanan-Brown, Bodley Head, 1966, Pantheon, 1967; *The Story of Jonah: Being the Whole of the Book of Jonah,* Bodley Head, 1968; Charles Perrault, *Puss in Boots; or, The Master Cat,* Bodley Head, 1968, World, 1969; Joseph Jacobs, *Lazy Jack,* Bodley Head, 1969, World, 1970.

Kathleen Lines, adapter, *The Story of Aladdin,* Walck, 1970; Naomi Mitchison, *Sun and Moon,* Bodley Head, 1970, T. Nelson (Nashville), 1973; R. Collinson, *Butch and Bax,* Chatto, Boyd & Oliver, 1970; David Mackay, Brian Thompson, and Pamela Schaub, *People in Stories,* Longmans for the Schools Council, 1970; D. Mackay, B. Thompson, and P. Schaub, compilers, *Sally Go Round the Sun, and Other Nursery Rhymes,* Longmans for the Schools Council, 1970; Walter Scott, *Kenilworth,* American Education, 1970; S. M. Lane and M. Kemp, *Myths and Legends,* Blackie & Son, 1972; K. Lines, reteller, *Agib and the Honey Cakes,* Walck, 1972; Margaret Howell, *The Mouse Who Wanted to Be a Man,* Longman, 1973; Charles Dickens, *A Tale of Two Cities,* abridged by Josephine Kamm, Collins, 1973; Phyllis Flowerdew, *Trug,* Oliver & Boyd, Books 1-4, 1973, Books 5-8 and Books 9-12, 1974; Aidan Chambers, *Great British Ghosts,* Pan Books, 1974; Robert L. Stevenson, *Kidnapped,* abridged by Olive Jones, Collins, 1974; Mary Cockett, *As Big as the Ark,* Methuen, 1974; (with Andrew Sier and Joanna Troughton) Jenny Taylor and Terry Ingleby, *The Scope Storybook,* Longman for the Schools Council Project in English for Immigrant Children, 1974; Ursula Moray Williams, *The Line,* Puffin, 1974; Marjorie Darke, *What Can I Do?,* Kestrel Books, 1975; Sheila Haigh, *Watch for the Ghost,* Methuen, 1975; Felicity Sen, *My Family,* Bodley Head, 1975, Bradbury, 1977; *Neil Grant's Book of Spies and Spying,* Kestrel Books, 1975; Dorothy M. Glynn, *Abracadabra!*, Oliver & Boyd, 1976; (with Gordon Melville and Jim Russell) D. M. Glynn, *Stories from Other Lands,* Oliver & Boyd, 1976.

S. Haigh, *Watch for the Champion,* Methuen, 1980; Ruth Silcock, *Albert John out Hunting,* Kestrel Books, 1980; R. Silcock, *Albert John in Disgrace,* Kestrel Books, 1981; Sybil Marshall, *Seafarers' Quest to Colchis* (anthology of fairy tales), Hart-Davis Educational, 1981; (with Eric Thomas) Sybil Marshall, *Tales the Greeks Told,* Hart-Davis Educational, 1982; Sheila McCullagh, *The Little Fox,* Hart-Davis Educational, 1982; Catherine Storr, reteller, *Jonah and the Whale,* Raintree, 1983; S. McCullagh, *The Magic People,* Hart-Davis Educational, 1983; S. McCullagh, *Sharon and the Great Horse,* Hart-Davis Educational, 1983; Ella K. Lindvall, *Jonah and the Great Fish,* 2nd edition, Moody, 1984. Also illustrator of *Old Chairs to Mend* by Noel Streatfeild, 1966.

All written by Michael Bond; all picturebooks, except as noted; all published by Collins: *Paddington at the Station,* 1976; *Paddington Goes to the Sales,* 1976; *Paddington Takes a Bath,* 1976; *Paddington's New Room,* 1976; *Paddington's Play Book: Things to Make, Games to Play, Pictures to Colour,* 1977; *Paddington's Counting Book: Learn the Numbers, Colour the Pictures,* 1977; *Paddington's Word Book: Words to Copy, Pictures to Colour,* 1977; *Paddington's First Book: An Object Recognition Book with Pictures to Colour,* 1977; *Paddington and Aunt Lucy,* 1980; *Paddington in Touch,* 1980; *Paddington on the River,* 1980; *Paddington Weighs In,* 1980.

Also illustrator of textbooks for Oliver & Boyd, Collins, and Ginn, and of a filmstrip about ancient Greece for BBC-TV. Contributor of illustrations to "Jackanory" (children's program), BBC-TV, and to magazines, including *Honey, New Society, Punch, Radio Times,* and *TV Times.* Designer of postage stamps.

WORK IN PROGRESS: Stories and illustrations for a television series; illustrations for educational readers.

SIDELIGHTS: "People are always saying to me that I must have been born with a gift for drawing and design, but I never have accepted this view. I do think one can be born with a natural sense of hand and eye coordination, but I believe the rest is due to a very early fascination for drawn images—'a photograph is easy—but *how* did the artist draw that? Could I possibly do the same? I'll have a try—not good, but not bad!' Early experiments with black and white, pen and ink, watercolour, crayons, etc. all helped to develop an ability which was fostered at art school ('fit for nothing else' was the attitude of the town I lived in) and then developed at the Royal College of Art in London. Teaching only helped to frustrate my creative impulses, but it *was* a help to mix with young people.

"After twenty-six years of practicing drawing and painting—mainly in illustration—I find that I am still learning, still trying to express more clearly my ideas and visions. Each new job comes to me as something entirely new with new problems. Never can one fall back on old successes. There is always a goal to aim for, something to strive after. I think this keeps one's work lively and never boring—difficult, worrying, puzzling, maybe—but never boring."

FOR MORE INFORMATION SEE: Lee Kingman and others, compilers, *Illustrators of Children's Books: 1967-1976,* Horn Book, 1978; Doris de Montreville and Elizabeth D. Crawford, editors, *Fourth Book of Junior Authors and Illustrators,* H. W. Wilson, 1978; Brigid Peppin and Lucy Micklethwait, *Book Illustrators of the Twentieth Century,* Arco, 1984.

SARAH WILSON

WILSON, Sarah   1934-

PERSONAL: Born October 18, 1934, in Syracuse, N.Y.; daughter of Homer Arthur (an engineer) and Elizabeth (an artist; maiden name, Remington) Turpin; married Herbert Eugene Wilson (an architect), September 30, 1956; children: Leslie Anne, Robert Murray. *Education:* University of Madrid, Spain, diploma de estudios Hispanicos, 1955; Ohio University, B.A., 1956. *Home:* Danville, Calif. *Office:* P.O. Box 2332, Dublin, Calif. 94568.

CAREER: Denver General Hospital, Denver, Colo., medical social worker, 1963-64; Laguna Pre-School, Laguna Beach, Calif., art teacher, 1965-77; Art Workshop West, Los Angeles, Calif., co-owner, 1971-73; free-lance artist and illustrator, 1977—. Has also worked as a workshop leader, and as a resource teacher in the Orange County public schools. *Exhibitions:* Craft and Folk Art Museum, Los Angeles, Calif.; Art Designs, Laguna Beach, Calif.; Laguna Beach Museum of Art; Coffee Garden Gallery, Corona Del Mar, Calif. *Member:* Author's Guild, Society of Children's Book Writers (past regional advisor), Bay Area Illustrators for Children, Virginia Kittredge Crosley Society. *Awards, honors:* Don Freeman Memorial Grant from the Society of Children's Book Writers, 1982, for *Beware the Dragons!*

*WRITINGS—*Self-illustrated: *I Can Do It! I Can Do It!,* Quail Street, 1976; *Beware the Dragons!,* Harper, 1985.

Illustrator: Elizabeth Rush, *The House at the End of the Lane,* Green Tiger, 1982.

Wrote and illustrated "The World of Food," a weekly newspaper column for children, 1981; also illustrator of "The Letter Bear," a monthly subscription letter for children, 1982-

86, and a children's calendar ''Amy's World,'' published by Green Tiger Press, 1982.

WORK IN PROGRESS: Three picture books; a middle-grade fiction book, *The McHenryville Comet;* illustrations for *Baby's First Year* by Phillis Hoffman and a snow story by Elizabeth Winthrop, both for Harper.

SIDELIGHTS: ''I have always loved children's books and illustrations from the time my mother read to me as a small child. From about the age of four, I put my own small books together—holding the pages with paper clips. At seven, I took my first art lessons outside of school (at the Boston Museum of Fine Arts), and they brought even more ideas for art work and stories. There was something very appealing to me about being able to carry art around in my pockets and enjoy it in a compact form.

''I grew up as an only child, and we moved a lot. My father was in the Navy, and when I was very small, I thought everyone moved like we did. It was a surprise to find out that they didn't! Wherever we went, I seemed to have at least one cardboard box full of papers—drawings, sketches, story ideas and of course, the little books I liked to put together. In the fifth

grade, a teacher pointed out that my art was becoming far more than a hobby, and that I might want to think about writing and illustrating children's books some day. His name was Max Barsis, and his special interest was illustrating for children. I felt very fortunate to be in his art classes.

''I went to several different elementary schools and three different high schools. There were things I didn't like about moving, but at the same time it was an opportunity for art enrichment. We lived in different parts of the east, the south and the midwest, all with their own regional colors and backgrounds. I became aware of light, and how the colors in other children's paintings (my own too!) varied with climate and surrounding. The greatest contrasts have been noticeable on the west coast, where I live now. Many of the children's paintings here have vivid color in them—bright blue skies and pink and yellow ice plant, for example. Some of the eastern paintings are softer and have warm greys and deeper hill and tree colors in them.

''There isn't space to tell you about the different places and houses I lived in when I was growing up, but I can describe one special house where I spent time visiting. It belonged to my grandparents in Rochester, New York, and it was large

When the bump leaned to one side, Tildy sat up, and looked around, and let out one wild whopping yell. ■ (From *Beware the Dragons!* by Sarah Wilson. Illustrated by the author.)

and rambling with interesting windows and stairways. The front stairway was wide and carpeted and like any other, but the back stairway was darker and twisting and strange—a good place for making up mystery stories when my cousins and I were brave enough to spend time there.

"My grandparents liked to travel at a time when people took big trunks with them and came back with all kinds of odds and ends from their trips. I also had a great-aunt and uncle who lived in Brazil and sent them things like native masks and snake skins and stuffed animals.

"There was armor from the Middle Ages at the foot of the front stairway in this Victorian house, a giant fascinating piece of petrified wood by the front door and a stuffed owl which sat on a bookcase in the front hall. At the top of the stairway was a large stuffed leopard rug, with head at eye level for anyone climbing the stairs. The leopard had glinting yellow-green glass eyes which shone every afternoon when the sun fell on them. I always felt sorry for him because his eyes looked so sad. Across from the leopard was a wide balcony and then a stuffed moose head with what seemed like extraordinarily large antlers. Everywhere were things like photographs of Roman ruins, renaissance madonnas, paintings of life in the English courts, tapestries, Chinese lamps with fringe on the shades and American Indian rugs. Scariest, was a closet in a back bedroom where one of my uncles kept his medical school skeleton as a joke. He thought it was funny, but even some of the adults were startled when they opened the door.

"Best, was the sunny attic with everything from a Civil War cannon to spinning wheels and years of *National Geographic* magazines and medical journals. My grandfather also kept medical supplies in his own pharmacy (including a jar of malted milk tablets for the children), and there were uncounted wonders in the long, long basement which stretched the length of the house. For a child, being in this grand hodgepodge was a great adventure. The drawing ideas were almost limitless. (I always used up a lot of paper when I visited!)

"The house apparently inspired my mother, too, because she drew and painted there when she was a girl. I wasn't used to such large spaces and so many things around me, though. As much as I liked exploring the house, I was always glad to go home to a smaller, more familiar surrounding!

"I always enjoyed looking through my grandparents' books and still am excited by early children's books and illustrations. I'm fortunate to have a small collection of them, most from family and friends, and especially like those with humor.

"Humor is something I'm drawn toward in artwork and in the world in general. I also enjoy spontaneous events, like the time I put on a tape cassette of birds singing in a field and suddenly a flock of real birds settled into a tree next to the open door to listen! (A wonderful chance to draw pictures of them, too!) I'm also happy in wilderness areas where I can sketch birds and animals in a natural surrounding. When I need to study an animal, I look at photographs and often go to a zoo, but it's much more fun to draw one in the wild—with exceptions, of course, like tigers!

"I believe that everyone is an artist. It's just a matter of finding the right medium, and that always takes time. When someone says, 'Oh, *I* can't draw!' I wonder if they've really given it much practice. Or maybe they're a sculptor inside, who hasn't found clay yet. Or a weaver of tapestries who has yet to try weaving. Anyone can carry a small sketchbook, too, and at least try a hand at whatever seems interesting. The

results are often surprising. I've also found that my own sketchbooks are like journals, celebrating people and events and all kinds of things. (I buy small inexpensive ones at a local drugstore—sometimes, even with lines on the pages— and use them up like memo pads.)

"The things which I enjoy most are probably the same things which nourish my artwork: oceans and water of all kinds, sun, good-natured people, the company of children, the seasons, holidays, dogs (we have a collie, Muffy), animals of all kinds, gardens, folk art, toys, seashells, adventure stories, humor, fantasy, nonsense, science fiction and so on.

"I feel very fortunate to be able to illustrate for children. It's the audience I would most like to work for in the world, one that I admire and enjoy and find full of resourcefulness, daring and an open, gentle heart.

"Too, I'm pleased (and still surprised, sometimes!) to have the chance to try to return some of the great pleasure I've had—and still have—from the well-loved children's books and illustrations of others."

WITTY, Paul A(ndrew) 1898-1976

PERSONAL: Born July 23, 1898, in Terre Haute, Ind.; died February 11, 1976, in Chicago, Ill.; son of William L. and Margaret (Kerr) Witty. *Education:* Indiana State Teachers College (now Indiana State University), A.B., 1920; Columbia University, M.A., 1923, Ph.D., 1931. *Residence:* Chicago, Ill.

CAREER: School psychologist in Scarborough-on-Hudson, N.Y., 1922; University of Kansas, Lawrence, associate professor, 1924-25, professor of educational psychology, 1925-30; Northwestern University, Evanston, Ill., professor of education and director of Psycho-Educational Clinic, 1930-66, professor emeritus, 1966-76. Lecturer. Chief educational consultant, D. C. Heath & Co., 1940-76; consultant, Western Publishing Co. *Military service:* U.S. Army, 1942-44; became major.

MEMBER: International Council for Exceptional Children, International Council for the Improvement of Reading Instruction (president, 1954), American Academy of Arts and Sciences (fellow), American Psychology Association (fellow), American Childhood Education Association, American Educational Research Association, American Association for Gifted Children, National Education Association, National Society for the Study of Education, National Council of Teachers of English, Association for Supervision and Curriculum Development, Society for the Advancement of Education, Sigma Nu, Phi Delta Kappa, Kappa Delta Pi.

WRITINGS: (With Harvay C. Lehman) *The Psychology of Play Activities,* A. S. Barnes, 1927; *A Study of Deviates in Versatility and Sociability of Play Interest,* Columbia University Press, 1931; (with David Kopel) *Reading and the Educative Process,* Ginn, 1939; (editor with Charles E. Skinner) Rose Alschuler, Harold Anderson, Nancy Bayley, and others, *Mental Hygiene in Modern Education,* Farrar & Rinehart, 1939.

The True Book of Freedom and Our U.S. Family, Childrens Press, 1948; *Reading in Modern Education,* Heath, 1949; *Streamline Your Reading,* Science Research Associates, 1949; (editor) *The Gifted Child,* Heath, 1951; *How to Become a Better Reader,* Science Research Associates, 1953; (with Anne Coomer) *Salome Goes to the Fair,* Dutton, 1953; (editor with Miriam E. Peterson and Alfred E. Parker) *Reading Roundup:*

A Reading-Literature Series, Heath, 1954; (editor) *Mental Health in Modern Education,* University of Chicago Press, 1955; (with Margaret Ratz) *A Developmental Reading Program for Grades 6 Through 9,* Science Research Associates, 1956; *How to Improve Your Reading,* Science Research Associates, 1956; *Creativity of Gifted and Talented Children: Addresses,* Columbia University Press, 1959.

(With Edith Grotberg) *Developing Your Vocabulary,* Science Research Associates, 1960; (editor) *Development in and through Reading,* University of Chicago Press, 1961; (editor with Alma Moore Freeland) *Silver Web,* Heath, 1964; (wtih A. M. Freeland) *Peacock Lane,* Heath, 1964; (wtih Mildred Bebell) *Reading Caravan,* Heath, 1965, revised edition, 1968; (with E. Grotberg and A. M. Freeland) *The Teaching of Reading: A Developmental Process,* Heath, 1966; (editor) *Educationally Retarded and Disadvantaged,* University of Chicago Press, 1967; (with Thomas Barensfeld) *Life and Times of Eight Presidents,* Highlights for Children, 1969; (with E. Grotberg) *Helping the Gifted Child,* Science Research Associates, 1970; *Adventures in Discovery Program,* Western Publishing, 1970; *Helping Children Read Better,* Science Research Associates, 1970; (editor) *Reading for the Gifted and the Creative Student,* International Reading Association, 1971.

Associate editor, *Highlights for Teachers,* and *Highlights for Children;* advisory editor, *My Weekly Reader;* member of editorial board, *Exceptional Children.*

SIDELIGHTS: As author and educator, Paul Witty pioneered the application of psychological principals to education. His work focused specifically upon gifted children, and served to dispel the myths that a gifted child is unhealthy, asocial, generally undesirable, and necessarily unitalented.

FOR MORE INFORMATION SEE: Library Quarterly, April, 1958; *Indiana Authors and Their Books, 1917-1966,* Wabash College, 1974. Obituaries: *New York Times,* February 14, 1976; *Publisher's Weekly,* March 22, 1976; *AB Bookman's Weekly,* April 26, 1976.

ASHLEY WOLFF

(From *The Bells of London* by Ashley Wolff. Illustrated by the author.)

WOLFF, (Jenifer) Ashley   1956-

PERSONAL: Born January 26, 1956, in Boston, Mass.; daughter of Klaus Heinrich (a professor) and Deane (a porcelain restorer; maiden name, Ibold) Wolff; married William Sabin Russell (a journalist), September 6, 1980; children: Brennan. *Education:* Rhode Island School of Design, B.F.A., 1979. *Home:* San Francisco, Calif. *Office:* c/o E. P. Dutton, 2 Park Ave., New York, N.Y. 10016.

CAREER: Valley Voice, Middlebury, Vt., staff artist, 1979-80; *Pacific Sun,* Mill Valley, Calif., staff artist, 1980-82; writer and illustrator, 1983—. *Awards, honors: A Year of Birds* was chosen a Notable Children's Book by the Association for Library Service to Children, 1984; *The Bells of London* was exhibited at the Bologna International Children's Book Fair, 1985.

WRITINGS—Juvenile; self-illustrated: *A Year of Birds,* Dodd, 1984; *The Bells of London* (Junior Literary Guild selection), Dodd, 1985; *Only the Cat Saw,* Dodd, 1985; *A Year of Beasts,* Dutton, 1986.

Illustrator: *The Country Christmas Advent Calendar,* Dutton, 1986.

WORK IN PROGRESS: Illustrations for "Block City" by Robert Louis Stevenson, for Dutton.

SIDELIGHTS: "I'm drawing on memories of my own happy childhood in the sixties to create my books for children. Without trying to idealize the nuclear family too much, I try to show the relationships of a loving, two-parent family through the everyday activities of life. I'm trying for a universal feeling that won't seem either dated or too contemporary.''

WOOD, Audrey

PERSONAL: Born in Little Rock, Ark.; daughter of Cook Edwin (an artist) and Maegerine (an antique historian; maiden name, Thompson) Brewer; married Don Wood (an illustrator), November 21, 1969; children: Bruce Robert. *Education:* Attended Arkansas Art Center, special studies in drama and art. *Home:* Santa Barbara, Calif. *Agent:* Heacock Literary Agency, 1523 Sixth St., Suite 14, Santa Monica, Calif. 90401.

CAREER: Author and illustrator of children's books, 1978; The Blue Moon (book and import shop), Eureka Springs, Ark. and Fayetteville, Ark., owner and operator, 1970-75. *Member:* Society of Children's Book Writers. *Awards, honors:* Golden Kite Award for illustration from the Society of Children's Book Writers, one of *New York Times* Ten Best Illustrated Children's Books of the Year, both 1984, one of International Reading Association/Children's Book Council's Children's Choices, and Southern California Council on Literature for Children and Young People Illustration Award for significant contribution in illustration, both 1985, Certificate of Merit from the Society of Illustrators, 1985, and Young Reader Medal from the California Reading Association, 1985, P.E.N. Los Angeles Center "Younger Children" Literary Award, 1985, all for *The Napping House; King Bidgood's in the Bathtub* was chosen one of Child Study Association of America's Children's Books of the Year, 1985, one of *School Library Journal*'s Best Books, 1985, Parents' Choice Award from the Parents' Choice Foundation, 1985, Certificate of Merit from the Society of Illustrators, 1985, Caldecott Honor Book from the American Library Association, 1986, and Colorado Children's Book Award, 1987.

WRITINGS—Juvenile; self-illustrated except as indicated: *Magic Shoelaces,* Child's Play International, 1980; *Tickleoctopus* (illustrated by Bill Morrison), Houghton, 1980; *Twenty-Four Robbers,* Child's Play International, 1980; *Scaredy-Cats,* Child's Play International, 1980; *Orlando's Little-While Friends,* Child's Play International, 1980; *Moonflute* (illustrated by husband, Don Wood), Green Tiger Press, 1980; *The Princess and the Dragon,* Child's Play International, 1981; *Quick as a Cricket* (illustrated by D. Wood), Child's Play International, 1982; *Balloonia,* Child's Play International, 1982; *Tugford Wanted to Be Bad,* Harcourt, 1983; *Presto Change-O,* Child's Play International, 1984; (with D. Wood) *The Big Hungry Bear* (illustrated by D. Wood), Child's Play International, 1984; *The Napping House* (ALA Notable Book; illustrated by D. Wood), Harcourt, 1984.

King Bidgood's in the Bathtub (ALA Notable Book; illustrated by D. Wood), Harcourt, 1985; *Tooth Fairy,* Child's Play International, 1985; *The Three Sisters* (illustrated by Rosekrans Hoffman), Dial, 1986; *Detective Valentine,* Harper, 1987; *Heckedy Peg* (illustrated by D. Wood), Harcourt, 1987; *Elbert's Bad Word* (co-illustrated by D. Wood), Harcourt, 1988.

ADAPTATIONS: "The Napping House" (filmstrip with cassette), Weston Woods, 1985; "King Bidgood's in the Bathtub" (filmstrip), Random House/Miller-Brody, 1986; audiocassette, including "Heckedy Peg," "King Bidgood's in the Bathtub," "The Napping House," "Moonflute," and "Elbert's Bad Word," Caedmon, 1987.

SIDELIGHTS: "My first memories are of Sarasota, Florida in the winter quarters of the Ringling Brothers Circus. There my father, a young art student, earned extra income by repainting the twelve-foot murals that decorated the big top and sideshows. My mother would often take me to watch him work, and made up wonderful stories about the people on the brightly colored murals—the tallest man in the world, the snake woman, and the fat lady who couldn't stand up. Later many of these people became our neighbors. The tallest man in the world bounced me on his knee, and the fat lady who couldn't stand up held me in her arms. My first babysitters were a family of little people who lived in a trailer lined with tropical aquariums. They never tired of telling me stories about the animals they worked with in the circus: Chi Chi the Chimp, Elder the

AUDREY WOOD

Elephant, and, of course, the most famous animal of the time, Gargantua the Gorilla.

"All of that happened during the first year of my life, a period I remember with extraordinary vividness. I think the reason for the unusual reach and power of my memory is that from the time I was conscious I lived in a heightened reality—the world of the circus—in which the fantastic was the stuff of day-to-day life.

"When I was about two, my father won an art scholarship to go to San Miguel, Mexico, about six hours north of Mexico City. We made our way to San Miguel in a trailer, and along the way met up with a band of gypsies and traveled with them. At that time, San Miguel had a very progressive art program. My first language was Spanish. Again, my memories of this period are terribly vivid. We lived in Mexico until I was five. By the age of three, I was a voracious reader in both English and Spanish.

"Ours has been a family of artists since the fifteenth century. I spent a lot of time in my grandfather's studio as a child. A magical place, canvases covered with beautiful images and colors were stashed all over. I used to love to watch the paintings emerge. Classical music filled the air along with the wonderful scents of paint, turpentine, linseed and a host of other oils. Like a chemist, or a wizard, he mixed his pigments from powders and oils. In junior high school I won third prize in a science fair for a project in which I showed where various pigments come from—yellow, for instance, comes from cow's urine.

"I also painted with my father. I had access to all his materials, in addition to my own. He guided me very subtly, giving me a feeling of working freely rather than being instructed. As a working artist, I represent the fourth consecutive generation to do so, but as a woman, I break the mold. By the time I reached first grade I had decided to be an artist.

"My mother never actively pursued a career as an artist, but is extremely talented in a number of areas, from sewing all of my ballet costumes to restoring antiques. She became director of the Little Rock Historical Landmark Preservation Society. She spun marvelous tales, something which had a very great effect on me.

"My parents owned an extensive library. By the age of three I was a bookworm with my own collection of picture books, many of which I still have. Later on, I loved Hans Christian Andersen and books that had an edge of fantasy, like *The Borrowers* and *The Rescuers*. I also read a lot of adult novels.

"As the eldest of three sisters, I quite naturally fell into the role of storyteller. I would open one of my parents' lavishly illustrated art books and make up stories about the paintings. The nature encyclopedia was also one of our favorites, especially the section on reptiles and amphibians. I remember these story sessions as idyllic, but recall my youngest sister's cries of alarm: 'Mommy! Mommy! Audrey's making the snakes crawl off the page again!'

"By the time I reached fourth grade, I had two burning ambitions: to live in Dr. Dolittle's house and to write and illustrate children's books. Earlier thoughts of becoming a veterinarian ended with a chipmunk dissection in the fourth grade.

"My parents had all of us involved in the arts. We took dance lessons, drama lessons, and classes in sculpture and painting. We would put on plays of our own creation complete with a

"Did you see that lady's face?" whispered Dot. ■
(From *The Three Sisters* by Audrey Wood. Illustrated by Rosekrans Hoffman.)

little stage and an old set of footlights. We designed and made our costumes and built the set using a lot of our father's paints and materials. A small admission would gain entrance to anyone in the neighborhood.

"Because of my early interest in reading, my mother enrolled me in one of the first Montessori Schools in the United States. The school's approach was geared toward the creative and independent child. Eventually I attended public elementary school, and had a very difficult and unhappy time. I remember becoming passionately interested in a particular assignment and devoting myself entirely to it to the exclusion of everything else. In fourth grade, I wrote a twenty-five page report, and let all my other subjects slide. There was never any middle ground, I either got 'A's or 'D's. And because I was often bored with what was going on in the classroom, I learned to *totally* tune it out. I kept a cigar box in my desk filled with little objects—paper clips, a crackerjack toy, tiny knobs, and so on. I would set them on my desk and make up stories about them. My involvement with these would put me in a trance-like state, causing my teachers to think there was something wrong with me. For *their* intents and purposes, I was *absent*. Socially, it was a nightmare as well. I was so different from the other kids—they taunted and ostracized me. My mother was very upset by all of this, but never lost faith in me, and always encouraged me to be an individual and to believe in myself.

"After elementary school I decided that I wanted to go to Mount St. Mary's Girls Academy, a Roman Catholic school. As a non-Catholic, I was again something of an outsider. The quality of education was excellent, however, and I was left alone to do my art and dream my dreams.

"Age fifteen saw me very involved in Little Rock's Art Center, an art and drama institute founded by a group of people that included my grandfather and father. They brought in artists from Europe and New York; the atmosphere was distinctly European and highly-charged. We produced plays that New York critics came to see. I considered the Art Center my real school, while putting in my time at St. Mary's. At the Center we did college-level work."

In the late 1960s, Wood moved to Berkeley, California, where she pursued her art independently, and where, in 1969, she met Don Wood, who became her husband and collaborator. "I was experimenting with my art and teaching children's art part time. My work consisted mostly of narrative paintings and large sculptures. I was also writing stories.

I'm as loud as a lion,

(From *Quick As a Cricket* by Audrey Wood. Illustrated by Don Wood.)

"We spent the first four months of our marriage in a cottage in the redwoods where Don worked as a logger, and I spent my time doing art and caring for a family of baby golden eagles that had been knocked from their nest. Once that happens the parent birds won't have anything to do with them. We hand-fed them raw meat until they were big enough to be released.

"We traveled all over—Mexico, the Yucatan, and Guatemala, seeking traditional Indian artists and craftspeople. We visited their homes, sat on their dirt floors and eventually brought a

lot of their work to Eureka Springs, a town in the Ozarks where we opened a shop. We had lots of hammered copper pieces, sculpture, pottery, weaving and ritual objects. After our initial four-month trip, we went down about every two months to keep in touch with the artists who supplied us. In addition to art and crafts, we sold books—philosophy, anthropology, metaphysics, children's books, whatever was interesting to us.

"Eureka Springs, where our family often spent the summer during my teens, is in the Ozark mountains. The front door of a house is often on one level, the back door on another. The

Just where do you think that balloon is going, Matthew?

To Balloonia Land, Jessica, where balloons live.

(From *Balloonia* by Audrey Wood. Illustrated by the author.)

town is filled with Victorian houses with lots of 'gingerbread.' Don and I lived there for about five years.

"I continued writing and drawing and by the time we left the Ozarks, I knew what I wanted to do. My childhood ambition to write and illustrate children's books had come back to me in full force. Having my own child by now, helped. I spent many hours reading to our son, Bruce, and becoming a part of his child world.

"My first impulse was to go to New York, the center of the publishing industry. But Don intervened, asking me to try Santa Barbara for a year, and if I didn't like it, we'd head for New York. I trusted him, so I agreed. As soon as we arrived in Santa Barbara, I fell in love with the place. We bought a house and have been here ever since.

"It may have taken us a little longer to break into publishing from the West Coast, but we did it. I made a point of talking with writers, librarians and publishers' representatives at the American Library Association and the American Booksellers Association. I wanted to know who was publishing what, and where my work might fit in. My research paid off. I had been submitting a manuscript entitled *Moonflute* and always got the same response:'Well-written but too romantic.' At a book convention I was able to locate a publisher who accepted my book within a week.

"I usually work from something I call my 'idea box,' something I'm sure goes back to the cigar box I kept in my desk all those years in elementary school. Whenever an idea comes to me in the form of a title, a character sketch, an image, a description of something I've seen or a place I've been, I jot it down and put it in the idea box. I have my sensors out all the time. Not only does this keep me attuned and attentive, but it eliminates the specter of writer's block. I go through the idea box when I sit down to write and put together a number of ideas—characters, images, bits of stories. Often during the process an entirely new idea emerges and takes over.

"I also carry a lot of ideas in my head, using a system that I believe originated with the Greeks. I construct in my mind a memory house with ten doors. On each door is a symbol indicating what is inside. I periodically go through the doors to see what's there. I store my ideas in the room behind the proper door. If I get too many ideas in a given room I make sure I write them down and put them in an idea box."

Wood will play classical children's songs or re-read *Mother Goose* to set the mood for writing and establishing rhythm. "Rhythm is terribly important in picture books. Some of my stories—*The Napping House* and *King Bidgood's in the Bathtub,* for example—began with a melody I heard deep inside myself. I actually sang these books as I wrote them. I am very lucky that my younger sister, a talented musician, makes musical compositions from my stories, and we sign them together. If a story translates easily into music, then I know it will make a wonderful book.

"Recently I have been doing life-sized papier maché sculptures of characters from my imagination. Victoria, for example, is dressed completely in a Victorian costume. She holds a teacup and saucer and sits, leaning forward slightly as if anticipating a witty remark or a pleasant compliment. She is

(From *Tugford Wanted to Be Bad* by Audrey Wood. Illustrated by the author.)

a palpable presence in our living room, except when local stores put her on display in their windows. She receives cards from people who have met her. My editor brought her a box of chocolates on a recent visit. Lately I have been getting lots of stories from Victoria—I sit watching her and ideas just come.

"My art work is very expressionistic. I do not work from models. While drawing *Elbert's Bad Word*, I surrounded my-self with images of high society, usually Europe in the 20s. I make the images part of my world, but when I begin to work on paper, I take the pictures down and draw from imagination and memory. For my work to convey humor, it must be spontaneous and free.

"I have matured as a writer. Not that I'll ever stop growing, but I've reached a point where I feel at home in that mysterious place where the stories come from. As an illustrator I feel that

They shook hands and agreed to change places that very night.

(From *The Princess and the Dragon* by Audrey Wood. Illustrated by the author.)

I still have a long way to go, however. Style is a problem for me, perhaps because my work tends to be expressionistic and moody. It may be that many years of working as a painter and sculptor has somehow made it harder for me to be an illustrator. I don't know. When you're illustrating a book, you're obliged to work with editors and art directors. That can be hard, as it can limit your sense of freedom, particularly if you're accustomed to working on your own.''

Audrey and Don Wood's first collaborative effort was born in *Moonflute,* for which she wrote the story and he did the illustrations. ''*Moonflute* was my second book. Shortly after it was accepted, my publisher sent me a list of potential illustrators. But I really thought that Don was the artist for the job. He did a sample, which was accepted as soon as they saw it.''

''Don and I approach our work very differently, but agree on certain basic things—rhythm is crucial in a picture book, a children's book should be delightful for the adults, who often read to their children. I usually come up with a concept for a book and I discuss it with him at this early stage. It's wonderful to have his feedback and encouragement when a story is just a 'seed.' Then I generally ask him to read my first draft. Here he wears the editor's hat and gives me concrete suggestions. I do the same for his art work. I have a lot of input into how the characters look. We 'cast' the book, much as if it were a stage play, and discuss page lay-out and type design. Don likes to work from models, often of people we are close to and generally I, too, appear in his paintings. I put on make-up and a costume and go through the lines as though it were a performance. Don makes sketches and takes photographs and uses them as a basis for his illustrations. It's thrilling. By virtue of having written the story, worked with the artist and appeared in the book, my entire creative self is involved in the process.

''Our collaboration is total. When one of us is 'in deadline,' the other one takes up the slack with regard to housework, cooking, and similar responsibilities.

''For years we shared the same studio, back to back. But now we're building a separate space behind our house that will allow us to have individual, but adjacent studios. I need a very large work space for research, writing and drawing, and space for all my books. Also, I keep a pet mouse, a pigeon, a parrot and a tortoise in my studio, and they, too, must be accommodated.

''Growing up I always had animals and as my life has increasingly reflected the realization of my dreams and ambitions, I have more animals than ever. Not only do I have those I already mentioned, but guinea pigs, koi fish, two cats and over 150 birds in our backyard. I belong to an animal rehabilitation network that specializes in abandoned and wounded birds. We have an excellent survival rate, and as I mark the birds I take in, I know that many of them return to the huge pepper tree in our backyard. In the case of babies that have fallen from the nest, I get them to the fledgling stage by feeding them with an eyedropper. The tricky part is releasing them into nature. You must do so in an area where there is a big flock of their kind, so that they will be adopted and have the benefit of the group's protection. Birds who have been separated from their parents are not as naturally savvy about predators as are those fledged from the nest.

''I read all the time—everything from science fiction and fantasy (which I particularly love) to the classics, nature books and poetry. I avoid the bestseller, preferring instead books that are out of the mainstream.''

When asked if she had any advice to aspiring writers and artists, Wood added: ''Just write, make drawings. Do a lot of dreaming. Maybe make your own idea box. Above all, don't get discouraged. It takes many years to master the art of making picture books. I can tell you, it is the most difficult task I have ever attempted. And because it is, I continue, for love of the challenge. I don't want to do something that doesn't make ultimate demands on me. And if you are truly an artist, you won't, either.''

—Based on an interview by Marguerite Feitlowitz

WOOD, Don 1945-

PERSONAL: Born May 4, 1945, in Atwater, Calif.; son of Elmer B. (a farmer) and Elizabeth (a teacher; maiden name, Smith) Wood; married Audrey Brewer (an author and illustrator of children's books), November 21, 1969; children: Bruce Robert. *Education:* University of California—Santa Barbara, B.A., 1967; California College of Arts and Crafts, M.F.A., 1969. *Home:* Santa Barbara, Calif. *Agent:* Heacock Literary Agency, 1523 Sixth St., Suite 14, Santa Monica, Calif. 90401.

CAREER: Editorial illustrator, graphic designer, and illustrator for magazines and children's books, 1976—; Blue Moon (book and import shop), Eureka Springs, Ark. and Fayetteville, Ark., owner and operator, 1970-75. Has worked as a logger, a sailmaker, a substitute art teacher, and has executed paintings for cable television series ''Faerie Tale Theatre.'' *Exhibitions:* ''The Artist as Illustrator,'' Metropolitan Museum of Art, New York, N.Y. 1982; Annual Exhibition of the Society of Illustrators, New York, 1986. *Member:* Society of Children's Book Writers.

AWARDS, HONORS: Golden Kite Award for illustration from the Society of Children's Book Writers, and one of *New York*

DON and AUDREY WOOD

Ohhh, how that Bear
loves red, ripe strawberries!

(From *The Big Hungry Bear* by Don and Audrey Wood. Illustrated by Don Wood.)

Times Ten Best Illustrated Children's Books of the Year, both 1984, Southern California Council on Literature for Children and Young People Award for significant contribution in illustration, and one of International Reading Association/Children's Book Council's Children's Choices, both 1985, Certificate of Merit from the Society of Illustrators, 1985, and Young Reader Medal from the California Reading Association, 1985, all for *The Napping House; King Bidgood's in the Bathtub* was chosen one of Child Study Association of America's Children's Books of the Year, 1985, one of *School Library Journal's* Best Books, 1985, Parents' Choice Award from the Parents' Choice Foundation, 1985, Certificate of Merit from the Society of Illustrators, 1985, Caldecott Honor Book from the American Library Association, 1986, and Colorado Children's Book Award, 1987.

WRITINGS—Self-illustrated: (With wife, Audrey Wood) *The Big Hungry Bear*, Child's Play International, 1984.

Illustrator; all written by A. Wood: *Moonflute*, Green Tiger Press, 1980; *Quick as a Cricket*, Child's Play International, 1982; *The Napping House* (ALA Notable Book), Harcourt, 1984; *King Bidgood's in the Bathtub* (ALA Notable Book), Harcourt, 1985; *Heckedy Peg*, Harcourt, 1987; (with A. Wood) *Elbert's Bad Word*, Harcourt, 1988.

ADAPTATIONS: "The Napping House" (filmstrip with cassette), Weston Woods, 1985; "King Bidgood's in the Bathtub" (filmstrip), Random House/Miller-Brody, 1986; audiocassette, including "Heckedy Peg," "King Bidgood's in the Bathtub," "The Napping House," "Moonflute," and "Elbert's Bad Word," Caedmon, 1987.

WORK IN PROGRESS: "The book on which I'm presently working has sent me back to the Dutch and Flemish masters to study light and shadow. Although I love strong contrast, I always want the reader to be able to go into even the darkest corners and see what goes on there."

SIDELIGHTS: Born May 4, 1945 in Atwater, California. "I was born and raised on a farm in the central San Joaquin Valley. We grew peaches, oranges, apricots, almonds and sweet potatoes. It was foggy and cold in the winter; in summer the heat could be devastating. The central valley was originally semi-desert, but after irrigation it became one of the most fertile farming areas in the country. Growing up on a farm, there was always lots of work. By the time I was in sixth grade or so, I had forty acres of potatoes to take care of by myself—irrigating, weeding, tending them day by day. The farm began pretty small, but eventually grew to encompass hundreds of acres. My father was a self-made man whose first job in the valley was picking grapes. Before his death he had worked his way into a position of prominence in California agriculture. I remember living in a little house and then moving to a bigger house when the farm became successful. But our daily life didn't change much—my dad was frugal and we never lived lavishly. My brother, half-brother and I were doing a man's work by the time we were twelve and thirteen. During the summer that often meant eighteen-hour shifts, seven days per week—during the day we worked in the fields, at night we loaded trucks with produce for market. With our earnings we bought our own clothes, cars, college tuition, room and board. This made us independent, which I think is a very good thing.

"I have no idea where the urge came from, but in the sixth grade I made a hard-and-fast decision to become an artist. It was unusual for me to take such a firm stand; I was basically a 'good' kid and pretty much did everything I was told. I faced up to some tough pressure to pursue other careers, such as architecture. Luckily, I had older brothers who wanted to run the farm, so it wasn't as though my artistic ambition would compromise or endanger the family business. Also, as the youngest kid, I had some 'black sheep' flexibility.

"My mother died when I was in second grade, and I think perhaps she is the 'missing piece' in my artistic 'puzzle.' Her

A street cleaner looked up from his broom and thought he saw a star falling from the sky. ■
(From *Moonflute* by Audrey Wood. Illustrated by Don Wood.)

brother was very artistic, and she herself used to sketch. Oddly enough, I have no recollection of her illness and death. But I do remember her. My dad remarried a very nice woman, Marjane Locher, an honors graduate in chemistry with a keen interest in languages.

"Winter was my time to draw, and I did so constantly (there was no time during the summer). I always drew stories, which I would make up. Looking back, they were quite primitive—usually a space ship going to another planet, an enormous conflict the hero would have to surmount, etc. I would do the whole story on one sheet of paper, almost like a mural. I started out working in pencil but eventually switched to ink and watercolors.

"I could never find paper big enough to draw what I wanted. My mother ingeniously solved my problem by giving me the tan paper the laundry came wrapped in. Laundry day was art day. When I unfolded one of those sheets, it covered the entire kitchen table. What a luxury! I remember surveying that panoramic blank surface, basking in its infinite potential, and gradually allowing grand and heroic plans to form as I drew.

"I loved comic books. In fact, I built an entire ritual around them. When I would buy one, I would bring it home, make sure no one was around to hassle me, make myself a peanut butter sandwich with a tall glass of milk, and just let the fantasy take over. Although I was an active kid—working on the farm, later playing football, which I loved—I had a dreamy side to my nature. I would go to bed quite a while before I was sleepy, so I could lie there and make up stories. For me,

bedtime was the time I consciously set aside for daydreams and fantasy.

"I took art all through high school although there wasn't a very ambitious art program. The most significant art instruction I received was private art lessons back in the sixth grade. We worked on such technical things as perspective: how to make a flat surface appear three-dimensional, etc. Unfortunately, these lessons lasted only one year—I think the teacher was unavailable after that. Still, that year was significant not only in terms of my technical growth, but the compliments I received reinforced my ambition.

"I went to the University of California at Santa Barbara where I majored in fine art. My first year was a revelation. It was a different world from the one in which I had grown up. It was wonderfully stimulating. I also got involved in theater, and was part of a big USO tour through Asia in 1966. I did so much with the theater department that I ended up with a minor in theater. That experience, I realized later, was important in terms of the way I approach picture books.

"But in terms of my art I became confused. I went to college in the mid-1960s. In my six years of art studies, there was only one teacher, Irma Cavat, whose work was frankly representational. In fact, her work was narrative and illustrative. She did series in which there were implied stories. She was a good and strong influence, however, she was a sort of a 'lone ranger,' and I think I pretty much buckled in to prevailing styles. Literary content was to be purged—according to the wisdom of those times—and so I more or less purged literary content from my work. I kept nothing from my college years—nothing I did then interests me.

"When I went to the California College of Arts and Crafts for a Masters in Fine Art, I began to realize that literary content was what had first inspired me and that stories had always been an integral part of my impulse to draw. I started doing things that looked almost like comic strips. But I was unsure of what I wanted and kept changing styles. For six years after I graduated, I hardly put pen to paper.

"I met Audrey Brewer in Berkeley in 1968, and we married in 1969. On our honeymoon Audrey, who had quite an extensive collection of children's books, read me some of her favorites, including George MacDonald's *At the Back of the North Wind*. I was immediately impressed, but didn't realize the enormous part in our lives children's literature would eventually play.

"The first summer we were married I worked as a logger in northern California. We were the 'good guys,' that is, we were clearing the forest of trees that were choking off the growth of the more spectacular varieties. Because I'd grown up on a farm and knew how to handle myself outdoors, they made me foreman, which amused me. I was the head chain saw operator, not owing to my extraordinary skill, but to the fact that I was the only guy over the age of nineteen.

"For about a year, we lived in Little Rock where I was a substitute art teacher. I had never intended to teach, but it

DON WOOD

seemed a better job than stacking bricks in a factory, which I was doing at the time. That was a really tough stint, but I am glad to have given it a try. I taught in a very poor school in which many families lived on welfare. I had virtually no art budget; art supplies consisted of pencil and paper. But we had fun. I worked a lot with music and the kids would dance as well as draw from whatever inspirations they got from the music.

"Eventually, we went to Mexico where we started a business bringing the work of traditional Indian artists and craftspeople to the U.S. It was wonderful. We traveled through Mexico, Yucatan and Guatemala and got to know a number of the artists quite well. Each family and each piece of art had a story behind it. Our first trip lasted about four months, after that we made shorter trips every two months.

"We decided to open a shop in which we would sell Mexican and Guatemalan art and books. We went to visit Eureka Springs, a unique town in the Ozarks where Audrey used to spend her summers. I was knocked out. I had never been to the South and certainly never expected to see anything quite like Eureka Springs. It's built right into the mountains, without a single intersection in the whole place. And within the city limits there are over 200 natural springs. We stayed in the area for five years.

"We decided to leave the Ozarks in order to get into publishing. I had always loved Santa Barbara—it's beautiful and has a vibrant artistic community—so we settled there. I started doing freelance magazine illustration, Audrey was writing and beginning to sell children's books."

Don and Audrey Wood have collaborated on a number of books for children. "To date I have only illustrated books written by Audrey, and will probably continue this pattern. *Moonflute*, the first of her books I illustrated, had been sold, but the publisher was having trouble finding an illustrator. At Audrey's request, I did a sample illustration and they accepted it within a day. As if that weren't enough 'beginner's luck,' the paintings from that book were selected for inclusion in an exhibit entitled 'The Artist as Illustrator/Children's Literature,' at the Metropolitan Museum of Art in New York. That was a thrill."

When questioned about his artistic process, Wood replied, "I'm a fumbler and a fiddler and a doer-over. That's why my favorite medium is oil. Because it dries so slowly, you have lots of time to change things. You can sand down and start again from scratch if you want to. I begin with lots of pencil sketches. I usually prepare about five different dummies before I do final pencil drawings. I transfer these onto the final surface and then begin to paint. It takes me one to two years to do a picture book. I work in a heat, but it's a very slow heat.

"Although Audrey and I work differently, we see picture books the same way. A picture book is at least half theatre or half film. Rhythm is an extremely important element. Also critical is point of view. When I'm planning my illustrations, I often pretend I have a camera and am moving it around, or deliberately keeping it still, as the case may be. It's fun to play with point of view. In *The Napping House*, for example, the 'camera' moves, but in a very restricted space. The audience is locked into what is essentially a one-room setting but the 'point of view' moves to the ceiling, then falls to the floor. In *King Bidgood*, the 'camera' is stationery. Keeping it still was very appealing to me. As I've said, I am not a very spontaneous painter and tend to pick mediums and styles that give me a lot of control. The idea of having infinite options regarding point of view, and then selecting the simplest solution was very appealing.

(From *King Bidgood's in the Bathtub* by Audrey Wood. Illustrated by Don Wood.)

"I tend to work with models, and most of the characters in our books are people we know. Audrey has done a lot of posing for me, and so has our son, Bruce. For the mouse in *The Napping House,* I worked for weeks with one crawling all over my drawing table! I also do a lot of library research. One of the more fascinating things I learned—this was during *Bidgood*—was that in medieval times people fished with hu-

man hair wound into lines. They preferred gray hair because it was translucent and difficult for the fish to see.

"With each book I set for myself a particular artistic challenge: the dynamics of light and dark masses; a certain narrative slant, or point of view, or perspective. In *Napping House,* the challenge was to establish what is basically an elaborate car-

(From the animated filmstrip "The Napping House." Produced by Weston Woods.)

toon style. Light plays an extremely dramatic role and denotes the passage of time. The progression of colors is essentially, though subtly, from monochrome to full color. In *King Bidgood,* I wanted a lavishly theatrical effect, almost operatic. The style is somewhat cartoon-like, but much more realistic than *Napping House.*

"Audrey and I work very closely. She'll originate an idea, or a draft and then present it to me to see if I would be interested in illustrating it. Sometimes we don't know. Sometimes it's a book that she could illustrate better. *Bidgood* we knew immediately was mine. That staginess is right up my alley. And I based the King on an old friend of mine, a craftsperson who lives in northern California. The entire cast of characters is based on our family and friends. Our editor at Harcourt Brace Jovanovich has a role, as well.

"*The Napping House* was a different case. When Audrey first read it to me, I thought it was beautiful. But when I began to work on the dummy, the drawings were dull. I gave the text back to her feeling that it wouldn't work visually. Undaunted, Audrey went back to work on the story, and made a small change that turned the whole thing around. She had everyone in the house fall asleep stacked in a pile, one atop the other. Suddenly the comic and cozy possibilities seemed endless.

"We're each other's best critics, I think. Audrey has saved me a lot of time by identifying problems in paintings early on. I think timing is our strongest asset. Maybe because we've both worked in theater—though Audrey more extensively than I—we're sensitive to split-second nuances that can make or break a show, or a picture book. For us, the page is a stage.

"As far as artists go, I like to look at people who work very differently than I do. People who work fast, loose, spontaneously. William Steig is one, James Marshall, Quentin Blake, Ralph Steadman, and Garth Williams are others.

"Picture books are about drama." Aspiring illustrators should "expose themselves to the theatre, learn how to tell a story in pictures, and do it dramatically."

"As I contemplate illustrating a new picture book, I get the same feeling of exhilarating potential that used to come over me as a kid when I was given the huge sheet of tan paper the laundry came wrapped in. A new world, complete with complex human relations, economic and social structures, as well as geology, flora and fauna, architecture and costume, is waiting to be discovered. What I find most rewarding, however, is entering into this new world as it comes to life through illustration, and happily anticipating that my work will inspire the reader to do the same."

—*Based on an interview by Marguerite Feitlowitz*

ZENS, Patricia Martin 1926-1972

BRIEF ENTRY: Born August 27, 1926, in Chicago, Ill.; died December 8, 1972. Author of children's books and lecturer. Zens graduated from Rosary College in 1948 and received her M.A. from Marquette University in 1950. Her first children's book, *I Like Orange* (F. Watts), appeared in 1961. She rewrote the classic children's tale *Gingerbread Man* (Whitman, 1963), as well as *The Bremen Town Musicians* (Whitman, 1964), and produced her own works, such as *Animals to See, 1, 2, 3* (Whitman, 1964), *A Funny Alphabet* (Whitman, 1965), *The Happy Book* (Whitman, 1965), and *The Thank You Book* (Golden, 1967). Zens also contributed short stories to children's magazines, including *Golden,* and feature and spiritual writings to religious magazines. Her hobbies included tennis, sewing, hiking, and nature lore.

FOR MORE INFORMATION SEE: Contemporary Authors, Volumes 5-8, revised, Gale, 1969; *Foremost Women in Communications,* Bowker, 1970. Obituaries: Date of death provided by son, Martin R. Zens.

Cumulative Indexes

Illustrations Index

(In the following index, the number of the volume in which an illustrator's work appears is given *before* the colon, and the page on which it appears is given *after* the colon. For example, a drawing by Adams, Adrienne appears in Volume 2 on page 6, another drawing by her appears in Volume 3 on page 80, another drawing in Volume 8 on page 1, and another drawing in Volume 15 on page 107.)

YABC

Index citations including this abbreviation refer to listings appearing in *Yesterday's Authors of Books for Children,* also published by the Gale Research Company, which covers authors who died prior to 1960.

Aas, Ulf, *5:* 174

Abbé, S. van. *See* van Abbé, S.

Abel, Raymond, *6:* 122; *7:* 195; *12:* 3; *21:* 86; *25:* 119

Abrahams, Hilary, *26:* 205; *29:* 24-25

Abrams, Kathie, *36:* 170

Abrams, Lester, *49:* 26

Accorsi, William, *11:* 198

Acs, Laszlo, *14:* 156; *42:* 22

Adams, Adrienne, *2:* 6; *3:* 80; *8:* 1; *15:* 107; *16:* 180; *20:* 65; *22:* 134-135; *33:* 75; *36:* 103, 112; *39:* 74

Adams, John Wolcott, *17:* 162

Adamson, George, *30:* 23, 24

Adkins, Alta, *22:* 250

Adkins, Jan, *8:* 3

Adler, Peggy, *22:* 6; *29:* 31

Adler, Ruth, *29:* 29

Adragna, Robert, *47:* 145

Agard, Nadema, *18:* 1

Agre, Patricia, *47:* 195

Ahl, Anna Maria, *32:* 24

Aichinger, Helga, *4:* 5, 45

Aitken, Amy, *31:* 34

Akaba, Suekichi, *46:* 23

Akasaka, Miyoshi, *YABC 2:* 261

Akino, Fuku, *6:* 144

Alain, *40:* 41

Alajalov, *2:* 226

Albrecht, Jan, *37:* 176

Albright, Donn, *1:* 91

Alcorn, John, *3:* 159; *7:* 165; *31:* 22; *44:* 127; *46:* 23, 170

Alda, Arlene, *44:* 24

Alden, Albert, *11:* 103

Aldridge, Andy, *27:* 131

Alex, Ben, *45:* 25, 26

Alexander, Lloyd, *49:* 34

Alexander, Martha, *3:* 206; *11:* 103; *13:* 109; *25:* 100; *36:* 131

Alexeieff, Alexander, *14:* 6; *26:* 199

Aliki. *See* Brandenberg, Aliki

Allamand, Pascale, *12:* 9

Allan, Judith, *38:* 166

Alland, Alexander, *16:* 255

Alland, Alexandra, *16:* 255

Allen, Gertrude, *9:* 6

Allen, Graham, *31:* 145

Allen, Pamela, *50:* 25, 26-27, 28

Allen, Rowena, *47:* 75

Allison, Linda, *43:* 27

Almquist, Don, *11:* 8; *12:* 128; *17:* 46; *22:* 110

Aloise, Frank, *5:* 38; *10:* 133; *30:* 92

Althea. *See* Braithwaite, Althea

Altschuler, Franz, *11:* 185; *23:* 141; *40:* 48; *45:* 29

Ambrus, Victor G., *1:* 6-7, 194; *3:* 69; *5:* 15; *6:* 44; *7:* 36; *8:* 210; *12:* 227; *14:* 213; *15:* 213; *22:* 209; *24:* 36; *28:* 179; *30:* 178; *32:* 44, 46; *38:* 143; *41:* 25, 26, 27, 28, 29, 30, 31, 32; *42:* 87; *44:* 190

Ames, Lee J., *3:* 12; *9:* 130; *10:* 69; *17:* 214; *22:* 124

Amon, Aline, *9:* 9

Amoss, Berthe, *5:* 5

Amundsen, Dick, *7:* 77

Amundsen, Richard E., *5:* 10; *24:* 122

Ancona, George, *12:* 11

Anderson, Alasdair, *18:* 122

Anderson, Brad, *33:* 28

Anderson, C. W., *11:* 10

Anderson, Carl, *7:* 4

Anderson, Doug, *40:* 111

Anderson, Erica, *23:* 65

Anderson, Laurie, *12:* 153, 155

Anderson, Wayne, *23:* 119; *41:* 239

Andrew, John, *22:* 4

Andrews, Benny, *14:* 251; *31:* 24

Angel, Marie, *47:* 22

Angelo, Valenti, *14:* 8; *18:* 100; *20:* 232; *32:* 70

Anglund, Joan Walsh, *2:* 7, 250-251; *37:* 198, 199, 200

Anno, Mitsumasa, *5:* 7; *38:* 25, 26-27, 28, 29, 30, 31, 32

Antal, Andrew, *1:* 124; *30:* 145

Apple, Margot, *33:* 25; *35:* 206; *46:* 81

Appleyard, Dev, *2:* 192

Aragonés, Sergio, *48:* 23, 24, 25, 26, 27

Araneus, *40:* 29

Archer, Janet, *16:* 69

Ardizzone, Edward, *1:* 11, 12; *2:* 105; *3:* 258; *4:* 78; *7:* 79; *10:* 100; *15:* 232; *20:* 69, 178; *23:* 223; *24:* 125; *28:* 25, 26, 27, 28, 29, 30, 31, 33, 34, 35, 36, 37; *31:* 192, 193; *34:* 215, 217; *YABC 2:* 25

Arenella, Roy, *14:* 9

Armer, Austin, *13:* 3

Armer, Laura Adams, *13:* 3

Armer, Sidney, *13:* 3

Armitage, David, *47:* 23

Armitage, Eileen, *4:* 16

Armstrong, George, *10:* 6; *21:* 72

Arno, Enrico, *1:* 217; *2:* 22, 210; *4:* 9; *5:* 43; *6:* 52; *29:* 217, 219; *33:* 152; *35:* 99; *43:* 31, 32, 33; *45:* 212, 213, 214

Arnosky, Jim, *22:* 20

Arrowood, Clinton, *12:* 193; *19:* 11

Arting, Fred J., *41:* 63

Artzybasheff, Boris, *13:* 143; *14:* 15; *40:* 152, 155

Aruego, Ariane, *6:* 4

See also Dewey, Ariane

Aruego, Jose, *4:* 140; *6:* 4; *7:* 64; *33:* 195; *35:* 208

Asch, Frank, *5:* 9

Ashby, Gail, *11:* 135

Ashby, Gwynneth, *44:* 26

Ashley, C. W., *19:* 197

Ashmead, Hal, *8:* 70

Assel, Steven, *44:* 153

Astrop, John, *32:* 56

Atene, Ann, *12:* 18

Atherton, Lisa, *38:* 198

Atkinson, J. Priestman, *17:* 275

Atkinson, Wayne, *40:* 46

Attebery, Charles, *38:* 170

Atwood, Ann, *7:* 9

Augarde, Steve, *25:* 22

Austerman, Miriam, *23:* 107

Austin, Margot, *11:* 16

Austin, Robert, *3:* 44

Averill, Esther, *1:* 17; *28:* 39, 40, 41

Axeman, Lois, *2:* 32; *11:* 84; *13:* 165; *22:* 8; *23:* 49

Ayer, Jacqueline, *13:* 7

Ayer, Margaret, *15:* 12; *50:* 120

B.T.B. *See* Blackwell, Basil T.

Babbitt, Bradford, *33:* 158

Babbitt, Natalie, *6:* 6; *8:* 220

Bachem, Paul, *48:* 180

Back, George, *31:* 161

Bacon, Bruce, *4:* 74

Bacon, Paul, *7:* 155; *8:* 121; *31:* 55; *50:* 42

Bacon, Peggy, *2:* 11, 228; *46:* 44

Potter, Miriam Clark, *3:* 162
Powers, Richard M., *1:* 230; *3:* 218; *7:* 194; *26:* 186
Powledge, Fred, *37:* 154
Pratt, Charles, *23:* 29
Price, Christine, *2:* 247; *3:* 163, 253; *8:* 166
Price, Edward, *33:* 34
Price, Garrett, *1:* 76; *2:* 42
Price, Hattie Longstreet, *17:* 13
Price, Norman, *YABC 1:* 129
Price, Willard, *48:* 184
Primavera, Elise, *26:* 95
Primrose, Jean, *36:* 109
Prince, Leonora E., *7:* 170
Prittie, Edwin J., *YABC 1:* 120
Provensen, Alice, *37:* 204, 215, 222
Provensen, Martin, *37:* 204, 215, 222
Pucci, Albert John, *44:* 154
Pudlo, *8:* 59
Purdy, Susan, *8:* 162
Puskas, James, *5:* 141
Pyk, Jan, *7:* 26; *38:* 123
Pyle, Howard, *16:* 225-228, 230-232, 235; *24:* 27; *34:* 124, 125, 127, 128

Quackenbush, Robert, *4:* 190; *6:* 166; *7:* 175, 178; *9:* 86; *11:* 65, 221; *41:* 154; *43:* 157
Quennell, Marjorie (Courtney), *29:* 163, 164
Quidor, John, *19:* 82
Quirk, Thomas, *12:* 81

Rackham, Arthur, *15:* 32, 78, 214-227; *17:* 105, 115; *18:* 233; *19:* 254; *20:* 151; *22:* 129, 131, 132, 133; *23:* 175; *24:* 161, 181; *26:* 91; *32:* 118; *YABC 1:* 25, 45, 55, 147; *YABC 2:* 103, 142, 173, 210
Rafilson, Sidney, *11:* 172
Raible, Alton, *1:* 202-203; *28:* 193; *35:* 181
Ramsey, James, *16:* 41
Rand, Paul, *6:* 188
Ransome, Arthur, *22:* 201
Rao, Anthony, *28:* 126
Raphael, Elaine, *23:* 192
Rappaport, Eva, *6:* 190
Raskin, Ellen, *2:* 208-209; *4:* 142; *13:* 183; *22:* 68; *29:* 139; *36:* 134; *38:* 173, 174, 175, 176, 177, 178, 179, 180, 181
Ratzkin, Lawrence, *40:* 143
Rau, Margaret, *9:* 157
Raverat, Gwen, *YABC 1:* 152
Ravielli, Anthony, *1:* 198; *3:* 168; *11:* 143
Ray, Deborah. *See* Kogan, Deborah
Ray, Ralph, *2:* 239; *5:* 73
Raymond, Larry, *31:* 108
Rayner, Mary, *22:* 207; *47:* 140
Raynor, Dorka, *28:* 168

Raynor, Paul, *24:* 73
Razzi, James, *10:* 127
Read, Alexander D. "Sandy," *20:* 45
Reed, Tom, *34:* 171
Reid, Stephen, *19:* 213; *22:* 89
Reinertson, Barbara, *44:* 150
Reiniger, Lotte, *40:* 185
Reiss, John J., *23:* 193
Relf, Douglas, *3:* 63
Relyea, C. M., *16:* 29; *31:* 153
Rémi, Georges, *13:* 184
Remington, Frederic, *19:* 188; *41:* 178, 179, 180, 181, 183, 184, 185, 186, 187, 188
Renlie, Frank, *11:* 200
Reschofsky, Jean, *7:* 118
Réthi, Lili, *2:* 153; *36:* 156
Reusswig, William, *3:* 267
Rey, H. A., *1:* 182; *26:* 163, 164, 166, 167, 169; *YABC 2:* 17
Reynolds, Doris, *5:* 71; *31:* 77
Rhead, Louis, *31:* 91
Rhodes, Andrew, *38:* 204; *50:* 163
Ribbons, Ian, *3:* 10; *37:* 161; *40:* 76
Rice, Elizabeth, *2:* 53, 214
Rice, James, *22:* 210
Rice, Eve, *34:* 174, 175
Richards, George, *40:* 116, 119, 121; *44:* 179
Richards, Henry, *YABC 1:* 228, 231
Richardson, Ernest, *2:* 144
Richardson, Frederick, *18:* 27, 31
Richman, Hilda, *26:* 132
Richmond, George, *24:* 179
Rieniets, Judy King, *14:* 28
Riger, Bob, *2:* 166
Riley, Kenneth, *22:* 230
Ringi, Kjell, *12:* 171
Rios, Tere. *See* Versace, Marie
Ripper, Charles L., *3:* 175
Ritz, Karen, *41:* 117
Rivkin, Jay, *15:* 230
Rivoche, Paul, *45:* 125
Roach, Marilynne, *9:* 158
Robbin, Jodi, *44:* 156, 159
Robbins, Frank, *42:* 167
Roberts, Cliff, *4:* 126
Roberts, Doreen, *4:* 230; *28:* 105
Roberts, Jim, *22:* 166; *23:* 69; *31:* 110
Roberts, W., *22:* 2, 3
Robinson, Charles, *3:* 53; *5:* 14; *6:* 193; *7:* 150; *7:* 183; *8:* 38; *9:* 81; *13:* 188; *14:* 248-249; *23:* 149; *26:* 115; *27:* 48; *28:* 191; *32:* 28; *35:* 210; *36:* 37; *48:* 96
Robinson, Charles [1870-1937], *17:* 157, 171-173, 175-176; *24:* 207; *25:* 204; *YABC 2:* 308-310, 331
Robinson, Jerry, *3:* 262
Robinson, Joan G., *7:* 184
Robinson, T. H., *17:* 179, 181-183; *29:* 254
Robinson, W. Heath, *17:* 185, 187, 189, 191, 193, 195, 197, 199, 202; *23:* 167; *25:* 194; *29:* 150; *YABC 1:* 44; *YABC 2:* 183
Roche, Christine, *41:* 98

Rocker, Fermin, *7:* 34; *13:* 21; *31:* 40; *40:* 190, 191
Rockwell, Anne, *5:* 147; *33:* 171, 173
Rockwell, Gail, *7:* 186
Rockwell, Harlow, *33:* 171, 173, 175
Rockwell, Norman, *23:* 39, 196, 197, 199, 200, 203, 204, 207; *41:* 140, 143; *YABC 2:* 60
Rodegast, Roland, *43:* 100
Rodriguez, Joel, *16:* 65
Roever, J. M., *4:* 119; *26:* 170
Roffey, Maureen, *33:* 142, 176, 177
Rogasky, Barbara, *46:* 90
Rogers, Carol, *2:* 262; *6:* 164; *26:* 129
Rogers, Frances, *10:* 130
Rogers, Walter S., *31:* 135, 138
Rogers, William A., *15:* 151, 153-154; *33:* 35
Rojankovsky, Feodor, *6:* 134, 136; *10:* 183; *21:* 128, 129, 130; *25:* 110; *28:* 42
Rorer, Abigail, *43:* 222
Rosamilia, Patricia, *36:* 120
Rose, Carl, *5:* 62
Rose, David S., *29:* 109
Rosenbaum, Jonathan, *50:* 46
Rosenblum, Richard, *11:* 202; *18:* 18
Rosier, Lydia, *16:* 236; *20:* 104; *21:* 109; *22:* 125; *30:* 151, 158; *42:* 128; *45:* 214
Ross. *See* Thomson, Ross
Ross, Clare Romano, *3:* 123; *21:* 45; *48:* 199
Ross, Dave, *32:* 152
Ross, Herbert, *37:* 78
Ross, John, *3:* 123; *21:* 45
Ross, Johnny, *32:* 190
Ross, Larry, *47:* 168
Ross, Tony, *17:* 204
Rossetti, Dante Gabriel, *20:* 151, 153
Roth, Arnold, *4:* 238; *21:* 133
Rotondo, Pat, *32:* 158
Roughsey, Dick, *35:* 186
Rouille, M., *11:* 96
Rounds, Glen, *8:* 173; *9:* 171; *12:* 56; *32:* 194; *40:* 230; *YABC 1:* 1-3
Rowe, Gavin, *27:* 144
Rowell, Kenneth, *40:* 72
Roy, Jeroo, *27:* 229; *36:* 110
Rubel, Nicole, *18:* 255; *20:* 59
Rubel, Reina, *33:* 217
Rud, Borghild, *6:* 15
Rudolph, Norman Guthrie, *17:* 13
Rue, Leonard Lee III, *37:* 164
Ruff, Donna, *50:* 173
Ruffins, Reynold, *10:* 134-135; *41:* 191, 192-193, 194-195, 196
Ruhlin, Roger, *34:* 44
Ruse, Margaret, *24:* 155
Rush, Peter, *42:* 75
Russell, E. B., *18:* 177, 182
Russo, Susan, *30:* 182; *36:* 144
Ruth, Rod, *9:* 161
Rutherford, Meg, *25:* 174; *34:* 178, 179
Rutland, Jonathan, *31:* 126
Ryden, Hope, *8:* 176
Rymer, Alta M., *34:* 181
Rystedt, Rex, *49:* 80

Author Index

The following index gives the number of the volume in which an author's biographical sketch, Brief Entry, or Obituary appears.

This index includes references to all entries in the following series, which are also published by Gale Research Company.

YABC—*Yesterday's Authors of Books for Children: Facts and Pictures about Authors and Illustrators of Books for Young People from Early Times to 1960,* Volumes 1-2
CLR—*Children's Literature Review: Excerpts from Reviews, Criticism, and Commentary on Books for Children,* Volumes 1-12
SAAS—*Something about the Author Autobiography Series,* Volumes 1-4

Author Index

Ashley, Ray
  See Abrashkin, Raymond
Ashton, Warren T.
  See Adams, William Taylor
Asimov, Issac 1920- 26
  Earlier sketch in SATA 1
  See also CLR 12
Asimov, Janet
  See Jeppson, J(anet) O(pal)
Asinof, Eliot 1919- 6
Astley, Juliet
  See Lofts, Nora (Robinson)
Aston, James
  See White, T(erence) H(anbury)
Atene, Ann
  See Atene, (Rita) Anna
Atene, (Rita) Anna 1922- 12
Atkinson, Allen
  Brief Entry 46
Atkinson, M. E.
  See Frankau, Mary Evelyn
Atkinson, Margaret Fleming 14
Atticus
  See Davies, (Edward) Hunter
  See Fleming, Ian (Lancaster)
Atwater, Florence (Hasseltine
  Carroll) 16
Atwater, Montgomery Meigs
  1904- 15
Atwater, Richard Tupper 1892-1948
  Brief Entry 27
Atwood, Ann 1913- 7
Atwood, Margaret (Eleanor)
  1939- 50
Aubry, Claude B. 1914-1984 29
  Obituary 40
Augarde, Steve 1950- 25
Augelli, John P(at) 1921- 46
Ault, Phillip H. 1914- 23
Ault, Rosalie Sain 1942- 38
Ault, Roz
  See Ault, Rosalie Sain
Aung, (Maung) Htin 1910- 21
Aung, U. Htin
  See Aung, (Maung) Htin
Auntie Deb
  See Coury, Louise Andree
Auntie Louise
  See Coury, Louise Andree
Austin, Elizabeth S. 1907- 5
Austin, Margot 11
Austin, Oliver L., Jr. 1903- 7
Austin, Tom
  See Jacobs, Linda C.
Averill, Esther 1902- 28
  Earlier sketch in SATA 1
Avery, Al
  See Montgomery, Rutherford
Avery, Gillian 1926- 7
Avery, Kay 1908- 5
Avery, Lynn
  See Cole, Lois Dwight
Avi
  See Wortis, Avi
Ayars, James S(terling) 1898- 4
Ayer, Jacqueline 1930- 13
Ayer, Margaret 15
Aylesworth, Jim 1943- 38

Aylesworth, Thomas G(ibbons)
  1927- 4
  See also CLR 6
Aymar, Brandt 1911- 22
Ayres, Carole Briggs
  See Briggs, Carole S(uzanne)
Ayres, Patricia Miller 1923-1985
  Obituary 46
Azaid
  See Zaidenberg, Arthur

B

B
  See Gilbert, W(illiam) S(chwenk)
B., Tania
  See Blixen, Karen (Christentze
  Dinesen)
BB
  See Watkins-Pitchford, D. J.
Baastad, Babbis Friis
  See Friis-Baastad, Babbis
Bab
  See Gilbert, W(illiam) S(chwenk)
Babbis, Eleanor
  See Friis-Baastad, Babbis
Babbitt, Natalie 1932- 6
  See also CLR 2
Babcock, Dennis Arthur
  1948- 22
Bach, Alice (Hendricks)
  1942- 30
  Brief Entry 27
Bach, Richard David 1936- 13
Bachman, Fred 1949- 12
Bacmeister, Rhoda W(arner)
  1893- 11
Bacon, Elizabeth 1914- 3
Bacon, Joan Chase
  See Bowden, Joan Chase
Bacon, Josephine Dodge (Daskam)
  1876-1961 48
Bacon, Margaret Frances 1895-1987
  Obituary 50
Bacon, Margaret Hope 1921- 6
Bacon, Martha Sherman
  1917-1981 18
  Obituary 27
  See also CLR 3
Bacon, Peggy 1895- 2
  See Bacon, Margaret Frances
Bacon, R(onald) L(eonard)
  1924- 26
Baden-Powell, Robert (Stephenson
  Smyth) 1857-1941 16
Baerg, Harry J(ohn) 1909- 12
Bagnold, Enid 1889-1981 25
  Earlier sketch in SATA 1
Bahr, Robert 1940- 38
Bahti, Tom
  Brief Entry 31
Bailey, Alice Cooper 1890- 12
Bailey, Bernadine Freeman 14
Bailey, Carolyn Sherwin
  1875-1961 14
Bailey, Jane H(orton) 1916- 12
Bailey, Maralyn Collins (Harrison)
  1941- 12

Bailey, Matilda
  See Radford, Ruby L.
Bailey, Maurice Charles
  1932- 12
Bailey, Ralph Edgar 1893- 11
Baird, Bil 1904- 30
Baird, Thomas P. 1923- 45
  Brief Entry 39
Baity, Elizabeth Chesley
  1907- 1
Bakeless, John (Edwin) 1894- 9
Bakeless, Katherine Little
  1895- 9
Baker, Alan 1951- 22
Baker, Augusta 1911- 3
Baker, Betty (Lou) 1928- 5
Baker, Charlotte 1910- 2
Baker, Elizabeth 1923- 7
Baker, Eugene H.
  Brief Entry 50
Baker, Gayle C(unningham)
  1950- 39
Baker, James W. 1924- 22
Baker, Janice E(dla) 1941- 22
Baker, Jeannie 1950- 23
Baker, Jeffrey J(ohn) W(heeler)
  1931- 5
Baker, Jim
  See Baker, James W.
Baker, Laura Nelson 1911- 3
Baker, Margaret 1890- 4
Baker, Margaret J(oyce)
  1918- 12
Baker, Mary Gladys Steel
  1892-1974 12
Baker, (Robert) Michael
  1938- 4
Baker, Nina (Brown)
  1888-1957 15
Baker, Rachel 1904-1978 2
  Obituary 26
Baker, Samm Sinclair 1909- 12
Baker, Susan (Catherine)
  1942- 29
Balaam
  See Lamb, G(eoffrey) F(rederick)
Balch, Glenn 1902- 3
Baldridge, Cyrus LeRoy 1889-
  Brief Entry 29
Balducci, Carolyn Feleppa
  1946- 5
Baldwin, Anne Norris 1938- 5
Baldwin, Clara 11
Baldwin, Gordo
  See Baldwin, Gordon C.
Baldwin, Gordon C. 1908- 12
Baldwin, James 1841-1925 24
Baldwin, James (Arthur)
  1924- 9
Baldwin, Margaret
  See Weis, Margaret (Edith)
Baldwin, Stan(ley C.) 1929-
  Brief Entry 28
Bales, Carol Ann 1940-
  Brief Entry 29
Balet, Jan (Bernard) 1913- 11
Balian, Lorna 1929- 9
Ball, Zachary
  See Masters, Kelly R.

R

Rabe, Berniece 1928- 7
Rabe, Olive H(anson)
  1887-1968 13
Rabinowich, Ellen 1946- 29
Rabinowitz, Sandy 1954-
  Brief Entry 39
Raboff, Ernest Lloyd
  Brief Entry 37
Rachlin, Harvey (Brant) 1951- 47
Rachlis, Eugene (Jacob) 1920-1986
  Obituary 50
Rackham, Arthur 1867-1939 15
Radford, Ruby L(orraine)
  1891-1971 6
Radlauer, David 1952- 28
Radlauer, Edward 1921- 15
Radlauer, Ruth (Shaw) 1926- 15
Radley, Gail 1951- 25
Rae, Gwynedd 1892-1977 37
Raebeck, Lois 1921- 5
Raftery, Gerald (Bransfield)
  1905- 11
Rahn, Joan Elma 1929- 27
Raible, Alton (Robert) 1918- 35
Raiff, Stan 1930- 11
Rainey, W. B.
  See Blassingame, Wyatt Rainey
Ralston, Jan
  See Dunlop, Agnes M. R.
Ramal, Walter
  See de la Mare, Walter
Rana, J.
  See Forrester, Helen
Ranadive, Gail 1944- 10
Rand, Ann (Binkley) 30
Rand, Paul 1914- 6
Randall, Florence Engel 1917- 5
Randall, Janet [Joint pseudonym]
  See Young, Janet Randall and
  Young, Robert W.
Randall, Robert
  See Silverberg, Robert
Randall, Ruth Painter
  1892-1971 3
Randolph, Lieutenant J. H.
  See Ellis, Edward S(ylvester)
Rands, William Brighty
  1823-1882 17
Ranney, Agnes V. 1916- 6
Ransom, Candice F. 1952-
  Brief Entry 49
Ransome, Arthur (Michell)
  1884-1967 22
  See also CLR 8
Rapaport, Stella F(read) 10
Raphael, Elaine (Chionchio)
  1933- 23
Rappaport, Eva 1924- 6
Rarick, Carrie 1911- 41
Raskin, Edith (Lefkowitz)
  1908- 9
Raskin, Ellen 1928-1984 38
  Earlier sketch in SATA 2
  See also CLR 1, 12
Raskin, Joseph 1897-1982 12
  Obituary 29

Rasmussen, Knud Johan Victor
  1879-1933
  Brief Entry 34
Rathjen, Carl H(enry) 1909- 11
Rattray, Simon
  See Trevor, Elleston
Rau, Margaret 1913- 9
  See also CLR 8
Rauch, Mabel Thompson 1888-1972
  Obituary 26
Raucher, Herman 1928- 8
Ravielli, Anthony 1916- 3
Rawlings, Marjorie Kinnan
  1896-1953 ....*YABC 1*
Rawls, (Woodrow) Wilson
  1913- 22
Ray, Deborah
  See Kogan, Deborah
Ray, Deborah Kogan
  See Kogan, Deborah
Ray, Irene
  See Sutton, Margaret Beebe
Ray, JoAnne 1935- 9
Ray, Mary (Eva Pedder)
  1932- 2
Raymond, James Crossley 1917-1981
  Obituary 29
Raymond, Robert
  See Alter, Robert Edmond
Rayner, Mary 1933- 22
Rayner, William 1929-
  Brief Entry 36
Raynor, Dorka 28
Rayson, Steven 1932- 30
Razzell, Arthur (George)
  1925- 11
Razzi, James 1931- 10
Read, Elfreida 1920- 2
Read, Piers Paul 1941- 21
Ready, Kirk L. 1943- 39
Reaney, James 1926- 43
Reck, Franklin Mering 1896-1965
  Brief Entry 30
Redding, Robert Hull 1919- 2
Redway, Ralph
  See Hamilton, Charles H. St. John
Redway, Ridley
  See Hamilton, Charles H. St. John
Reed, Betty Jane 1921- 4
Reed, Gwendolyn E(lizabeth)
  1932- 21
Reed, Kit 1932- 34
Reed, Philip G. 1908-
  Brief Entry 29
Reed, Thomas (James) 1947- 34
Reed, William Maxwell
  1871-1962 15
Reeder, Colonel Red
  See Reeder, Russell P., Jr.
Reeder, Russell P., Jr. 1902- 4
Reeman, Douglas Edward 1924-
  Brief Entry 28
Rees, David Bartlett 1936- 36
Rees, Ennis 1925- 3
Reeve, Joel
  See Cox, William R(obert)
Reeves, James 1909- 15
Reeves, Joyce 1911- 17
Reeves, Lawrence F. 1926- 29

Reeves, Ruth Ellen
  See Ranney, Agnes V.
Regehr, Lydia 1903- 37
Reggiani, Renée 18
Reid, Alastair 1926- 46
Reid, Barbara 1922- 21
Reid, Dorothy M(arion) (?)-1974
  Brief Entry 29
Reid, Eugenie Chazal 1924- 12
Reid, John Calvin 21
Reid, (Thomas) Mayne
  1818-1883 24
Reid, Meta Mayne 1905-
  Brief Entry 36
Reid Banks, Lynne 1929- 22
Reiff, Stephanie Ann 1948- 47
  Brief Entry 28
Reig, June 1933- 30
Reigot, Betty Polisar 1924-
  Brief Entry 41
Reinach, Jacquelyn (Krasne)
  1930- 28
Reiner, William B(uck)
  1910-1976 46
  Obituary 30
Reinfeld, Fred 1910-1964 3
Reiniger, Lotte 1899-1981 40
  Obituary 33
Reiss, Johanna de Leeuw
  1932- 18
Reiss, John J. 23
Reit, Seymour 21
Reit, Sy
  See Reit, Seymour
Rémi, Georges 1907-1983 13
  Obituary 32
Remington, Frederic (Sackrider)
  1861-1909 41
Renault, Mary
  See Challans, Mary
Rendell, Joan 28
Rendina, Laura Cooper 1902- 10
Renick, Marion (Lewis) 1905- 1
Renken, Aleda 1907- 27
Renlie, Frank H. 1936- 11
Rensie, Willis
  See Eisner, Will(iam Erwin)
Renvoize, Jean 1930- 5
Resnick, Michael D(iamond)
  1942- 38
Resnick, Mike
  See Resnick, Michael D(iamond)
Resnick, Seymour 1920- 23
Retla, Robert
  See Alter, Robert Edmond
Reuter, Carol (Joan) 1931- 2
Revena
  See Wright, Betty Ren
Rey, H(ans) A(ugusto)
  1898-1977 26
  Earlier sketch in SATA 1
  See also CLR 5
Rey, Margret (Elizabeth)
  1906- 26
  See also CLR 5
Reyher, Becky
  See Reyher, Rebecca Hourwich

Author Index

Author Index

Author Index

Character Index

The following index lists selected characters from books and other media created by the authors and illustrators who appear in *Something about the Author (SATA)* and in its companion series, *Yesterday's Authors of Books for Children* (noted below as *YABC*). This index is intended to help readers locate a *SATA* (or *YABC*) entry when they know the name of a character but not the name of its creator.

In this limited space it would be impossible to cite every character; yet there is no final authority that might determine the "most important" characters. (Several hundred important characters might be taken from Dickens alone, for example.) Therefore, the *SATA* editors have used their best judgment in selecting those characters that are most likely to interest *SATA* users. Realizing that some favorite character may not appear in this index, the editors invite all users, and librarians in particular, to suggest additional names, thereby helping to build a uniquely useful research tool for young people.

Each entry in this index gives the character's name followed by a "*See*" reference to the character's creator and the *SATA* (or *YABC*) volume number in which the creator's bio-bibliographical sketch can be found. If a character's name is not part of the title of the work in which the character appears, the title of the work is also listed below the character's name in this index. Character names are given in non-inverted form. For example: "Bartholomew Cubbins" is listed in the B's; "Captain Nemo" is listed in the C's.

Mock Turtle, The
in *Alice's Adventures in Wonderland*
(book)
See Dodgson, Charles
Lutwidge ....*YABC 2*
Modestine
in *Travels with a Donkey* (book)
See Stevenson, Robert
Louis ....*YABC 2*
Moffats, The
See Estes, Eleanor 7
Mog the Cat
See Kerr, Judith 24
Mokey Fraggle
See Henson, James Maury 43
Mole
in *The Wind in the Willows* (book)
See Grahame, Kenneth .....*YABC 1*
Mole, The
See Gould, Chester 49
Mole and Troll
See Johnston, Tony 8
Moll Flanders
See Defoe, Daniel 22
Mollie
See Blyton, Enid 25
Mollie Maria Toodlethwaite Carruthers
See Nesbit, E. ....*YABC 1*
Mollie Stone
in *Nothing Rhymes with April* (book)
See Karp, Naomi J. 16
Molly Bell
See Storey, Margaret 9
Molly Cameron
in *Keeper of the Bees* (book)
See Stratton-Porter, Gene 15
Molly Dudgeon
in *No-one Must Know* (book)
See Sleigh, Barbara 3
Molly Flower
in *The White Sea Horse* (book)
See Cresswell, Helen 48
Earlier sketch in SATA 1
Momo
in *The Great Gentleman* (book)
See Ende, Michael 42
Mona
See Vestly, Anne-Cath 14
Mona O'Rourke
See Lynch, Patricia 9
Monarch [bear]
See Seton, Ernest Thompson 18
Monks
in *Oliver Twist* (book)
See Dickens, Charles 15
Monsieur Beaucaire
See Tarkington, Booth 17
Monsieur Bon-Bon
in *Chitty-Chitty-Bang-Bang* (book)
See Fleming, Ian 9
Monsieur (C. Auguste) Dupin
See Poe, Edgar Allan 23
Monsieur Le Blanc
in "*Marie Roget*" (short story)
See Poe, Edgar Allan 23
Monsieur Racine
See Ungerer, Thomas 33
Earlier sketch in SATA 5

Monster
See Mueller, Virginia 28
Montgomery
in *The Island of Dr. Moreau* (book)
See Wells, H. G. 20
Monty Fletcher
in *Frank and Francesca* (book)
See Martin, David Stone 39
Mooch the Messy
See Sharmat, Marjorie
Weinman 33
Earlier sketch in SATA 4
Moomins, The
See Jansson, Tove 41
Earlier sketch in SATA 3
Moon Dance [horse]
in *Good Luck Arizona* (book)
See Benedict, Rex 8
Moon Man
See Ungerer, Thomas 33
Earlier sketch in SATA 5
Moon-Eyes [cat]
See Chapman, Jean 34
Moon-Face
See Blyton, Enid 25
Moonflower
See Nesbit, E. ....*YABC 1*
Moon-Watcher
in *2001: A Space Odyssey* (book)
See Clarke, Arthur C. 13
Moonta
in *Far Out the Long Canal* (book)
See DeJong, Meindert 2
Moors, The
in *Durango Street* (book)
See Bonham, Frank 49
Earlier sketch in SATA 1
Mophead
in *The Size Spies* (book)
See Needle, Jan 30
Moppet [kitten]
See Potter, Beatrix ....*YABC 1*
Mopsa the Fairy
See Ingelow, Jean 33
Morad
in *Two Greedy Bears* (book)
See Reeves, James 15
Morag MacKenzie
See Fidler, Kathleen 3
Morella
See Poe, Edgar Allan 23
Morgan Knight
in *Flying Horseman* (book)
See Cumming, Primrose 24
Morlocks
in *The Time Machine* (book)
See Wells, H. G. 20
Morna Mackellaig
See Allan, Mabel Esther 32
Earlier sketch in SATA 5
Morris Brookside
See Sharmat, Marjorie
Weinman 33
Earlier sketch in SATA 4
Morris the Moose
See Wiseman, B. 4
Mortimer J. Titmouse
See Eisner, Will 31

Mortimer Lightwood
in *Our Mutual Friend* (book)
See Dickens, Charles 15
Mortimer the Raven
in *Tales of Arabel's Raven* (book)
See Aiken, Joan 30
Earlier sketch in SATA 2
Mortimer Thynne
in *Botany Bay* (book)
See Hall, James Norman 21
See also (co-creator) Nordhoff,
Charles 23
Morton Children
See Saville, Malcolm 23
Moses, Mickser, and Michael
in *The Flight of the Doves* (book)
See Macken, Walter 36
Moshie [cat]
See Griffiths, Helen 5
Mossy
in *The Golden Key* (book)
See MacDonald, George 33
Mother Carey
See Wiggin, Kate
Douglas ....*YABC 1*
Mother Carey
See Mother Holly
Mother Farthling
See Morgan, Helen 29
Mother Gothel
in *The Stone Cage* (book)
See Gray, Nicholas Stuart 4
Mother Holle
See Mother Holly
Mother Holly
See Grimm, Jacob Ludwig
Karl 22
See also (co-creator) Grimm,
Wilhelm Karl 22
Mother Shipton
in "The Outcasts of Poker Flat"
(short story)
See Harte, Bret 26
Mother Wolf
in "Jungle Books" (series)
See Kipling, Rudyard ....*YABC 2*
Moti
See Lang, Andrew 16
Motor Boys
See Stratemeyer, Edward L. 1
Motorcycle Boy
in *Rumble Fish* (book)
See Hinton, S. E. 19
Mouldiwarp, The
See Nesbit, E. ....*YABC 1*
Mouse
See Park, Ruth 25
Mouse
in *The Eighteenth Emergency* (book)
See Byars, Betsy 46
Earlier sketch in SATA 4
Mouse
See Baker, Margaret J. 12
Mouse King, The
See Hoffmann, E. T. A. 27
Mouse Woman
See Harris, Christie 6
Mousekin
See Miles, Patricia 29

Character Index

Q